Political Power and Corporate Control

Political Power and Corporate Control

THE NEW GLOBAL POLITICS OF

CORPORATE GOVERNANCE

PETER ALEXIS GOUREVITCH
AND JAMES J. SHINN

PRINCETON UNIVERSITY PRESS

PRINCETON AND OXFORD

Library of Congress Cataloging-in-Publication Data

Gourevitch, Peter Alexis.
Political power and corporate control : the new global politics of corporate governance /
Peter Alexis Gourevitch and James J. Shinn.
p. cm.
Includes statistical evidence from a sample of 39 countries, with detailed narratives of
nine specific country cases.
Includes bibliographical references and index.
ISBN-13: 978-0-691-12291-5 (alk. paper)
ISBN-10: 0-691-12291-1 (alk. paper)
1. Corporate governance. 2. Corporations—Investor relations. 3. Business and politics.
4. Corporations—Political activity. 5. International finance. I. Title: Global politics of
corporate governance. II. Shinn, James. III. Title.

HD2741.G677 2005
338.6+—dc22   2004065435

British Library Cataloging-in-Publication Data is available
This book has been composed in Goudy
Printed on acid-free paper. ∞
pup.princeton.edu
Printed in the United States of America
1 2 3 4 5 6 7 8 9 10

CONTENTS

LIST OF ABBREVIATIONS   vii

PREFACE   xiii

CHAPTER ONE
Introduction and Summary Argument   1

Why Fight about Corporate Governance?   3
Great Variance and the "Great Reversals"   4
Putting the Pieces Together: In Search of a Political Explanation   10
Policy Consequences   12
Plan of Attack   14

CHAPTER TWO
Governance Patterns: What Causes What?   15

Outcomes: Dependent Variables and Patterns of Control   16
Capitalist Economic Policies, Minority Shareholder Protections, and Degrees
  of Coordination   20
Politics: Preferences and Institutions   22
Conclusion   26

CHAPTER THREE
Framing Incentives: The Economics and Law Tradition   27

Origins of the Debate   28
Incomplete Contracts and Private Order   30
Law and Regulation: Minority Shareholder Protections—Information, Oversight,
  Control, and Incentives   39
Varieties of Capitalism: Degrees of Coordination in Market Economies   51
Conclusion   55

CHAPTER FOUR
Politics: Preferences and Institutions   57

Mapping Financial Interests on Political Processes: A Causal Model   57
Preferences and Coalitions among Owners, Managers, and Workers   59
Political Institutions: Majoritarian and Consensus Mechanisms   67
Alternative Arguments: Legal Family and Economic Sociology   83
Conclusion   93

CHAPTER FIVE
Preference Cleavages 1: Class Conflict   95

Section 1: Owners and Managers Dominate Workers   96
  The Investor Model   96
  Analytic Narrative   123
    Korea: Changing Institutions, Shifting Preferences   123

Section 2: Workers Dominate Owners and Managers   132
   The Labor Power Model   132
   Analytic Narrative   140
      Sweden: The Exemplar of the Labor Power Model?   140
   Conclusion   147

CHAPTER SIX
Preference Cleavages 2: Sectoral Conflict   149

   Section 1: Cross-Class Coalitions   149
      The Corporatist Model: Workers and Managers Dominate Owners 150
      Analytic Narrative   159
         Germany: From Corporatist Bargain to a Transparency Coalition   160
         Japan: Concentration without Owners   167
         The Netherlands: The Evolution of "Poldermodel" Corporatism   177
   Section 2: Building Coalitions in Authoritarian Systems   187
      The Oligarchy Model: Owners Dominate Workers and Managers   187
      Analytic Narratives   189
         Russia: Oligarchs and Politics   190
         China: "Selectorate–Electorate" Coalition   192
         Singapore: Shareholder Protections with "Guided" Democracy   199
   Conclusion   203

CHAPTER SEVEN
Preference Cleavages 3: Transparency, Voice, and Pensions   205

   Section 1: Workers and Owners Dominate Managers   205
      From Class Conflict to Corporatist Compromise   206
      Analytic Narratives   228
         Chile: Authoritarian Roots of the Transparency Coalition 228
         Malaysia: Ethnicity and Democracy in Governance Politics 232
   Section 2: Managers Dominate Owners and Workers   237
      "Managerism"   237
      Analytic Narratives   241
         The United States: A Contested Path from Oligarchy to MSP 241
         United Kingdom: The Power of Majoritarian Political Institutions?   259
         France: Without the State, Who Is in Control?   262
   Conclusion   273

CHAPTER EIGHT
Conclusion: Going Forward   277

   Questions and Answers: What Explains Variance?   277
   Shortcomings and Guideposts for Future Research   285
   Conclusion: Fighting over the Governance Debate   287

DATA APPENDIX   297

BIBLIOGRAPHY   313

INDEX   333

ABBREVIATIONS

A&P:	Atlantic and Pacific Company
ABN AMRO:	Large banking firm headquartered in the Netherlands.
ABP:	Algemeen Burgerlijk Pensioenfonds (Netherlands)
ABRASCA:	Associação Brasileira das Companhias Abertas
ACWI:	All Country World Index
ADRs:	American depositary receipts
AEGON Nederland:	Dutch financial institution
AFG:	Association Française de la Gestion Financière
AFL:	American Federation of Labor
AFL-CIO:	American Federation of Labor-Congress of Industrial Organizations
AFP:	Administradora de Fondos de Pensiones
AGF-Paribas:	Assurances Générales de France and Paribas
AGM:	Annual general meetings
AKZO Nobel:	Large multinational firm headquartered in the Netherlands, dealing in chemicals, coatings, and healthcare products
AOW:	Algemene Oudermans Wet (Netherlands)
ARRCO:	Association pour le Régime de Retraite complémentaire de Salariés (France)
ASC:	Accounting Society of China
ASEAN:	Association of Southeast Asian Nations
AT:	Austria
ATP:	Allmänna Tilläggspension (Sweden)
AU:	Australia
BADC:	Kigyô Kaikei Shingikai (Business Accounting Discussion Council) (Japan)
BASF:	Badische Anilin und Soda-Fabrik AG, a large chemicals multinational headquartered in Germany
BDI:	Bundesverband der Deutscher Industrie (Germany)
BE:	Belgium
BIS:	Bank for International Settlements
CA:	Canada
CAC-40:	Compagnie des Agents de Change, a broad-based stock index for the Paris Bourse, since 1998 part of SBEF, Société de Bourse Francaise (SBEF)
CalPERS:	California Public Employees' Retirement System
CAS:	Chinese accounting standards
CCP:	Chinese Communist Party
CDU:	Christian Democratic Party (Germany)

CEO:	Chief executive officer
CEP:	Capitalist Economic Policies
CES:	Creative Electronic Systems (Germany)
CH:	Switzerland
CI:	Coordination Index
CICPA:	China Institute of Certified Public Accountants
CII:	Council of Institutional Investors (U.S.)
CIO:	Congress of Industrial Organizations (U.S.)
CL:	Chile
CME:	Coordinated Market Economies
CNAVTS:	Caisse Nationale d'Assurance Vieillesse des Travailleurs Salariés (National Fund for Salaried Workers' Old Age Insurance) (France)
CNC:	Conseil National de la Comptabilité (France)
CPA:	Certified public accountant
CPF:	Central Provident Fund (Singapore)
CRC:	Comité de la Reglementation Comptable (France)
CSRC:	China Securities Regulatory Commission
CSX:	CSX Corporation, a large freight transportation company (U.S.)
DASC:	Disclosure and Accounting Standards Committee
DB:	Defined benefits
DE:	Germany
DK:	Denmark
DoC:	Degrees of Coordination
DPI:	Database of Political Indicators
DRSC:	Deutscher Rechnungslegungs Standards Committee (Germany)
DSM:	Large multinational chemical manufacturer, based in the Netherlands
DSR:	Deutscher Standardisierungrat (Germany)
EPF:	Employees Provident Fund (Kumpulan Wang Simpanan Pekerja) (Malaysia)
ERISA:	Employee Retirement Income Security Act
ESOPs:	Employee Stock Option Plans
EU:	European Union
EVA:	Economic value added
FASB:	Financial Accounting Standards Board
FDI:	Foreign direct investment
FDP:	Free Democratic Party (Germany)
FESE:	Federation of European Stock Exchanges
FI:	Finland
FIBV:	Federation Internationale des Bourses de Valeurs (International Federation of Stock Values)
FKI:	Federation of Korean Industry

FPI:	Foreign portfolio investment, distinct from FDI, foreign direct investment
FR:	France
FSA:	Financial Services Agency (Japan)
FSA:	Financial Services Authority (United Kingdom)
FSC:	Financial Supervisory Commission
GAAP:	Generally accepted accounting principles (U.S.)
GB:	United Kingdom
GCGF:	Global Corporate Governance Forum
GDP:	Gross domestic product
GLCs:	Government-linked companies
GTE:	General Telephone and Electronics
HGB:	Handelsgesetzbuch (commercial code) (Germany)
HK:	Hong Kong
IAS:	International Accounting Standard
IASB:	International Accounting Standards Board
IASC:	International Accounting Standards Committee
IBM:	International Business Machines
ICC:	International Chamber of Commerce
ICPAS:	Institute of CPAs of Singapore
IDC:	International Data Corporation (U.S.)
IDR:	International depository receipts
IE:	Ireland
IFO:	International financial organization
IFRS:	International Financial Reporting Standards
IMF:	International Monetary Fund
ING:	Dutch Financial services firm. Originally Internationale Nederlanden Group, now officially ING Group.
IO:	International organization
IPCOH:	Index of political cohesion
IPD:	Implicit pension debt
IPD:	Integrated project development
IPO:	Initial public offering
IRS:	Internal Revenue Service (United States)
IT:	Italy
JCGA:	Japan Corporate Governance Association
JICPA:	Japanese Institute of Certified Public Accountants
JP:	Japan
KapAEG:	Kapitalaufnahmeerleichterungsgesetz (the law on facilitating raising capital) (Germany)
KASB:	Korean Accounting Standards Board, or Hanguk hoegye kisun wiwon
Keidanren:	Keizaidantai-rengokai (Japan)
KEPCO:	Korea Electric Power Company
KFAS:	Korean Financial Accounting Standards

KLM:	Royal Dutch Airlines (Netherlands)
KLSE:	Kuala Lumpur Stock Exchange (Malaysia)
KonTraG:	Gesetz zur Kontrolle und Transparenz im Unternehmens-bereich (the law on control and transparency of corporations)
KOSDAQ:	Korea Association of Securities Dealers Automated Quotation
KPN:	Netherlands telecommunications company
KSE:	Korean Stock Exchange
LDP:	Liberal Democratic Party (Japan)
LG:	Lucky-Goldstar (Korea)
LLSV:	La Porta, López-de-Silano, Shleifer, and Vishny
LME:	Liberal market economy
LSE:	London Stock Exchange
M&A:	Mergers and acquisitions
MACPA:	Malaysian Association of Certified Public Accountants
MASB:	Malaysian Accounting Standards Board
MCA:	Malaysian Chinese Association (Persutuan China Malaysia)
MGAAP:	Malaysia's generally accepted accounting principles
MIA:	Malaysian Institute of Accountants
MITI:	Ministry of International Trade and Industry (Japan)
MOF:	Ministry of Finance (Japan)
MOFE:	Ministry of Finance and Economy (Japan)
MSCI:	Morgan Stanley Capital International, Inc.
MSP:	Minority shareholder protection
NASDAQ:	National Association of Securities Dealers Automated Quotations
NBFI:	Non-bank financial intermediaries
NCR:	National Cash Register Corporation (U.S.)
NED:	Non-executive director
NL:	Netherlands
NLRB:	National Labor Relations Board
NO:	Norway
NRE Bill:	loi sur les Nouvelles regulations economiques de 2001 (New Economic Regulations Bill of 2001, France)
NV:	Naamloze Vennootschap (Netherlands)
NYSCRF:	New York State Common Retirement Fund (U.S.)
NYSE:	New York Stock Exchange (U.S.)
NZ:	New Zealand
O:	Owners
OECD:	Organization for Economic Cooperation and Development
OLS:	Ordinary least squares
OME:	Organized market economy

PAP: People's Action Party (Singapore)
PAYGO: Pay-As-You-Go pension system
PBGC: Pension Benefits Guarantee Corporation
PGGM: Stichting Pensioenfonds voor de Gezondheid, Geestelijke en Maatschappelijke Belangen (Netherlands)
PRA: Personal retirement account
PSA: Port of Singapore Authority (Singapore)
QCL: Quality of corporate law
R&D: Research and development
RIETI: Research Institute of Economy, Trade, and Industry (Japan)
SAF: Svenska Arbetgivarforening (Sweden)
SCGOP: Stichting Corporate Governance Onderzoek voor Pensioenfondsen (Netherlands)
SE: Sweden
SEC: Securities and Exchange Commission (United States)
SER: Sociaal Economische Raad (Consultative tripartite Social and Economic Council)
SIB: Securities and Investment Board (United Kingdom)
SIPO: Share initial public offering, used in place of IPO
SK: Sankyong (Korea)
SNCF: Syndicat National des chemins de fers (the National Train Authority, France)
SOE: State-owned enterprise
SPD: Sozialedemokratische Partei Deutschland (German Social Democratic Party)
SSE: Singapore Stock Exchange
SVS: Superintendencia de Seguros y Valores (Chile)
TEFRA: Tax Equity and Fiscal Responsibility Act of 1982
TIAA-CREF: Teachers Insurance and Annuity Association-College Retirement Equities Fund
TLCs: Temasek listed companies
TransPuG: The Corporate Sector Transparency and Publicity Act
TVA: Tennesee Valley Authority
UAP-BNP: Unions des Assurances de Paris and Banque Nationale de Paris
UMNO: United Malays National Organization (Pertubuhan Kebangsaan Melayu Bersatu)
US: United States
US-GAAP: U.S. generally accepted accounting principles
VoC: Varieties of Capitalism
W: Workers
WWI: World War I
WWII: World War II
WWTR: Worldwide total remuneration

PREFACE

THE LIMITED LIABILITY company is approaching its four hundredth birthday.[1] Its creation provided a powerful engine for economic growth by mobilizing capital and rewarding risk-taking. Economies with deep capital markets and healthy corporate structures grow faster than those with weak financial and corporate structures. At the same time, corporations are vulnerable to problems of accountability and responsibility. Recent scandals (Enron, Parmalat, Adelphia, Ahold, etc.) are repeats of events familiar to historians of the corporation.

Looking at corporate structures around the world would fascinate Darwin. There is no single form, but many. The United States has strict rules on insider trading, hostile takeovers, the composition of boards, the process of proxy voting; it ranks high on most indicators of "shareholder protection." Japan, by contrast, has substantial cross-shareholding across firms, so that there is no effective market for control. In Germany, firms are supervised by institutionalized blockholders. In many parts of the world, external shareholders have few protections, while most firms are supervised by closely knit owners, linked by family, ethnicity, religion, or community.

The U.S. pattern is not the typical one. If we measure the concentration of shareholding within firms, or the regulations on shareholder protection, or the rules on board organization, the United States lies at one end of the scale. This was not always the case. In the late nineteenth century, U.S. corporations resembled those of continental Europe. Then policy forced change. The U.S. political system enacted laws against monopolies and concentrated financial institutions and created institutions for the regulation of securities. Other countries did not pass such laws.

This book seeks to explain that divergence. It focuses on the politics of law and regulation concerning corporate structure. There are certainly variables in technology and competition that work regardless of the formal laws, and private bonding or trust mechanisms are quite real. But some important element of what drives the behavior of firms lies in the incentives that law and regulation structure. Explaining law and regulation is thus central to any account of corporate governance.

---

[1] In March 1602 the Netherlands Republic chartered the United East India Company (Vereenigde Oost-Indische Compagnie, or VOC) as a limited liability joint stock company, the prototype of the listed multinational trading enterprise. Renaissance merchants in Florence and Genoa had experimented with joint stock arrangements before this date, but with a limited term and a "complete contract" between the investors and managers. The VOC, in contrast, raised 6.45 million guilders (over a billion dollars in current terms) from more than a thousand investors, on the basis of an ambitious corporate charter with uncertain return and (initially) a 10-year operating horizon. Arguments among owners, shareholders, and employees regarding the governance of the VOC fill its corporate archives for the 300 years until its demise. See Paul Frentrop, *Corporate Governance, 1602–2002* (Amsterdam: Prometheus, 2002) chap. 2.

Our book is not about recent scandals, though they are important and revelatory and produce considerable suffering in lost pensions and jobs. They also tell us something about how the system works—the scandals are bad for people but good for social science. We do not offer a "how to fix it" analysis, though we have some ideas about the problem. We do offer something essential to a repair manual: a realistic analysis of the politics that shape what actually happens, not just what ought to happen. Politics drives regulations, and regulations shape corporate governance patterns, which then protect or abuse investors. When we design solutions, we have to think about what is likely to happen given political processes, not what is abstractly ideal.

Our motives mix moral with practical concerns. Shareholding provides an important asset for individual and institutional savings. As such, it becomes a vital part of a person's security, life plan, and goals. Widows and orphans, retirees, charities and educational institutions, foundations and nonprofits, along with the wealthy, or the comfortable, or the seekers of pleasure, or people with modest goals—all use securities markets. The ability to attract those savings fuels the economy. Thus we care about "what works" because we care about the aims of people and institutions.

That concern makes us intensely curious. What are the politics of the regulation of corporate governance? We find this topic curiously underdeveloped in the study of firms. There is a rich literature on all the related topics—law, economics, history. Without that literature we could not undertake this project. However, until recently, political variables have not been seriously considered as important elements of an explanation. That is changing as colleagues in several fields look at such variables. We seek to contribute to this growing literature.

Corporate governance, we are convinced, lies at the core of comparative and international political economy. Much of what happens and who benefits is driven by it. Patterns in corporate governance substantially covary with labor markets, education and training, social services, and income distribution. They affect the rates of economic growth and adjustment, the good and the bad. They are intertwined with issues of corruption, the rule of law, and political democracy. They mingle with trade disputes and international economic coordination. Corporate governance is not the sole driver in these areas of policy, but it is an important component, thus important to understand.

We both became interested in this topic well before the recent scandals. Different experiences and reasons brought each of us here. Gourevitch has been studying comparative and international political economy: how countries respond to changes in the international economy and to the pressures they cause. His book *Politics in Hard Times* examined how countries picked policies when faced with challenges of what we now call globalization—the crises of the 1880s, 1930s, and 1970s.

This led to an interest in why countries perform so differently: why, in the 1980s, the U.S. economy was doing badly, while Germany and Japan were doing so well. Gourevitch became convinced that a key element lay in corporate governance, in how firms were run and how they related to subcontractors, banks, investors, workers. This, rather than the formalized role of the state in the economy (a strong or weak state, the role of the bureaucracy), seemed the key variable. He wrote several papers on this theme.

Shinn came to the topic of corporate governance from a different route—from the bottom up. Over the course of a (checkered) career in business, he worked sequentially as a union employee, a line worker, middle and general manager, chief executive, entrepreneur, then inside and outside director. At the first firm he cofounded, he established and then supervised corporations in 16 countries, including Argentina, Belgium, Brazil, China, France, Germany, India, Italy, Hong Kong, Israel, Japan, Korea, Malaysia, Singapore, Spain, and the United Kingdom. This exposed him to the details of corporate governance "on the ground"—and impressed him (sometimes uncomfortably) with the wide variance in company law, financial reporting standards, and governance rules among countries. He decided to finish a Ph.D. and wrote his dissertation at Princeton on corporate governance and capital market integration in several of the countries in which he had operated as a manager. Some of the material and data in this book draws upon that dissertation.

We discovered our common interest in 1999–2000 at a conference in San Diego, introduced by mutual friend and Gourevitch's University of California–San Diego colleague Miles Kahler, whom Shinn knew when both were Fellows at the Council on Foreign Relations. We decided to work together. We persuaded Les Gelb, then president of the Council on Foreign Relations, that there were international issues in this topic of relevance to foreign policy. He authorized us to run a workshop on this topic at the CFR in 2002–3, which formed the basis of our coauthored *How Shareholder Reforms Can Pay Foreign Policy Dividends*. We are deeply obliged to the participants of that workshop, especially the practitioners from Wall Street, portfolio managers, underwriters, accountancy firms, lawyers, and economists, whose knowledge on corporate governance stemmed from both practical experience and public policy interest, and who were gracious with their (very expensive) time.

Convinced there was much more to say, we turned then to develop this book. We wrote the first draft during 2002–3. Gourevitch had a sabbatical from UCSD that he spent at the Harvard Center for European Studies in 2001–2, and then at the Center for Advanced Studies in the Behavioral Sciences for 2002-3. He thanks these institutions for their remarkable assistance, and the William and Flora Hewlitt Foundation for support while at CASBS. In 2002, Gourevitch published with Michael Hawes an early statement of ideas about the importance of political institutions in shaping corporate governance outcomes. In 2003 Gourevitch developed further some of the ideas about coalitions and alignments that contributed to this book in his *Yale Law Journal* essay, "The Politics of Corporate Governance Regulation," a review of Mark Roe's fine study of this topic.

Both of us mix public policy concerns with empirical ones. We seek here to write a piece of social science—an analysis of reality, an effort to understand, and to develop theories about, why things happen, and to test those theories.

At the same time, we do have practical and ethical concerns about the topic. What corporate governance system is most efficient? Which system promotes growth, protects investors, and at the same time encourages employment and equality of opportunity? We have learned in this project that these variables are interconnected. Those connections influence the politics that shape corporate governance, and more needs to be done to understand those connections.

Many people have helped us with this project.

Peter Gourevitch thanks students in several classes who warmed to the topic, read chapter drafts, did some research of their own, and helped track down references; he notes in particular Jacob Allen, Adriana Bejan, Chris Chan, Willi Hao, and Gonzalo Islas.

For assistance with data analysis, we thank Pablo Pinto, especially for work in preparation of the appendix, and for checking many of our calculations; Mike Hawes for helping to develop the data on political institutions, used for chapter 4 (and for help in the paper coauthored with Gourevitch published in the French journal *Régulation*, which was an early version of these ideas); Rob Knacke, then at the Council on Foreign Relations, who helped us with the conferences and did much of the hard work on the subsequent CFR publication; and Philip Novack at Princeton University, who provided superb research assistance. At UCSD, Marina Green helped as research assistant in the final stages of manuscript preparation. Lynne Bush used her great editorial skills to save us from many errors.

Thanks to the many colleagues who read drafts of the book. We are awed by the brilliance and engagement they showed, the kind of thing that makes research exciting! We note especially Suzanne Berger, Frank Dobbin, Peter Hall, Peter Katzenstein, David Lake, Margaret Levi, Mark Roe, Krislert Samphantharak, Yves Tiberghien, Nicolas Véron, Nicholas Ziegler, and people who read chapters or sections of the manuscript, including Ruth Aguilera, Patrick Bolton, Marco Becht, John Cioffi, Julian Dierkes, Pepper Culpepper, Ronald Dore, Michel Goyer, Martin Höpner, Takeo Hoshi, David Soskice, Brian Cheffins, Aseem Prakhesh, Ailsa Röell, Ulrike Schaede, Vivien Schmidt, and John Zysman. Several anonymous reviewers provided extremely valuable comments.

We are also obliged to the many individuals who contributed key ideas or data to our project, and were gracious with their time during the course of our research and interviews, including Jamie Allen, Bruno Amable, Gavin Anderson, Theodore Baums, John Biggs, Robert Boyer, Carolyn Brancato, Ken Burkhardt, Peter Butler, Kent Calder, Peter Clapman, Peter Clark, Andrew Clearfield, Gerald Curtis, John Davey, Stephen Davis, Simeon Djankov, Cho Dong-sung, Alexander Dyck, Hart Fessenden, Julian Franks, Richard Frederick, Mitsuhiro Fukao, Jeffrey Garten, Leo Goldschmidt, Chang Ha-joon, Ryozo Hayashi, Takeo Hoshi, Miles Kahler, Merit Janow, Kiattisak Jelatianranat, Lee Jung-hong, Andrew Kim, Masao Konomi, John Langlois, Rafael La Porta, Andy Lawrence, William Lazonick, Fernando Lefort, John Lemasters, Pierre-Henri Leroy, Steve Levitt, Sophie L'Helias, Florencio López-de-Silanes, Jon Lukomnick, Andy Martin, Kathy Matsui, Colin Mayer, Kathleen McNamara, Barry Metzger, Ira Millstein, Nell Minow, Robert Monks, Yoshiaki Murakami, Taggart Murphy, William Megginson, Roberto Newell, Roger Noll, Charles Oman, Steve Orlins, Barbara O'Toole, William Overholt, Robert Palacios, Hugh Patrick, Robert Pozen, Geert Raaijmakers, Rhyu Sang-young, Fritz Scharpf, Erich Schneiderman, Yasuhisa Shiozaki, Steve Smaha, Anne Simpson, Benn Steil, Wolfgang Streeck, Somo Subramajian, Stoyan Tenev, Paul Theil, Alan Timblick, Shan Turnbull, Jing Ulrich, Michael Vatikiotis, Paolo Volpin, Rudiger Von Rosen, Eduardo Walker, Guy Wyser-Pratte, Youn Young-mo, and Nick Zwick.

We thank the participants in several seminars who patiently listened to our ideas as they were being developed. We are particularly grateful to Margaret Levi for organizing a daylong seminar to discuss an early draft of the manuscript at the University of Washington in the fall of 2003 and to her colleagues who participated. For their comments we thank colleagues at the Center for European Studies in fall 2001, Harvard Business School in the winter of 2002, the WissenshaftsZentrum Berlin (WZB) in Berlin in fall 2003, the Center for Advanced Studies in the Behavioral Sciences in November 2002, the American Political Science Association meetings of 2001, 2002, 2003, and 2004, the University of California, Berkeley in 2000 and 2004, the University of North Carolina in fall of 2001, the CEBREMAP Group in Paris in June 2003, the Max Planck Institute in Cologne in July 2003, the Council for European Studies meeting of March 2004, the University of British Columbia in May 2003, and Duke University and Brigham Young University in the fall of 2004.

Thanks to UCSD for sabbatical leave support for parts of 2001–3, to the Graduate School of International Relations and Pacific Studies for research support; to the UCSD Senate for travel funds and manuscript preparation; to the Council on Foreign Relations for help with the workshop; to the East-West Center of the University of Hawaii, for their kind hospitality over several summers of research and writing; to Princeton's Woodrow Wilson School and Georgetown's School of Foreign Service, for their logistical support, fine colleagues, and high-speed computer systems.

Above all, we thank our ladies and our children for putting up with us for several years as we mumbled and growled and emailed at the keyboard. It has been a pleasure (at least for us), and an intellectual adventure. We thank each other for a fine collaboration; from the beginning to the end, we remain convinced neither could have written the book without the other.

Political Power and Corporate Control

Introduction and Summary Argument

ENRON, WORLDCOM, TYCO, Adelphia, Ahold (a Dutch firm), Hollinger (Canadian), Vivendi (French), Parmalat (Italian)—these names have long been staples of the *Financial Times* and *Wall Street Journal*, but more recently they have become scandalous and exotic fare on news dailies and TV networks. Since the Enron scandal began in the fall of 2001, these firms, their bankruptcies, and their miscreant executives have become "above the fold" headlines and evening news clips.[1]

In addition to providing entertainment, these examples of financial failure have graphically demonstrated that there is, in fact, what some delicately refer to as a "corporate governance problem." Scholars and media mavens alike frequently dismissed the corporate implosions that followed in the wake of the financial crises in the mid-1990s—mostly in Latin America and developing Asia—as a regional problem specific to the "crony capitalism" of developing regions. By the turn of the millennium, it became clear the problem was more widespread. Scandals of one kind or another were occurring around the world. At first, people saw Enron as a "one-off" case, a singular event caused by unscrupulous or incompetent people and requiring no special response.[2] As more scandals emerged, however, it became clear that something deeper was at work.

This book is not about these scandals, but about the underlying structures of corporate accountability. We will not try to say why any specific individual abused trust, but rather are interested in the variance among systems of corporate governance around the world. There was a "corporate governance problem" long before Enron and Parmalat. Fiske and Gould were famous nineteenth-century American examples of stock manipulation, with counterparts around the world. Their behavior led to efforts, private and public, to protect investors. Those efforts are the central concern of this book.

Corporate governance is about power and responsibility. It is the structure of power within each firm that determines who allocates money: who gets the cash flow, who allocates jobs, who decides on research and development, on mergers

---

[1] Media in the West focused on these firms, but Asia and Latin America witnessed a parallel series of high-profile corporate governance scandals, including Korea's SK Corp and LG Card debacles; China's Shanghai Land and Far East Pharmaceutical; Hong Kong–listed CNOOC Finance and China Life; Thailand's Thai Petrochemical Industry; Indonesia's Asian Pulp and Paper; an apparently endless series of Japanese bank abuses; Mexico's TV Azteca; Chile's Endesa/Enersis squabble; and Brazil's COPEL case.

[2] In addition to news stories, this observation is based on comments made over the fall and winter of 2001–2 by participants at a Roundtable on Corporate Governance, organized by the authors of this book at the Council on Foreign Relations, leading to publication of Peter A. Gourevitch and James P. Shinn, *How Shareholder Reforms Can Pay Foreign Policy Dividends* (New York: Council on Foreign Relations, 2002).

and acquisitions, on hiring and firing CEOs, on subcontracting to suppliers, on distributing dividends or buying back shares or investing in new equipment. Corporate governance is also about accountability: who takes the blame for corruption, misuse of funds, or poor performance.

Corporate governance systems reflect public policy choices. Countries pass laws that shape incentives, which in turn shape governance systems. Some countries have rigorous prohibitions on insider trading, vigorous markets for control, strong protection of minority shareholders (rules on accounting, corporate boards, securities), and effective rules for product-market competition and antitrust. These countries have diffuse patterns of share ownership and managerial supervision through boards elected by their shareholders. Other countries encourage block-holding by allowing pyramid leveraging and cross-shareholding, restricting markets for control, limiting competition, and offering weak protection to minority shareholders.

Such different regulatory policies concerning corporate governance turn on political differences among countries—on the interest groups that press for one set of rules or another and on the political institutions that aggregate preferences to produce policies. This book is about choices of corporate governance in countries around the globe. We make extensive reference to the United States, where the give-and-take of interest groups as they press their preferred arrangements for corporate accountability has been particularly visible. American political processes produced the Sarbanes-Oxley bill of 2002, the most extensive U.S. reform of rules on corporate governance in several decades.

Indeed, politics explains the great U.S. "reversal" in corporate governance. In the late nineteenth century, the U.S. system resembled those of Europe: large "trusts" or oligopolies were controlled by shareholder blocks in the hands of individuals and banks; minority shareholder protection was weak, insider trader scandals common. Then laws were passed: the Sherman Antitrust Act in 1890, several laws following the 1905 Armstrong Commission on the insurance industry, the Glass-Steagall Act on banking in 1933, the Securities and Exchange Act of 1934, and now Sarbanes-Oxley of 2002. It is this legislation, regulatory structure, and their enforcement that changed corporate governance in the United States.

In the United States, *interest groups* fought over these laws and regulations: owners; investors as outsiders and investors as insiders; workers as employees and workers as pension fund holders; managers of various kinds; the so-called reputational intermediaries consisting of accountants, lawyers, bond-rating agencies; and institutional investors. These groups fought through *political institutions* whose structure influenced the outcome: the separation of power between the U.S. Congress and the presidency, federalism, political parties, and electoral laws.

These elements of politics—interests, institutions, and political conflict—are in play all over the world. In Korea greater democratization in the 1990s broke the link between the big firms (*chaebols*) and the authoritarian government, leading to rules for greater transparency and accountability in corporate governance, backed by a coalition that included labor, previously excluded businesses, and regional reformers. In Germany, the various political parties have been battling over legislation that would create markets for control, shareholder rights, and transparency; contrary to most expectations, it is labor and the Social Democrats who are often on the side of the external investors, while the conservative Christian Democrats defend the established insider system preferred by managers and inside blockholders. In Italy, the Parmalat scandal, in France, the Vivendi controversy, and in the Netherlands, the Ahold case have all pushed issues of governance to the fore. The financial crisis of 1997 exposed weaknesses in governance mechanisms for several countries in Asia, particularly in Korea, Thailand, Indonesia, and Malaysia. In Europe, disagreement on takeover legislation and a variety of other measures has slowed development of European Community–wide policies on corporate governance.

WHY FIGHT ABOUT CORPORATE GOVERNANCE?

That corporate governance provokes political debate should not surprise us. Corporate governance—the authority structure of a firm—lies at the heart of the most important issues of society. That authority structure decides who has claim to the cash flow of the firm, who has a say in its strategy and its allocation of resources. As such, corporate governance affects the creation of wealth and its distribution into different pockets. It shapes the efficiency of firms, the stability of employment, the fortunes of suppliers and distributors, the portfolios of pensioners and retirees, the endowments of orphanages and hospitals, the claims of the rich and the poor. It creates the temptations for cheating and the rewards for honesty, inside the firm and more generally in the body politic. Corporate governance influences social mobility, stability, and fluidity: the openness of economic systems to new entrants and outsiders from established social structures, and the rewards to entrepreneurial initiative. It shapes the incentives firms have to invest in their labor force; thus it intersects with education and training systems, and with social welfare, health, and retirement plans. Corporate governance interacts with hostile takeovers, antitrust, economic competition, international trade disputes, and trade unions. It structures pension systems, social security, and retirement plans.

It is no wonder, then, that corporate governance provokes conflict. Anything so important will be fought over. Anything that shapes wealth, opportunities, stability, and corruption is sure to attract the concerns of the powerful and provoke the anxiety of the weak. Everyone has a stake in the corporate governance system, and everyone has an interest in how it is structured.

We believe that, like other decisions about authority, corporate governance structures are fundamentally the result of political decisions. Corporate governance systems reflect policy choices. They are shaped by a mixture of laws, rules, regulations, and the degree of their enforcement. These laws define the obligations of managers, the rights and duties of owners, the claims of shareholders, and the powers of boards. Researchers often group these rules under the label of *corporate governance law*, dealing largely with the composition and obligations of the board, separating these from *securities law*, dealing with shareholding processes. We use a broader label, increasingly recognized as more comprehensive, *minority shareholder protections*, covering issues of accounting, takeovers, reporting, and control issues—all the legal factors that control a firm's cash flow.

We take our concerns a step farther than the firm itself. A firm's authority system is also shaped by processes outside what are normally called governance rules within the firm. Labor market regulations shape employees' job protection (how easy or difficult it is to fire workers): strong job protection gives workers substantial influence on how the firm is run. Other rules shape the connection of firms to suppliers and distributors, defining the claims and obligations of each.[3] Still other rules define antitrust, banking and finance, competition from other countries and within each country, and pension plans, all of which can have an impact on corporate governance.[4]

Nor is it enough to know the "law on the books." Much depends on whether and how these laws are enforced. Many countries have extensive codes and shareholder protections—but these are not enforced. Or, if enforced, their interpretation can alter their meaning substantially. The actual application of law turns, again, on politics and choices.

That corporate governance reflects political choices is not the standard perspective. Most treatments look at law, economics, and contractual issues between parties as if they were separate from politics. That is not our view. Law and economic policies have an impact on what happens, but the content of those laws, policies, and regulations needs to be explained. For example, some countries forbid insider trading, allow hostile takeovers, and compel substantial reporting of information to shareholders (the United States has done all of these for many years), while other countries do not. Some countries have substantial cross-shareholding among firms (Japan), or vertical pyramid control (Chile), while other countries forbid these practices. Germany requires firms to have union representatives on the board; the United Kingdom and the United States do not.

GREAT VARIANCE AND THE "GREAT REVERSALS"

Countries vary substantially in the way they organize authority in the firm. To simplify, we can contrast two models: an external, diffuse *shareholder* model and an internal concentrated *blockholder* model. In the external or diffuse shareholder

---

[3] In this respect corporate governance resembles other forms of "nested authority," where relationships within a unit are influenced by the larger structures in which they operate. See Miles Kahler and David Lake, eds., *Governance in a Global Economy: Political Authority in Transition* (Princeton: Princeton University Press, 2003).

[4] Mark Roe has been a leader in asserting the importance of politics in shaping corporate governance. His most recent book, *Political Determinants of Corporate Governance: Political Context, Corporate Impact* (New York: Oxford University Press, 2003), stresses the limits of corporate law in fully explaining the patterns.

model, managers are supervised by a board of directors elected by shareholders; the board members hold relatively small portions of the total stock, but their vote is required on major decisions, and they are supposed to discipline or reward the managers. Rewards of stock options are one way to align managers with the many diffuse shareholders—in theory. Managerial performance is assessed by information provided through "reputational intermediaries" such as accountants and market analysts; the market price of the stock provides an ongoing evaluation of the company's prospects and its managers' competence. An active market for corporate control, allowing hostile takeovers and inhibiting barriers like poison pills, provides an important tool for punishing managerial incompetence and neglect by the board. The United States has moved the farthest down the path toward this system, famously described by Berle and Means as the separation of ownership and control.[5]

By contrast, the blockholder model tightly links ownership and control. Managers are supervised by "insiders" (concentrated blockholders), with little formal protection of the outsiders, or minority shareholders. This model disciplines managers through direct supervision and intervention by insider owners who control large blocks of shares. The blockholder approach has several variants. In one version, large shareholder blocks are held by financial institutions, banks, or other firms. The family or ethnic network is another variant, in which personal or group ties are used to control managers. Yet another form of blockholding is the state ownership model, where public authorities use a variety of instruments to supervise firms. For the blockholder category generally, some influential theorists, such as Ronald Dore, use the label *stakeholder model* to convey the range of groups besides shareholders with claims on the firm; we reserve this term to consider the politics of choosing the form, rather than the governance system itself.[6]

Most of the world operates through the blockholder model. It exists in Germany and Japan, in most of continental Europe, and, indeed, in a variety of forms throughout Latin America and Asia.[7] The diffuse shareholder model found in the United States is relatively unusual. And even in the United States, it is rather recent in the evolution of organizational forms. There is much talk in the business press and among researchers about change around the world, about convergence toward the American model. We need to consider, then, what causes governance systems and what causes them to change.

What explains this difference among countries and over time? It is only recently that observers have come fully to appreciate how great the variance is. In the United States at least, it was thought that the Berle-Means separation— the American model—was the inevitable path for all countries. This was how markets worked, it was argued, and as all countries engaged in the market, they

    [5] Adolf A. Berle and Gardiner C. Means, *The Modern Corporation and Private Property* (New York: Commerce Clearing House, 1932).

    [6] Ronald Dore, *Stock Market Capitalism, Welfare Capitalism: Japan and Germany versus the Anglo-Saxons* (New York: Oxford University Press, 2000).

    [7] Though technically Japan has diffuse ownership, cross-shareholding makes it function like a blockholding system. See discussion of Japan in Dore 2000.

too would look this way. So long as the U.S. economy seemed to be the world's most dynamic, this attitude prevailed, among pundits and (most) scholars alike.

Then, in the 1980s, the U.S. economy stumbled. Japan and Germany grew rapidly, exports penetrated the United States, there was talk of the "rust belt" and economic decline. "American's Failing Capitalist System" was the title of a *Harvard Business Review* essay by Michael Porter, which indicted (among other alleged sins) the U.S. corporate governance system as a factor in this "decline."[8]

Much was written about the German and the Japanese models, and many labels were generated for these models with their allegedly superior institutional endowment: "Rhenish capitalism," "coordinated market economy," "regulatory market," "social market," "stakeholder capitalism." Michel Albert's *Capitalism versus Capitalism* pointed out to the public that key debates in comparative political economy were not about state versus market, but among different forms of market economies, and that choices had to be made. France, he argued, had to choose between the Rhenish model of Germany and the neoliberal model of the United States and the United Kingdom.[9]

Then the pendulum swung back. By the late 1990s, the U.S. economy was booming, while Japan and Germany stagnated. The U.S. model re-acquired both political and intellectual status. This time the U.S. model would indeed triumph, wrote many observers, and the world would conform to its practices, including corporate governance. Two prominent specialists even proclaimed "The End of History for Corporate Law."[10] And then, yet another shift: Enron set off the chain reaction of governance scandals with which we began this book, revealing structural flaws in corporate governance in so many countries that triumphalism with regard to the virtues of any corporate model—U.S., European, or Japanese—appeared increasingly silly.

When we compare countries, we do not find the same corporate governance system in each. Even with a single country, a sense of history is useful, for we rarely find consistency over time. The United States, so strongly identified with the Berle-Means pattern now, was not always thus. In the late nineteenth century, patterns of ownership of large firms looked far more like Germany than they do now. U.S. firms began with concentrated inside owners, the blockholding model, as have most firms around the world. The United States then began to create shareholder protections through listing requirements on stock exchanges.

---

[8] Michael Porter, "Capital Disadvantage: America's Failing Capital System," *Harvard Business Review* 72 (1992): 65–83. Porter was a leader in encouraging comparative rather than U.S.-centric study of countries and firm strategy.

[9] See Michel Albert, *Capitalism versus Capitalism: How America's Obsession with Individual Achievement and Short-Term Profit Has Led to the Brink of Collapse* (New York: Four Walls Eight Windows, 1993); Masahiko Aoki, *Information, Corporate Governance, and Institutional Diversity: Competitiveness in Japan, the United States, and the Transitional Economies* (New York: Oxford University Press, 2001); Peter A. Hall and David Soskice, eds., *Varieties of Capitalism: The Institutional Foundations of Comparative Advantage* (New York: Oxford University Press, 2001); and Dore 2000.

[10] See Henry Hansmann and Reinier Kraakman, "The End of History for Corporate Law," *Georgetown Law Journal* 89 (2000): 439–67.

Legislation, stimulated in part by earlier scandals, produced financial separation of firms from insurance companies and banks. Antitrust rules, securities regulation, and accounting rules institutionalized these practices to generate what we now call the Anglo-American model.

The pattern we call American was not given as part of the natural contours of the North American tectonic plate. It was created by people. It came out of specific, identifiable decisions, made over time, in the various pieces of legislation we noted earlier, from the Sherman Antitrust Act of 1890 to Sarbanes-Oxley of 2002.

These "great reversals," to use the phrase of Rajan and Zingales, belie the notion found in the literature that governance patterns are "hard-wired," as the most prominent theory in the law-and-economics literature—the "legal family school"—strongly suggests.[11] Countries have long been classified according to their legal system of either "common" or "civil" law; case law has been associated with the United Kingdom and its colonial descendants, and civil law with France and its colonial or cultural descendants. La Porta, López-de-Silanes, Shleifer, and Vishny did important research on the differences in corporate law and in securities law, and found that they correlated with the degree of ownership concentration or diffusion, thus with corporate governance practices.[12] They then found that these practices, in turn, correlated with the distinction between common and civil law, the former producing the diffusion model, the latter producing block-holding. This analysis became thereby a widely cited theory of variance: country legal families shape corporate governance practice.

That theory, however, does not explain change: countries have shifted over time. Rajan and Zingales show that France and Japan had vibrant, diffused securities markets before World War I. After the war, policy and law changed: political factors—stronger trade unions, protectionist lobbies, "rent-seeking" business groups, banks—all pushed for a system that regulated markets and favored insider control. Corporate governance in the two countries became more blockholder oriented. At the same time, the United States went the other way, toward more diffuse shareholder patterns and stronger instruments of minority shareholder control.

Thus, corporate governance systems vary among countries around the world, and over time, corporate governance systems within countries change. We need robust, rigorous explanations of these changes, rather than shallow triumphalism (of any flavor) until the next swing of the pendulum. These explanations have to look at variables that themselves change: if corporate governance outcomes are the dependent variable, something in the independent variables must have produced the change. The decisive independent variables cannot therefore be "constants"

[11] See Raghuram Rajan and Luigi Zingales, "The Great Reversals: The Politics of Financial Development in the Twentieth Century," *Journal of Financial Economics* 69 (2003): 5–50.

[12] See Rafael La Porta, Florencio López-de-Silanes, Andrei Shleifer, and Robert Vishny, "Legal Determinants of External Finance," *Journal of Finance* 52 (1997): 1131–50; "Law and Finance," *Journal of Political Economy* 106 (1998): 1113–55; "Investor Protection and Corporate Governance," *Journal of Financial Economics* 58 (2000): 3–27; and "Investor Protection and Corporate Valuation," *Journal of Finance* 57 (2002): 1147–70.

in a country—for example, its legal family, something created centuries ago, which rarely changes and only very slowly. It cannot be the enduring "cultural" components of a country, its value systems, or habits, which define its essence, as these two also change very slowly, and cannot account for variance within the culture's practices. Thus change from one period to another, such as France from the 1940s to the present, cannot be explained by the enduring and continuous features of French civilization. Instead, in this book we seek an explanation of both static and dynamic variation in governance among countries, rooted in economic preferences and political institutions—in short, in politics.

Corporate governance practices reflect law and regulation. Laws express the outcome of political processes—a broad political bargain among the major players contesting a variety of policies that influence incentives, which in turn produce corporate governance outcomes. Our causal model looks at *preferences*—at interest groups that advocate policies that promote their goals—and at *political institutions*—the machinery that refracts the preferences and that aggregates them into policy outcomes.

Who are the players that produce these bargains? We start with the law-and-economics tradition, which focuses on owners and managers. These are key players in the problems of authority within the firm. They face the problem of the "incomplete contract," that is, how to handle the impossibility of specifying all future contingencies with a contract. This uncertainty creates a risk of moral hazard, the ability of an agent (here, the manager) to act against the goals of the principals (here, the owners). Owners need managers, but how do they know the managers will not abuse the discretion they are given? At the same time, outside investors seek protection from abuse by insiders. These conflicting goals shape policy preferences about rules. Managers and insider blockholders want autonomy. External investors want protection. The two groups will battle in the private and public spheres over the rules that shape governance of the firm.

To this mix we add workers, the employees of the firm. They are often left out of models of corporate governance, largely because the labor contract is assumed to be complete, fully specifying the conditions that merit either payment of a wage or dismissal. The completeness of the labor contract is contestable and does not at any rate fully cover the power of employees or the need for management and owners to have a well-functioning workforce. Workers have their own concerns about governance: how much of the firm's cash goes to protect job security, the level of pay, working conditions, health benefits, and, increasingly in some countries, the protection of their firm-related pension benefits.

"Owners" (O), "Managers" (M), and "Workers" (W) thus develop alternative preferences for a corporate governance regime. As there is more than one dimension in the preference functions of each group, they can combine in different coalitions. Owners and managers ally to contain workers' demands on wages and job security; workers and managers combine to secure employment and stable wages in the firm; and workers and owners combine to contain managerial agency costs and preserve the security of their investments and pensions, and even jobs. These coalitional alignments of O, M, and W are summarized in table 2.4, and the reasoning behind the preferences, the coalitions, and their consequences is developed in chapter 3.

To get what they want in law and regulation, however, these actors must move disagreements inside the firm out into the public arena. To obtain their preferred corporate governance outcome, they have to win in politics. To do that, they have to mobilize allies outside the firm. Each type of player—owners, managers, workers—has counterparts in society: fellow owners, managers, and workers. To some degree players make their appeal based on some common ground—for example, all workers may be assumed to have a common interest, and all owners a common interest in opposition to workers (see chapter 5). But there may be cleavages within each group and other criteria of attraction across class bounds. Workers in a vigorous export industry may diverge from those in a declining or uncompetitive one or from those in nontradables. They may ally with managers and owners on sectoral rather than class grounds (see chapter 6). Workers with substantial pension holdings may have preferences different from those of workers wholly dependent on PAYGO (pay as you go) public-sector social security. Indeed, we see the growth of pension funds as a substantial driver of new coalitional possibilities, drawing worker-based pension funds into alliance with minority shareholder groups against insider managers and blockholders. This approach is contrary to most scholarly treatments, which see workers in direct opposition to outside investors. In order to convey these relationships we provide an analysis of the structure of pension fund systems (see chapter 7). Blockholders with substantial assets in a specific firm may think differently than owners with dispersed, diffuse shareholdings. We therefore will need to make our model more complex, at the expense of parsimony.

As workers, owners, and managers turn to society, they find a complex structure. Many voters and interest groups interact with the firm but are not part of it—indeed, vertical "disintegration" is so extensive that more and more relationships are enacted across firms rather than within them. Firms have many relationships "upstream" and "downstream," with suppliers above, distributors below. They are located in cities and districts that care about the success of particular firms. Lawyers, accountants, bond-rating agencies, banks, and financial intermediaries all make a living dealing with firms.

These groups thus have a double interest: in one guise, they identify with the firm that gives them business. In another, they are a group unto themselves, a caste, or a corps within the system, with its own sectoral interests, interest groups, and concerns. Thus the accounting industry has its own lobbies that defend goals in the system, to preserve the profitability of the industry as a whole or of specific firms. The same can be said for the other groups—the so-called reputational intermediaries that provide information to investors, shaping the financial image of the firm.[13]

Some researchers call these many groups with an interest in the firm "stakeholders," actors with a stake in the firm. The label contrasts with the "shareholder"

---

[13] See Timothy J. Sinclair, *The New Masters of Capital: American Bond Rating Agencies and the Politics of Creditworthiness* (Ithaca, N.Y.: Cornell University Press, 2004); and "Global Monitor: Bond Rating Agencies," *New Political Economy* 8 (2003): 147–61.

approach, where a fiduciary hierarchy gives a clear primacy to shareholders and their agents, managers. The distinction is both descriptive and normative. For our purposes, all society has some voice in the firm because the rules are made by a political system in which the "citizens" of society are far more numerous than the "citizens" of the firm. The players in the firm, as they turn to politics to get the regulations they prefer, have to appeal to a broad set of external stakeholders. Unraveling the politics of regulation obligates us to look at instruments of linkage and aggregation, methods of combining citizens, voters, and interests into a political process.

For this we look at political institutions, which aggregate preferences into a process that produces outcomes. These include the formal constitutional institutions of a political system, such as legislative-executive relations, electoral laws, and federalism, and the private ones, such as political parties and interest groups. Researchers on a variety of policy issues find that the type of political system influences the content of policy. For example, single-member winner-take-all electoral systems are more likely to generate consumer-oriented policies, with more competition and lower prices, than are electoral systems with proportional representation or multiseat districts.

We apply these ideas about institutions to corporate governance. Following Arend Lijphart and others, we sort political systems into "majoritarian" and "consensus" types.[14] The first is typified by the U.K. Westminster system, where the government rests on a majority of deputies in the lower house, chosen by single-member plurality districts. The second is typified by Sweden and a number of democracies in continental Europe, where the government relies on a majority of deputies provided by a coalition of political parties chosen through proportional representation.

Majoritarian systems are more likely to generate policies that encourage patterns of diffuse governance, while consensus systems generate blockholding. The effect seems to lie in the greater continuity of policy within consensus systems. This stability reassures actors, who then are more likely to invest in relationship-specific assets, which in turn sustain the more stable governance model of blockholding. Majoritarian systems produce greater swings in policy, which reward investment in more flexible strategies, which sustain the diffuse governance model. These ideas are developed further in chapter 4 and in the country narratives.

PUTTING THE PIECES TOGETHER: IN SEARCH OF A POLITICAL EXPLANATION

To sum up: we explain corporate governance outcomes through public policy that is generated by the interaction of interest group preferences and political institutions. Our argument puts great emphasis on public policy and incentives. Corporate governance patterns reflect strategic choices among players seeking to realize some kind

---

[14] See Arend Lijphart, *Patterns of Democracy: Government Forms and Performance in Thirty-six Countries* (New Haven: Yale University Press, 1999).

of gain: money, security, and so on. Players pick institutional forms according to what suits those preferences. If we know the relevant laws and regulations that structure the incentives, we know what happens in corporate governance.

Which are the relevant laws? We cast this question more broadly than much of the literature. Certainly corporate governance law matters, but so do measures normally excluded from that label, which we group together as *minority shareholder protections* (MSPs). We extend the discussion to include *degrees of coordination* (DoC), the rules that structure markets more broadly, including labor law, antitrust law, price determinations, supplier–distributor relations, all elements of the economy that correlate very highly with patterns of corporate governance. A growing body of research comparing market economies notes the strong covariance of corporate governance with these other arenas of policy. Knowing a country's policies on labor, or welfare, or competition gives us substantial power to predict its laws on diffusion or blockholding and on MSP. In their influential book *The Varieties of Capitalism*, Peter Hall and David Soskice sort advanced industrial countries into two categories: liberal market economies (LMEs) and coordinated market economies (CMEs).[15] Its type of economy influences a country's politics affecting corporate governance. This is the variable we call degrees of coordination, which measures the differences between these two categories of economic systems.

The connection between the DoC variables derived from the varieties-of-capitalism literature and MSP is suggestive. MSP provides some important explanations for corporate governance, but it leaves numerous outliers, and correlations are weak, especially for the CME countries. There we find blockholding even if MSPs are reasonably strong. Sweden and Germany are notable examples. It is possible that the reason lies with the DoC variables: countries that produce high levels of coordination are dampening the incentives for shareholder diffusion.

We find empirically that MSP and the DoC variables influence the pattern of corporate governance. This helps us frame the core question: What explains the provision or lack of high MSP and the provision or lack of policies that favor different DoC? Since MSP and DoC originate in policies, we need to look at the politics that explain the policies.

This is where we turn to interest group preferences, partisan conflicts, and political institutions. We examine interest group and political party variables, following different principles of cleavage: class conflict (left versus right, labor [workers] versus capitalists [investors]); sectoral cleavage (along industry rather than class lines); and a cross-class coalition of labor and minority shareholders against inside blockholders. We also examine the way institutions influence the likely winners of these contests.

This examination gives us a strong picture of the "comparative statics" of the story. It helps us pinpoint whether, at specific moments in time, the corporate governance pattern correlates with specific political variables. This is important, as many of the disagreements over explanations of corporate governance turn on such "point in time" comparisons.

---

[15] Hall and Soskice, 2001.

The preceding step does not, however, allow us to explore the dynamics of change: What causes movement from one system to another? For that question we need a dynamic comparison, to see if change in the variables leads over time to change in outcomes. A perfect world of information would allow us to perform that analysis, but the data is flawed. For key variables, such as patterns of diffusion, we do not have good historical comparative data. On some dimensions we can show change over time, and we can supplement this evidence with analytic narratives that highlight the interactions at play. Thus we integrate country case narratives into our discussion.

These narratives suggest a complex causal pattern. We doubt a perfect comparative statics will achieve a satisfying explanation. Historical context makes for twists and turns that require something more flexible for causal understanding. Countries make choices at key moments that have long-standing effects. Early and late development à la Gerschenkron, world wars and depression, dictatorship and democracy—all enter the story and need to be integrated into our account.[16]

Our account of incentives makes us skeptical about arguments that predict convergence toward a single model. Much talk about the world economy assumes a single, optimal pattern, a single equilibrium, a unique and perfect way of combining all the ingredients of the economy, so that market competition will force all countries to converge. We are doubtful. The economy is too complex; there are too many ways of putting the pieces together. Convergence assumes a relentless and powerful selection mechanism, clearly rewarding some behaviors as it clearly punishes others.

We don't see this mechanism at work in corporate governance. At times the German and Japanese model has performed very well, at other times not. At times the U.S. model has done superbly, at other times not. Some governance mechanisms do better under certain conditions and worse under others. And conditions change, often faster than the relevant policies, so countries have choices to make. Changing circumstances change the incentives that affect policy—the inducements to change or preserve the rules. Countries may be politically efficient, but not economically so: they respond to political forces pushing for change or preventing it.

Since countries vary in their internal political dynamics—institutions, preferences, parties, and interest groups—their policy outcomes vary. And thus their corporate governance systems will differ. Change may occur, but not necessarily toward convergence on a single model of governance.

POLICY CONSEQUENCES

This book is primarily about the causes of corporate governance systems, rather than a careful study of the consequences. The two are linked in our argumentation:

---

[16] Alexander Gerschenkron, *Economic Backwardness in Historical Perspective* (Cambridge: Harvard University Press, 1962).

people fight about corporate governance because it affects their lives. Their motives in caring about governance are connected to how it affects their income, their jobs, and their security. We do not, however, provide a systematic exploration of those consequences. We have studied them, but we leave to others exploration of the output in detail.

However, the profound consequences of corporate governance systems have, in our opinion, been insufficiently appreciated. They have not been at the center of investigation in several fields where we think they actually have substantial effects. The literature on comparative capitalisms, for example, was for many years dominated by discussion about the role of the state, comparing the strong state to the weak state. This was an interesting question, but insufficient. The state operates less by picking winners and industrial policy than by structuring the relationships among actors in the market economy, in which the relationships within and between firms is central. The type of state intervention is shaped by the type of governance; it is a prior important choice.

Much literature in comparative capitalism has also looked at social services, the welfare state, income equality, education, labor, and training. All are important topics, but again the role of corporate governance in shaping them has been underplayed (though that is changing). The firm's incentives to invest in worker training, health, and job stability are connected to the governance system: diffuse shareholder firms have limited incentives to invest in workers, while the blockholder system has more.

Trade disputes are rarely studied from the perspective of corporate governance, yet underlying many of these disagreements is the system of relationships structured by governance rules, broadly understood. Japanese firms rely on their network of suppliers, not because they are Japanese but because they are interlinked by cross-shareholding.

Corruption, democracy, and accountable governments both reflect and shape corporate governance patterns. In some countries, blockholding mingles with authoritarianism to mask structures and events. Transparency in politics is needed to sustain transparency in the economy, and each can stimulate the other. The Korean experience, where democratization led to governance reform, is an example that we examine in later chapters. International corruption is also affected by transparency or the lack thereof. For example, money laundering is more difficult when the corporate governance reporting standards are high.

We do not have a strong conviction about the virtues of one system over another. We resist the triumphalism of the Washington consensus that the American way is the only way, and we are skeptical about Japanese or German triumphalism as well. The best version of each type of governance has strong virtues as well as characteristic weaknesses. A stakeholder system can be efficient and honest, a diffusion system can be corrupted and perverted in its operation—and vice versa. We think diversity is a good thing. Each system can provide strengths to the international division of labor. Organizational form complements comparative advantage; having more than one kind can increase productivity. Organizational diversity is inevitable in any case. It behooves us to understand its causes.

PLAN OF ATTACK

The book is organized as follows:

Chapter 2 provides a schematic plan for our book and the data on which it relies. It describes the variance of governance patterns around the world, the logic of the argumentation, and the data sources we use to test our explanation of variance.

Chapter 3 examines economic theories of the governance of firms: a technological competition view drawn from Chandler, and the "nexus of contracts" view in law and economics derived from Coase. From this examination we derive the major policy variables that require explanation: the provision or absence of MSP, and the economic policies grouped under DoC.

Chapter 4 lays out the political variables, the preferences of interest groups, and the aggregating mechanisms of political institutions. It evaluates the legal family interpretation associated with La Porta et al., and the economic sociology tradition.

Chapters 5 through 7 examine the three preference group cleavages: workers versus owners and managers in the class conflict cleavage, workers and managers versus owners in the sectoral cleavage, and workers and owners versus managers in the transparency coalition. In each of these chapters we provide detailed case studies of some of the 39 countries whose data we have gathered: Chile, China, France, Korea, Germany, Japan, Malaysia, the Netherlands, Singapore, Sweden, the United Kingdom, and the United States.

Chapter 8, the conclusion, analyzes the patterns we observe in these case studies, the implications of the findings for debates about explanation of governance patterns and about convergence, and issues for further research.

We expect that diverse readers may choose different paths through the book. Many will prefer to read the theoretical setup first before the application and the country cases, and thus will read it in the order presented. Others may explore more effectively by inference from cases and political context, and could move therefore from here to chapters 5–7 and selected country cases, and then move backward. There are many paths through the trees to the forest, or the forest to the trees.

Governance Patterns: What Causes What?

How DO POLITICS shape the type of corporate governance we find in various countries? The previous chapter summarizes our ideas. This chapter lays out the operationalization of those ideas and presents a schematic summary of the sequence of causality in our argument.

We expose the reader to a plethora of numbers and data sets in this book and believe it is wise to introduce at the outset the kinds of data we are using. Different data sets are used to establish both correlation and causation throughout the subsequent chapters, so we think it helpful to lay out the sources of these numbers in advance. Readers more interested in the results than the empirical process may wish to skip this chapter and, perhaps, return later.

The *dependent variable*—what we are trying to explain—is the pattern of corporate governance in countries around the world, both a snapshot of the whole sample today, and within a given country over time. Our prime indicator of corporate governance consists of shareholder ownership—*diffusion* versus *concentration* in blockholding. These terms are explained more fully in chapter 1 and chapter 3.

The pattern of governance worldwide, we argue, is caused by two groups of *variables* (what we are explaining with): the *policies* that shape corporate governance (intervening variables) and the *politics* (independent variables) that shape those policies.

The politics independent variable is composed of *preferences* and *institutions*. Interest groups have preferences, which are then aggregated by political institutions. This process generates "winners," coalitions that obtain corporate governance policies they prefer. This, the policy variable (an *intermediate*, or intervening, variable in scholar-speak), consists of sets of regulations sometimes known as *capitalist economics patterns*, or CEPs. We focus on two principal policy components of the CEPs: minority shareholder protections (MSPs) and degrees of coordination (DoCs): liberal versus highly coordinated, derived from the varieties-of-capitalism literature.

Our causal model is represented in figure 2.1, with the independent variables on the left side, dependent variable outcomes on the right. There is also a feedback loop from outcomes back to independent variables; more on this later.

This chapter explains, for each block in the model, how the variable is defined ("operationalized"), how we measure it, the distribution of our country sample for this variable, and our approach to the statistical relationship between these variables and the next block in the causal sequence.

Some of the data we use are drawn from firm-level, microeconomic analysis. Others are macro data, such as on capital flows and aggregate savings, and yet

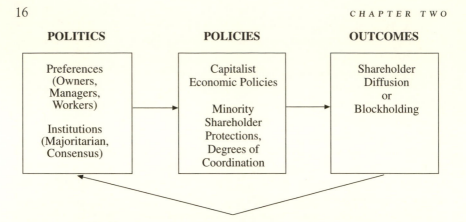

| POLITICS | POLICIES | OUTCOMES |

Figure 2.1 Causal Schema (also reproduced as figure 4.1, p.58)

others are composite indices of national-level politics. We draw on several political science indices describing political institutions. These data sets are familiar to the specialists in each field, but are rarely (to our knowledge) used together, so it is important for the reader to understand where all these numbers come from, as well as their analytic strengths and weaknesses. We dwell in more detail on shortcomings of this data, as well as the robustness of evidence for our tests, in the concluding chapter 8.

Outcomes: Dependent Variables and Patterns of Control

We measure patterns of governance in this book primarily with a data set that measures control of the firm: how concentrated or diffuse is the shareholding of listed firms.

Close managerial supervision by owners requires that they have substantial direct control: for that, they need to have a concentration of voting shares, sometimes referred to as *blockholding*. If shareholding is diffuse, then diffuse owners use other mechanisms of supervision (a board of directors they elect, information made public, a market for control and other instruments) to protect their interests.

In the last decade, particularly in the last five years, scholars have made enormous progress deciphering the puzzle of corporate ownership. Following breakthrough research by Mayer and Franks, who argued that U.S.-style diffuse ownership was more the exception than the rule, several ambitious projects analyzed listed companies in Europe, Asia, and most emerging markets, in search of ultimate ownership.[1] These efforts included a survey of 10 countries by the

[1] Julian R. Franks and Colin Mayer, "Capital Markets and Corporate Control: A Study of France, Germany, and the UK," *Economic Policy* 5 (1990): 191–231; "Hostile Takeovers and the Correction of Managerial Failure," *Journal of Financial Economics* 40 (1996): 163–81; "Corporate Ownership and Control in the UK, Germany, and France," *Bank of America Journal of Applied Corporate Finance* 9 (1997): 30–45.

European Corporate Governance Network team, reported by Barca and Becht; research by a team under the direction of La Porta, López-de-Silanes, Shleifer, and Vishny, whose database ultimately grew to 49 countries; a World Bank study led by Stijn Claessens, who applied similar methods to firms in 9 Asian countries; and refinement of the European countries data by Faccio and Lang.[2]

Sifting through ownership records, company reports, and regulatory filings, these scholars worked backwards up the chain of ownership to trace out control of firms and assign them one of several ownership "buckets"—individually held (which includes families), government held, or widely held. The threshold defining control in these studies varies, at either 10 percent or 20 percent of total shares. In this book, we use the 20 percent threshold for assigning a firm as block-held, versus diffusely owned.

The ownership buckets are then used to calculate a single concentration figure for a whole country. For example, in the case of Japan, the market value of all the listed firms controlled by individual blockholders amounts to 4.1 percent of the total stock market capitalization of Japanese stock markets. In the case of Chile, on the other hand, the market value of all the listed firms controlled by individual blockholders accounts for 90 percent of the country's total stock market capitalization.

Japan and Chile are at opposite ends of a continuum running from the diffusion to the blockholder pattern, with other countries falling between. The United States, the United Kingdom, Canada, and Australia fall towards the diffuse shareholding end. Italy, Germany, Sweden, most of the rest of continental Europe, Asia, and Latin America are closer to the blockholding end. Table 2.1 lists countries by degree of ownership concentration.

Our sample of 39 countries accounts for 99.5 percent of the total world equity markets—virtually the complete universe of public corporations—so we are confident that the tests against the sample are representative of the underlying domain. The sample has the additional virtue of being geographically representative, including countries from Europe, North and South America, South and East Asia, and a few data points from the Middle East and Africa.

There is considerable variance of control by blockholders in this country sample around a mean value of 47, with a high of 90 and a low of 4. This sample is negatively skewed, with most countries falling between the 40 and 70 percent levels, as figure 2.2 shows.

Despite this clumping around the 40 to 60 percent level of blockholding, variation among countries is substantial. For example, concentration levels in countries such as Argentina and Hong Kong are five times higher than in the United

[2] Stijn Claessens, Simeon Djankov, Joseph P. H. Fan, and Larry H. P. Lang, "Diversification and Efficiency of Investment in East Asian Corporations," World Bank Working Paper, 1998, "Expropriation of Minority Shareholders: Evidence from East Asian Corporations," World Bank Working Paper, 1998; Rafael La Porta, Florencio López-de-Silanes, and Andrei Shleifer, "Corporate Ownership around the World," *Journal of Finance* 54 (1999): 471–517; Fabrizio Barca and Marco Becht, *The Control of Corporate Europe* (New York: Oxford University Press, 2001); Mara Faccio and Larry H. P. Lang, "The Ultimate Ownership of Western European Corporations," *Journal of Financial Economics* 65 (2002): 365–95.

TABLE 2.1
Ownership Concentration

Concentration	Country	Concentration	Country
4.1	Japan	49	Venezuela
5	China	51.5	Belgium
15	United States	51.9	Thailand
20	Netherlands	52	South Africa
23.6	United Kingdom	52.8	Austria
24.6	Ireland	55	Israel
27	New Zealand	55.8	Spain
27.5	Australia	58	Turkey
27.5	Canada	59.6	Italy
31.8	South Korea	60.3	Portugal
37.5	Denmark	63	Brazil
38.6	Norway	64.6	Germany
42.6	Malaysia	64.8	France
43	India	66	Mexico
44.8	Singapore	67.3	Indonesia
45.5	Taiwan	71.5	Hong Kong
46.4	Philippines	72.5	Argentina
46.9	Sweden	75	Greece
48.1	Switzerland	90	Chile
48.8	Finland		

Source: Claessens et al. 1998a, 1998b, 2,980 public corporations in 9 countries; Barca and Becht 2001; Faccio and Lang 2002, 5232 listed firms; La Porta, López-de-Silanes and Shleifer 1999, 20 largest firms for "large," 10 largest "small" firms for large; for Korea, Jang 2003, table 10; for Chile, Lefort and Walker, 1999; for China, Lin, "Public Vices in Public Places: Challenges in Corporate Governance Development in China," In *The History of Corporate Governance around the World: Family Business Groups to Professional Managers*. Randall Morck, ed. Chicago: University of Chicago Press, forthcoming.

Note: The full table of concentration from which table 2.1 is drawn is reproduced in the data appendix.

States, the United Kingdom, and Japan. Variation within the Organization for Economic Cooperation and Development (OECD) countries runs from Greece at 75 percent to Japan at 4 percent, a ratio of 1:18.

Only three countries—the United States, Japan, and China—fall below the 20 percent concentration ratio. Only six countries fall below 25 percent, meaning that diffuse ownership is relatively rare.

Some readers will object to our characterization of Japan or China as low-concentration countries, given the well-known fact of *keiretsu* cross-shareholdings on the Tokyo Stock Exchange, and the somewhat less known fact that the Chinese government owns 95 percent of the firms by value listed on both domestic and foreign (mostly Hong Kong) exchanges. This is a crucial distinction: a large percentage of the shares of Japanese and Chinese firms may be owned by other firms or by state-controlled entities, but when the network of ownership is traced and no individual or family owns 20 percent or more of the shares, then the firm is dropped into either the diffuse or the state-owned bucket. Japan and China are

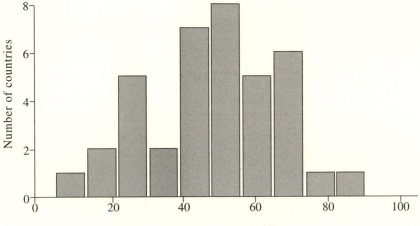

Figure 2.2 Blockholding Histogram

therefore correctly classified according to shareholding concentration, but their cases show a limit to the accuracy of this indicator in fully revealing the character of control in governance mechanisms.

The numbers presented so far represent the pattern in the late 1990s. This static snapshot does not show changes in patterns of ownership over time. As noted in the previous chapter, "great reversals" have taken place, to use the phrase of Rajan and Zingales. Countries have not simply held to one system but have changed over time.

Evidence comes largely from longitudinal studies of ownership concentration in specific countries. A group of scholars headed by Morck is reconstructing historical trends of blockholding in Japan, France, the Netherlands, Italy, Canada, the United States, and the United Kingdom.[3] These materials show striking changes over time within countries.

Rajan and Zingales present data on the size of equity markets in relation to GDP over time. This measure is not the same as concentration of ownership, for it leaves aside the key question of how that shareholding is structured for the

[3] The materials are planned to be published by University of Chicago Press as *The History of Corporate Governance around the World: Family Business Groups to Professional Managers*, edited by Randall Morck, and can be found in draft via the NBER: http://www.nber.org/books/corp-owner03/index.html. On the United Kingdom, Julian Franks, Colin Mayer, and Stefano Rossi, "Spending Less Time with the Family: The Decline of Family Ownership in the UK"; on the Netherlands, Abe de Jong and Ailsa Roell, "Financing and Control in the Netherlands: A Historical Perspective"; on Canada, Randall Morck, Michael Percy, Gloria Tian, and Bernard Yeung, "The Rise and Fall of the Widely Held Firm: A History of Corporate Ownership in Canada"; on China, William Goetzmann and Elisabeth Koll, "The History of Corporate Ownership in China"; on France, Antoine E. Murphy, "Corporate Ownership in France—the Importance of History"; on France, Caroline Fohlin, "The History of Corporate Ownership and Control in Germany"; on Sweden, Peter Hogfeldt, "The History and Politics of Corporate Ownership in Sweden"; and on the United States, Marco Becht and J. Bradford DeLong, "Corporate Control in the United States: An Historical Perspective."

Table 2.2
The "Great Reversals": Evolution of Equity Markets' Capitalization to GDP (%)

	1913	1960	1999
France	.78	.28	1.17
Germany	.44	.35	.67
Japan	.49	.36	.95
Netherlands	.56	.67	2.03
Sweden	.47	.24	1.77
United Kingdom	1.09	1.15	2.25
United States	.39	.61	1.52
Japan	.08	.15	.08

Source: Adapted from Rajan and Zingales 2003, table 3.

purpose of supervision.[4] It is, however, one of the few indicators on which data can be gathered over time. It was also a mainstay of an earlier wave of research that measured governance systems by the role of banks, as distinguished from stock markets, the debt/equity ratio. Table 2.2 is a summary; we provide in the data appendix a full table from their work (see appendix table A.3).

We stress that the data available for measuring variance of shareholder concentration over time is not robust. The sample size is small, the data points are few, or the measures are indirect. As a result, the principal measure we use for correlations and causal tests in this book is the snapshot of concentration in table 2.1, which is largely based on data from the late 1990s. However rough, the data suggests major changes over time within countries.

CAPITALIST ECONOMIC POLICIES, MINORITY SHAREHOLDER PROTECTIONS, AND DEGREES OF COORDINATION

In the policy block of our causal schema, we use two areas of policy, each with its own data sets: one for minority shareholder protections and another set of values known as the degrees of coordination index, drawn from the varieties-of-capitalism literature.

We argue that the incentives for blockholding and diffusion are influenced by a variety of rules, regulations, formal institutions, and informal practices set by public policy. The elements of MSP are the most well known and frequently used

---

[4] "A more stable measure of the importance of the equity market is the total stock market capitalization. A drawback is that this measure captures the amount of equity listed, not the amount of equity raised. Thus, the presence of a few companies that have greatly appreciated in value can give the impression of an important equity market even when the amount of funds raised in the market is tiny. On the positive side, however, this measure is less cyclical than the previous one and thus is better for making comparisons across countries and across time periods." Rajan and Zingales 2003, 11.

variables in research on governance, with the best-developed, if still flawed, data. In this book we extend the analysis to a wider set of policies than MSP, which also shape incentives on governance, including labor relations, product market competition, coordination among employers, education and training systems, and some supplier-producer relationships.[5]

Minority Shareholder Protections (MSPs)

Central to major debates on corporate governance is the role of minority share-holder protections (MSPs). These shield external investors from the abuse of inside blockholders and managers. They provide information: disclosure and audit, oversight (boardroom composition), control (the market for control of the firm), and managerial incentives (most notably, compensation). These are the most important shareholder protections. MSPs are critical to the willingness of block-holders to give up controlling positions in the firm, and (by the same token, on the other side of the transactions) of outside investors to purchase a minority stake in the firm.

We codify four dimensions for MSP in chapter 3, table 3.1, drawing on standardized measures provided by corporate governance scholars, and backfilling for a few missing values to fill out our country sample. This table shows the level of protection for each dimension, a composite for that country, and international ranking by country. As with concentration, there is a high degree of variation in MSP in our sample. On the high end of the MSP scale are the United States, Singapore, Canada, United Kingdom, Australia, Hong Kong, and Ireland; on the low end are China, Indonesia, Turkey, Italy, and Portugal. For the 39 countries for which we were able to collect these data, the minimum value is China (11) and the maximum value is the United States (97).

In chapter 3 we test the correlation between MSP and concentration. As predicted, these values are negatively correlated, with a value of −.33 for the whole sample. The graphical distribution is scattered around a 45-degree line in figure 3.3, with the United States and the United Kingdom (GB) on the lower-right-hand side, and countries such as Italy (IT) on the upper left. But there are many prominent outliers: Chile (CL), Hong Kong (HK), and France (FR) have high protections but also high concentration, while Japan (JP), Netherlands (NL), and China (CN) have low protections but also low concentration. We later explore factors that might explain the outliers and the fact that the negative correlation is relatively weak.

Degrees of Coordination (DoC)

To measure these relationships, for a subset of our country sample we use data developed in the varieties-of-capitalism literature, which compares countries by

[5] Luigi Zingales, "In Search of New Foundations," *Journal of Finance* 55 (2000): 1623–53; Paul Milgrom and John Roberts, "The Economics of Modern Manufacturing: Technology, Strategy, and Organization," *American Economic Review* 80 (1990): 511–28; Bengt Holmstrom and Paul Milgrom, "The Firm as an Incentive System," *American Economic Review* 84 (1994): 972–91.

the degree of coordination in their economies. The levels of coordination are in turn shaped by regulations, which are in turn the product of politics. Coordination levels are thus in market economics a proxy for policies and laws that shape the structure of market relationships. They extend the arena of regulation that affects corporate governance beyond the domain covered by MSP. Societies with high levels of coordination have incentives toward shareholding concentration. Coordinated economies (CMEs) provide incentives toward blockholding, whereas noncoordinated economies (LMEs) encourage diffusion.

These measures tell us something about "institutional complementarity": how the pieces of an economy fit together. LMEs have diffuse corporate governance mechanisms, while CMEs have blockholding systems. We provide measures of institutional complementarity as indicators of LME versus CME patterns and show their correlation with corporate governance indicators. In this book, primarily in chapter 3, we use the coordination index developed by Gingerich and Hall as shown in table 3.2.[6] For the 20 countries for which this index is measured on a scale from 0 to 1, the lowest value is the United States (0), the maximum value is .95, the mean is .51 and the standard deviation is large, .35. As expected, we find that the coordination index has a strong negative correlation with minority shareholder protections (−.89) and a strong positive correlation with ownership concentration (+.62).

POLITICS: PREFERENCES AND INSTITUTIONS

The politics box in our causal schema produces the MSP and CEP values in the policy box in figure 2.1. Political coalitions take control of the policy machinery to set the rules of the corporate governance game. Which coalitions form, and which ones win in the political contest, depends in turn on the interaction of preferences and institutions. Preferences reflect the distributional consequences of difference corporate governance patterns for individuals and groups; institutions shape how those preferences are aggregated in politically potent, mobilized groups of actors.

Preferences

We have no direct evidence, nor any convenient index, to measure the *ex ante* preferences for corporate governance on the part of owners, managers, or workers. These are worked out deductively in chapter 3, based on the distributional consequences for these three groups of different mechanisms of governance. We assume these distributional preferences are invariant among countries—a simplifying, and not entirely arbitrary, assumption.

[6] Peter A. Hall and Daniel W. Gingerich, "Varieties of Capitalism and Institutional Complementarities in the Macroeconomy: an Empirical Analysis," paper presented to the Annual Meeting of the American Political Science Association, August 2001, San Francisco.

Table 2.3
Political Coalitions and Governance Outcomes

Coalitional Lineup	Winner	Political Coalition Label	Predicted Outcome
Pair A: Class Conflict:			
Owners + managers vs. workers	Owners + managers	Investor	Diffusion
Owners + managers vs. workers	Workers	Labor	Blockholding
Pair B: Sectoral:			
Owners vs. managers + workers	Managers + workers	Corporatist compromise	Blockholding
Owners vs. managers + workers	Owners	Oligarchy	Blockholding
Pair C: Property and Voice:			
Owners + workers vs. managers	Owners + workers	Transparency	Diffusion
Owners + workers vs. managers	Managers	Managerism	Diffusion

Note: Also reproduced as table 4.1, p. 60.

Over time, these preferences are interactive. A policy generates support for its continuance by eliminating its opponents and strengthening its beneficiaries and their commitment to the policy. This is the reason for the feedback loop from outcomes back to politics in the causal schema in figure 2.1.

The various arguments we examine suggest different mechanisms of how owners, managers, and workers come together or conflict in shaping policy. These coalitions are depicted schematically in table 2.3.

Since we have no direct way of measuring preferences empirically, and since there are two variables at work in coalition formation, we employ indirect measures to test our sample of countries in order to determine which coalition is successfully shaping corporate governance outcomes in its favor. This is tricky work; the measures are embedded in sometimes elaborate theories of finance or politics with different assumptions and rules of evidence.

In this book we examine six alternative coalitions, which fit into three overall categories sharing common assumptions about the fundamental cleavage in distributional preferences. The first category is "class conflict," which includes the "investor" model and "labor" model. The second category is "sectoral," which includes a "corporatist compromise" model and (a rather less common) "oligarchy" model. The third category is "property and voice," including both the "transparency" coalition and its default state, a rather clumsily termed "managerism" model.

PAIR A: CLASS CONFLICT MODELS

The class conflict models we measure with indicators of capital flows for the investment version, and of partisan political conflict for the labor power version.

For the investment models we analyze data on the growth of institutional investor assets and their "penetration ratio" in stock markets around the world in tables 5.1 and 5.2.

Table 5.3 shows the substantial growth of institutional investor assets.[7] According to this table, institutional investors in the United States and the United Kingdom control three-quarters of the total assets, and allocate between two and three times the proportion of their assets invested in equities. Anglo-American investors account for 80 percent of total equity holdings among the 10 countries in this data sample. We have good data on institutional investor assets for only 10 of the 39 countries in our sample. The high-income countries clearly dominate this list, but Anglo-American investors' weight far exceeds their GDP weight on this list, so something is at work beyond income levels: we examine the crucial role of the financial sector in forming these assets pools at several points in the book.

The mean weight of foreign penetration of stock markets doubled in the 1990s for those countries for which data is available, from 12 percent in 1990 to 25.1 percent in 2000. For developed countries, the mean value grew from 15 percent in 1990 to 28.6 percent a decade later; for emerging countries, foreign penetration increased fivefold, from 2.3 percent in 1990 to 13 percent in 2000.

There is considerable variation in penetration levels among countries, determined by many variables, including the absolute size of stock market capitalization, the correlation of these markets with U.S. and U.K. securities markets (the less correlated, the more attractive from a portfolio standpoint), investment regulations, country risk, and so forth. But it is striking that the trend is uniformly in one direction—towards greater penetration of foreign investors, often to very high levels.

The labor side of the class conflict model looks at electoral outcomes to provide a measure of coalitional formation. Mark Roe, the pioneer in work of this kind, measures labor power (he calls it *social democratic power*) with "left" governments; the more years government lies with the "left," the greater the labor power, and the less likely is diffusion.[8] Like Roe, we draw on Cusack's measure of left versus right, though we use a wider time frame of 1960–96, our MSP index rather than his QCL (quality corporate law; see chapter 3) index drawn from La Porta et al., and a composite diffusion index consistent with our other tables. Our results, shown in table 5.4, are not as strong as Roe's, but we do find a statistical relationship between partisanship and governance outcomes.

Roe also tests social democratic strength by looking at job security legislation and at income inequality. We find a similar relationship using our MSP index (figures 5.6 and 5.7) but in chapter 6 offer a different interpretation of the politics that produces it: cross-class coalitions rather than left versus right.

The shortcoming of the measure we use for the labor power model is the relatively small country sample for which this data is available—the small-n problem

---

[7] Carolyn Brancato, "International Patterns of Institutional Investment," *Conference Board Institutional Investment Report*, April 2000, 26–31.

[8] Roe 2003b.

that bedevils us throughout this book. The labor power model is based primarily on a handful of western European countries, yet our intention in this book is to tease out a model with more global applicability.

PAIR B: SECTORAL MODELS

As alternatives to the class-based coalitions, we examine two cross-class possibilities, the corporatist bargain and the transparency coalition. In this pair, we have one cross-class coalition, that of corporatism, and its opposite, an oligarchic outcome.

To measure corporatism we rely principally on the Hicks-Kenworthy measure. (See appendix and table 6.1, which shows Sweden, Austria, Norway, Finland, Germany, and Japan as high in corporatism, with the United States, Canada, Ireland, United Kingdom and New Zealand as low.)

We have no empirical measure with which to probe oligarchic outcomes, and instead rely on a handful of descriptive country cases to illustrate what it looks like.

PAIR C: PROPERTY AND VOICE

The transparency coalition derives its potential from the growing importance of equity holdings in pension systems around the world. Countries differ considerably in the extent to which they rely on tax-financed PAYGO systems, with zero equity content, and securities-based, defined contribution systems.

We probe the transparency coalition with measures of pension asset accumulation, including a macro indicator of implicit pension debt (IPD), which has been calculated for a 25-country subset of the sample, and another index of institutional investor assets to GDP. These are contained in chapter 7.

We do not have a separate indicator for the default case of managerism in this pair. We argue that large equity pools are a precondition for both models, but that other variables, specifically regulations regarding institutional investors and reputational intermediaries (the structure of financial institutions), play a pivotal role in determining which outcome prevails.

In our analysis of preferences and coalitional politics, we frequently observe cleavages within our major group categories, and not only between them: owners divide into more than one type with different preferences, as do workers and managers. We explore some of the causes of these differences and their meaning for coalition formation in politics toward the end of chapter 7. For clarity of presentation and empirical testing throughout the book we use the simplified owners (O), workers (W), managers (M), diagram, table 2.3.

Institutions

Political institutions influence the way preferences are aggregated. We contrast "consensus" and "majoritarian" institutions. These are measured by data that deal with legislative matters—executive relations, electoral law, and party systems—which together measure veto players: the people whose consent is needed for policy to prevail. Consensus systems extend the net farther than do majoritarian ones: more groups are guaranteed a voice in them, whereas in majoritarian systems, groups can be more easily excluded. We provide these measures in chapter 4; see table 4.2.

The Scandinavian countries are predictably grouped together, towards the consensual end of the spectrum. But there are some counterintuitive results. Japan, for example, often considered an archetypical consensus political system, in fact falls quite close to the United States when measured objectively by this method.

We correlate our indicator with shareholder diffusion. The relationship is weak for the sample as a whole, stronger for the OECD countries, and meaningless for the emerging countries (see figures 4.2 and 4.3).

CONCLUSION

This chapter laid out the causal schema and highlights the data sources of our argument. The analysis and data are developed further in the relevant chapters. Gluttons for statistical punishment are encouraged to probe the data appendix at the end of the book, and the material on our website at http://www-irps.ucsd.edu/politicalpower.php.

Framing Incentives: The Economics and Law Tradition

WE REPEAT THE key question of this book: Why is there variance among governance systems? We have seen in the previous chapter that governance patterns vary substantially across countries and across time. Awareness of this variance is relatively recent—only a decade or so old—in the academic literature on corporate governance, though references to variance among countries and over time can be found in a few historical and comparative treatments. With that awareness has come a vigorous debate over explanations of the phenomenon. In this book we wade into the fray.

The assumptions of our approach are consistent with those of the so-called law-and-economics tradition, which sees corporate governance systems as a rational response to economic incentives. All the relevant players in the firm—managers, owners, and workers—are pursuing a strategy of optimizing their utility function. According to the logic of this approach, then, variation in corporate governance outcomes reflects variance in incentives.

We share this incentives-centered perspective, and set out to critique it from within: to explain the structure of incentives requires that we look at policies generated by political economy, not by law or economics as separate systems. The rules that create these incentives arise from the political process.

We draw on several strands of law and economics in order to identify which policies, laws, and regulations matter in shaping corporate governance, and thus which require explanation. In our model, these policies are the intervening independent variables—the policies produced by the political system, which in turn shape corporate governance outcomes. We call these policies *capitalist economic practices* (CEP), which consist of two components: (1) minority shareholder protections (MSP) and (2) degrees of coordination (DoC), the pattern of economic policy in each country, that is, market liberalism or coordination. DoC shape the way countries handle "institutional complementarity" in such fields as labor markets, price setting, antitrust, and product-market competitiveness.

As Zingales notes, the conceptualization of the governance problem turns on conceptualization of the firm.[1] We anchor our inquiry in debates from the law-and-economics tradition concerned with the "nexus of contracts," incomplete contracting, transactions costs, and principal-agent theories. It is from these approaches that we derive the importance of policies dealing with shareholder protection and institutional complementarity. We begin with an account of the origins of the debate, then examine the nexus of contracts framework, explore minority shareholder protections, and end the chapter with a discussion of degrees of coordination and institutional complementarity.

[1] Zingales 2000.

ORIGINS OF THE DEBATE

Interest in opening up the "black box" of the firm is relatively recent, and comparing boxes across countries even newer. Berle and Means's famous book published in the 1930s spoke of the separation of ownership and control in the United States, but initially prompted little exploration of this possibility in other countries.[2]

An important framework for thinking about structure of the firm arose from Alfred P. Chandler's pathbreaking *Strategy and Structure*, which examined the authority structure of the firm and its relationship to markets and technology.[3] As the complexity of the firm grew, it compelled a system of governance. Owners had to delegate. They needed managers able to grasp the complexity of the task, break activities into pieces, assign tasks, monitor behavior—the modern bureaucracy theorized by Max Weber. The structure varied with scale and complexity of technology. Complex tasks requiring huge amounts of capital, and high vertical integration required large firms with substantial bureaucratic delegation. Simpler technology, lower capital intensity, a less vertical integration required smaller firms with simpler organizational forms: compare, for example, a steel mill, auto plant, or integrated circuit manufacturer, all capital intensive and technically complex, with a hamburger stand, dry cleaner, or yard service.

Chandler did not focus on corporate governance, the problem of shareholders or issues of external finance. His major concern was with organizational capacity. The growing complexity of scale and scope of firms created a substantial challenge, how to structure delegation to make it work. As the firm developed in complexity owners needed professional managers: thus was born the problem of managerial agency costs. How could owners be sure that managers would promote their goals as owners—profits, growth—rather than steal (though tunneling, outright theft, or other means), or shirk (poor performance)? The bigger and more complex the firm, the greater the challenge to contain agency costs.[4]

Neither Chandler nor Berle and Means initially focused on a comparison across countries, thus on why the divergence in patterns of control occurred. But Chandler's ideas about organization of the firm laid the groundwork for thinking about its structure in ways that predicted how patterns of organizational form would spread: the firm's structure derived from the technology, scale, and scope of its activities. This would—in theory—be true around the world. Firms having similar economic conditions would look alike—the logic of efficiency required as

---

[2] Berle and Means 1932.

[3] Adfred Chandler, *Strategy and Structure: Chapters in the History of the Industrial Enterprise* (Cambridge: MIT Press, 1990).

[4] As we discuss below, blockholding was the first solution to this problem. Founders of firms held controlling numbers of shares and monitored managers directly. They were either on the board themselves or able to put trusted monitors (such as family members) on the board. Blockholder owners from the nineteenth-century United States (such as John D. Rockefeller of Standard Oil) to twentieth-century Korea (such as Chung Ju Yung of Hyundai) employed these solutions.

much. Thus, whatever was happening in the United States—the most advanced economy in the world and the largest—would generalize and spread as the technology of production spread around the world.

In this theoretical tradition, variance in governance patterns was explained by purely economic conditions: variation in technology, market size, scale and scope, and so on. Firms with similar characteristics in these variables would look alike, regardless of which country they called home. Countries undergoing economic development moved down the same path, a sequence of basic accumulation, takeoff, growth, and maturity, as schematized in Rostow's *Stages of Economic Growth*. Countries at similar levels of growth, technology, and markets would have similarly governed firms. Economists by and large did not consider variations in local conditions: national histories, institutions, politics, culture, and law. These variables are hard to measure and even harder to use as the foundation for predictions and empirical testing.

Some researchers, including economic historians, country specialists, and policy analysts, did consider local conditions. Gerschenkron's famous essay saw important differences in the role of banks across countries, leading to differences in governance structures; he explained this pattern with an economic argument, albeit a historically contextualized one, highlighting what was later called *path dependence*.[5] Germany developed a strong bank-centered economy because it was a late developer facing competition from the United Kingdom; similar logic could be applied to Japan. Schonfield's *Modern Capitalism* explored patterns of economic management and structure across industrial countries.[6] A European "national economy" tradition paid attention to structural differences, and a political economy literature took them seriously.

But by and large these ideas were not powerful in economics until the 1980s, at least not in the United States, and were marginalized in the scholarly mainstream. In the 1980s, the intellectual climate started to change. Economic reality was one cause: the rapid growth of Japan, the emergence of the East Asian tigers, the revival of Germany, and troubles in the American economy all raised questions about the American model, leading to a torrent of writing such as Michael Porter's "America's Failing Capital System," published in 1992 and the MIT study of U.S. manufacturing *Made in America*.[7]

The expectations of the Chandlerian school, that the corporate structure of firms, including corporate governance practices, would follow a similar trajectory in all countries as a function of industrial development, were undermined by several waves of comparative research and careful measurements in the 1980s and 1990s.

[5] Gerschenkron 1962.

[6] Andrew Schonfeld, *Modern Capitalism: The Changing Balance of Public and Private Power* (New York: Oxford University Press, 1965).

[7] Porter 1992; Michael L. Dertouzos, Richard K. Lester, Robert M. Solow, and the MIT Commission, *Made in America: Regaining the Productive Edge* (Cambridge: MIT Press, 1989); and Suzanne Berger, Michael L. Dertouzos, Richard K. Lester, and Robert M. Solow, "Toward a New Industrial America," *Scientific American* 260 (1989): 39–47.

"Structural Determinism" Debunked

Firms of similar size and technology in the same industry did not, in fact, look alike across countries. Mayer and Franks demonstrated that ownership structures in the United States were not the model for the rest of the world, for many countries were not developing the Berle-Means separation of ownership and control.[8] La Porta et al. produced a more comprehensive set of data that firmly established this fact for economists.[9] Sellier and other European researchers showed that French and German factories making the same product were organized quite differently.[10] The Sloan Foundation–sponsored book *The Machine That Changed the World* showed that Toyota's corporate governance structure was very different from that of General Motors.[11]

Along with a changed picture of the reality of economic performance emerged new theoretical perspectives. Microeconomics became substantially more important, calling attention to the institutions of the firm. This led to the second family of economic explanations of variance in corporate governance: the problem of incomplete contracts and its various solutions in private bonding, shareholder protections, and the nexus of contracts.

INCOMPLETE CONTRACTS AND PRIVATE ORDER

If the firm is, as neoclassical theory treats it, a black box production function that seeks to maximize profits, how are we to understand the division of revenues among the parties within the firm, including workers, managers, and shareholders? According to neoclassical economical theory, competitive markets will force firms to adopt the most efficient rules for structuring authority and distributing outputs. As inefficient forms are destroyed, convergence of governance forms takes place. At this level of abstraction in neoclassical economics, there is no sustained variance in corporate governance to be explained, and thus many classical economists disdain corporate governance as "epiphenomenal."

[8] Franks and Mayer 1990, 1996, 1997.

[9] La Porta et al. 1997, 1998, 2000; Rafael La Porta, Florencio López-de-Silanes, and Andrei Shleifer, forthcoming, "What Works in Securities Law?" *Journal of Finance*.

[10] Marc Maurice, François Sellier, and Jean-Jacques Silvestre, *The Social Foundations of Industrial Power: A Comparison of France and Germany*, trans. Arthur Goldhammer, (Cambridge: MIT Press, 1986). On the Italian model, see Richard Locke, *Remaking the Italian Economy* (Ithaca, N.Y.: Cornell, 1995). On choice among organizational forms, Michael Piore and Charles Sabel, *The Second Industrial Divide: Possibilities for Prosperity* (New York: Basic Books, 1984). Albert 1993; Dore 2000; and Aoki 2001 contrast economic organization in Japan and Germany with that of the United Kingdom and the United States. Some business schools paid serious attention to variance in firms' organization and cross-country differences; Michael Porter published work comparing country production systems, *The Competitive Advantage of Nations* (New York: Free Press, 1990).

[11] James P. Womack, Daniel T. Jones, and Daniel Roos, *The Machine That Changed the World: The Story of Lean Production* (New York: Harper Perennial, 1991). ·

In recent years, economists looking inside the black box raised some important questions. Coase had written about transactions costs: why, he asked, do we have firms rather than millions of independent entrepreneurs contracting with each other? The answer for Coase was that firms overcome the costs of the transactions involved in making these contracts.[12] Williamson stressed the importance of transactions costs; the greater the cost, the more reliance on hierarchy than markets. Alchain and Demsetz argued contracts could solve many of these problems in the market.[13] Jensen and Meckling pushed the idea of contracts further and posited the firm as "nexus of contracts"—"a legal fiction which serves as a nexus for a set of contracting relationships among individuals."[14] A firm is the equilibrium outcome that specifies the set of contracts. Facing agency problems, the optimal contracts can be designed and enforced. Although these contracts do not lead to the first-best allocation, they are comprehensive in the sense that they specify all parties' obligations to all future contingencies.

Grossman and Hart noted, by contrast, the problem of incomplete contracts, arguing that it is impossible to specify fully all the important issues of the future.[15] They stressed the cost of writing contracts, such as the cost of negotiations and of enforcement, among others, costs that emerge even without agency problems. Some solutions focus on transaction costs, others on agency issues. Kester, for example, characterizes the Japanese system as reducing transaction costs at the expense of higher agency costs, and the U.S. system as reducing agency costs at the expense of higher transaction costs.[16]

In this tradition, the search for a solution to contractual ambiguity results in organizations, hierarchies of authority, structured groups able to specify who has residual control in the unspecified situation.[17] The key challenge in governance, according to the contracterian view, arises from the asymmetric possession of information by the shareholder, the principal in terms of ownership of capital, and by the agents, the managers and other employees of the firm whom the

[12] Ronald H. Coase, "The Nature of the Firm," *Economica* 4 (1937): 386–405.

[13] Armen A. Alchian and Harold Demsetz, "Production, Information Costs, and Economic Organization," *American Economic Review* 62 (1972): 777–95.

[14] Michael C. Jensen and William H. Meckling, "Theory of the Firm: Managerial Behavior, Agency Costs, and Ownership Structure," *Journal of Financial Economics* 3 (1976): 305–60.

[15] Sanford J. Grossman and Oliver D. Hart, "Disclosure Laws and Takeover Bids," *Journal of Finance* 35 (1980): 323–34; "Implicit Contracts, Moral Hazard, and Unemployment," *American Economic Review* 71 (1981): 301–7; "The Costs and Benefits of Ownership: A Theory of Vertical and Lateral Integration," *Journal of Political Economy* 94 (1986): 691–719.

[16] W. Carl Kester, "American and Japanese Corporate Governance: Converging to Best Practice?" in *National Diversity and Global Capitalism*, Suzanne Berger and Ronald Dore, eds., (Ithaca, N.Y.: Cornell University Press, 1996), 107–37.

[17] Oliver E. Williamson, *Markets and Hierarchies: Analysis and Antitrust Implications* (New York: Free Press, 1975); *Organization Theory: From Chester Barnard to the Present and Beyond* (New York: Oxford University Press, 1995); and Oliver Hart, *Firms, Contracts, and Financial Structure* (Oxford: Oxford University Press, 1995); "An Economist's Perspective on the Theory of the Firm," *Columbia Law Review* 89 (1989): 1757–74.

shareholders hire. While all of the other parties to this bundle of relationships can in principle enter into a more or less complete contract with the firm, shareholders necessarily face an incomplete contract. Shareholders cannot fully specify in advance all the behaviors they wish managers to undertake or to avoid. There is thus an irreducible element of uncertainty in managing a firm, an implicit risk that shareholders cannot contract away or hedge against. Their investment is sunk when they buy the stock, and they bear this residual risk until they are bought out by other shareholders, or write off their investment.

Residual Risk and Residual Control

As compensation for this residual risk, according to the contracterian theory, shareholder "principals" claim residual control over the firm, in order to ensure that managerial "agents" maximize shareholder value, rather than shirk or steal. Managers have many ways to pursue their own objectives in ways that may conflict with the goals of maximizing shareholders' value, in addition to garden-variety sins such as laziness or theft. Managers may engage in activities that are too risky or too pedestrian, as compared to the level of risk that the shareholder thinks he or she has bargained for when purchasing the stock.

For example, managers may engage in "empire building," acquiring firms to diversify risk across industries or within a vertical chain, whereas shareholders may prefer to engage in such diversification themselves, according to the dictates of portfolio theory—without the additional difficulty of observing managerial effectiveness that conglomerates induce. This is the notion of the "agency costs of free cash flow," developed in the corporate governance literature by Michael Jensen.[18]

Faced with the incomplete contract, the principals (owners) and agents (managers) need to resolve uncertainty and the problem of managerial agency costs. They can try purely private "ordering," mechanisms of reassurance or signaling that do not involve the state. Or they can use the coercive instruments of public authority: courts, law, and regulation. Coasians do not agree on the preferred instrument. Some claim his ideas argue against state intervention, some claim the opposite—"Coase vs. the Coasians," the title of an article by Glaeser, Johnson, and Shleifer, nicely encapsulates this divergence.[19]

This is the core of the governance problem as it arises in the contracterian tradition: how to manage the agency challenge that arises from the incomplete contract between owner (investor, be it insider or external) and the manager. Linked to problems of collective action among shareholders, transaction costs, and

[18] Michael C. Jensen, "The Agency Costs of Free Cash Flow: Corporate Finance and Takeovers," *American Economic Review* 76 (1986): 323–29; Eugene Fama and Michael Jensen, "Separation of Ownership and Control," *Journal of Law and Economics* 26 (1983): 301–25.

[19] Edward Glaeser, Simon Johnson, and Andrei Shleifer, "Coase vs. the Coasians," *Quarterly Journal of Economics* 3 (2001): 853–99.

agency problems more generally, it defines the area of policy that we address here. What policies can address these agency problems? And what politics produces those policies?

If, as some theorists believe, private "bonding mechanisms" are quite powerful, then the role of law and regulation diminishes and politics recedes in importance. If, as others argue, private bonding is insufficient and the solution of the agency problem requires law and regulation, then we need a theory of the provision of those laws, and a debate about which combination is the most effective. We take up the debate on bonding in the remainder of this chapter, and turn then to law and regulation.

Private Bonding and Governance Games

To reassure shareholders in purely "private" ways, managers can signal that they will neither shirk nor steal. They do this by investing in instruments of reputation building. They can issue commitments "bonding" themselves to good behavior: the more costly the bond to the issuer, the more reassuring to the target. When managers and shareholders engage in this private contracting repeatedly, managers find it rational to engage in reputation building as reliable agents.

Managers can buttress their reputation by engaging "reputational intermediaries" to monitor and reinforce their reputation as reliable agents. There is, for example, a temptation for the managers to mislead investors, given the asymmetry of information between the managers who issue stocks and the investors that buy them; the firm may issue stock only once or often. How do the investors know the managers are providing reliable information?

The reputational intermediaries, the accounting and securities firms, turn this one-time game of stock issuing into an iterative game, as game theory would call it, by monitoring the managers of issuing firms over time. The network of intermediaries renders a professional opinion on equity securities, in effect "renting" their reputation to the managers for a fee. They perform this same role in their ongoing scrutiny of publicly traded firms, the accountants auditing the financial statements with an "opinion letter," and the securities firms rendering a buy-or-sell recommendation.

Investors are the customers for these professional opinions (both the audit and the buy/sell recommendation), and they deal with the accountants and the securities intermediaries day in and day out. These investors presumably have long memories, and will punish accounting or securities firms that breach their professional reputation by siding with managers or misleading investors in any single deal. This complex process engages the reputational intermediaries, managers, and investors in a repeated game where reputation counts—rather than a "one-off" game in which both parties have low trust and an incentive to defect (especially the managers), with clearly defined mechanisms for monitoring and punishing defection. In addition to market sanctions from investors, reputational intermediaries are also kept honest by interfirm competition, self-policing, regulation, and (at the extreme) legal liability.[20]

Reputations First, Regulations Later

In this "pure" world of efficient markets and private order, corporate governance practices are the result of an ongoing principal-agent bargain between shareholders and managers. Any particular firm's rules for financial disclosure, audit, board oversight, control, and managerial compensation reflect an equilibrium bargain between shareholder principals and managerial agents. Managers provide the accounting, audit, and disclosure data that shareholders need to monitor their performance. The board of directors are a loyal intermediate agent for shareholders, monitoring managers, hiring and firing them, setting their compensation, and otherwise approving major decisions with a weather eye on maximizing shareholder value. Control rules ensure that shareholders get the last word on big decisions—including who serves on the board, and managerial compensation extends an incentive to management to "do the right thing."

Placing this process in historical perspective, legal scholars such as Cheffins, Black, Roe, and Coffee argue that private bonding mechanisms helped develop a credible stock market in the United States and the United Kingdom *before* the regulatory reform of the Securities and Exchange Commission came about, not afterward.[21] In an oft-cited example, managers such as J. P. Morgan demonstrated a credible commitment to investors by their actions, before reputational intermediaries or the SEC existed. In Morgan's case, these investors were European (largely British) banks seeking to find secure locations in the high-growth U.S. economy. Stock exchanges in the United States and the United Kingdom began imposing listing requirements for public disclosure and accounting.

The sort of private commitment extended by Morgan and developed by stock exchanges was eventually put into legislation, so for certain legal scholars, private bonding preceded law. Reputational intermediaries emerged to assist in this monitoring process, to supply the information needed to enhance the bonding

---

[20] This complex process engages the reputational intermediaries and investors in an iterated game in which reputation counts—rather than a "one-off" game in which both parties have low trust and an incentive to defect (especially the managers)—with clearly defined mechanisms for monitoring and punishing defection. Bernard Black, "Creating Strong Stock Markets by Protecting Outside Shareholders," paper presented to the OECD Conference on Corporate Governance in Asia, March 3–5, 1999, Seoul, 6–7.

[21] Bernard Black, "The Legal and Institutional Preconditions for Strong Securities Markets," UCLA *Law Review* 48 (2001): 781–855; Brian Cheffins, "Does Law Matter? The Separation of Ownership and Control in the United Kingdom," *Journal of Legal Studies* 30 (2001): 459–84; Cheffins, "Corporate Law and Ownership Structure: A Darwinian Link?" *University of New South Wales Law Journal* 25 (2002): 346–78; John Coffee, "The Rise of Dispersed Ownership: The Roles of Law and the State in the Separation of Ownership and Control," *Yale Law Journal* 111 (2001): 1–81.

mechanisms: accounting firms, bond-rating agencies, stock analysts, brokerage firms, and securities lawyers. Stock exchange rules further embedded the reputational intermediaries in the solution to the "incomplete contract" between manager and investor.

In this theoretical tradition, the more self-sufficient are private bonding mechanisms, the less important is politics. There is little role for policy, hence little role for political processes in producing policy. While bonding mechanisms can certainly be powerful—a flaw of legal and political "centrism" is to downplay what can be worked out by individuals and groups—it is not plausible that they act wholly autonomously from the "shadow of the state" and thus of politics.[22]

Private bonding arises when the state is too weak and sometimes when it is too strong. It arises where weak or predatory states make formal judicial and regulatory mechanisms ineffective or risky: family, ethnicity, or regional ties substitute as "credible" bonding mechanisms where contracts are not reliable; the literature on transition economies confirms this effect.[23] At the same time, private bonding may also rely on state action to back up contracts of certain kinds, and to keep orderly markets operating in predictable ways. The weakness of markets in so many countries with unstable or authoritarian governments confirms this point; private bonding works best when the rule of law is powerful— and as many studies suggest, establishing the rule of law rests on political foundations.[24]

Governance Regulation: Necessary, Useful, or Rent-Seeking?

For the strictest of the private-order theorists, the state is not necessary, not even courts. Less severe analysts acknowledge that orderly markets require that contracts be enforced through courts located in the state. Here another series of analytic divides appears: how minimal or developed should these courts be? Should there be a specialized body of rules concerning corporate governance, or is tort law sufficient? Can a regulatory body do something courts cannot?

The minimalist view of courts argues that regular tort law is sufficient without any specialized body of rules on corporate governance or securities. Clear law with strong penalties deters bad behavior. More law or regulation than this minimum cannot add to the efficiency of the market, and must therefore be a form of capture by some interest group seeking a rent,[25] or by politicians seeking

[22] Robert C. Ellickson, *Order without Law: How Neighbors Settle Disputes* (Cambridge: Harvard University Press, 1991).

[23] Theodore Groves, Yongmiao Hong, John McMillan, and Barry Naughton, "Autonomy and Incentives in Chinese State Enterprises," *Quarterly Journal of Economics* 109 (1994): 183–209; Avinash K. Dixit, *Lawlessness and Economics: Alternative Modes of Governance* (Princeton: Princeton University Press, 2004).

[24] Daron Acemoglu, Simon Johnson, and James Robinson, "Institutions as the Fundamental Cause of Long-Run Growth," NBER Working Paper No. 10481, 2004.

[25] For example, according to this line of thinking, recent corruption scandals in the United States were an example not of too little regulation but of too much: external audit was undermined by the SEC-mandated rule that listed firms must have their financial statements reviewed by third-party

a rent by providing regulation to interests who will pay them for it. At its most vigorous, the private bonding or private contract model cannot see the state doing anything better than contracts and courts can, and most likely worse—the state is assumed to be notoriously inefficient and regulatory goods very expensive.

Private Bonding and National Variance

What does this contracterian theory have to say about the variety of corporate governance forms across countries? This has not been a major preoccupation of such theory, so to some degree the discussion has to be inferred from the literature. One line of reasoning that can be derived from the Coasian school would predict considerable variation in governance because the conditions that shape contracts vary. The key driver, the incompleteness of the shareholder-manager contract, is a function of the business that the firm engages in. As those conditions are likely to vary across countries, so would the problems of bonding, thus their solutions in corporate forms. If the incompleteness of the contract is influenced in any way by law and policy, then other variables are creeping into the situation that the theory has not specified clearly.

If technology and market conditions are the driver, we might expect the following: private-order arrangements would be heterogeneous *within* any given country, but with a relatively homogeneous pattern by industry type *across* countries. Differences in the "average" sort of governance practices adopted by private ordering should stem from differences in the types of businesses that private actors contract over. Whatever differences do exist should *not*, according to the theory of private bonding, have any connection to regulatory or political differences.

For example, countries whose industrial structure is weighted towards firms with a high degree of inherent managerial initiative and which are difficult to monitor—such as designing semiconductor integrated circuits, for example—would have more elaborate reputation-building procedures, reputational intermediaries, and minority shareholder protections. Countries with industrial structures weighted towards primary processing—such as logging or mining—with less inherent room for managerial initiative and easier monitoring, would have less complex reputational intermediaries and sparser shareholder protections. By the same logic, blockholders and dispersed minority shareholders

---

accounting firms. This removed the incentives for firms (and managers) to compete with each other on the basis of the reliability of their financial figures and thus lulled investors with a false promise of mandated financial accuracy. With a huge market handed to auditing firms on a platter, this also dulled the incentive for these firms to compete with each other on the basis of stringent audit, encouraging a sort of one-size-fits-all approach with a virtually identical blessing from the "accountant's letter" at the end of the financial statements. With less regulation, firms would compete to provide stricter accounting and auditing services—or so this argument goes.

should coexist in varying patterns, from firm to firm, based on the underlying industrial sector. Pure contracterian theory relying entirely on private bonding predicts no particular trend towards enhanced minority shareholder protections, other than some waxing and waning as industrial structure varies over time.

Contrary to this line of reasoning, however, we find homogeneity in corporate governance practices within countries, and heterogeneity across them. Industry complexity does raise issues of contracting, but the way these are resolved is influenced by national conditions. There is a positive correlation between per capita GDP and shareholder protections for our country sample. Shareholder protections do partake of regulation and the law. But if private bonding were the driver of behavior, these regulations should not matter as much as they do.

Inconveniently for the "pure" contracterian model, governments through courts and regulations do play a central role in setting the rules for corporate governance, in every country in this sample. This does not falsify the logic of private-order models. They may indeed tell us a great deal about corporate behavior. But they may not do so well explaining variance across countries. That firms are constrained by governments in their corporate governance doesn't falsify the logic of the private-order model, but it makes it less useful in explaining variance among countries.

Hurdles to Private Order

The private-order model rests on assumptions about conditions the absence of which would cause several problems. The "grand bargain" of private order only works if shareholders and managers are in fact engaged in an iterative game; if the private market infrastructure of reputational intermediaries such as accountants, auditors, and stock market analysts has the incentives perform this role objectively; if the many minority shareholders can overcome the collective action problem of monitoring, bargaining with, and sanctioning managers; and if the regulatory system itself can be "captured" by one or more of the players in a private-order game. We revisit these assumptions in more detail in chapter 5 when we examine and test the investor model, which relies heavily on private order as the driver of corporate governance change and outcomes.

REPEATED INTERACTION VERSUS "TAKE THE MONEY AND RUN"

The temptation for managers to defect and "take the money and run" may be very high. Private order can thus be undermined if the basis for reputation building is corroded by "one-off" rather than iterative games between shareholders and managers. It can take time, several fiscal quarters at a minimum, to tell if a particular manager is having a positive or negative impact on the firm's value.

Managerial careers may be too short to make an investment in reputation worth building.[26]

Conflicted Reputational Intermediaries

Private order may also be undermined if the reputational intermediaries are undeveloped, or if they acquire incentives that put them in conflict with shareholders. As Black and others observe,[27] any country's network of accountants, analysts, and security lawyers is a complex and fragile ecology, built up over many years. The objective role of reputational intermediaries can be distorted by other incentives; what happens when securities firms and accountants can make more money by providing transactions services to managers than by paying attention to their credibility with investors?[28]

A CLASSIC COLLECTIVE ACTION PROBLEM

Dispersed shareholders face an immense problem of collective action. The many dispersed shareholders have limited incentives to review firms' financial disclosures, much less assure themselves that the reputational intermediaries (auditors and analysts) aren't colluding with managers to skew the data.

The contracterian model invokes several auxiliary mechanisms by which private ordering can remedy this collective action problem. The most straightforward mechanism is blockholding, in which one shareholder or a small group of shareholders retains voting control sufficient to provide both incentive and means to discipline managers and keep them acting as good-faith agents. Another mechanism is the "market for control"—the possibility of a hostile takeover, through which one or a small group of actors gathers together to acquire control of the firm as temporary blockholders, vote out the current board of directors and management in order to remedy whatever managerial defects annoyed them, and then sell their interest to dispersed shareholders. A third mechanism is large institutional investors who pool the shares of many dispersed investors into one voting block large enough to capture the attention of managers or support a takeover.

---

[26] Some critics, Blair and Roe notable among them, argue that employees (including managers) as well as shareholders have an incomplete contract with the firm, and that they, like shareholders, have made "firm specific" investments in the firm. While these players in the system may not be shareholders, they are "stakeholders": they have important commitment to the firm, not easily transferable to other firms. The firm benefits from this investment in firm-specific assets, so some way of protecting them needs to be found. This idea can be extended to managers, suppliers, distributors, communities, and others who contribute to the firm without owning a portion of it. Finance theory excludes these stakeholders. Margaret M. Blair and Mark J. Roe, eds., *Employees and Corporate Governance* (Washington, D.C.: Brookings Institution Press, 1999). This point is developed as well in Zingales 2000.

[27] Bernard Black and John C. Coffee, "Hail Britannia? Institutional Investor Behavior under Limited Regulation," *Michigan Law Review* 92 (1994): 1997–2087.

[28] Sinclair 2004.

This model would predict hostile takeovers, much invoked by contracterian theory as a central mechanism of efficiency. But they take place surprisingly rarely, even in the United States. Few countries in our sample permit hostile takeovers. The United Kingdom, Malaysia, Hong Kong, and the United States are the exceptions. Moreover, since the heyday of hostile takeovers in the United States in the 1980s, a wave of antitakeover legislation was passed in a majority of the 50 states. Since then there has been much activity in mergers and acquisitions, but hostile takeovers are rare.

REGULATORY CAPTURE?

Finally, private order requires at least some degree of public regulation, if only to enforce contracts. Regulation is inevitable. There are no pure markets, wholly devoid of law. The issue is not whether to regulate, but what and how. Dismissing regulation because it is "captured" fails to explain who, among competing groups seeking to capture, actually succeeds in doing so.

Faced with limits on private bonding and the reality of regulation, we need to explore which regulations matter and what explains their provision—that is, which regulations are actually enacted as law and enforced.

LAW AND REGULATION: MINORITY SHAREHOLDER PROTECTIONS—INFORMATION, OVERSIGHT, CONTROL, AND INCENTIVES

In the first part of this chapter, we summarized the issue of managerial agency, thought by many theorists to lie at the core of the corporate governance problem: how owners can monitor managers when it is difficult to specify a complete contract. We then analyzed the "private bonding" solution to this problem, the mechanisms of signaling that establish credibility to honor the contract. While such mechanisms do exist and can be quite effective in certain circumstances, they are weak in other conditions, and they do not help us make sense of the reality of regulation, law, and political intervention we see around the world.

Here we take up law and regulation. Few theorists think private bonding is sufficient without any public authority. Most agree that private mechanisms rely on the shadow of the state.[29] Private courts, such as arbitration agreements that managers and investors can invoke as an alternative to expensive public courts, still depend on the state as the ultimate reversion point: an expensive trial is always there as an inducement to accept the private arbitration results.[30]

Law matters (as the debate over private bonding shows). The question here is *which* law. Theorists are divided on this: for some, traditional *tort law* is sufficient; for others, a specialized body of law dealing with corporate governance is needed (labeled here as *quality corporate law*, or QCL). Yet others argue QCL is too narrow;

---

[29] Ellickson 1991.

[30] Andrei Shleifer and Robert W. Vishny, "A Survey of Corporate Governance," *Journal of Finance* 52 (1997): 737–83.

the distinction between corporate law and securities law does not fully specify the governance issues, they suggest. We need to look more broadly at *minority share-holder protections* (MSPs), provisions concerning information, oversight, control, and incentives. Finally, another set of theorists argue that even MSP is too narrow: governance relationships are influenced by the broader set of rules that determine the type of market economy at work, what some call the "production system" that includes labor relations, price setting, competition, education and training, and social welfare systems. We label this cluster of policies DoC, degrees of coordination between liberal and corporatist models of an economy.

We examine this literature here to specify the public policies that have the greatest bearing on corporate governance, the key intervening variables in our discussion. It is provision of these policies that requires a political explanation.

From Torts to Corporate Law

The first branch in the debate over "which law matters" is between tort law and specialized corporate law. A muscular tort law—one with clear standards, strong penalties, and an efficient bar—should, some argue, provide sufficient force to inhibit abuse. Tort law, about punishing wrongs, includes concepts of fiduciary responsibility. Case law can articulate the standards as they apply to corporate governance. Strong penalties are seen as effective deterrents.[31]

The opposing view argues that tort law cannot be clear enough to provide effective supervision of malfeasance in corporate governance. A special set of laws is needed to deal with the defects in private order. With unclear standards, protections are weak, punishment sporadic, and thus deterrence ineffective. A clearer body of law—most broadly, MSP (minority shareholder protections)—can produce enforcement both from public authorities and from private ones.[32] With clear law, public authorities can bring cases against managers or other abusers. At the same time, private actors can use the information provided by MSP to sue other private actors. Together public and private actors are more effective than either alone. Incentivizing private actors and providing them with information empowers more monitoring than public authorities can do on their own. Public authorities can work to overcome collective action limits on private action. Both public and private routes are key elements of the ability of law to control agency problems.

Another fork in the argument is between law and regulation. Are there things a regulatory body can do that laws alone cannot? Glaeser et al. argue the private bonding argument rests "on the possibility of effective judicial enforcement of complicated contracts. Judges must be able, and more importantly willing, to read complicated contracts, verify whether the events triggering particular clauses

---

[31] Gary Becker, "Crime and Punishment: An Economic Approach," *Journal of Political Economy* 76 (1968): 169–217; Richard A. Posner, *Economic Analysis of Law* (Boston: Little, Brown, 1972), chap. 7; John Coffee, "No Soul to Damn, No Body to Kick: An Unscandalized Inquiry into the Problems of Corporate Punishment," *Michigan Law Review* 79 (1981): 386–459.

[32] La Porta, López-de-Silanes, and Shleifer forthcoming.

have actually occurred, and interpret broad and ambiguous language."[33] But what incentive do judges actually have to undertake the work this involves? "Indeed, even when contracts are restricted by statutes, the courts may not have the resources or incentives to verify whether or how particular statutes apply. . . . These requirements on the judges apply as strongly to the judicial enforcement of laws, where the interpretation and application of particular statutes requires significant investment."[34]

Regulatory bodies can overcome these obstacles to the effective use of legislation and courts. If the system is properly structured, regulators have incentives to investigate, study, examine, and enforce: "reducing the costs of the investment in information by law enforcers can improve enforcement efficiency."[35] In the 1930s this logic inspired Judge Landis's design of the SEC: creating a regulator to do what civil suits would not, but also giving incentives to reputational intermediaries to provide information that could be used by the regulator, and by civil action.[36]

While the distinction between a regulator and courts-legislation is quite interesting, it is not our central concern here. For our purposes, the key distinction lies in the existence or absence of a substantial body of law and regulation, both providing protections to minority shareholders—MSP. The issue of torts, courts, specialized law and regulation separates from the pure private bonding argument. All of them involve law and regulation, while the bonding argument does not. Regulation is a mode of implementing MSP; whether it works better than a specialized body of law is important but is not central concern. We care about whether MSP makes a difference—does a strong body of rules and regulations designed to protect investors from managerial agency costs have an impact on corporate governance practices and thus on the development of financial markets and firms?

In what follows we lay out evidence that suggests it does. Strong MSP produces more diffusion in shareholding, less concentration among blockholders. As we present this evidence, we emphasize again that we are folding "quality corporate law" into the broader measure of MSP. Some of the important evidence on this issue was generated by looking at the narrower QCL measure. QCL focuses on the composition of the board and its powers. It does not include accounting, securities, the market for control, and other key issues.[37] These are important for understanding the incentives that face all the players.

[33] Glaeser, Johnson, and Shleifer 2001, 854.

[34] Glaeser, Johnson, and Shleifer 2001, 854.

[35] Glaeser, Johnson, and Shleifer 2001, 855.

[36] La Porta, López-de-Silanes, and Shleifer forthcoming.

[37] Rules on the structure of boards, proxy rights, legal rights toward directors, the right to call meetings, and full information disclosure are among the variables that La Porta et al. examine. In recent work, they look at the closely related provisions concerning securities law. QCL includes not only law on the books, but the "quality of the regulators and judges, the efficiency, accuracy and honesty of the regulators and the judiciary, the capacity of the stock exchanges to manage the most egregious diversions, and so on" (Roe 2003b, 167). If these protections are of high quality, buyers and sellers will consider the managerial agency problem as under control, and share trading will occur. The quality of corporate law is thus the main driver of the type of corporate governance system used in each country, and therefore the principal explanation of variance across countries.

The pioneering work of La Porta, López-de-Silanes, Shleifer, and Vishny began with measures of QCL. They developed a large data set of countries on two dimensions: the strength of QCL and the concentration or diffusion of shareholding. They showed a positive correlation: the greater the QCL, the higher the degree of shareholder diffusion. La Porta et al.'s work helped set off substantial further work on both measures. By providing a comparison across countries, they laid the foundation for research and for debates.

Recently, their work has moved toward the broader concept of MSP, as they are including securities law and other regulation in their work, and noting scholarship on the even broader idea of the capitalist profile by looking at labor legislation, social security, and other subsystems of market economies. Our point of disagreement is their particular claim about the causes of the differences in rules: they locate the origins and persistence in "legal family," common versus civil law. We disagree with that explanation of the differences across countries, but for now, we focus on the areas of analytic convergence with La Porta et al.: the role of minority shareholder protections. We return to the "legal family" debate in the next chapter, which examines political explanations.

We turn therefore to a statement of the provisions of MSP and the evidence on how it correlates with corporate governance patterns.

MINORITY SHAREHOLDER PROTECTIONS

The logic of the MSP argument is this: if a nation's law poorly protects minority stockholders, a potential buyer may fear that the majority stockholder will shift value to himself or herself and away from the buyer. The prospective buyer therefore "does not pay pro rata value for the stock. If the discount is deep enough, the majority stockholder decides not to sell, concentrated ownership persists, and stock markets do not develop."[38] The seller may wish to fragment ownership to prevent a controller from diverting value. But the buyers would still have reason to fear that an outside raider could capture control and divert value, so again the sale price is depressed.[39]

The MSP school argues that ownership concentration or diffusion is driven by the existence (or lack) of a bundle of practices, both informal norms and formal rules and regulations that protect the rights of minority shareholders. This school is grounded in principal-agent theory and subsumes many concepts of both private ordering and quality of corporate law; it combines market-based and regulatory-based practices in a company-specific set of rules that structure the relation between outside investors and insiders—both managers and blockholders.

A number of institutions exist to structure the way dispersed owners can monitor managers: financial disclosure, board structure and composition, rules on proxy. These are often called shareholder protections, the practices that serve to

[38] Roe 2003b, 165.
[39] Roe 2003b, 166.

ensure that the firm is operated to maximize the value of the shareholders' stock, rather than spent or wasted on something else. There are several such practices, including financial disclosure, oversight, control, and management compensation.

There is no canon in economic theory of precisely what practices constitute minority shareholder protections, nor agreement on how exactly these practices shape firms' performance and protect minority shareholders from expropriation (at the hands of blockholders) and agency costs (at the hands of managers and employees). Much of the discussion in the popular press of corporate governance is devoted to the roles and functions of the board of directors, though we use a much broader definition of the institutions involved in providing minority share-holder protections. For our purpose of constructing an aggregate index of MSP, we employ a broad definition of corporate governance practices, including infor-mation, oversight, control, and managerial practices.

Among these practices, some are formal, embedded in statute or regulatory procedures, while others are informal, a matter of convention or norm. The mix of formal and informal practices varies from country to country, as does the lati-tude for innovation that is granted to firms by the regulatory authorities.

Further muddying the waters, some practices are complements—for example, formal protections for minority shareholder voting rights can be overridden by takeover rules in several countries in this sample—whereas others may act as sub-stitutes; there is a considerable (and inconclusive) academic literature on the notion of complements and substitutes. The empirical evidence on the effective-ness of corporate governance practices in protecting the interests of minority shareholders is surprisingly thin; as Mayer observed, "Corporate governance has become a subject on which opinion has drowned fact."[40]

Just as there is no agreement on precisely which governance practices are most important, there is also no generally accepted method of measuring the degree of shareholder protections offered by each governance practice. Instead competing indices proliferate, sweeping in different features, arranged on different scales, some based on written laws and regulations, others incorporating the degree of enforcement, and so forth. In the next section we describe the full range of cor-porate governance practices as well as the index we use to assess them.

Information: Disclosure and Audit

Information practices include accounting rules and audit procedures.[41] Over the last decade an increasingly rigorous set of international accounting practices, the International Financial Reporting Standards (IFRS), has been emerging under the auspices of the International Accounting Standards Board (IASB). The IFRS

---

[40] Colin Mayer, "Corporate Governance, Competition, and Performance", OECD Working Paper No. 164, 1996, 3.

[41] Much of this section and the measurements that follow derive from James P. Shinn, "Globaliza-tion, Corporate Governance, and the State," Ph.D diss., Princeton University, 2000.

(conventionally referred to by the first three letters of the codifying organization, or IAS) is similar to the generally accepted accounting practices (GAAP), which is administered by the Financial Accounting Standards Board (FASB) in the United States. IAS is built on the GAAP but is considerably more streamlined and less grounded in U.S.-specific commercial and tax practices.

The closer a state's rules conform to the IAS or to GAAP, the more accurately a minority shareholder can assess agency or expropriation costs. Good rules for consolidation, asset valuation, and income recognition are important if there is a threat of expropriation by a blockholder through affiliated transactions.[42]

By the same token, objective audit by a competent third party—usually a professional accounting firm—is essential in verifying the accuracy of the reported accounting data, free of meddling from management or blockholders. Audit practices of vital interest include the scope of the audit, frequency, the recipients of the report, criteria for independence of the auditor, and the conditions for both selection and termination of auditors.[43]

The practices for accounting and audit are formal in most countries in this sample, that is, set by statute, usually in the company law. Sometimes the ministry of finance sets the rules, sometimes they are delegated to stock exchange regulators or the stock exchange itself. Either method provides little latitude for firms to innovate in terms of accounting systems, or to "shop around" for their favorite standards-setting body.[44] By the same token, most securities regulators or stock exchanges establish minimum standards for financial audit, though firms are usually free to choose between a prestigious or "no name" accounting firm for this audit.[45] For our index of accounting and audit we use two data series from La Porta et al., one for accounting quality, and the other for financial disclosure, which ranks all the countries in our sample on a score from 1 to 100.[46] We averaged these two measurements to derive a single index for our sample.

[42] "Because the controlling owner oversees the accounting reporting policies and is perceived to have strong opportunistic incentives to hold up minority shareholders, the market expects that the owner will not report high quality accounting information." Joseph Fan and T. Wong, "Corporate Ownership Structure and the Informativeness of Accounting Earnings in East Asia," Center for Economic Institutions Working Paper No. 2001-21, 2001, 3.

[43] Because accounting interpretations can have a profound impact on the banking sector, and on tax revenues more generally, central banks and ministries of finance traditionally take an intense interest in this practice. Prior to the IASC, the gold standard for objective standards setting has been the Financial Accounting Standards Board (FASB) in the United States, whose decisions are usually (but not always) dominated by accounting academicians and professionals, and subjected to close scrutiny by both the SEC and Wall Street.

[44] Firms have latitude to cross-list their shares on international markets, such as New York, Hong Kong, or the Euromarkets, which requires that they abide by the accounting rules of a foreign securities commission or stock exchange. American Depository Receipts (ADRs) provided the most popular arena for this type of innovation, though country authorities vary in their willingness to accept GAAP for statutory domestic reporting.

[45] For example, a small "captive" accounting firm in Toyota-City audits Toyota Motors' Japanese financial statements.

[46] http://iicg.som.yale.edu/data/datasets.shtml.

Oversight: Board Independence

Oversight practices include boards of directors and the rules governing their fiduciary responsibilities.[47] Outsider boards independent of management—nonexecutive directors, or NEDs in governance parlance—can protect minority shareholders from agency costs; outsider boards independent of the blockholder can protect them from expropriation costs. The precise definition of "independent" is critical since it is usually possible for management or the blockholder to stack the board with nominally independent NEDs who are nonetheless obliged either to the chief executive officer (CEO) or the blockholder.

Governments often require a minimum number of NEDs for listed firms, usually as a condition of listing on a stock exchange. Firms are usually free to appoint as many NEDs as they wish, though they may be limited by a regulation that specifies a minimum percentage of board seats be filled by employees or union representatives. An example is Germany's employee codetermination (or *Mitbestimmung*) law that employee representatives fill 49 percent of the seats on the supervisory board (*Aufsichtsrat*). It is more common for the state to impose a minimum percentage of independent board members, allowing firms to include additional NEDs as they wish.

For our index of board oversight we use the estimated percentage of NEDs on the boards of directors of listed firms in our sample. For the largest countries (by market value) we use data compiled by Davis Advisors as of 2002.[48] For other countries we use point estimates of the NED percentage from a variety of scholarly and professional sources, and then normalize the sample to a scale of 1 to 100.

Control Rules

Control practices include minority voting rights over important decisions such as changes in control, as well as takeover provisions. Blockholders or managers can employ many voting rules or procedures to weaken or eliminate the ability of minority shareholders to affect control decisions. These include voting caps that impose ceilings on minority or outside votes; shares with disproportionate (or no) voting rights; and restrictive voting procedures such as "tie-up" requirements or limited information or notice regarding annual general meetings. Most countries also provide blockholders and managers with an elaborate armamentarium of potential antitakeover practices, including "poison pills" (of which there are several flavors), "dead hand" provisions, staggered boards, stock transfer restrictions, and "golden shares" triggered only in a contest. These practices allow management

---

[47] The board's fiduciary obligation to shareholders can be narrow or broad; shareholders can pursue legal recourse for directors' performance on behalf of the company, known as a derivative suit, or on a shareholder "class action" basis. Derivative suits can limit agency costs; class action suits are more effective in limiting expropriation costs.

[48] Davis Global Advisors, *Leading Corporate Governance Indicators, 2002*, November 2002, 41.

or a blockholder to foil bona fide takeover offers that would otherwise enrich the minority shareholder, while possibly costing managers their jobs and blockholders their control.

In most countries in this sample, the government imposes a minimum amount of due process to protect minority voting rights, but firms are free to innovate beyond these minimums and to provide greater protection to the minority investor. By the same token, firms are free not to use antitakeover provisions; the commercial code in most countries requires an explicit vote by either the board or a shareholder majority in order to adopt antitakeover provisions. For our index we use an index compiled by La Porta et al. on so-called antidirector rights, which they base on the presence or absence of seven legal rights of minority shareholders.[49]

Managerial Incentives

Shareholders prefer to have managers compensated in ways that make them think like shareholders. The use of stock options is a common practice that can align the interests of managers with those of shareholders, including minority shareholders, although this method is open to abuse by poorly monitored or by entrenched managers. Firms are free to devise incentive compensation plans that align managers with shareholders, although as a practical matter the use of stock options is molded by the tax treatment of capital gains for the optionee (and the expense recognition requirements for the optioning firm).

For our index of managerial incentives we estimate the ratio of long-term incentive compensation (largely stock options in practice) to total compensation for CEOs in listed firms in each market. This is based on survey data from Towers & Perrin and Mercer, which cover the 30 largest countries; missing values for 9 countries are point estimates based on discussions with board search professionals.[50]

In order to combine these different measures into a common index, we averaged the accounting and disclosure values for each country to derive a single

[49] La Porta et al. 1997, table 2, "Shareholder Rights around the World," data set available at http://iicg.som.yale.edu/data/datasets.shtml. These include one-share, one-vote; proxy by mail; shares not blocked before a meeting; cumulative voting; oppressed minority rights; preemptive rights to new issues; and the quorum of share capital required to call an emergency general shareholders meeting.

[50] Towers & Perrin 1999 Global Survey: Total Cash Compensation, April 1999, for Argentina, Australia, Brazil, Canada, France, Germany, Japan, Malaysia, Mexico, Netherlands, Singapore, South Africa, Spain, Sweden, United Kingdom, and Unites States, and Mercer Human Resources Consulting, 2002 Total Remuneration Survey, for Argentina, Belgium, Chile, China, Denmark, Germany, Hong Kong, India, Indonesia, Ireland, Italy, Japan, New Zealand, South Korea, Switzerland, Thailand; where both surveys had a value for the same country, we average them for the index. Missing values filled by point estimates for Austria, Finland, Greece, Israel, Norway, Philippines, Portugal, Taiwan, and Turkey.

measure for information institutions, normalized each of the other three indices to 100, and then performed a simple arithmetic average. The results for a single index for minority shareholder protections are shown in table 3.1.[51]

As in the index of blockholder concentration, there is considerable variation in minority shareholder protections, around the mean of 45 for this sample. As the histogram in figure 3.1 shows, the sample is positively skewed, with most of the sample countries falling between 20 and 50 on our index.

On average, developed economies score higher than emerging markets. As with the index on concentration, these data must be interpreted with caution. The accounting index is dated, almost a decade old; things have changed since then. The disclosure index is more recent, but is based on required disclosures, usually by stock exchanges; it says nothing about the actual compliance or enforcement of this disclosure. The data on NEDs is also suspect, since true independence is hard to verify, and again, the enforcement of fiduciary duties towards minority shareholders is not picked up by this index. Finally, the incentive compensation data is based on a limited sample of firms in each country, biased towards larger and multinational firms.

As with the blockholding data, this minority protections data is a static snapshot. There have been recent, significant changes in minority protections in several sample countries that are not picked up by this index. Moreover, we have weighted all four groups of practices—information, oversight, control, and compensation—equally in creating this overall synthetic index.

A small survey of institutional investors performed by the authors in a previous study suggested that not all protections are equally important to foreign portfolio investors, and that their priority was (in descending order) information, compensation, control, and—at the bottom of the list—oversight.[52] Given the standard deviation in the oversight values, rescaling the numbers to reflect the notional priorities of portfolio investors would generate different ratings.

Predictions of MSP

The MSP school argues that ownership concentration can be predicted by minority shareholder protections. In the MSP school, ownership concentration is the result of low shareholder protections, and diffuse ownership only emerges as these protections become stronger. If this is an accurate portrayal of reality, then

---

[51] The indices used by La Porta et al. have a correlation coefficient with our composite index of .89. Accounting index from La Porta et al. 2000, which they based on Center for International Financial Analysis and Research, 1990; missing values for China, Ireland, and Indonesia estimated by authors from other sources. Disclosure index from La Porta et al. forthcoming; missing values for China estimated by authors from other sources. Control index from La Porta et al. 1997, table 2, "Shareholder Rights around the World," http://iicg.som.yale.edu/data/datasets.shtml. Missing values for China estimated by authors.

[52] Gourevitch and Shinn 2002.

TABLE 3.1
Minority Shareholder Protections Index

	Information	Oversight	Control	Incentive	Total MSP
United States	86	100	100	100	97
Singapore	89	71	80	97	84
Canada	83	71	100	78	83
United Kingdom	81	60	100	53	74
Australia	75	71	80	59	71
Hong Kong	85	14	100	81	70
Ireland	69	71	80	59	70
Malaysia	84	36	80	69	67
South Africa	73	43	100	41	64
Chile	35	14	100	66	54
France	64	37	60	47	52
New Zealand	56	71	80	0	52
Argentina	48	0	80	72	50
Spain	57	14	80	50	50
Israel	74	29	60	31	48
Norway	66	29	80	16	48
Sweden	67	36	60	22	46
Finland	60	36	60	16	43
Venezuela	49	14	20	81	41
India	50	7	100	0	39
Switzerland	59	36	40	16	38
Japan	66	0	80	0	37
South Korea	65	21	40	22	37
Denmark	44	43	40	16	36
Netherlands	57	0	40	47	36
Philippines	74	7	60	0	35
Taiwan	74	7	60	0	35
Belgium	43	32	0	59	34
Germany	44	29	20	41	33
Thailand	78	7	40	6	33
Brazil	27	0	60	41	32
Austria	40	36	40	6	30
Greece	53	14	40	0	27
Mexico	59	14	20	9	26
Portugal	43	0	60	0	26
Italy	69	7	20	0	24
Turkey	51	0	40	0	23
Indonesia	45	0	40	0	21
China	25	0	20	0	11

Source: Accounting from La Porta et al. 2000, which they based on Center for International Financial Analysis and Research 1990; disclosure from La Porta, López-de-Silanes, and Shleifer 2004; oversight NED estimates for Belgium, France, Germany, Netherlands, Portugal, UK, and US from Davis
Global Advisors, 2002, 41; Japan from Tokyo Stock Exchange, Survey on Directors, 2001; China
from Stoyan Tenev and Chang, 2001; Korea from Ha-sung Jang, unpublished; Turkey from Hakan
Orbay, Sabanci Universitesi, unpublished; Latin American countries from Lefort and Walker 1999.

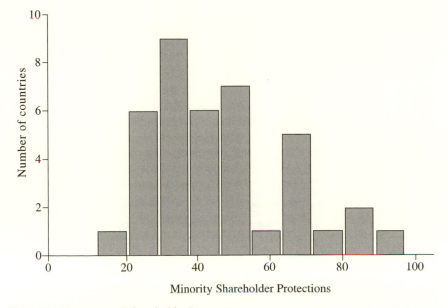

Figure 3.1 Histogram of Shareholder Protections

countries should scatter close to the 45-degree line, with ownership concentration on the y-axis and minority shareholder protections on the x-axis.[53]

How accurate are the predictions of the MSP model? For our sample of 39 countries, there is indeed a negative correlation between blockholding and shareholder protections, −.33 for the whole sample, and −.44 for the developed countries (defined as gross domestic product (GDP) per capita greater than $10,000).[54] But as figure 3.3 shows, there is an exuberant scattering of countries away from a linear relationship between blockholding and shareholder protections.[55]

[53] "[C]oncentrations of ownership and complex control vehicles are a response to inadequate protection of investors. Faced with a risk of exploitation by self-interested managers, investors require powerful mechanisms for exercising control and they do so through holding large ownership stakes in companies and exerting voting power that is disproportionate to the amount they invest in firms." Barca and Becht 2001, 4. Barca and Becht sketch out the linear trade-off of shareholder protections and ownership concentrations, with the additional refinement of noting that the 45-degree line can be bowed outward or inward by corporate governance rules that reflect a "private control bias" or a "market control bias."

[54] The countries in our sample account for 99.6 percent of the Morgan Stanley Capital International Index (99.8 percent of the index reweighted for free float)—virtually the entire global equity market. The sample includes Argentina, Australia, Austria, Belgium, Brazil, Canada, Chile, China, Denmark, Finland, France, Germany, Greece, Hong Kong, India, Indonesia, Ireland, Israel, Italy, Japan, Malaysia, Mexico, Netherlands, New Zealand, Norway, Philippines, Portugal, Singapore, South Africa, South Korea, Spain, Sweden, Switzerland, Taiwan, Thailand, Turkey, United Kingdom, United States, and Venezuela.

[55] Appendix table A.4 contains the data used to develop this figure.

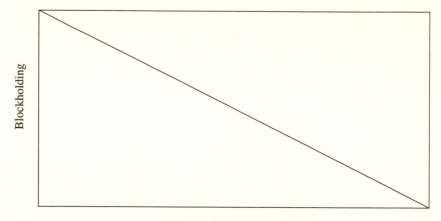

Figure 3.2 The MSP/Ownership Trade-off

The United States and United Kingdom (GB) anchor the lower-right-hand side of the distribution, with high protections and low concentration, as predicted by the conventional wisdom, and countries such as Italy (IT) anchor the upper-left-hand side of the distribution, with low protections and high concentration. Yet there are many prominent outliers, such as Chile (CL), Hong Kong (HK), and France (FR) with high concentration of ownership and high shareholder protections.

Conversely, Japan (JP) and the Netherlands (NL) are outliers in the other direction, with low concentration and low shareholder protections. China has even lower blockholder concentration, insofar as the state controls 95 percent of listed firms, and very low shareholder protections. Finally, the slope of a fitted OLS regression line to this sample is −.25, not −1, as would be the case in a simple 45-degree line; in any case, the relationship is not statistically significant (see appendix tables A.5 and A.6). Clearly, something more complex is going on here than a simple negative covariance of protections and ownership. Too many countries don't fit.

MSP theory has powerful insights. Without shareholder protection, investors will seek protection from the costs of managerial agency. They will therefore turn to one or another form of blockholding. With strong protections, investors can be reassured that they have means of monitoring and sanctioning managers. A strong institutional framework of protection allows investors to diversify and thus leads toward the external indicator method of monitoring and greater shareholder diffusion.

An explanation of the provision of MSP is thus a powerful part of any explanation of corporate governance. The next part of our book looks at political explanations of the provision of MSP. However, there is one more important step in establishing which policies require explanation. It is here with MSP as the key independent variable that most discussion of corporate governance stops. We do not. First, we treat MSP as an intervening variable—that is, while MSP is a powerful influence on corporate governance, we still need an explanation of MSP. Why do

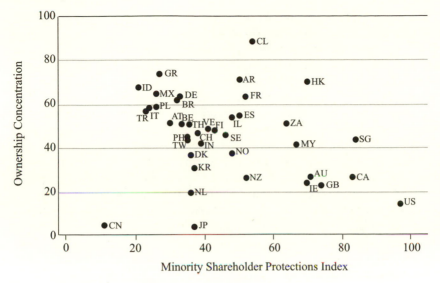

Figure 3.3 Blockholding and Shareholder Protections

some countries have strong MSP and others not? We take this up in the next chapter.

MSP is, moreover, necessary but insufficient as an "intervening variable." MSPs sit in a context. They operate within a framework of rules about the dynamics of the market economy itself. This effect varies with "degrees of coordination."

VARIETIES OF CAPITALISM: DEGREES OF COORDINATION IN MARKET ECONOMIES

Apparently MSP encourages ownership diffusion under some country conditions but not others. For example, Sweden and Malaysia rank high in MSP, but not high in shareholder diffusion. We argue that corporate governance patterns vary substantially with other features of the economy, among them job protections, product-market competition, education and training systems, price- and wage-setting mechanisms, financial structures, and income inequality. These country-wide economic features exhibit what Milgrom and Roberts called "institutional complementarity"[56]—a logic of fit that causes each to contribute to the other.

---

[56] "In general, two sets of institutions can be said to be complementary to each other when the presence of one set raises the returns available from the other." Gingerich and Hall 2002, 4, who derive the idea from Milgrom and Roberts 1990; Paul Milgrom and John Roberts, *Economics, Organization, and Management* (Englewood Cliffs, N.J.: Prentice Hall, 1992); and "Complementarities, Industrial Strategy, Structure, and Change in Manufacturing," *Journal of Accounting and Economics* 19 (1995): 179–208; and Ramchandran Jaikumar, "Postindustrial Manufacturing," *Harvard Business Review* 64 (1986): 69–76. The logic of institutional complementarity underlies the overall argumentation of the "varities of capitalism" literature as developed in Hall and Soskice 2001.

For example, in comparing Japanese and American firms, Aoki noted that the high job security characteristic of Japan was possible only because cross-shareholding shielded firms from the pressure of having to lay off workers in the face of fluctuating demand in order to conform to external shareholder demands for profitability.[57] Conversely, where governance models push managers toward maximizing share prices and dividends, pressure grows for flexibility in all relationships, from labor contracts, to wages and prices, to suppliers and distributors, to finance and research. Zingales notes that as human capital grows in importance, the vital assets of the firm shift, with implications for corporate governance.

A number of researchers have been exploring the degree of "fit" among economic practices.[58] Measuring institutional complementarity for countries leads to a dichotomous result. Hall and Soskice's *Varieties of Capitalism* volume, an important synthetic statement of this line of research, sorts countries into two groups, according to the degree of coordination that takes place: "liberal market economies" (LMEs) and "coordinated market economies" (CMEs).[59] In LMEs, firms coordinate through formal contracting in arm's-length relationships operating in highly competitive markets. In CMEs firms coordinate through information sharing, repeated interactions, and long-term relationships, all sustained by institutional arrangements that make the stability of these commitments credible. In CMEs, managers invest in worker training to sustain manufacturing that demands high levels of skill, and workers have incentives to engage in that training; in LMEs managers prefer flexibility and hence lack motive to invest in skill development, while workers lack incentives to upgrade.[60] Firms in LMEs have the diffuse shareholder governance model; in CMEs firms have the block-holder model.[61]

---

[57] Masahiko Aoki, "Toward an Economic Model of the Japanese Firm," *Journal of Economic Literature* 28 (1990): 1–27; "The Japanese Firm as a System of Attributes: A Survey and Research Agenda," in *The Japanese Firm: Sources of Competitive Strength*, Masahiko Aoki and Ronald Dore, eds. (Oxford: Clarendon Press, 1994).

[58] Porter 1990; Robert Boyer, *The Regulation School: A Critical Introduction* (New York: Columbia University Press, 1989); Bruno Amable, "Institutional Complementarity and Diversity of Social Systems of Innovation and Production," *Review of International Political Economy* 7 (2002): 645–87; Bruno Amable, Ekkehard Ernst, and Stefano Palombarini, "How Do Financial Markets Affect Industrial Relations: An Institutional Complementarity Approach," unpublished manuscript, 2001; Robert Boyer and J. P. Durand, *L'Après-fordisme* (Paris: Syros, 1997); Ekkehard C. Ernst, "Financial Systems, Industrial Relations, and Industry Specialization: An Econometric Analysis of Institutional Complementarities," OECD, February 2002.

[59] Hall and Soskice 2001; see Martin Höpner, "European Corporate Governance Reform and the German Party Paradox," Max-Planck-Institute for the Study of Societies, Program for the Study of Germany and Europe Working Paper Series 03.1, 2003; Gingerich and Hall 2002.

[60] Amable 2000.

[61] Roe notes the same pattern, that the "world's wealthy democracies have two broad packages: (1) competitive product markets, dispersed ownership, and conservative results for labor; and (2) concentrated product markets, concentrated ownership, and pro labor results. The three elements in each package mutually reinforce each other." Roe 2003b, 140.

TABLE 3.2
Coordination Index

Austria	1	Sweden	0.69
Germany	0.95	Netherlands	0.66
Italy	0.87	Spain	0.57
Norway	0.76	Switzerland	0.51
Belgium	0.74	Australia	0.36
Japan	0.74	Ireland	0.29
Finland	0.72	New Zealand	0.21
Portugal	0.72	Canada	0.13
Denmark	0.7	United Kingdom	0.07
France	0.69	United States	0

Institutional complementarity implies that we need to know policy outcomes in related areas in order to know the impact of any given variable. Corporate governance outcomes are influenced by what happens in other elements of the system. Knowing corporate law, MSP, and private bonding mechanisms is important, but not sufficient. We need to know as well what happens in other areas of the economy that have a functional relationship with corporate governance practices.

We use a measure of institutional complementarity developed by Hall and Gingerich, which they term the *coordination index* (CI).[62] It is constructed from country scores on six values: shareholder power (drawn from La Porta et al.), dispersion of control (a La Porta et al. measure of concentration), stock market capitalization, level of wage coordination (at what level wages are set: local, intermediate, or national), degree of wage coordination, and labor turnover (a proxy for job security). This index was calculated for 20 of our sample countries for the period 1990–95, as shown in table 3.2.

We are wary of the endogeneity between the CI and both our MSP and ownership data sets, because it incorporates values reflecting similar calculations (our data sets draw on some La Porta et al. values, and roughly correlate with those measures). For that reason (among others) we rely more on correlations between our own MSP index and the ownership data rather than on the CI data.

Predictions of Degrees of Coordination Logic

Prediction: The coordination index varies positively with ownership concentration, negatively with MSP.

As noted in chapter 2, the correlation between ownership and CI is positive (+.61). The same correlation between ownership and MSP is strongly

[62] Hall and Gingerich 2001.

negative (–.89). This is demonstrated graphically in the plots shown in figures 3.4 and 3.5.

In figure 3.4, Denmark and Austria are in the upper-right-hand corner, with high levels of coordination and correspondingly high levels of ownership concentration. The United States anchors the lower-left-hand quadrant, as expected. Two of our corporate governance outliers, Japan and the Netherlands, lie in the upper-left-hand quadrant, both combining relatively high coordination with low ownership concentration. We return to this puzzle in chapter 6.

Figure 3.5 reveals the inverse relation between CI and MSP, as predicted by our interpretation of CEP. In this scatter plot the country sample falls much more closely along the 45-degree line (as the high negative correlation coefficient indicates), with Japan and the Netherlands much less different from the rest of the pack. This suggests that CEP variables such as CI have a more direct effect on MSP and a somewhat more attenuated effect on ownership (though still of the predicted sign), consistent with our overall causal schema.

The positive correlation of CI with concentration and negative correlation with MSP is supported by data of other researchers. Höpner measures corporate governance against "industrial relations" system measures (such as trade union regulations, work hours, employment contracts, minimum wage, and codetermination), which are proxies for the LME/CME distinction.[63] Gingerich and Hall measure a similar relationship.[64] Both find that shareholder concentration correlates with patterns of economic coordination. There is endogeneity here, as corporate governance is one of the indicators of the economic coordination: but this is the point of the argument on institutional complementarity. Corporate governance and MSP do not operate in isolation from the other policy regimes in the economy and society.

Roe's work provides evidence that labor protections and income equality correlate strongly with corporate governance systems. Gourevitch and Hawes show correlation between corporate governance and policy patterns as well.[65] This data suggests that corporate governance is indeed nested in a set of relationships with other elements of the political economy.[66] From this we infer prima facie evidence that the explanation of MSP in any given country can be strengthened by reference to the economic policy context (DoC) in which it operates.

[63] Martin Höpner, "What Connects Industrial Relations and Corporate Governance? Explaining Institutional Complementarity," Max-Planck-Institute for the Study of Societies Working Paper, draft 2003; see table 1, "Correlations between Degrees of Organization in Corporate Governance and Industrial Relations, 21 OECD Countries," 35. Gingerich and Hall show a similar relationship (included as a measure in Höpner's table) presented graphically. Gingerich and Hall 2002, 34, figure 1, "Coordination in Labor Relations and Corporate Governance."

[64] Gingerich and Hall 2002.

[65] Peter Gourevitch and Michael Hawes, "The Politics of Choice among National Production Systems," in L'Année de la Régulation No. 6, Robert Boyer, ed. (Paris: Presses des sciences Po, 2002).

[66] Roe 2003b.

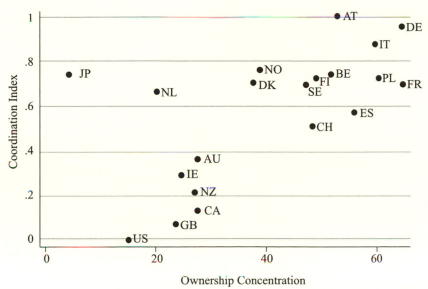

Figure 3.4 Coordination Index and Ownership Concentration

CONCLUSION

In this chapter, we have examined several theories of corporate governance in order to get leverage for the explanation of variance. We draw something important from each, and nest each point in an expanding structure of explanation. The scale and scope of technology analyzed by Chandler sets up some patterns for firm structure. The issue of contracts raised by Coase helps define the problem of transactions costs and of managerial agency costs. We then consider the various solutions to the agency problem: private bonding, then law and regulation, grouped under the broad range of minority shareholder protections, which include "quality of corporate law." That in turn leads to the issue of institutional complementarity and the full range of economic practices that shapes the incentives of players to accept the diffuse shareholder "bargain" or resist it and retain blockholding.

Working through this literature sets up the variables for which we then seek a "political" explanation. Corporate governance outcomes are shaped by policies toward the market: the interaction of MSP and DoC variables. MSP and DoC variables are shaped by public policy. What explains the choice of one set of policies over another?

Here we see the importance of politics. Legal protections and market structure are made by policy. They derive from decisions made in the political process: laws passed, laws enforced, regulations applied, courts sheltered from corruption—all deeply political variables.

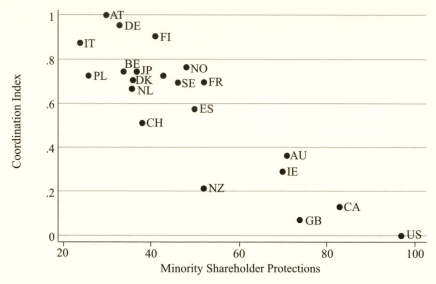

Figure 3.5 Coordination Index and MSP

Corporate governance confers advantages. It may provide social efficiency, but it does so by favoring some groups over others. It thus involves distribution of benefits and constraints and thus politics.[67] Owners, managers, and workers certainly do have contractual problems that law and regulation can assist. But their wanting them from inside the firm does not explain how they achieve their wishes outside the firm. Struggles inside the firm are connected to struggles outside of it. Power inside the boardroom connects to power outside in the polity at large: claims on the profits of the firm derive from obligations defined by a country's political processes.

In the next chapter we take up theories of political process that may help explain the choice of public policy relevant to corporate governance.

[67] Enrico Perotti and Ernst-Ludwig von Thadden, "The Poltical Economy of Bank and Market Dominance," European Corporate Governance Institute Finance Working Paper No. 21/2003, 2003.

Politics: Preferences and Institutions

CORPORATE GOVERNANCE CONFERS benefits: it distributes income, power, and authority. Different models of corporate governance distribute benefits differently across groups in society. Naturally enough, groups in any society will push for the system of corporate governance that helps them the most, and oppose the system that hurts them the most. They work through politics to create the public policy regime that reflects their preferences in corporate governance.

Efficiency considerations alone do not explain corporate governance outcomes. There may be several ways to govern an efficient firm. Distribution issues will influence the outcome. The struggle for power inside the firm is settled by the struggle for power outside the firm, in the political system that determines the rules. Efficiency may drive the game, but it is primarily political effectiveness rather than economic efficiency.

In this chapter, we set out a basic model of political variables that shape corporate governance rules. We focus on interest group preferences and the formal institutions of preference aggregation. We then locate our discussion with reference to two important bodies of literature about corporate governance, which treat political processes differently: the legal family school and economic sociology.

MAPPING FINANCIAL INTERESTS ON POLITICAL PROCESSES: A CAUSAL MODEL

Finance theory provides a sophisticated model of how players within the firm interact with investors outside the firm to strike governance bargains that accommodate their mutual interests. Finance theory does not show how these actors negotiating at the level of the business firm manage to operate in society at large to get the corporate governance rules that advantage them at the level of the firm. To obtain the most advantageous rules, each player needs a way of getting the political system to reflect its preferences. In the limit, it is therefore political process that sets the rules.

In order to make sense of these coalitional possibilities within a political system, we need a way of mapping the preferences generated from finance theory onto society, onto the preferences of social forces and the mechanisms of preference aggregation that produce policy outputs. We begin the story with the interests of players expressed by their interests in the firm. We need then to link these intrafirm interests to broader societal interests, to coalition building, and to the mechanisms of preference aggregation in political institutions.

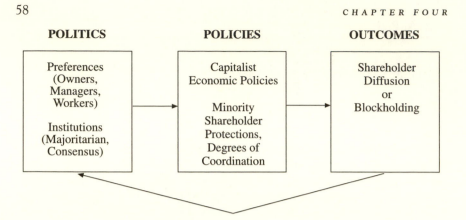

POLITICS   **POLICIES**   **OUTCOMES**

Figure 4.1 A Simple Model of Causality (also reproduced as figure 2.1, p.16)

In this chapter we develop ways of integrating politics into explanations of corporate governance patterns. We begin with a careful specification of the preferences of actors within the firm—owners, managers, and employees—toward policies regarding corporate governance that are made outside the firm. We examine the coalitions these groups can form to advance their goals for corporate governance. We then explore the political institutions that mediate the aggregation of these preferences to shape policy in the public arena.

Policy, we suggest in a simple causal model, is the output of preferences and power resources mediated by political institutions. Those policies shape the incentives that lead to patterns of corporate governance. Those patterns in turn have a feedback effect on preferences: being in one system or another influences what actors want. The impact of preferences on policy outcomes is refracted by political institutions. Political science has for many years been split into two camps, those emphasizing preferences and those emphasizing institutions.[1] Each school holds constant the variance of the other to explore the impact of what they study: holding preferences constant reveals the power of institutions; holding institutions constant reveals the power of preferences.

Each approach has virtue, but it is vital to explore the interactions of the two variables over time. We examine both, first by exploring the comparative "statics," modeling preferences, then institutions. We then add a dynamic element: how the institutions and preferences interact over time. We do this through analytic historical narratives of the patterns of countries' policies. We sketch out this simple model in figure 4.1.

Recall that the set of policies we seek to explain is the combination of minority shareholder protections (MSPs) and degrees of coordination (DoCs), which together comprise what we label as capitalist economic policies (CEPs). They

---

[1] Jeffrey Frieden, "Actors and Preferences in International Relations," Ronald Rogowski, "Institutions as Constraints on Strategic Choice," and Peter A. Gourevitch, "The Governance Problem in International Relations," in *Strategic Choice and International Relations*, David Lake and Robert Powell, eds. (Princeton: Princeton University Press, 1999).

define the incentives that shape the choice of corporate governance systems. Thus the final outcome is either a blockholding pattern of monitoring or a diffusion pattern. In what follows we seek to explain the politics that leads to the policy cluster.

The second section examines preferences: we provide a schematic outline of the major players, what they want, and the possible combinations they can form in coalitions. While important, preferences can be underdetermining. Political institutions can influence the outputs from preference aggregation; we analyze that possibility in the third section, and in the fourth section provide an analysis of political coalitions that support different outcomes in corporate governance. In the last section of the chapter we examine two important alternative explanations of political outcomes: the legal family school and the economic sociology literature.

Preferences and Coalitions among Owners, Managers, and Workers

Politicians respond to demands of their constituents. How they do so is a function of preferences—what varying constituencies want—and institutions—the mechanisms that aggregate preferences and link politicians to constituencies.

We begin with the actors within the firm identified by finance theory, owners, managers, and workers, and the preferences for corporate governance practices of each group.[2] These preferences can be combined in several possible ways.

The three actors contend with each other over the resources of the firm, each with a varying set of claims against the firm's revenue and profit stream. Each set of actors has preferences that set up a range of trade-offs, thus of possible alignments with the other players.

Workers seek good wages, job stability in the face of layoffs, even at the expense of profitability, and protection of their pension claims on the firm. They are in conflict with managers and owners over wages and with managers over agency costs that benefit only managers. They may be relatively indifferent to expropriation costs that help one set of shareholders at the expense of other shareholders unless self-dealing by a blockholder threatens the financial viability of the firm, job security, and the firm's ability to cover its pension claims.

Managers seek income, job security, and managerial autonomy. They want high payments of various kinds, from salary to options, and the greatest autonomy in directing the resources of the firm—which also gives them the greatest leeway to shirk. They dislike expropriation costs at the expense of the firm, for reasons similar to those of workers. Thus they have common interests with workers against some kinds of action by owners, and common interests with owners against workers' claims.

Owners prefer to minimize all the forms of agency costs paid to managers and workers, fearing that each of these groups is able to divert resources from profits, requiring the firm to pay above market prices to them. Owners may be concentrated or diffused. Concentrated owners incur the risk of exposure to a single firm, as compared to diffuse owners, who can spread the risk of their equity investment

---

[2] The basic formulation of the agency problem looks at owners and managers only, on the grounds that there is no problem of incomplete contract with workers. Concern with "human capital" undermines that distinction, and thus we include workers. See Zingales 2000.

TABLE 4.1
Preference Theories: Political Coalitions and Governance Outcomes

Coalitional Lineup	Winner	Political Coalition Label	Predicted Outcome
Pair A: Class Conflict:			
Owners + managers vs. workers	Owners + managers	Investor	Diffusion
Owners + managers vs. workers	Workers	Labor	Blockholding
Pair B: Sectoral:			
Owners vs. managers + workers	Managers + workers	Corporatist compromise	Blockholding
Owners vs. managers + workers	Owners	Oligarchy	Blockholding
Pair C: Property and Voice:			
Owners + workers vs. managers	Owners + workers	Transparency	Diffusion
Owners + workers vs. managers	Managers	Managerism	Diffusion

Note: Also reproduced as table 2.3, p. 23.

over several firms and assets. On the other hand, blockholders can help themselves to a variety of expropriation costs at the expense of minority shareholders. Diffuse owners don't share in expropriation costs; they focus on getting the best risk-adjusted rate of return on their investment, and assembling a diversified equity portfolio. A subset of owners may have common interests with workers against the expropriation claims of blockholders, while in other situations, blockholders may make common cause with managers and workers.

We see three possible alignments. Each group can make a bargain with another. Or each group can divide, one faction going in one direction, another faction the other. This helps us understand "coalitional potential," the possible alliances of the intrafirm players as they move outside to politics. Which one coalesces in a given country, and which side wins, cannot be understood by knowing their preferences alone. In order to translate these preferences into real coalitions, we must understand the forces at work that decide which coalitions will coalesce.

Political Coalitions

We have sketched out a simple model of groups within the firm and their preferences concerning corporate governance practices. To get a regulatory regime that fits their preferences, these groups have to mobilize support in the political arena. In so doing they can combine or conflict with each other in various coalitions. With three groups, owners, managers, workers, we can identify three combinations of pairs, and two outcomes for each, depending on who wins. We list them in table 4.1, the expected policy outcome for each set of winners.

The schema in table 4.1 derives from basic theories of preferences common in political economy. Class conflict models, derived from political economy and from Marx, posit owners of capital in conflict with workers possessing only labor power. Managers are allied with capital. This cleavage structure underlies a classic theorem of trade economics, the Stolper-Samuelson analysis of returns to the factors of production, which can be used to predict preferences in economic policy debates.[3] It also reflects debates in corporate finance about the role of labor in claims on the firm; do incomplete contracts apply only to the owner-manager relationship, or to the human value contribution labor can make to the firm?[4]

Sectoral cleavage shows alliances between members of different "classes" as a function of their investment in specific assets proper to that sector. In trade economics the Ricardo-Viner theory, based on asset specificity and mobility, is used to explain why workers and managers cooperate to protect "their" industries from foreign competition, or support free trade. Similar ideas appear in discussions of the firm that consider the value of information held by suppliers, distributors, and employees, and the difficulty shareholder-centered theories have in accounting for the effect on governance of this difference in level of information.

The third cleavage derives from a mixture of factor and asset specificity arguments applied to various circumstances. Workers, to protect their pension funds or to protect their jobs, may find it strategically useful to challenge managers with the aid of external investors. Owners may be internally divided over the advantages to diversification by outside investors and the advantages to blockholding by insiders. These conflicts within groups make possible, as happens with the sector model, different alignments or coalitions that cut across class lines.

These theories of coalitions have been used by researchers to study corporate governance. We can integrate them into a coherent analytic approach that stresses historical and situational variables to explain which coalition prevails. At one time or another, in different places, each of the coalitions has triumphed. We ask why it has done so.

The investor model derives from our reading of conventional ideas about the goals of investors and of blockholders.[5] It assumes investors want shareholder protections and that firms will provide them. There is no specified role for politics

---

[3] See applications by Ronald Rogowski, *Commerce and Coalitions: How Trade Affects Domestic Political Alignments* (Princeton: Princeton University Press, 1989); Stephen P. Magee, William A. Brock, and Leslie Young, *Black Hole Tariffs and Endogenous Policy Theory in General Equilibrium* (Cambridge: Cambridge University Press, 1989); Peter A. Gourevitch, *Politics in Hard Times: Comparative Responses to International Economic Crises* (Ithaca, N.Y.: Cornell University Press, 1986); Gourevitch, "International Trade, Domestic Coalitions, and Liberty: Comparative Responses to the Crisis of 1873–1896," *Journal of Interdisciplinary History* 8 (1977): 281–313; Jeffrey Frieden, "Sectoral Conflict and U.S. Foreign Economic Policy, 1914–1940," *International Organization* 42 (1988): 59–90; Michael Hiscox, "Class versus Industry Cleavages: Inter-industry Factor Mobility and the Politics of Trade," *International Organization* 50 (2001): 1–46.

[4] Zingales 2000; Andrei Shleifer and Larry Summers, "Breach of Trust in Hostile Takeovers," in *Corporate Takeovers: Causes and Consequences*, Alan J. Auerbach, ed. (Chicago: University of Chicago Press, 1988).

[5] Hansmann and Kraakman 2000; Henry Hansmann and Reinier Kraakman, "The Essential Role of Organizational Law," *Yale Law Journal* 110 (2000): 387–440; La Porta et al. 1997.

here—that is, no explanation of why the political system provides MSP. Adding some political assumptions to the standard view gives us the investor model. The pendant to the investor model is the labor model, the other side of the class divide, developed by Roe's important work.[6]

The sectoral model has a long tradition in political economy, especially the trade literature. Writing on the political economy in the advanced industrial countries after World War II discusses at some length the "corporatist compromise" to describe the historical compromise of the mixed economy, the welfare state, market forces, and regulation that emerged after 1945. We use that label for this pattern, which has been applied by Pagano and Volpin to the specific issue of corporate governance patterns.[7] The oligarchy model is the obverse of the investor model: it is what happens if shareholders lack protection, and by implication, workers are politically weak.

The property and voice model is suggested by Höpner and colleagues writing on new trends in Germany and Europe. We link it as well to the literature on pensions (Drucker).[8] The managerism model (we are tempted to refer to it as the managerial agency failure model) was invoked positively by Chandler, negatively by Berle and Means, and resurrected by critics of contemporary governance scandals.[9]

Coalitional Pair A: Class Conflict

The first coalitional divide consists of owners and managers on one side, workers on the other. As translated by politics, this coalitional struggle has two possible outcomes. In the investor model, owners and managers prevail, while in the labor model workers succeed in having their preferences embedded in corporate governance practices, and owners must adjust accordingly. We examine each of these possibilities in turn.

THE INVESTOR MODEL

This explanation posits that investors want high-quality minority shareholder protections and pay a premium (or assign a discount) for governance when they invest in firms. Blockholders find it in their interest to trade expropriation costs

[6] Roe 2003b.

[7] Marco Pagano and Paolo Volpin, "The Political Economy of Corporate Governance," Centre for Economic Policy Research Working Paper Series No. 2682, 2001; "The Political Economy of Finance," *Oxford Review of Economic Policy* 17 (2001): 502–19; Perotti and von Thadden 2003.

[8] Höpner 2003a; Peter Drucker, *The Unseen Revolution: How Pension Fund Socialism Came to America* (New York: Harper and Row, 1976).

[9] John Coffee, "Understanding Enron: It's about the Gatekeepers, Stupid," Columbia Law and Economics Working Paper Series No. 207, 2002; "What Caused Enron? A Capsule Social and Economic History of the 1990s," Columbia Law and Economics Working Paper Series No. 214, 2003. Writing critical of managerial "excess" in recent years includes Robert A. G. Monks and Nell Minow, *Power and Accountability: Restoring the Balance of Power between Corporations, Owners, and Society* (New York: Harper Business, 1991); Monks and Minow, eds., *Corporate Governance*, 2nd ed. (Oxford: Blackwell, 2001); Robert A. G. Monks, *The Emperor's Nightingale: Restoring the Integrity of the Corporation in the Age of Shareholder Activism* (Reading, Mass.: Addison-Wesley, 1998).

in exchange for higher valuation by these outside investors, and lobby their political system to enhance minority shareholder protections. In this model, owners and managers combine together; workers' possible objections to these changes in governance rules are mere obstacles to be overcome.

The outcome of corporate governance practices in a dominant investor coalition is low agency and expropriation costs, across the board, as reflected in strong minority shareholder protections, with decreasing concentration until diffuse shareholding becomes the predominant case for listed firms.[10]

It is this link between investors and politicians that lies at the heart of the investor demand model. Without protections, capital will not come. Investors seek firms that proffer these assurances (if private ordering does its job), but prefer investing in firms in countries that provide these protections. They will avoid or discount firms in countries that don't provide these protections. This drives up the costs of capital and hurts the economy. Competitive pressure thus rewards the provision of minority shareholder protections and hurts countries that do not provide them. The Darwinian logic does its job. Politicians seek economic health to stay in office. They seek, therefore, the confidence of investors. The result is the system of minority shareholder protections. Thus the investor demand model produces results by assuming that politicians, the makers of regulation, respond to the demands of investors.

This view is common both to conservative supporters of investment models of the economy, who like it, and to left-wing critics of neoliberal models, who don't. Both see the flow of money as the driver of politics and policy. Both call attention to the immense flow of money in the contemporary world economy, especially from Anglo-American institutional investors who have entered economies all over the world in recent years, and have induced some change of behavior in both the private and the public sectors.[11]

---

[10] This model is reflected, for example, in E. Philip Davis and Benn Steil's comprehensive *Institutional Investors* (Cambridge: MIT Press, 2001). In a similar tone, in *Capital Markets and Corporate Governance in Japan, Germany, and the United States* (New York: Routledge, 1998), 41, Helmut Dietl attributes variance in corporate governance practices across countries to variance in capital market inefficiencies across these countries, which in turn are embedded in different regulatory compromises. In an adventuresome departure from their quality-of-corporate-law approach with La Porta et al., Andrei Shleifer and Robert Vishny explain corporate governance (or the lack of it) in terms of an equilibrium bargain between rent-seeking politicians and protection-seeking investors: "institutions supporting property rights are created not by the fiat of a public-spirited government but, rather, in response to political pressure on the government exerted by owners of private property." Andrei Shleifer and Robert Vishny, *The Grabbing Hand: Government Pathologies and Their Cures* (Cambridge: Harvard University Press, 1998), 10.

[11] Examples can be given from many countries. The literature in France is quite lively on these points: Suzanne Berger, *The First Globalization: Lessons from the French* (Paris: Seuil, 2003); Pepper Culpepper, Peter Hall, and Bruno Palier, eds., *The Politics That Markets Make: Economic and Social Change in France* (Palgrave MacMillan, forthcoming); Frédéric Lordon, *Fonds de pension, pièges à cons? Mirage de la démocratie actionnariale* (Paris: Raisons d'agir, 2000); Robert Boyer, "The Diversity and Future of Capitalisms: A *Régulationnist* Analysis," in *Capitalism in Evolution: Global Contentions—East and West*, Geoffrey M. Hodgson, Makato Itoh, and Nobuharu Yokokawa, eds. (Cheltenham: Edward Elgar, 2001); Amable 2000.

THE LABOR MODEL

Workers prefer governance systems that maximize their share of the firms' profits (or "quasi rents" in economic jargon). They demand employment protection in labor markets, good wages and stability of wage levels, work rules, health insurance, and often a voice in the boardroom. These preferences put them in conflict with owners and managers. The labor model is the opposite side of the class divide from the investor model. As Roe argues, where labor is weak, the investment model prevails and diffuse governance patterns develop.[12] Where labor is strong, blockholding prevails. Thus conflicts within the boardroom over power and economic share are resolved in the political marketplace.

The corporate governance outcome of the labor model is less protection for minority shareholders and greater concentration of ownership. Both the demand for regulation model and the labor model are based on the same coalitional divide, with owners and managers on one side and workers on the other, but the outcomes in terms of corporate governance are radically different, the difference being explained by politics. But this particular coalitional divide does not exhaust the opportunities for coalitional formation. In the corporatist compromise, managers switch sides, as it were, casting their lot with workers rather than with owners.

Coalitional Pair B: Sectoral Conflict

The second coalitional divide cuts across class lines. It puts managers and workers together in seeking to preserve jobs, firm size, and income to employees as a whole, rather than the income stream to shareholders. We call this form sectoral because this pattern of alliance has been found to be common in trade politics, where employees join with managers to lobby for tariff protection or other subsidies for "their" firm.

THE CORPORATIST COMPROMISE

Managers and workers have common cause in promoting the stability and size of the firm as well as their insiders' claims on the profit stream. Owners accommodate this pattern, seeing some benefit in the stability and the protection it can provide for their private benefits of control. The minority shareholders are left out.

In the political sphere, this coalitional bargain seeks regulations that assure stability of relationships: they allow blockholder-favorable rules in corporate governance law, employment protection and other elements of the social democratic package. This is the corporatist model in several countries of continental Europe and (to some degree) Japan. The results in terms of corporate governance are similar to those of the social democratic model, but the underlying politics are explained differently: it is a cross-class coalition, not the victory of one class (workers) over another (owners).

The application of this coalition to corporate governance is most clearly laid out by Pagano and Volpin.[13] Support is found as well in interest group arguments

---

[12] Mark J. Roe, *Strong Managers, Weak Owners: The Political Roots of American Corporate Finance* (Princeton: Princeton University Press, 1994); Roe 2003b.

[13] Pagano and Volpin 2001a.

that explore cross-class alignments, such as interest groups examined by Rajan and Zingales, by Krozner, and by Hall and Soskice in *Varieties of Capitalism*. The notion of institutional complementarity helps explain the formation of common preferences across class lines. These solidarities are often based on sectors, on "bosses and workers" within a particular business sector who share interests, along with the inside blockholders who join them.

The predicted outcome of the corporatist model is few minority shareholder protections and high concentration of ownership.

OLIGARCHS

The reverse of the corporatist model is the defeat of the manager-worker coalitions by the owners. This leads to direct ownership control. It is the outcome preferred by blockholders, not by minority investors. It reflects a point neglected by the standard investor model—that the preferences of owners are not uniform; they divide on desire for MSP and diffusion patterns of ownership. Without concern for minority shareholders, the political victory of the owners can thus lead to blockholding, the opposite of the outcome predicted by the investor model.

Coalitional Pair C: Voice

The third pair of coalitions divides the interest pairing around the classic concern of managerial agency, the rents for the managers themselves. The problem of managerial agency costs is indeed the very issue that drove finance theory and the conceptualization of the problem dating back to Berle and Means. The investor model washes away the problem by assuming owners will prevail. But they may need help overcoming managerial action. They may find it among "workers," leading to the little-studied but potentially important pattern of owners and workers against managers, with two possible winners.

THE TRANSPARENCY COALITION

In this model, owners and workers join together to constrain managerial agency costs. Owners' interests express a desire to control managers, increase share price, and get the benefits of diversification at the price of giving up blockholding.

Why would workers join this coalition? We see two reasons, each based on different aspects of their economic situation. As employees, workers may seek to protect their jobs through greater involvement in decision making. The lack of transparency in the corporatist model is double edged for workers. It has helped the manager-worker coalition, but at some cost for workers. The obscurity in the model makes it difficult for workers to participate in managerial decisions, as managers are able to construct systems that hide decisions. Höpner sees transparency for preservation of jobs and wages as the major factor in shifting German Sozialedemokratische Parte: Deutschlands and trade unions positions.[14]

The other reason focuses on pension funds, the property stake workers acquire as shareowners. Drucker called attention to this point in the mid-1970s in *The*

---

[14] Höpner 2003a.

Unseen Revolution: How Pension Fund Socialism Came to America.[15] Several other studies by Clowes, Williams, Useem, and Sykes explore the roots of this "fiduciary" capitalism, while Monks and Minow show the work of "investor-activists."[16]

The substantial growth of worker-owned pension funds invested in equities alters workers' incentives with respect to corporate governance. Under conditions that we explore in chapter 7 involving pension fund ownership, workers can become broadly interested in corporate governance, and organizations representing worker funds can become activists on behalf of shareholder rights and transparency. Whether this happens turns in large measure on the actual institutions that handle worker pensions and their incentives to be active in issues of managerial agency. How much a worker is concerned about the effect of corporate governance on his or her pension depends upon who is the ultimate payer of that pension and who controls it.

MANAGERISM

If owners and workers fail, then managers prevail. This is sometimes referred to as *managerial agency failure*, the very problem that motivates much of the work on this topic. The managers' victory can happen for a variety of reasons: collective action by owners and workers, for example, is a problem within the firm (organizing leverage at board meeting) but also in society and politics. Workers' groups are organized around wages and job issues, not necessarily around voice, and even less about pension rights. Owners are similarly individualistic on the shareholder side, rather than the firm side.

Firms can be active lobbyists, and goals of this lobbying are controlled by managers. This is the source of managerial power in politics, not votes, as their numbers are smaller than the ranks of employees, but the ability to use the resources of the firm in political action. Business associations are important lobby groups around the world, but often they are controlled by the top executives, not the shareholders.

We would expect managerial triumph to result in weak minority shareholder protections, and also low blockholding. Managers' ideal world is a balance between the two: enough minority shareholder protections to weaken powerful blockholders who might otherwise discipline them, but not enough to make shareholding democracy effective—which is to say, enough to dilute the blockholders, but not enough to permit a hostile takeover.

We have here sketched out coalitional patterns: the possible ways in which the various actors can combine and the policy patterns they support. This is an

---

[15] Drucker 1976.

[16] Michael Clowes, *The Money Flood: How Pension Funds Revolutionized Investing* (New York: Wiley, 2000); James Hawley and Andrew Williams, *The Rise of Fiduciary Capitalism: How Institutional Investors Can Make Corporate America More Democratic* (Philadelphia: University of Pennsylvania Press, 2000); Michael Useem, *Investor Capitalism: How Money Managers Are Changing the Face of America* (New York: HarperCollins, 1996); Allen Sykes, *Capitalism for Tomorrow: Reuniting Ownership and Control* (Oxford: Capstone, 2000); Monks 1998, and Robert Monks, *The New Global Investors: How Shareholders Can Unlock Sustainable Prosperity Worldwide* (Oxford: Capstone, 2001).

important step in understanding the politics of corporate governance policy, but it is not enough. Sketching the possible combinations does not tell us who wins, which combination prevails. To determine that we need to know more: the impact of political institutions as mechanisms of aggregation in influencing outcomes.

Fragmented Actors

Having laid out this coalition pattern, we alert the reader to an important complication: each of our three major actors, owners, managers, workers, turns out to be a composite. The analytic interest in these actors derived from a realization that the firm is not a monolithic whole, but a composite of underlying units. Not all members of each category behave in lock step with their fellow members, especially across firms. For example, owners cleave into insider blockholders and external minority shareholders. Both are owners, indeed both are shareholders.[17] "Old money" blockholders and "new money" entrepreneurs have different preferences (including very different stakes in equity markets) and behave differently in the arena of corporate governance.

Similarly, workers face possible conflicts between concern for their jobs and concern for their pension investments. Without substantial savings workers' major assets are their jobs; thus they will worry about job preservation. That may motivate them to worry about voice in the firm so as to preserve jobs. Historically that concern has motivated worker representatives toward the corporatist stakeholder bargain with managers and blockholders for stability in the firm and job protection. Conversely, where workers have substantial savings invested in the firm or in shares generally, they acquire the concerns of minority shareholders. The greater their savings, the more worried they are about managerial actions that could threaten those assets. As investors in the firm, they care about profitability—like other investors. But as minority shareholders they care about managerial agency costs.

Managers divide along choice of strategies. Some managers prefer the security and predictability of dealing with "patient" blockholders; other prefer the autonomy of dealing with diffused shareholders in financial markets. Some are willing to commit to high MSP in exchange for high remuneration (through stock options, among others); others prefer job security to remuneration and will do anything to avoid a contest for control.

We alert readers to these distinctions among workers, owners and managers, as we develop the argument and particularly in the country case studies. We return at the end of chapter 7 to consider these distinctions.

POLITICAL INSTITUTIONS: MAJORITARIAN AND CONSENSUS MECHANISMS

The next step in analyzing the political process involves political institutions. Preferences, even adjusted for consideration of political resources such as money

[17] This is what makes the *stakeholder* and *shareholder* labels potentially confusing. Both include shareholders; the differences lies in the way they are organized and their relationship to other players.

and votes, can by themselves be indeterminate. Institutions affect outcomes. Hold preferences constant, vary the institutions, and you will often get a different result. The reverse may also be true: vary the preferences of those who use the same institutions and the results may differ. Political science has been fighting about preferences versus institutions for some time. Having paid serious attention to the preferences argument, we turn to institutions as a way of seeing how preferences combine.[18] Institutional change may encourage preference changes as the payoff matrices change; preferences push institutions to change so as to conform to the desired result.

Institutions can thus affect coalition formation and policy victory. A particular institutional arrangement may favor one side over another. By institutions, we mean the set of rules that determine the processes of rule making and enforcement.[19] Institutions can affect outcomes. If preferences are assumed to be constant, varying the rules will produce different policy outputs. Proportional representation in electoral law (as in Japan) produces different electoral results than do single-member districts with plurality winners.[20] The supermajority rules of the United States Senate, colloquially known as the "filibuster" rule, whereby a small group or even a single senator can bring the legislative machinery to a halt as long as long as he or she can keep talking on the floor is another famous example. Both of these institutions derive from laws, not constitutional items, as they can be changed by a legislature. More permanent are constitutional provisions such as federalism in the United States and separation of powers.

Political institutions can therefore influence the outcome of policy disputes concerning regulation of corporate governance. Since countries differ in their political institutions, it may well be that differences in corporate governance structures reflect differences in political institutions. We explore this relationship here by correlating corporate governance outcomes with political form. Following a substantial literature in political science, we sort country institutions into "majoritarian" and "consensus" types. High levels of MSP and a liberal production regime will, we predict, correlate with majoritarian political institutions. Low levels of MSP and an organized or regulated production regime will correlate with consensus institutions. We analyze first the classification of political systems and then the causal mechanisms that produce a relationship.

---

[18] See David Stasavage's criticism of the well-known paper by North and Weingast. The latter argues that Parliament's triumph over the Crown in seventeenth-century Britain reassured investors that royal will could not corrupt public finance, thereby lowering interest rates. Stasavage argues we cannot evaluate the ability of Parliament to produce policies favorable to creditors without looking at who controlled Parliament. David Stasavage, "Credible Commitment in Early Modern Europe: North and Weingast Revisited," *Journal of Law, Economics, and Organization* 18 (2002); 155–86; Douglass C. North and Barry R. Weingast, "Constitutions and Commitment: The Evolution of Institutions Governing Public Choice in Seventeenth-Century England," *Journal of Economic History* 69 (1989): 803–32.

[19] Our usage of institutions here is that of political scientists speaking largely of "parchment institutions," the documents more or less formal; this is different from the usage found often in sociology, for which institutions means established practices, separate from any formalism.

[20] Gary Cox, *Making Votes Count: Strategic Coordination in the World's Electoral Systems* (New York: Cambridge University Press, 1997).

Mechanisms of Interest Aggregation

Specialists in comparative political institutions such as Lijphart have focused attention on differences among democratic regimes in electoral laws, party systems, and legislative-executive relations.[21] We can stylize their findings as two contrasting systems, majoritarian and consensus.[22]

Majoritarian systems magnify the impact of small shifts of votes, thus allow large swings of policy; consensus systems reduce the impact of vote shifts by giving leverage to a wide range of players through coalitions, and thus have lesser swings of policy. Consensus systems have many "veto players," majoritarian ones have few. In a consensus system, a wide range of opinion has to be included in decisions. The coalition nature of the government assures this, as all participants in the cabinet have to agree to important decisions. In a majoritarian system, large blocks of opinion can be overridden by a narrow majority; thus small shifts of votes can have big consequences.

In Lijphart's classification, the United Kingdom is the closest to a pure majoritarian model, where a single party controls a cabinet that controls the legislature.[23] Consensus systems (in Scandinavia and Austria) also have cabinet dominance over the legislature, but within the context of a multiparty system. The connection between institutions and outcomes emerges clearly in an examination of the impact of electoral rules. Electoral rules have a big impact on how preferences are articulated and represented.[24] Single-member districts, with victory to the plurality winner, reward coalitions formed before an election. Groups of varying opinions have an incentive to combine forces so as to get the plurality needed for victory.

Conversely, proportional representation systems reward the articulation of divergent preferences at the time of election. It is after the election that combinations or coalitions are formed. The electoral system is not the only logic at work: in a population there are sometimes cleavage lines in preferences, such as religion or ethnicity, that do not follow this logic, but even there it can have substantial force.

The formal organization of authority influences the degree of fragmented or unified authority.[25] Where legislatures are unicameral, or where the second chamber has little power, as in the United Kingdom, power can be concentrated. In the

---

[21] See Lijphart 1999; Thorsten Beck, George Clarke, Alberto Groff, Philip Keefer, and Patrick Walsh, "New Tools in Comparative Political Economy: The Database of Political Institutions," *World Bank Economic Review* 15 (2001): 165–76; Matthew S. Shugart and John M. Carey, *Presidents and Assemblies: Constitutional Design and Electoral Dynamics* (New York: Cambridge University Press, 1992); see chapter 9 for development of this classification scheme.

[22] Preferences do not influence policies unless the preference holders have political resources to compel attention by the decision makers: votes, money, ideas, force. We appreciate the importance of this point, all too often neglected in arguments about institutions versus interests or preferences as explanations. But we do not analyze these power resources here. We make the usual excuse of parsimony, space, and measurement problems. Instead we incorporate resources into the other two variables: the holders of preferences have to have resources that are effective in a particular institutional setting. Thus political resources are incorporated in an analysis of preferences and interests and of institutions.

[23] Lijphart 1999, 10–21 for specification of the archetypal majoritarian (Westminster) system.

[24] Electoral laws play an important role in shaping the system. Cox 1997.

[25] Lijphart 1999, 10–21.

United Kingdom, the legislature is effectively unicameral, as the House of Lords has little power. The constitution can be amended by a simple majority in the House of Commons, there is no effective judicial review, and the central bank is dominated by the executive. In Japan, the upper house has more power than the British House of Lords.

The contrast with presidential systems is considerable. In the United States, as in much of Latin America, the separation of powers makes the presidential executive independent from the legislature.[26] The president is independently elected, has veto power over legislation, and makes appointments. The U.S. legislature is fully bicameral, so that each house could be controlled by a different party. Thus the United States can have divided government (presidency and legislature in different hands). In addition, the United States is federal, with considerable power in the hands of separately chosen state governments that may again differ politically from the national government. Judicial review gives the U.S. Supreme Court substantial autonomy from both president and Congress.

Where the majority is solid, minorities have few protections. Whoever controls the majority in the House of Commons has enormous policy latitude. These are not dictatorial powers; the majority is elected, and is concerned with winning the next election. The majority can turn against the party leader, as happened to Margaret Thatcher when she pushed for an unpopular poll tax and was forced to resign. Within those limits, however, the prime minister with a large majority has substantial discretion, a wide range of behaviors at his or her disposal. A relatively small shift in votes by the electorate replacing one major party with another, allows the new party to change policy quite dramatically.

By contrast, consensus systems have substantial power sharing. Italy, the Netherlands, and Sweden are notable examples. Instead of single-party control, several political parties form coalition governments. The executive is therefore secure only so long as the coalition holds together. Prime ministers have less control over the members of that coalition than would the head of a single party who had considerable leverage over that party machinery (picking candidates for office, for example). Policy making thus reflects a constant process of bargaining and accommodation among the parties. The members of the coalition have more leverage, more voice, more ability to make their demands heard and to be effective brakes on policy change. Electoral laws and intraparty rules have a substantial effect on how these systems work. Proportional representation encourages a multi-party system where bargains are formed after the election. Single member plurality systems encourage two party systems with bargaining before the election. Strong rules of party discipline within each political grouping encourage centralized bargaining process within a coalition, as well as Cabinet control within one-party majorities.

Many countries are hybrids of these dimensions. The United States, for example, has a strong majoritarian element in its electoral law, which leads to a two-party system. At the same time, it separates the executive from the legislature so it can have divided government (each branch under control of a different party). Japan and Germany mix proportional representation with single member districts.

---

[26] Shugart and Carey 1992.

Germany is federal, with a more important upper house whose composition reflects party dynamics within the German states. France has both a prime minister responsible to the legislature and an independently elected president. If the president's party has a majority in the National Assembly, power shifts to that office; if the majority lies with the opposition, power shifs to the prime minister.

Veto Points and Consensus Politics

In analyzing these systems, researchers focus on the way institutions define the capacity to block or to pass legislation, thus to exercise a "veto."[27] While different terms are used to articulate this concept, we focus on veto "points" rather than two common alternatives, veto "gates" and veto "players."[28]

Majoritarian systems have fewer veto points than consensus systems; thus governments are able to make important decisions on a narrower base of support. Because consensus systems contain more veto points, governments depend on a broader base of support. We would expect, therefore, narrower policy swings in consensus than in majoritarian systems, on the same swing of votes in an election.

This is, we note, an argument about continuity as well as about creation. Once a policy is adopted in consensus systems, it is likely to be kept. Consensus systems may make it harder to get things adopted in the first place.[29] Alternatively, majoritarian systems are indeed able to make decisions, but they may be of a substantively different kind: consumer oriented rather than producer oriented, as Rogowski suggests.

[27] Several commonly used institutional measures deserve some attention here. They usually relate to the formal rules of the system. Two such measures, veto gates and the distinction between presidential and parliamentary systems, do not produce any meaningful relationship. As we discussed above, we believe these measures are too formally institutional and do not adequately examine the issue of party composition of government—the ability of a single cohesive political party to integrate veto gates, for example, or the potential for multiple parties to exercise veto power within a single institutional veto gate. Since we believe that consensual or majoritarian policymaking is a function of the de facto veto points, not the de jure ones, we have focused on the number of veto points in the system, and have found statistically significant correlations.

[28] The phrase *veto gates* refers to formal institutional points where legislation can be blocked, such as a presidential veto, or a legislative committee, or the Supreme Court. A *veto player* is any person or group who has the capacity to block legislation (a specific committee chair, or party leader, or interest group). A *veto point* combines the notion of institution (a de jure concept) and individual or group; it is thus any point in a political system where legislation can be blocked, be it veto gates or veto players.

Thus, a presidential system with a bicameral legislature has three veto gates, but the number of veto players depends on the division of government and the degree of party unity. If such a system had a strong party system and the same party controlled all three veto gates, there would be only one veto player. But, if there was divided government, there could be two or three veto players (depending on the organization of the parties controlling the two chambers of the legislature).

Similarly, a unicameral parliamentary system would have only one veto gate, but could have any number of veto players depending on how many parties are included in the governing coalition. So majoritarian and consensus systems could both have any number of veto gates. What distinguishes them is that consensus systems have many veto players, while majoritarian systems have few veto players. Consensus systems, which have multiparty coalition government, have many groups that can veto legislation, while majoritarian systems lack these multiple de facto veto players.

[29] Guiliano Bonoli suggests that this restraint explains why the United States and Switzerland have less extensive welfare states than Sweden. Guiliano Bonoli, *The Politics of Pension Reform: Institutions and Policy Change in Western Europe* (New York: Cambridge University Press, 2000).

We explore the second of these ideas: that institutions influence not whether a decision is made, but what coalition wins, thus what the content of the decision may be.

MEASURING INSTITUTIONAL DIFFERENCE

To quantify the countries in our sample in terms of consensus or majoritarian politics, we use an index of political cohesion derived from and modified from the Beck et al. World Bank database of political indicators (DPI).[30] In our index, 0 equals a unified presidential or a one-party parliamentary government; 1 equals a divided presidential government, a two-party coalition parliamentary government, or a minority party parliamentary government; and 2 equals a multiparty coalition parliamentary government. Since the number of veto points can change with each election, these scores are the average across all the years available in the DPI. Table 4.2 shows the 32 countries in our sample for which we have data with which to calculate this index, ranked from most majoritarian (lowest value) to most consensual (highest value).

The Scandinavian countries are predictably grouped together, towards the consensual end of the spectrum. But there are some counterintuitive results. Japan, for example, often considered an archetypical consensus political system, in fact falls quite close to the United States on the cohesion index. France and Thailand, both with a reputation for a strong executive, are actually more consensual than the Netherlands, by this measure.

Predicting the Effects of Consensus or Majoritarian Politics

We sort the countries out further according to institutional differences having to do with degree of democratic stability and vitality. We identify countries with functioning democracies of several decades in duration, with established highly functioning economies. We differentiate them from countries with less stable and transitional or authoritarian political systems, with less deeply developed market economies, and lower income levels.

Our expectation is that in established democracies

• Consensus systems favor corporatist coalitions and correlate positively with blockholding and negatively with minority shareholder protections.
• Majoritarian systems inhibit corporatist coalitions, thus correlate negatively with blockholding and positively with shareholder protections.

[30] The index of political cohesion used here is a recoding of the Beck et al. 2001 material, done to measure our definition of veto players. We recoded the instances of minority parliamentary government from 3 to 1, i.e., from the highest score on the list, to the same score as two-party parliamentary government. The justification for this is that though minority governments are forced to find support from other parties in order to pass legislation, they have the ability to shop around for that support and usually only need one other party to get things through. Thus, they are coded by us as equivalent to two-party government (IPCOH = 1), rather than multiparty (IPCOH = 2), or even higher, as they had initially been (IPCOH = 3). There are several other potential variables from the Beck DPI database that we probed for use as a measure of consensus or majoritarian institutions, including type of election, political fractionalization, and so forth. We believe that the measure of veto players captured by our index is the most effective measure.

TABLE 4.2
Modified Index of Political Cohesion

Canada	0.043478	Brazil	0.73913
New Zealand	0.130435	Ireland	0.826087
United Kingdom	0.130435	Malaysia	0.956522
India	0.391304	Chile	1
Philippines	0.478261	Denmark	1.086957
Spain	0.565217	Norway	1.086957
Australia	0.608696	Sweden	1.173913
Austria	0.608696	Netherlands	1.304348
Greece	0.608696	France	1.347826
Portugal	0.608696	Thailand	1.391304
South Korea	0.608696	Israel	1.521739
Venezuela	0.608696	Italy	1.521739
United States	0.652174	Belgium	1.652174
Argentina	0.695652	Germany	1.652174
Japan	0.695652	Finland	1.913043
Turkey	0.695652	Switzerland	2

Number of observations	38
SD	.5772191
Mean	.771167

Source: Beck 2001.

TABLE 4.3
Correlations of Political Cohesion

	All Countries	Developed	Emerging
Blockholding	20	0.34	0.26
Shareholder protections	−0.16	−0.46	0.33

On the other hand, we predict that in authoritarian regimes or weak democracies:

- Strong governments, with few veto points, have a high capacity for policy change and predation, thus correlate positively with blockholding, even if they correlate positively with shareholder protections.
- Weak governments, with many veto points, are ineffective in responding to crises, and frightening to investors, thus correlate positively with blockholding.

Established Democracies

For the sample as a whole (both democratic and authoritarian regimes), consensual political systems tend to have higher ownership concentration and lower shareholder protections, and majoritarian countries have the reverse, being correlated with lower concentration and higher shareholder protections, as shown by table 4.3 and figure 4.2.

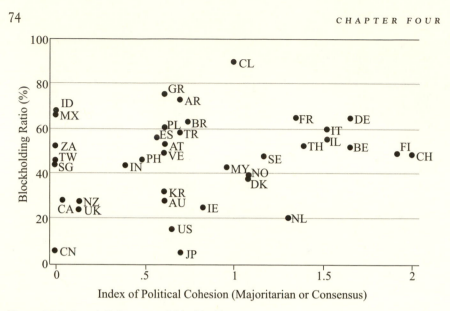

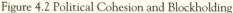

Figure 4.2 Political Cohesion and Blockholding

These correlations have the correct sign (as predicted) but are weak for the sample as a whole. They are somewhat stronger for the developed democracies as a group, and statistically insignificant for the emerging countries (defined as GDP per capita below $10,000). (See appendix table A.7 for an expanded table.)

To stress institutions, rather than income levels, we measure the robustness of democracies. We factor into the equation another variable from the World Bank DPI database, which captures the duration of a political system. This variable ("tensys") is the mean number of years that the country's political system has existed in its current institutional form.

For the sample as a whole, a bivariate regression of blockholding against both the index of political cohesion and the tenure variable is significant at $t = 2.42$ with an adjusted $r^2 = 24$. Similarly, regressing the minority shareholder protections index against both the index of political cohesion and the tenure variable is significant at $t = 2.24$, adjusted $r^2 = 25$. (See appendix table A.8.) Thus the consensus/majoritarian distinction is strong among the well-established, institution-heavy industrial democracies—those places where effective markets in both politics and the economy operate, where the actors in the firm are able to mobilize resources for political action in society.

This provides stronger support for the predictions of the effects of consensual or majoritarian political systems on corporate governance outcomes. In countries with weak or short-lived democratic systems and poorly functioning economic markets, one result is that political markets are also sketchy—it is difficult for preference coalitions to form and press their case through public political action.

Other treatments of political institutions stress the relationship among the variables differently. Pagano and Volpin show that proportional representation

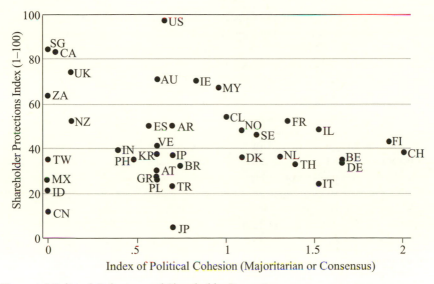

Figure 4.3 Political Cohesion and Shareholder Protections

encourages blockholding, while plurality systems correlate with diffusion.[31] This goes very much in the direction of our analysis, as electoral law contributes to the pattern of political cohesion we analyze. On its own, however, the impact of electoral law is muted by partisanship. Countries that code as plurality electoral systems are the United Kingdom, Canada, Australia, and France. If we look at all the rest, with proportional representation or mixed-member districts, we note that they spread rather widely on the left-right variable. The "work" of the correlation is thus being done by the clumping of the diffusion countries on the strong "right" indicators. We note as well that the impact of the left-right marker on the degree of diffusion is strong—the United States, United Kingdom, and Canada are quite strongly above the clumping of the other countries toward the bottom of the diffusion index. Thus the partisan spread is greater among the blockholding countries.

Similar effects appear when we look at the number of political parties. The United States, United Kingdom, Canada, and Australia are all on one side of the party indicator and the diffusion indicator—few parties, high diffusion—while there is a big spread in the party variable among the countries that concentrate toward low diffusion.

Electoral law interacts with societal preferences and the fractionalization of issue space to generate the number of political parties, and this is in turn quite important in shaping how formal institutional arrangements operate. Thus in our view electoral law and the number of political parties work through the political

[31] Pagano and Volpin 2001a.

cohesion mechanisms to generate the pattern of majoritarian and consensus systems. Electoral law influences the number of parties, which in turn enters into the cohesion index. The variables produce their results by their impact on the diffusion cases. The blockholding countries vary more greatly in type of political institution.

The Causal Mechanism of Credibility

We have established a correlation between majoritarian or consensual political institutions and outcomes on corporate governance, at least for the advanced democracies. What is the causal mechanism at work?

The logic is this: the organized production regime rests on a high degree of interdependence among the various players in the firm: it rests on an arrangement among the stakeholders, managers, blockholders, and workers to preserve the institution of the firm against outsiders. In so doing they seek a high degree of stability in the policy regime that favors this outcome—to protect their stake in the high level of specific assets they have invested in that regime. Consensus systems are more likely to do that than majoritarian systems, as they give a "veto" to all players on the shape and rate of change. It is not that consensus systems necessarily produce a CME, but once one is in place, for historically contingent reasons, such a system is more likely to preserve it. Thus consensus political systems protect blockholding/stakeholder corporate governance systems.

Conversely, majoritarian institutions undermine the incentives of producers to commit to specific assets. These political systems have greater policy variance than do consensus systems. As a result, firms want flexibility, the ability to hire and fire, to cut production, shift assets, sell, close, move as market conditions require in the moment. They prefer policies that support the liberal governance model, hence policies that stress the primacy of the external shareholder, not the various stakeholders.

The driving force is the capacity of consensus institutions to make credible commitments among coalition partners in a bargain. "Credible commitment" indicates the probability that partners think the other side will hold to an agreement.[32]

Consensus institutions increase the probability because the system provides a greater degree of "veto" to the players. Their consent to change is needed; thus they can enter an agreement with greater confidence that the bargain will be held. This process then becomes self-enforcing. Participants make decisions based on the degree of stability of policy, and then seek to preserve that system.

Majoritarian systems, conversely, experience greater swings of policy because small shifts of votes can produce bigger swings of control over policy. As a result, players in economic and political life cannot be sure agreements will last. They pursue, therefore, economic and political strategies that assume greater variability of policy.

[32] Our reasoning here is influenced by Hall and Soskice 2000, chap. 1; Stewart Wood, 1997, "Capitalist Constitutions: Supply-Side Reform in Britain and West Germany, 1960–1990, Ph.D. dissertation, Department of Government, Harvard University. Keefer 2005 and Keefer and Stasavage 2003 explore the issue of credible commitment in the provision of public goods.

The credible commitment argument affects both the forming of a bargain and underlying preferences for policy. It affects the bargain because political actors calculate strategy on the basis of the capacity for bargains to be made and held. The corporatist model described in chapter 7 involves cooperation among heterogeneous players across class, economic sector, and religious divides. These are difficult to bring about and support. They are induced by the consensus institutional pattern and supported by it.

Overall, it is the aspects of institutional systems having to do with credibility of commitment that influence the coalitional patterns that affect shareholding patterns. We underscore the fact that institutional "credibility" is not a normative judgment; the effects of various arrangements may be good or bad (efficient or inefficient) from an economic standpoint. For example, the varieties-of-capitalism literature argues that corporatist understandings of employment continuity may allow firms and employees to invest in firm-specific training that would otherwise not make sense in an economy with higher labor mobility; this may be a good thing. On the other hand, the private benefits of control that blockholders can extract under equally credible understandings of the corporatist compromise may not be a good thing.

The capacity of a coalitional system to make credible the corporatist compromise leads to blockholding. The workers, managers, and blockholders cement a deal that excludes minority shareholders. Systems with low credibility of commitment to political bargains cause policy variance, which undermines the arrangements all participants demand. This creates privatizing incentives, which induce blockholders to defect from the worker-manager corporatist alliance in favor of practices that protect minority shareholders.

Thus in the worker-manager-blockholder alignment against minority owners, a high-credibility system leads to the corporatist understanding whereby managers and workers smooth over the differences in their joint incentives in a corporatist deal, whereas a low-credibility system makes the elaborate cross-sector deals of corporatism unsustainable because of the risk of change or defection.

Consumers or Producers?

We infer additional support for this approach to institutions from research on other issues. If variance in outputs in other issue areas can be linked to differences in political institutions, and particularly to the distinctions we have explored here between consensus and majoritarian systems, that linkage gives additional reason to have confidence in our findings. Recent research in several areas indeed links policy outputs to political institutions, and we observe substantial covariance between corporate governance and other social patterns.

Roe suggests that the difference between policies that favor diffuse shareholding and those that favor blockholding resonates strongly with the distinction between policies that favor consumers and those that favor producers.[33] If we

---

[33] Roe 2003b, 133.

could explain the politics of proconsumer and proproducer interests, he observes, we would gain greater insight into the corporate governance.

The institutionalists offer just that. Ronald Rogowski and Mark Keyser find that while majoritarian electoral systems reward consumers, proportional representation rewards producers. Countries with majoritarian systems have low product prices, while countries with proportional representation have "high voter turnout; less strategic voting; less political violence, greater cabinet instability and shorter lived governments; higher governmental expenditures and budgetary deficits; more welfare spending; greater dependence on trade; and greater equality of income."[34] This pattern corresponds to our distinction between majoritarian and consensus systems.

This suggests that similar processes are at work across a range of issues; giving us confidence in the explanatory utility of institutions in general and their observed pattern in particular.

We cited Roe earlier to say that openness to trade, a high degree of competition, income inequality, low employment protection, and diffuse shareholding all correlate. Hall and Soskice extend the interconnections to include education and training systems, welfare and social services, price setting in labor markets and the economy, and economic coordination generally.[35] Governance systems fit into national production systems, and these in turn appear to correlate with the same patterns of political institutions we note here, consensus and majoritarian.[36]

---

[34] Ronald Rogowski and Mark A. Kayser, "Majoritarian Electoral Systems and Consumer Power: Price-Level Evidence from OECD Countries," *American Journal of Political Science* 46 (2002): 562–39.

[35] For example, the German training system links workers to specific jobs. Firms are willing to invest in the workers, because they know they will not leave the job; thus there is little chance of their paying the costs of worker training without reaping the rewards. The regulation of the labor market by the government makes it difficult to discharge workers. The welfare system, furthermore, is tied to employment so that workers have little incentive to leave. Corporate governance laws (many shares owned by single owners, such as banks or other firms) shield managers and firms from takeovers, stock price pressures, and short-term concerns that might pressure them to reduce the workforce.

[36] In education and training, LMEs stress general skills (for all employers) vs. specific ones (for a particular industry or firm). The LMEs stress the former, the OMEs the latter. In labor relations and labor markets, the LME systems have low rates of union participation and weak regulations on discharging employees. The OME systems have high union participation and highly regulated labor markets. In economic decision-making the OME countries have highly organized and centralized business and trade-union structures; the LMEs are quite decentralized and market-driven. In welfare and social service policy, the OME countries have highly developed welfare state services in health, retirement, etc.; they divide into the social democratic (Scandinavian) model, where benefits are decommoditized from jobs and located in individuals, and the Christian democratic model, where benefits are connected to the job. Torben Iversen and Anne Wren, "Equality, Employment, and Budgetary Restraint: The Trilemma of the Service Economy," *World Politics* 50 (1998): 507–46. In the arena of economic policy, if countries face trade-offs among economic growth, equality, and balanced budgets (Torben Iversen, "Wage Bargaining, Central Bank Independence, and the Real Effects of Money," *International Organization*, 52 [1998]: 469–504; Geoffrey Garrett, *Partisan Politics in the Global Economy* [Cambridge: Cambridge University Press, 1998]; Geoffrey Garrett and Peter Lange, "Internationalization, Institutions, and Poltical Change," in *Internationalization and Domestic Politics*, Robert Keohane and Helen Milner, eds. [New York: Cambridge University Press, 1996]), the LME systems favor balanced budgets and growth (with high employment rates) at the cost of equality, while the OMEs again divide between the social democratic model of equality and growth at the cost of deficits, and the Christian democratic model of balanced budget and equality at the cost of growth.

Feedback Loop to Preferences

Institutional interdependence has quite significant implications for our evaluation of preferences. We noted earlier that the major actors in governance politics can cleave along several principles of differentiation: class, sector, or "voice." Once systems are created at a specific moment, expressing the preferences of the time, they generate incentives that perpetuate those alliances. In CME systems for example, workers and employers acquire an interest in preserving welfare and training systems, in price and employment stability, and in "managing" market competition. This observation, well developed by varieties-of-capitalism authors, compels us to be careful about imputations of left-right alignments by social actors on policy issues in political economy. There is certainly a class element in disputes about wage levels and taxes, but there are also reasons for cooperation that shifts political alignments.

Institutions also influence preferences dynamically, so that the institutions facilitate commitments that then generate incentives to hold the preferences that keep them in place—they become self-enforcing. Actors in the blockholding model see stable commitment to the system. They are thus able to invest in production strategies that assume that stability. They invest in worker training, expensive machinery, supplier relationships—the whole complex web characteristic of blockholder systems—because the political system protects its stability. They then acquire an interest in preserving the system.

Conversely, a change in preferences can induce a demand for institutional change. If policy outputs do not correspond with what is wanted, groups push for institutional change. The demand for universal suffrage is one example. Democratization is another, in our sample notably in Korea.

We see, thus, a dynamic feedback loop at work: institutions shape policies that influence preferences. At the same time preferences induce institutional arrangements that increase the chances of preserving the policies desired by the preferences.

Authoritarian and Transitional Countries

The institutional argument has been worked out above for a specific set of countries: the economically advanced OECD countries, with stable democratic institutions. We can compare the impact of institutions in these countries via the assumption of holding preferences constant because certain important features are true across them: levels of wealth able to sustain high savings, thus an investor class; welfare systems and well-paid workers; well-developed capital markets and financial institutions; competitive, accountable political institutions responsive to the demands of populations organized through political parties and elections. With all these ingredients, we can conceptualize a political process common to this set of countries in which the map of interests in the firm interacts with the map of interests in society by constitutional and democratic means.

As we move away from countries in this set, the comparisons become more difficult. Lower levels of wealth reduce the size of capital markets, weaken financial institutions, and reduce the class of investors and the prosperity of workers. Weaker democracies reduce the impact of elections and democratic methods of preference aggregation. Authoritarian systems respond to cues or political incentives differently. They are not immune to social preferences, but the incentives of their leaders to respond to those preferences differ in important ways. We can examine the impact of institutions on governance in authoritarian countries, but the categories of institutional comparison will not be the same. It makes little sense to look at the veto gates in legislatures, which have no real power in an authoritarian political system.

Overall, we expect that the more authoritarian the political system, the weaker are minority shareholder protections and the more likely are blockholding patterns of ownership. Political transparency as well as firm-level transparency is a crucial ingredient of investor confidence. Without political transparency, property rights are in doubt; the rules may be administered in biased ways, and investors will be wary. Some minimum degree of external political transparency is a necessary (though not sufficient) condition for effective firm-level corporate governance. There are limits to the effectiveness of private order in providing for corporate governance, as we learned in chapter 3.

Authoritarian rulers are not immune to social pressures. They do need support to govern. Even the most authoritarian rulers need soldiers, secret police, administrators, and party members. In exchange these supporters are given special privileges, such as money, access to schools, housing, and medical care. One-man rule is not possible; even it relies on a cadre of supporters.

That set of supporters has been called by some analysts the "selectorate"—the set of people upon whom the ruler relies for support.[37] The ruler is able to some degree to select his support base, excluding most people, while rewarding a few. Democratic rulers have more difficulty excluding people from power, though they may try to broaden or limit political participation.

Authoritarian systems can be classified by the nature of the selectorate, the degree of power dispersion and power sharing. North Korea and Myanmar are extremes at one end of centralized power. China no longer fits that model despite one-party rule. It has opened up parts of the economy to the market. This makes the state dependent on investors, consumers, and workers for economic support, even if they are not able to vote in competitive elections to select the rulers. Economic actors can refuse to invest, buy, or work, and that means rulers have to follow policies that induce some kind of acceptance or support.

To that extent, nondemocratic rulers who seek market support have to provide some minimal protections to investors, to provide assurances of capital repatriation and other basic exercises of property rights of investors. The challenge for

---

[37] Susan Shirk, *The Political Logic of Economic Reform in China* (Berkeley and Los Angeles: University of California Press, 1993); Philip G. Roeder, *Red Sunset: The Failure of Soviet Politics* (Princeton: Princeton University Press, 1993).

authoritarian rulers is to make such guarantees credible in the absence of political mechanisms that can sanction the rulers for noncompliance. Authoritarianism always leaves the possibility of interference, thus greater uncertainty to investors than occurs in stable democracies with predictable rules that are followed. Investors may still invest in authoritarian countries, of course, but with a high-risk premium and a shorter time horizon.

Democracies, it must be noted, are by no means always stable or effective. Weak democracies have formalized elections and means of leadership succession, but are quite vulnerable to manipulation by elites and special groups. Money, guns, poverty, weak civil service systems, and ignorance can all contribute to a system unable to enforce its rules and regulations. Again, law on the books is not the same as law in practice. The diffuse shareholding model of governance depends on effective public regulation, on a vigorous system of regulation and enforcement to make sure players of the complex game play their part. In a corrupt democracy, investors feel insecure, and diffusion will not take place.

Governmental authority may thus pose a trade-off between adaptability and effectiveness with regard to corporate governance. McIntyre suggests a U-shaped curve.[38] Governments with many veto gates can be stable in policy because groups are able to inhibit substantial change, but ineffective because they cannot respond to crises. Conversely, authoritarian governments with few veto gates can respond quickly, but are not consistent because their leaders can switch direction with little restraint.

An interesting contrast with the European experience may be noted: there we found that majoritarian systems encouraged diffusion because they undermined the policy stability that the highly interlocked production system of the blockholding countries required; policy volatility there breaks the bonds among actors, leading to production strategies that prefer flexibility, in turn undermining the logic of blockholding. This may be an effect that happens only where there is substantial protection and confidence in the regulatory system. In many countries, of which Malaysia may be an example, the regulatory process may not be stable enough to provide those protections. There, policy volatility may also threaten the adequacy of shareholder protection. If that is in question, blockholding retains support. Thus centralized institutions can be too powerful, leading to blockholding.

The impact of consensus/majoritarian and veto gate models thus may vary according to the degree, length, and duration of democratic regimes. In longstanding democracies, consensus regimes with few variations in policy have in the past produced coalitions around blockholding. Majoritarian systems with great variation in policy may produce diffusion. Conversely in less established democracies or in authoritarian regimes, policy variance may lessen confidence in shareholder-protecting regulation, and, at the same time, numerous veto gates may lessen confidence in the effectiveness of government. In both cases we will find blockholding.

[38] Andrew McIntyre, "Institutions and Investors: The Politics of the Financial Crisis in Southeast Asia," *International Organization* 55 (2001): 81–122.

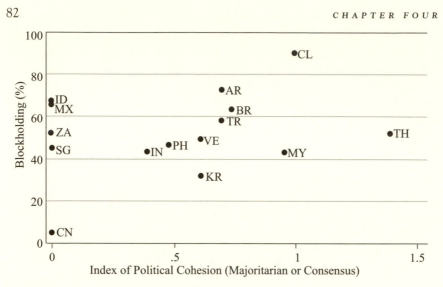

Figure 4.4 State Strength and Blockholding U-Curve

Investor confidence may thus be highest at the bottom of the U shape—some important balance between the capacity to act and limits on arbitrary rule, the goal of democratic theorists for centuries.

For example, McIntyre pairs Malaysia with Indonesia as having few veto points, in contrast with Thailand, with many veto points, and the Philippines, between the extremes but closer to Thailand. While Thailand also has a multiparty system, there the parties fight during the election and form volatile coalitions afterwards, while in Malaysia, "the parties divide the electoral map among themselves before each election to avoid competing with each other."[39] Politically, Malaysia has the capacity to take decisive action to change policy if the leaders find it useful to do so. In this respect Malaysia lies with the majoritarian countries of Europe—policy change can be sharp. This can be threatening to investors, as they cannot be sure of the stability of the policies in place. It can also mean strong response to problems and crises: McIntyre classifies Malaysia as having taken decisive action in response to the Asia financial crisis because its institutions allowed it.

Figure 4.4 from our emerging countries in the sample provides a graphical hint (although no statistical evidence) that a U-shaped curve may exist with respect to corporate governance outcomes in authoritarian or weak democratic states, with blockholding still high at the upper and lower ends of the index of political cohesion on the x-axis, and lower in the middle of the distribution.

We are less sure about how to measure the impact of political institutions in other types of systems. Much of the research in institutions has looked only at processes in relatively well established democracies, generally in wealthy countries.

We need ways of thinking about what happens in authoritarian regimes, or poorly functioning democracies. We expect that in those cases, the quality of law is weak. Governments are able to intervene without adequate restraint by the rule

[39] McIntyre 2001, 92.

of law. Property rights are thus suspect, courts vulnerable to political interference. Under those conditions, the external monitoring model for corporate governance will not function well and investors will not feel reassured. The result will be block-holding. This may often take place with strong "ascriptive" mechanisms, that is, family, religion, or ethnicity providing ties that function something like reputational bonding mechanisms among the members of a production network.

Authoritarian regimes do experience pressures from constituents, and so there is a politics to their policy. If they engage in trade and seek foreign investment, they have to worry about the views of potential investors. They will also generate domestic constituencies that can have influence—not an electorate, but a "selectorate," key actors who control or administer important resources. The decision-making structures can have some impact on this process.

Some of the countries in question are transitional, from authoritarian to democratic, or are democracies that function at somewhat higher levels. Something can be learned by comparing these institutions and by comparing processes of transition. Our work here is tentative. We provide some statistical comparison, but turn as well to tracing processes in different cases of countries that have passed through authoritarian political systems, such as Korea and Chile, and—though the jury is still out—China.

ALTERNATIVE ARGUMENTS: LEGAL FAMILY AND ECONOMIC SOCIOLOGY

In our quest to explain corporate governance patterns, we focus on public policy. We identify the policies that produce outcomes and what explains the shape of those policies. We focus on interest group preferences and political institutions (showing our background as political scientists). Two influential bodies of work present alternative understandings of law, regulation, and social processes: the legal families school, deriving from law, though presented by a group of economists, and the economic sociology school, developed substantially by sociologists. Because of the importance of these arguments in current discussions of corporate governance, we pause here to consider these bodies of work. We indicate where we converge with this literature, indeed where we rely on its findings, and where we disagree or offer alternative findings.

Legal Family: Civil versus Common Law

The most widely known explanation of divergence on corporate governance policy is the legal family school, developed by La Porta, López-de-Silanes, Shleifer, and Vishny. We have already referred to their important work on measuring aspects of MSP. That work makes two vital contributions to our enterprise. First, it measures the variance in corporate governance outcomes around the world; it establishes a vital dependent variable and weakens ideas of convergence. Second, it argues the importance of law, regulations, and policies in shaping those outcomes. It helps establish the importance of one of our two intervening variables, MSP (and in recent work on labor, our other intervening variable, production regimes).

TABLE 4.4
Legal Family and Corporate Governance

Legal family	Mean	Median	Market Capitalization
Common law			
English-origin average	.43	.42	6,586
Civil law			
French-origin average	.54	.55	1,844
German-origin average	.34	.33	8,057
Scandinavian-origin average	.46	.45	4,521

Source: La Porta et al. 1998, table 7. 1147–48.

La Porta et al. then make another move: to explain the provision or absence of MSP, they turn to the concept of "legal family," the distinction between "common" and "civil" legal systems. This is a familiar distinction in legal scholarship, generating considerable research considering the impact of the difference. La Porta et al. see a causal connection with corporate governance, namely that common-law countries are more likely to follow diffuse shareholding models, civil-law countries blockholder models. The driving mechanism is MSP. Shareholder protection is more likely in common-law countries, and less likely in civil-law countries. We alert the reader again to the distinction between QCL and MSP. The first round of work by La Porta et al. examined the narrower QCL, not the fuller MSP. For this discussion about legal family, the distinction does not matter; we will take up the impact of the difference in the next chapter.

Table 4.4, reproduced from La Porta et al., sorts countries into legal family, measures the concentration of ownership among the three largest shareholders, and notes their mean and median. It also presents the per capita market capitalization among the sampled countries.

The force of the relationship lies in the contrast between English common law and French civil law. The French examples include all its former colonies, mostly in Africa and those of the former Spanish empire, mostly in South America. The English group includes its former colonies, scattered around the world, comprises both the countries of English-European settlement and the colonies of conquest in Asia and Africa. Note that the civil law category has variance with the grouping: Scandinavian civil law has high shareholder protection, as does Germany, but both have blockholding.

What mechanisms explain these results? La Porta et al. have suggested several. For example, they offer (as one candidate) judicial discretion, the notion that judges in common-law countries have stronger principles of fiduciary duty than do civil judges applying general principles farther removed from specific cases.[40]

[40] La Porta et al. 2000; John Coffee, "Privatization and Corporate Governance: The Lessons from Securities Market Failure," Journal of Corporation Law 25 (1999): 1–39; Simon Johnson, Rafael La Porta, Florencio López-de-Silanes, and Andrei Shleifer, "Tunneling," American Economic Review, Papers and Proceedings of the One Hundred Twelfth Annual Meeting of the American Economic Association 90 (2000): 22–27.

Common-law judges rely on precedent and experience; thus they have more lee-way and are more inclined to be permissive. As civil law is more detailed, it spec-ifies and prohibits, rather than permits and encourages. Civil-law countries may be more involved in regulating business than are common-law ones. The civil code is a toolbox, inclined to regulate and restrict—thus when situations arise, the countries regulate.[41] They inhibit the development of free and open capital markets, and the bonding mechanisms that began the process of shareholder dif-fusion. Civil law allows the state to interfere with business activities and inhibits the free play of the market in ways that would encourage the diffusion model.

Recent work by Djankov et al. suggest a "torts" model of what happens. Legal protections, like those we have called MSP, facilitate two channels of enforce-ment.[42] One channel works through public authorities, who use their powers to bring suit against wrongdoers. The other channel allows private individuals to sue, using the information provided by MSP. This mechanism economizes on the public resources. It uses a market of enforcement by allowing individuals to work through the judicial system.[43]

Outcomes without Explanations

While the distinction between two legal families provides an intriguing stylized fact, the correlation between MSP and legal family, it is not in our view convincing. If civil law is more regulatory, why does that regulation appear to favor blockholding rather than supply effective protection to shareholders? A regulatory system could be strong in MSP. The fact of greater regulation does not establish by itself the con-tent thereof.

If the mechanism is judicial discretion, La Porta et al. themselves note that judges could apply their discretion in different ways to protect insiders as much as outsiders, or to bar all intervention. It is therefore not enough "to focus on judicial power; a political and historical analysis of judicial objectives is required."[44] Common-law countries can pass legislation that suffocates markets, and civil-law countries can pass laws that protect MSP if they so choose. Common-law Britain

[41] Juan C. Botero, Simeon Djankov, Rafael La Porta, Florencio López-de-Silanes, and Andrei Shleifer, "The Regulation of Labor," *Quarterly Journal of Economics* 119 (2004). 1339–82.

[42] Botero et al. 2004.

[43] Mathew D. McCubbins, and Thomas Schwartz, "Congressional Oversight Overlooked: Police Patrols versus Fire Alarms," *American Journal of Political Science* 28 (1984): 165–79.

[44] From the seventeenth century onward, for example, the British Crown lost influence over the courts to Parliament and the property owners who dominated it, so common law evolved to protect property against the Crown. John Brewer, *The Sinews of Power: War, Money, and the English State, 1688–1783* (New York: Knopf, 1989); Barrington Moore, *Social Origins of Dictatorship and Democracy: Lord and Peasant in the Making of the Modern World* (Boston: Beacon Press, 1966). While many observers classify the English state as weak in comparison to highly bureaucratized French and Pruss-ian examples, Brewer argues that the English state was in fact stronger because parliamentary super-vision of the executive reassured social groups the state was being used as they desired, and not at the monarch's whim. See also North and Weingast 1989 (showing that England paid lower interest rates on loans because investors had confidence in a supervised executive).

became more interventionist under a Labour government in 1945, while civil-law France became less regulatory after 1985. Common-law countries can have effective rule of law, or weak rule if the common-law legacy does not prevent political interference with markets and courts, as in Pakistan, for example, and several countries in Africa.

Legal tradition can evolve in different directions, depending on the politics that shapes legislation and enforcement. La Porta et al. note that while "political factors affect corporate governance through channels other than the law itself[,] . . . the law remains a crucial channel through which politics affects corporate governance."[45] Indeed, law is a channel, but this confirms the point about the centrality of politics: politics picks the law and shapes its enforcement.

Pister and colleagues note that the effect of transplantation, how law moved from one country to another, thus how common and civil law moved from France and the United Kingdom to their former colonies or related empires, turns on local conditions. We interpret the transplant effect as an argument calling attention to politics, the way in which receiving societies want to use their legal legacy, according to local politics, institutions, and cultures.[46]

Laws Come from Politics

Law and regulation come from politics. If Pakistan has weak shareholder protection and thus blockholding, while the United Kingdom has the opposite, the difference lies in the political use of their common-law tradition. This is the implication of Glaeser, Johnson, and Shleifer's comparison of regulation with courts as enforcers in "Coase vs. the Coasians." The choice of regulator (as in Poland) rather than courts (as in the Czech Republic) was a political one, not explicable by legal family.[47] Similarly, they place politics at the center of the evolution of the U.S. system: the United States turned to regulation because nineteenth-century courts were deeply corrupted by big lobbies, especially the railroads. These examples contradict the legal family argument: holding constant its common-law tradition, the United States has gone through periods of poor shareholder protection and of good protection. Contemporary scandals suggest just how variable the system really is.

What changes over time within countries of any legal tradition is politics and political processes. Is legal family in fact a political interpretation? Yes, but only in the initial move to pick a legal family. At some point decision makers selected a legal tradition, voluntarily in some cases, through coercion (colonialism) in others. At that moment, we could say, there was a political process that influenced corporate governance. But a weakness of the legal family school is that political processes disappear thereafter. How certain laws are enacted

[45] La Porta et al. 2000.

[46] Daniel Berkowitz, Katharina Pistor, and Jean-François Richard, "Economic Development, Legality, and the Transplant Effect," *European Economic Review* 47 (2003): 165–95. Keefer (2005) finds that when political context is specified, the impact of legal family fades in the data.

[47] Glaser, Johnson, and Shleifer 2001.

and enforced to give higher or lower protections disappears from the analysis. Judges seem to make decisions because of the logic of the legal tradition, but again this insulates the process from politics. La Porta et al. do study laws and regulations—extensively, again a major contribution—but they offer no account of why and when these laws are passed or enforced. The entire legal structure flows from legal family, thus from a single political act in a distant past.

Interpretations based on legal tradition seem to leave countries trapped in their founding moment. They cannot explain "the great reversals," the changes that have taken place within one country over time. The argument has odd implications for policy: are civil-law countries unable to develop effective MSP? If they can, then legal family cannot be decisive in its impact.

Several researchers have challenged the legal family school on empirical as well as philosophical grounds. Roe compares legal family to three indicators of political forces—partisan location of governments (left vs. right), labor employment protection, and income inequality.[48] The three political variables do better in correlations than legal family. Roe goes on to challenge MSP (actually, QCL, the measure La Porta et al. use in the work Roe considers) as an explanation more generally. He helps develop the policy package or production system argument, as we call it here: that the policies that shape labor markets, product competition, antitrust, and so on, influence corporate governance. MSP alone is an insufficient explanation. We return to some of Roe's measurements in chapters 5 and 6.

Legal family is thus, in our view, not a political model. Whatever its classification, it does not persuasively explain why we have high- or low-quality MSP nor why we have different patterns of production systems.

ECONOMIC SOCIOLOGY ANALYSIS

A substantial body of research on market economies has been generated by economic sociology in recent years, informative for our enterprise. These researchers share our desire to locate economic practices and behaviors in social processes. Work in this tradition includes studies of changes in corporate forms,[49] the influence of investors in the breakup of conglomerates in the 1980s,[50] the diffusion of poison pill and antitakeover laws,[51] the role of law firms in the development of

---

[48] Roe 2003b.

[49] Neil Fligstein, *The Architecture of Markets: An Economic Sociology of Twenty-First-Century Capitalist Societies* (Princeton: Princeton University Press, 2001).

[50] Neil Fligstein and Linda Markowitz, "Financial Reorganization of American Corporations in the 1980s," in *Sociology and the Public Agenda*, William J. Wilson, ed. (Newbury Park, Calif.: Sage, 1993); Gerald Davis, Kristina Diekmann, and Catherine Tinsley, "The Decline and Fall of the Conglomerate Firm in the 1980s: The De-institutionalization of an Organizational Form," *American Sociological Review* 59 (1994): 547–70; Michael Useem, *Executive Defense: Shareholder Power and Corporate Reorganization* (Cambridge: Harvard University Press, 1993); Useem 1996.

[51] Gerald F. Davis and Michael Useem, "Top Management, Company Directors, and Corporate Control," in *Handbook of Strategy and Management*, Andrew Pettigrew, Howard Thomas, and Richard Whittington, eds. (London: Sage, 2002); Gerald F. Davis and Gregory E. Robbins, "The Fate of the Conglomerate Firm in the United States," in *How Institutions Change*, Walter W. Powell and Daniel L. Jones, eds. (Chicago: University of Chicago Press, forthcoming); Tracy A. Thomson and Gerald F. Davis,

high-technology industry in Silicon Valley,[52] decision-making processes in firms (on General Motors); the implementation of legislation, the emergence of the chief financial officer in American firms,[53] shareholder activism as a social movement,[54] the role of networks in developing and enforcing norms,[55] labor market and labor training in shaping production systems,[56] international patterns of corporate governance,[57] the diffusion of corporate governance structures,[58] and the roles of legitimacy and efficiency in the spread of governance codes.[59]

This work contributes substantially to our understanding of the processes that shape firms and the actors in them. It challenges a pure "efficiency" account of economic life, conforming to deductively derived principles of optimality, wholly autonomous from the society in which it takes place. Economic activities are "embedded," sociology argues. They emerge out of the same process by which social practice arises in such realms as family, ethnicity, religion, education, and social structure. Behavior and practice derive from social forces and processes, such as

---

"The Politics of Corporate Control and the Future of Shareholder Activism in the United States," *Corporate Governance* 5 (1997): 152–59; Gerald F. Davis, "Agents without Principles? The Spread of the Poison Pill through the Intercorporate Network," *Administrative Science Quarterly* 36 (1991): 583–613; Davis, "Networks and Corporate Control: Comparing Agency Theory and Interorganizational Explanations for the Diffusion of the Poison Pill," in *Academy of Management Best Papers Proceedings, 1991*, 173–77; Davis, "The Significance of Board Interlocks for Corporate Governance," *Corporate Governance* 4 (1996): 154–59; John Meyer and Brian Rowan, "Institutionalized Organizations: Formal Structure as Myth and Ceremony," *American Journal of Sociology* 83 (1977): 340–63.

[52] Mark C. Suchman, On Advice of Counsel: Law Firms and Venture Capital Funds as Information Intermediaries in the Structuration of Silicon Valley, Ph.D. diss., Department of Sociology, Stanford University; Mark C. Suchman and Mia L. Cahill, "The Hired Gun as Facilitator: Lawyers and the Suppression of Business Disputes in Silicon Valley," *Law and Society Inquiry* 21 (1996): 679–712.

[53] Dirk Zorn, Frank Dobbin, Julian Dierkes, and Man-Shan Kwok, "Managing Investors: How Financial Markets Reshaped the American Firm," in *The Sociology of Financial Markets*, Karin Knorr Celina and Alex Poole, eds. (Oxford: Oxford University Press, 2004).

[54] Gerald F. Davis and Douglas McAdam, "Corporations, Classes, and Social Movements," in *Research in Organizational Behavior 22*, Barry Straw and Robert I. Sutton, eds. (Oxford: Elsevier Science, 2000).

[55] Davis 1991b.

[56] Wolfgang Streeck, *Industrial Relations in West Germany: A Case Study of the Car Industry* (London: Heinemann, 1984).

[57] Ruth Aguilera and Gregory Jackson, "Institutional Changes in European Corporate Governance," *Economic Sociology* 3 (2002): 17–26; Aguilera and Jackson, "The Cross-National Diversity of Corporate Governance: Dimensions and Determinants," *Academy of Management Review* 28 (2003): 447–65; Ruth Aguilera and Michal Federowicz, eds., *Corporate Governance in a Changing Economic and Political Environment: Trajectories of Institutional Change on the European Continent* (London: Palgrave Macmillan, 2003).

[58] Marie-Laure Djelic, *Exporting the American Model: The Postwar Transformation of European Business* (Oxford: Oxford University Press, 2001); Marie-Laure Djelic and Sigrid Quack, eds., *Globalization and Institutions: Redefining the Rules of the Economic Game* (Cheltenham, U.K.: Edward Elgar, 2003); Mauro Guillén, "Corporate Governance and Globalization: Is There a Convergence across Countries?" *Advances in International Comparative Management* 13 (2000): 175–204.

[59] Alvaro Cuervo-Cazurra and Ruth Aguilera, "The Worldwide Diffusion of Codes of Good Governance," in *Corporate Governance and Firm Organization*, Anna Grandori, ed. (Oxford: Oxford University Press, 2004); Peer Fiss and Edward Zajac, "Corporate Governance and Contested Terrain: The Rise of the Shareholder Value Orientation in Germany," *Administrative Science Quarterly* (forthcoming).

political dynamics and social emulation and the interaction of the economy with other social subsystems, such as the state, bureaucracy, political and other organizations. Ensminger shows how norms, social structure, and institutions fuse to make markets.[60]

A growing number of people across several disciplines have recognized the nature of "embedded" economies. Some specialists in law and finance and corporate governance have been examining the role of interest groups, electoral systems and political institutions, social structures, the media, and human capital. Rajan and Zingales; Kroszner; Perotti and van Thadden; and Pagano and Volpin are all economists working on finance and governance writing in this vein. Other economists have been exploring political institutions and interest groups more generally (Grossman and Helpman, Persson and Tabellini), while others examine the interaction of social structures and path dependence on the evolution of institutions (North; Acemoglou, Johnson, and Robinson).

Conversely, many sociologists studying the economy explore the impact of incentives and utilitarian calculations on economic behavior. Davis, Dobbin, and Useem all note that changes in antitrust policy by the Reagan administration and the development of financial institutions following legislation helped set loose processes that undermined the conglomerates that had emerged in World War II. Streeck's work on labor and training systems, Dobbin on railroad building in the United States, France, and the United Kingdom, Aguilera and Jackson on corporate governance, all pay careful attention to the incentives of actors as embedded in a social context. Sociologists contribute important quantitative work on ownership patterns, on connections across firms among directors, and the diffusion of practices across firms. "There is now a large literature documenting the role of board interlocks in the spread of governance practices such as adopting a poison pill (Davis and Greve, 1997), creating an investor relations office (Rao and Sivakumar, 1999), making particular types of acquisitions (Haunschild, 1993), and others."[61] Davis and McAdam examine the politics of shareholder activism and locate it in the framework of social movements.[62]

But while there is often substantial overlap, there are differences in emphasis among the disciplines of sociology, economics, and political science. In some places those differences are substantial. We see disagreements on two key points. If regulations and policy shape economic action, rather than derive from an independent economic calculus, what explains the content of policy and regulation? In this book we stress politics and political processes. Many economic sociologists also point to political processes and resource mobilization, but quite frequently they subordinate politics as a subsystem of a larger society and social action. This is an old quarrel among the social sciences going back at least to Parsons, Durkheim, Weber, Marx, Mill, and even before them to Aristotle and Plato.

---

[60] Jan Ensminger, *Making a Market: The Institutional Transformation of an African Society* (New York: Cambridge University Press, 1992).

[61] Davis and Useem 2002.

[62] Davis and McAdam 2000.

To many sociologists, the political processes themselves reflect some more funda-mental social process, a mixture of value systems, family, culture, and institutions. We do not make an effort to survey the boundaries between politics and other social processes, but do point out differences in emphasis. Our goal is to clarify just where political choices are operative.

The second disagreement between political economy and economic sociology has to do with incentives and interests. Do economic incentives sufficiently capture the richness of the motivations of economic actors? Many sociologists doubt they do. Drawing on the work of John Meyer and others, Dobbin writes in a major liter-ature survey, "Sociology's core insight is that individuals behave according to scripts that are tied to social roles."[63] Individuals and firms construct a world out of these scripts. They negotiate an understanding built out of incentives, to be sure, but interpreted through past experience, cultures, and frames of understanding. It is not possible to model "interests" and incentives, therefore, without knowing the scripts that give meaning and motive to them. Dore questions the adequacy of "allocative efficiency" in explaining behavior: "overall output maximization is achieved less by allocative efficiency than by productive efficiency which involves organizational learning and willing cooperation."[64] Incentives and their efficacy cannot be dis-cussed without reference to the latent patterns of motivation that the incentive devices appeal to. Is it indeed true that the prospect of material gain and the threat of legally enforced sanctions to which incentive mechanisms relate are the only rel-evant motives? "It requires only a small amount of reflection," Margaret Blair has written recently, "to realize that financial incentives and enforceable legal con-straints cannot possibly be what holds most cooperative relationships together. They simply do not bind tightly enough. Most business relationships involve, and indeed require, a substantial amount of voluntary cooperation and trust among par-ticipants in the enterprise."[65]

---

[63] Frank Dobbin, ed., *The New Economic Sociology: A Reader* (Princeton: Princeton University Press, 2004), 4.

[64] Ronald Dore, "Pros and Cons of Insider Governance," REITI Working Paper, 2004:

> within all societies *individuals* differ in their propensity to be cooperative, trusting and trust-worthy, absent strong material incentives to be so. (That is to say human beings are capable of "natural inclination" trust—though differing in the extent to which they have it—and not just the "calculative trust" which transaction economists consider (a) universal because rational, and (b) the only kind of trust worth bothering with). . . .

> But over and above those individual differences, there is also considerable *national* variation in *modal* patterns of such inclinations—variations in the social norms about trusting and cooperation which are subscribed to by the average individual and which hence provide the motivational resources which can make the incentives implicit in institutional arrangements work. . . .

> Organisational tinkering in the name of reforming corporate governance interacts with, and can sometimes reinforce changes in social structures and class interest, as well as, increasingly, changes in the international environment and the society's degree of exposure to that environ-ment. But in the long run what really changes corporate governance (reverting to this paper's opening definition of corporate governance as being about the distribution of power) is the social structural changes themselves.

[65] Margaret M. Blair, "Post-Enron Reflections on Comparative Corporate Governance," *Journal of Interdisciplinary Economics* 14 (2003): 113–24.

Shareholder value, a core concept in the "nexus of contracts" approach, is for many sociologists "constructed." It "is intrinsically impossible, given human nature, to calculate the intrinsic value of a share."[66] Forecasting earnings prospects for specific companies is indeed a prodigious challenge for securities analysts. "Financial forecasting appears to be a science that makes astrology respectable. Pricing in practice can only mean intersubjective agreement, and intersubjective agreement is embodied in the price assigned by the stock market."[67]

Firms are engaged in "impression management. They in act in accord with the models various constituencies hold of best practice."[68] The wording of announcements can shape their impact on stock prices.[69] "[G]overnance reforms are themselves rhetorical performances, intended to persuade activists and other players in the financial markets of the corporation's fitness for investment. Creating 'the kind of firm, governance structure, and securities the customers in capital markets want' involves marketing through rhetoric, from the letter to the shareholders in the annual report, to how diversified the corporation portrays its operations on the income statement, to the choice of directors."[70] The concepts of signaling and status help explain firms' behavior in this context.

> What is important to recognize is that standards that apply [for evaluating change in governance] do not concern whether the theory is true (this governance structure will create earnings growth into the future), but whether it is persuasive (this governance structure is rhetorically plausible). Truth in this case is in principle unknowable: the vast body of recent research on corporate governance provides no consistent support for any particular "best practice" that has worked well in the past, much less insight into what will work well in the future. The relevant question, however, is not is the defendant "really" guilty, but how did the jury vote.[71]

> Corporations are *legal fictions*. In the sophisticated version of contractarianism, shareholders are as much a legal fiction as the corporation itself. It just happens that they are, by hypothesis, part of a social welfare-maximizing genre of corporate governance. As Allen (1992) puts it, this conception of the corporation "is not premised on the conclusion that shareholders do 'own' the corporation in any ultimate sense, only on the view that it can be better for all of us if we act as if they do."

[66] Burton G. Malkiel, *A Random Walk Down Wall Street: The Time-Tested Strategy for Successful Investing*, 6th ed. (New York: W. W. Norton, 1996), 103.

[67] Malkiel 1996, 169. Cited in Davis and Useem 2002, 246.

[68] Edward J. Zajac and James D. Westphal, "The Costs and Benefits of Managerial Incentives and Monitoring in Large U.S. Corporations: When Is More Not Better?" *Strategic Management Journal* 15 (1994): 121–42, cited by Davis and Robbins, 1999; see also Edward J. Zajac and James D. Westphal, "The Social Construction of Market Value: Institutionalization and Learning Perspectives on Stock Market Reactions," *American Sociological Review* 69 (2004): 433–57.

[69] "The announcement of a new long-term incentive plan for executives on a proxy statement produces a significantly higher stock price increase when described in terms of incentive alignment than the same plan described as a means to attract and retain qualified executives even if there is no change in operating performance." James D. Westphal and Edward J. Zajac, "Symbolic Management of Stockholders: Corporate Governance Reforms and Shareholder Reactions," *Administrative Science Quarterly* 43 (1998): 127–53, cited by Davis and Useem 2002, 250.

[70] Davis and Useem 2002, 293.

[71] Davis and Robbins 1999, 33.

As a corporate genre, the contractarian approach is as distinctive to the US as Faulkner and Hemingway. The emphasis on voluntarism and individual liberty, and the suspicion of viewing the corporation as a social entity with obligations to constituencies other than shareholders, are recurrent themes in American law and economics.[72]

"[C]ustom among law and economics scholars—if not the law itself—treats the shareholders as the sole owners and legitimate 'stakeholders' of the corporation, and this notion has achieved the status of doxology among American corporate managers in the 1990s."[73]

The sociologists note divergence in judgments on whether concentrated or diverse ownership is beneficial. Davis and Useem cite Rajan and Zingales, "The opacity and collusive practices that sustain a relationship-based system entrench incumbents at the expense of potential new entrants."[74] Moreover, economies characterized by concentrated wealth in the hands of "old money" families grow more slowly than economies without such families, again suggesting a political entrenchment that limits economic adaptability.[75]

> Recent research in financial economics thus suggests that social welfare is enhanced by a strong independent state and undermined by concentrated inherited wealth and power. The implications are ironic. Whereas Berle and Means feared that dispersed ownership would create a class of managers with control over large corporations but little accountability to shareholders, the late twentieth-century assessment suggests that *concentrated* ownership leads to cronyism, political favoritism, and weak economic growth. The irony runs deep. "Managerialist" firms in the United States pursue shareholder value with little regard for other stakeholders, while firms with concentrated ownership elsewhere in the world cannot help but attend to other stakeholders. Yet the explicit ignoring of other stakeholders may ultimately yield more favorable benefits for them.[76]

The importance of scripts and ideology surely matters. Finance theorists like Zingales note that alternative theories of the firm lead to varying views of value, governance, and finance.[77] By implication, the choice of theory is a construct. Some political scientists have applied the concepts of scripts and discourse to political economy: Schmidt on European economic policymaking, Katzenstein on economic regionalism, and Sinclair on bond-rating agencies are but some examples. March and Olson write about the logic of appropriateness and the logic of consequences in a noted volume on international relations. Suzanne Berger stresses the element of choice as firms and countries select strategies for dealing with common pressures of international competition. Hancké stresses the leeway managers have in devising solutions to new situations they confront; policy and

---

[72] Davis and Useem 2002, 250.
[73] Davis and Useem 2002, 252.
[74] Davis and Useem 2002, 250.
[75] Morck et al., forthcoming.
[76] Davis and Useem 2002, 251.
[77] Zingales 2000.

economic shifts change the parameters, but firms and their leaders pick among alternative paths.[78]

We do not take this approach. We stress incentives and interests in shaping policies and the response to them. MSP and the rules of the production system *do* influence behavior. On that we agree with the finance economists, the legal family school, and our economic sociology colleagues who study the impact of policies upon economic behavior. Where we disagree on emphasis is in explaining the origins of those rules (politics for us, not legal family, or the "autonomous" economy pure and simple), and we disagree about which rules matter (tort law alone, or MSP and/or rules of the production system). We agree with Roe, the *Varieties of Capitalism* authors, many of the sociologists, and some of the finance economists in saying that the broader set of rules matter. Where we disagree, at least in emphasis, is on the inadequacy of an incentive model and the sufficiency of separateness of scripts.

We stress change over time in a country's regulatory regime and its practices. To the extent that a "national script" explains behavior, we are not sure how to explain change by a country over time. Ideas about Confucian patterns in China or the French or American model do not capture the way those countries changed. We agree with the economic sociologists who note the self-interest of various actors in bringing about change: the financial analysts who make money encouraging conglomerates, then in breaking them up. The swirl of competing interests both makes a case for scripts—in confusing situations, one's "priors" are a guide to action—and against them—in confusion, actors advance their particularistic goals. Either way, an abstract concept of optimum efficiency has substantial weaknesses as an explanation.

Just how to integrate these alternative arguments remains an open theme for the future. We see advantages to specialization, to each school working out the logic of its inquiry, and then comparing. That seems better than assembling all the pieces into a collage or a laundry list of factors.

Conclusion

With this analytic apparatus in place we now turn to evaluate the arguments in detail. In the next three chapters, we examine the coalitional pairings, the ideas that support them, and the evidence for and against each of them.

---

[78] Vivien Schmidt, "The Politics of Adjustment in France and Britain: When Does Discourse Matter? *Journal of European Public Policy* 8 (2001): 247–264; Schmidt, "Does Discourse Matter in the Politics of Welfare State Adjustment?" *Comparative Political Studies* 35 (2002): 168–193; Peter Katzenstein and Takashi Shiraishi, eds., *Beyond Japan: East Asian Regionalism* (Ithaca, N.Y.: Cornell University Press, forthcoming); James G. March and Johan P. Olsen, "The Institutional Dynamics of International Political Orders," *International Organization* 52 (1998): 943–969; Suzanne Berger, *The First Globalization: Lessons from the French* (Paris: Seuil, 2003); Bob Hancké, *Large Firms and Institutional Change: Industrial Renewal and Economic Restructuring in France* (Oxford: Oxford University Press, 2002).

Chapter 5 looks at the class conflict pair of models: the investor-dominant model that predicts diffuse shareholder outcomes, and its counterpart, the worker-dominant model, which predicts blockholding. Chapter 6 looks at the cross-class sectoral models: the corporatist compromise around blockholding and the oligarchy model, also around blockholding. Chapter 7 examines the voice models, the transparency model of workers and owners and the managerialist model, both of which predict diffusion, albeit with different distribution of the benefits.

In each of these chapters we examine specific countries in analytic narratives designed to both test and highlight the argument.

Preference Cleavages 1: Class Conflict

CORPORATE GOVERNANCE PRACTICES are the result of policies, which in turn are created by political processes. Policy thus reflects the preferences of social actors as processed by political institutions in each country. Scholarly debates about which political variables really count in determining outcomes often turn on more basic disagreements about the structure of social actors' preferences, arguments about the pattern of *cleavages* that sort people into opposing camps on the policy issues.

Chapter 4 laid out in condensed form our understanding of those cleavage patterns in preferences for corporate governance outcomes. In the next three chapters we probe these models more deeply, exploring their logic, setting up their empirical predictions, and, where possible, testing them against our country data set. In each chapter, we also construct a handful of detailed country case studies, *analytic narratives* in scholarly parlance, which offer another way of developing the argument and examining the evidence.

Throughout we will consider the impact political institutions have on the outcomes—which side of a cleavage actually prevails. The class model pits labor against capital (owners and managers together). The sectors model sees elements of labor and managers in alliance against external investors, pushing insider blockholders into a bargain with them to preserve the firm and their place it in; their opposition consists of the oligarchs or founders, to use contrasting value-laden terms, who want complete freedom to run the firm. The voice model sees workers, worried about their pensions and voice in the firm to preserve jobs, in alliance with external investors (minority shareholders) in conflict with managers and inside blockholders.

Each cleavage has two outcomes, depending on which pole wins. In the class model, if the investors win, we get (in theory) high levels of MSP and reduced concentration of ownership, with monitoring by diffuse external shareholders. If labor wins, we get low MSP and, in reaction to labor pressures, the high concentrations typical of blockholding. In the sectoral model, a labor-management victory should give us blockholding with high stakeholder involvement and, in theory, low MSP. Conversely, if the oligarchs prevail (or a manager-labor coalition has not emerged, which amounts to the same thing), we have blockholding under owner control and little or no MSP. In the voice model, a labor–external investor bargain produces high MSP and diffuse shareholder governance. Conversely, a management victory "rolls back" MSP while retaining low concentration.

These models derive, as noted before, from both academic theory and popular discourse on corporate governance. In this book we make these models clear by examining their embedded assumptions about the way the world works, tease out their logic into testable propositions, and then see if these predictions actually comport with the way the "real world" works—at least the real world of our country sample.

In each case our goal is to understand the political lineups for or against the policy package that shapes corporate governance outcomes: high or low minority shareholder protection and liberal or regulated degrees of coordination in policy affecting the economy. Our streamlined argument is that high MSP and liberal market regulation produce diffusion, while low MSP and highly coordinated market patterns produce blockholding.

This chapter looks at coalitions formed by class cleavage: owners and managers on one side, workers on the other. In the investor model, corporate governance outcomes reflect the preferences of owners and managers more than those of workers. In the labor power model, these outcomes reflect the preferences of workers. In this chapter, we describe the theoretical and practical roots of these two models in turn; derive their predictions for our sample; compare them with the data from our sample; and explore in narrative detail the cases of Korea and Sweden, both of which dramatically illustrate the dynamic coalitional jockeying at work in these models.

Section I: Owners and Managers Dominate Workers

The Investor Model

We turn first to corporate governance as viewed by the owners of capital, the group whose preferences economists have modeled extensively and formally. In the investor model, the owners of firms and external providers of capital work out a "good governance" bargain through a combination of private ordering and public regulations, thus providing protections for minority shareholders. In its most schematic form, this deal is made by inside blockholders and outside investors; managers are assumed to be the "hired hand" agents of blockholders, allied with owners from the standpoint of forming coalitions. Workers are mere bystanders to this "deal," in a political alignment of owners plus managers versus workers.

The "political theory" of the investor model consists, baldly, of the power of capital. To produce the public regulations this bargain requires, capital is able to get the political process to produce what it wants. Outside investors and insider owners are presumed to have the power to have their respective corporate governance preferences adopted by democratic countries with market economies. The theorists of the bargain often are not clear about how the desired rules come into being, but their discussion at a minimum implies that they do. MSP and private bonding come about, it is presumed, because the investors want them as the efficient bargain, the optimum solution to the incomplete contract noted by Coase. How that efficient bargain is translated into politics is rarely specified. This may be the appeal of the private-bonding argument: it claims not to require political action, though it avoids specifying the politics that produced the conditions that make bonding possible.

The investor model specifies or implies this political logic: the blockholder always has the option of keeping the firm to herself, in which case she can do what she wants with it. But if she wants to sell shares to outside investors, perhaps to diversify assets or raise additional capital, she must reckon with outside investors' preferences for minority shareholder protections. Investors seeking higher returns choose the system that protects their interests most clearly. Some countries lack these safeguards, so investors demand a premium compared to other countries with better minority shareholder protections. This price discount puts pressure on blockholders in countries with lesser protections, who then turn to their political systems and lobby for a change in the rules to satisfy these external investors and convince them to reduce the "governance discount."

Despite its analytic force, the investor model does not survive our empirical tests very well. The many acolytes of the investor model (knowingly or not) frequently invoke the vast flows of Foreign Portfolio Investment (FPI) and the proliferation of enhanced "good governance codes" as prima facie evidence that the former caused the latter, further assuming that enhanced protections for minority shareholders in turn will emerge more or less automatically from these codes. But although we have ample evidence of demand for minority shareholder protections from foreign portfolio investors, our data set and country cases provide little corresponding evidence on the other side that private blockholders stepped up to supply these enhanced minority shareholder protections. Where enhanced MSPs have followed in the wake of growing FPI penetration, we find other, more subtle shifts in preferences and political institutions at work, which we explore in more detail in chapters 6 and 7.

POLITICS OF THE GOOD-GOVERNANCE DEAL

In the investor model, shareholders on one side and blockholders on the other both turn to the state to the same end. Shareholders want minority shareholder protections. Blockholders want to reap the economic benefits of higher share prices through enhanced protections, but without giving up their private benefits of control. For theorists who believe in the sufficiency of private order, state action is not necessary: markets will compel firms to provide guarantees that managerial and blockholding agency costs are under control. But almost everywhere investors find private ordering guarantees insufficient; they want the arm of the state on their side in various ways. Nor, generally, are the mechanisms available under standard tort law seen as sufficient; laws and enforcement mechanisms dealing directly with securities, financial institutions, accounting, mergers, and corporate control apparently are required to reassure minority shareholders that they are protected.

State action of some sort thus appears necessary to strike a good-governance deal between investors and blockholders. The challenge is to explain *how* this state action is provided. Why do some countries provide it, while others do not, and when do they do so? Saying investors want shareholder protections does not prove they will be provided, a common functionalist fallacy. A linkage neglected by finance theory needs to be made overt—the link between investors' preferences and policy outcomes.

In a private ordering model, state action is not needed and politics not directly involved. Investors pay a premium for shares in firms with good-governance practices, and they discount the price they pay for shares in firms (and countries) with "substandard" minority shareholder protections. In this process, portfolio investors, particularly large, foreign portfolio investors, are particularly important. By combining many individual shareholdings into a smaller number of large institutional investors, some of the collective action problems of private order are overcome. Price discrimination by investors provides private blockholders with an incentive to supply enhanced minority protections in exchange for higher valuation by foreign investors, adopting better governance practices at the level of the firm while lobbying their governments for regulatory reform.

When legislation or regulatory modification is required to change formal practices, politics is involved. It is these steps between the preferences of players in the firm and the political process that are not well specified in finance models. They are implied; by drawing out the implications we can clarify the strengths and weaknesses of the argument. How exactly is it that outside investors and inside blockholders are able to influence the complex public actors who make laws, write regulations, and execute enforcement?

Interest groups such as blockholders are deliberate about seeking policies. They seek to influence politicians by mobilizing their constituencies, engaging in direct lobbying, seeking votes, giving campaign contributions, and pursuing a host of other practices familiar in democratic politics. In the investor model, private blockholders form a political coalition to push through the changes in corporate governance demanded by outside investors.

When the investor model shifts from preferences to the field of political action, it assumes that the interests of owners and investors take precedence in determining what the owners of capital and the firm will seek in terms of regulatory changes. This model also assumes that "capitalists" are united in their goals, that all of them want the same good-governance deal. Managers are the agents of owners; they can be monitored, incentivized, or disciplined in order to accept the outcomes sought by owners. As for workers, they are passive bystanders in the investor-driven model.

As a result of this political bargaining, therefore, both informal and formal governance regulations change to provide enhanced minority investor protections. Private blockholders gradually sell down their concentrated holdings to portfolio investors, trading their private benefits of control for higher valuation by portfolio investors, often foreign. The presumed end point is diffuse shareholding and more minority shareholder protections, as all countries realize that they, too, can "reap the full benefits of the global capital market" that the OECD principles proffer.

Where countries have evolved strong minority shareholder protections and the external monitoring model is already in place, investors reinforce the pattern by watching to see that governance standards are maintained, and rewarding or punishing behavior by firms and countries through their stream of buy or sell orders. We will explore later how breakdowns and other market failures occur in these mechanisms.

Where large blockholdings remain, the prevailing case in most countries in our sample, the process is different. Blockholders have many advantages over outside investors in terms of access to the firm and controls over decision making. As part of a notional good-governance deal predicated by the investor model, they reassure outside investors by voluntary compliance with good-governance procedures, such as independent oversight and executive compensation that aligns managers with shareholders. These changes in informal practices are a variant of private order, whereby blockholders overcome the potential problems of reputation building and bonding through their direct control over managers and firms. Blockholders must also then lobby their government to change those formal governance practices that are fixed by statute or official regulations, such as rules on accounting, financial disclosure, and contests of control.

These changes do not amount to giving up controlling interest. Blockholders can offer shareholder protections without giving up their controlling position, as in Korea (where protections are weak, though increasing) and in Sweden (where protections are relatively strong). Why then would blockholders be motivated to give up that kind of control in favor of diffusion?

Blockholders need reassurance. In order to strike a bargain with external investors, to adopt new practices of corporate governance, they need motivation. They have to be sure that their return will be better, both in the short run and the long. They need new practices, some through law and regulation as enhanced MSP, others through strong private bonding mechanisms. The limits of private order without state action push toward the need for MSP. It seems doubtful that investors and blockholders can be persuaded to construct the deal without change in formal state rules; thus the private ordering model does not lead inevitably to investors driving the system toward diffusion.

THE ESSENTIAL REPUTATIONAL INTERMEDIARIES

Elaborations of the investor model include other actors such as reputational intermediaries and international financial organizations (IFOs). In this view, the reputational intermediaries (accounting firms, bond-rating agencies) and securities markets, particularly stock exchanges, are seen as the prime transmission belt for minority shareholder protections, and as an intermediary in the bargain between blockholders, who want the best price, and external investors, who want the best price as well as minority shareholder protections. Listing requirements influence governance: firms are obligated to assure investors in order to qualify for a stock exchange listing. Accounting firms, rating agencies, and others provide key information about managerial performance to investors.

To attract firms to do business with, and to list on, their exchanges, reputational intermediaries are tempted to lower their requirements for minority shareholder protections. But to attract capital, to attract the mobile investors, the exchanges must satisfy these investors' demand for protections. Reputational intermediaries and exchanges that tilt too far towards blockholders, or managers, will lose business because of investor dissatisfaction.

Thus competition among reputational intermediaries and exchanges adds a further impetus to competition among countries to provide enhanced minority shareholder protections.[1] The reputational intermediaries thus join the lobby for shareholder protections, and push governments to provide strong regulation.

INTERNATIONAL FINANCIAL ORGANIZATIONS WEIGH IN

An even more elaborate version of the investor model adds the influence of supranational actors such as the International Monetary Fund (IMF), World Bank, Bank for International Settlements (BIS), and the OECD to the mix of actors with a preference for enhanced minority shareholder protections around the world.

In this view, the ultimate bargain is still between blockholders and minority shareholder protections, but international financial organizations have a partic-ular interest in better corporate governance, which they advance by acting as midwife to the broad emergence and consolidation of a good-governance deal between blockholders and outside investors, especially international investors. Development organizations such as the World Bank or OECD are interested in enhancing minority shareholder protections in order to foster cap-ital market development, which in turn promotes higher economic growth rates. The IMF and the BIS have a vital interest in reducing moral hazard in financial sector firms as part of the global challenge of prudential regulation—a challenge that came to a head during Korea's experiences in the Asian finan-cial crisis of 1997–98, which had profound consequences for Korean corporate governance.

PREDICTIONS OF THE INVESTOR MODEL

The investor model makes several predictions about the variance in governance practices among countries, for which we should be able to find evidence of the following:

- Portfolio investors pay a premium for shares in firms in countries with greater minority shareholder protections, and assign a discount for shares in firms in countries with weaker protections.
- Blockholders unilaterally adopt minority shareholder protections on the firm level, within the scope permitted by informal rules, such as putting NEDs on the board and adopting management incentives that align them with shareholders in general.[2]

---

[1] John Coffee, "Competition among Securities Markets: A Path Dependent Perspective," Colum-bia Law and Economics Working Paper Series No. 192, 2002.

[2] Some moves for minority shareholder protections are "private," that is, under the authority of firms to offer without state regulation. For example, the ratio of NEDs on a firm's board and the use of executive compensation that may align managers' interests with those of minority shareholders are usually set by "industry practice" or norm, which means that in the limit they are under the control

- Blockholders lobby their governments to adopt formal minority shareholder protections, by regulation or statute, in the areas of corporate governance that involve the state, such as accounting standards, disclosure, and voting rules.[3]

- Blockholders' concentrated holdings fall as shareholder protections are put in place, a good-governance premium is applied to the shares in these firms by investors, and blockholders sell down their holdings to reap higher valuation from foreign portfolio investors.

- Blockholders in markets with low or lagging MSPs cross-list in markets with higher MSPs in order to reap the investor model's valuation premium.

- Reputational intermediaries and stock exchanges take the lead in lobbying governments to provide greater minority shareholder protections, with support from international financial institutions.

- The weight of portfolio investors, particularly foreign portfolio investors, in a given country's stock market covaries positively with greater minority shareholder protections.

What does the evidence show for our country sample?

THE GOOD-GOVERNANCE PREMIUM (AND DISCOUNT)

A growing body of empirical research suggests that the relationship between minority shareholder protections and a firm's share price is positive, in line with the first prediction of the investor model.[4] Gompers et al. established a significant correlation between minority investor protections and stock market valuation in the United States, based on an index including 24 oversight, control, and management institutions for 1,500 firms between 1990 and 1999. Firms in the lower deciles of the index (stronger protections) earned returns of 8.5 percent higher than those in the upper deciles (weaker protections).[5]

On a comparative basis, a growing body of statistical, survey, and anecdotal evidence suggests that investors, particularly portfolio investors, do care about minority shareholder protections in international equity markets and are willing to pay a premium for firms in countries that provide these protections. Recent

---

of blockholders. Conversely, other measures do involve state action: rules for accounting, audit, and disclosure are more formal, set forth by statute or explicit regulatory prescription, as are most of the rules for control, although blockholders are generally free to adopt (or dissolve) antitakeover devices such as staggered boards or variants of the infamous "poison pill."

[3] Blockholders will try not to "lead" the formal changes too much, insofar as they will be exposed to some loss of private benefits of control prior to reaping the good-governance premium.

[4] This literature is summarized in several excellent surveys: Marco Becht, Patrick Bolton, and Ailsa A. Roell, "Corporate Governance and Control," European Corporate Governance Institute Finance Working Paper No. 02/2002, 2002; Maria Maher and Thomas Andersson, "Corporate Governance: Effects on Firm Performance and Economic Growth," in *Corporate Governance Regimes: Convergence and Diversity*, Joseph A. McCahery, Piet Moerland, Theo Raaijmakers, and Luc Renneboog, eds. (Oxford: Oxford University Press, 2002); Shleifer and Vishny 1997.

[5] Paul Gompers, Joy Ishii, and Andrew Merrick, "Corporate Governance and Equity Prices," NBER Working Paper No. 8449, 2001. The authors make no claims about the arrow of causation between good governance and performance, however.

studies by Claessens et al., La Porta et al., and several regional research teams have established similar evidence for a good-governance premium (and discount) in European and Asian equity markets, including Korea.[6]

For example, Chen et al. established a significant relationship between minority shareholder protections and the cost of capital, which includes stock market valuation (as part of the capital asset pricing model), for a sample of firms from nine Asian countries; their data suggests that a shift from the 25th to the 75th percentile of their corporate governance ranking reduces the total cost of capital by 1.26 percent, which roughly corresponds to a 20 percent corporate governance premium.[7]

The magnitude of the premium estimated by Chen et al. is consistent with a much-cited McKinsey survey of 200 investors, which found the average good-governance premium for a sample of 22 countries to be 21.6 percent, with a low of 17.9 percent and a high of 27.6 percent; for the 10 countries used in the McKinsey sample, the average premium was 20.9 percent.[8] In this survey, the good-governance premium is calculated as the difference between current market price per share of firms in these markets and the price institutional investors say they would be willing to pay if these firms adopted minority investor protections.[9]

The relation between the *firm*-level corporate governance premium or discount and the *country*-level premium or discount is ambiguous. It is difficult to disentangle these two empirically; most studies simply calculate the country-level premium as the sum of the individual premiums of a sample of listed firms from that country's equity market. The study by Chen et al. suggests that both firm-level and country-level effects are at work, but the country-level premium (associated with nondisclosure protections) is almost three times larger than the firm-level premium (associated with disclosure) in terms of cost of capital.[10]

[6] Stijn Claessens, Simeon Djankov, Joseph P. H. Fan, and Larry H. P. Lang, "Disentangling the Incentive and Entrenchment Effects of Large Shareholdings," *Journal of Finance* 57 (2002): 2741–71; Stijn Claessens, Simeon Djankov, and Larry H. P. Lang, "The Separation of Ownership and Control in East Asian Corporations," *Journal of Financial Economics* 58 (2002): 81–112; La Porta et al. 2002; Bernard Black, Hasung Jang, and Woochan Kim, "Does Corporate Governance Affect Firms' Market Values? Evidence from Korea," Stanford Law and Economics Olin Working Paper No. 237, 2003.

[7] Kevin Chen, Zihong Chen, and John Wei, "Disclosure, Corporate Governance, and the Cost of Equity Capital: Evidence from Asia's Emerging Markets," working paper, 2003. The authors use a CLSA index of minority shareholder protections for nine Asian countries for 2001 and 2002. On a pooled basis, the coefficient of the effect of all governance institutions on cost of capital (using capital asset pricing model) is −.24 for 2000 and −.16 for 2001, both statistically significant ($t = 4.13, 2.91$ respectively). On a country basis, these values are statistically significant for Hong Kong, India, Indonesia, Philippines, Singapore, Thailand, and Taiwan. CLSA Emerging Markets, www.clsa.com.

[8] Robert Felton, Alec Hudnut, and Jennifer van Heeckeren, "Putting a Value on Board Governance," *McKinsey Quarterly* 4 (1996): 170–75; McKinsey Investor Opinion Survey, June 2000, www.gcgf.org. In this survey, "good governance" was defined as a majority of outside directors, extensive disclosure, and use of stock options for directors—a rather narrow range of governance institutions.

[9] There are many problems with this evidence: portfolio investors' preference for minority shareholder protections may be too small to emerge from the evidence, or it may be swamped by other more important pricing factors such as relative return or diversification gains provided by spreading their equity portfolios across many markets. And portfolio investors may engage in other risk-spreading strategies such as derivative or indexed investments, that blur their interest in firm-specific minority shareholder protections.

[10] Chen, Chen, and Wei 2003.

On the other hand, anecdotal evidence suggests that large institutional investors and stock market analysts have been moving away from country-based portfolios in favor of a global industrial sector view.[11] For example, they analyze the performance and structure of pharmaceutical firms or automobile firms against their global peers, rather than against other firms from their home stock market. We revisit this knotty question later in this chapter when we look at the sequence of informal versus formal governance reforms adopted by firms in our country sample, but there are two indirect ways of looking at country premiums.

One way of looking at the country premium is to examine what happens to firms' share prices when they cross-list on a different exchange. The most common method of cross-listing is issuing American Depository Receipts (ADRs) on the New York Stock Exchange (NYSE) or the NASDAQ. Foreign firms that issue ADRs have a higher average valuation than firms from their domestic market that do not, suggesting a country discount at work, although it is hard to get around the selection bias of the sample; it may be that firms with better minority shareholder protections, or better growth prospects, decide to issue ADRs.[12]

Another indirect measure is the relation between market capitalization and minority shareholder protections; on average, the ratio of market capitalization to GDP should closely covary with our index of shareholder protections. The ratio of market capitalization to GDP is the result of a host of other variables besides shareholder protections, including macroeconomic conditions and the debt-equity structure of each country's capital markets, but it provides a gross indicator of the governance premium or discount.

The prediction that market capitalization to GDP should covary positively with minority shareholder protections is substantiated by our country sample, with a moderately positive correlation of .46, and a positive slope of .10 in a fitted OLS regression line ($t = 3.06$, $r^2 = .20$). There are also several outliers such as Hong Kong and Switzerland, both with a high market capitalization to GDP ratio, reflecting their roles as international financial entrepôts and tax havens. (See also Appendix tables A.10 and A.11.)

FLOOD TIDE OF FOREIGN PORTFOLIO INVESTORS

Table 5.1 shows the increasing weight of foreign portfolio investors' ownership in the sample countries over the decade from 1990 to 2000, measured as the percentage of the total market capitalization of listed firms held by foreign investors.

---

[11] Authors' interviews with money managers in New York and London, 2001–2; Nicolas Mottis and Jean-Pierre Ponssard, "L'Influence des investisseurs institutionnels sur le pilotage des enterprises," Ecole Polytechnique Laboratoire d'Econometrie Working Paper No. 2002-020, 7–8; Dominique Plihon, Jean-Pierre Ponssard, and Philippe Zarlowski, "Quel scenario pour le gouvernement d'enterprise? Une hypothèse de double convergence," Ecole Polytechnique Laboratoire d'Econometrie Working Paper 2001-008, August 2001.

[12] Karl Lins, Deon Strickland, and Marc Zenner, "Do Non-U.S. Firms Issue Equity on U.S. Stock Exchanges to Relax Capital Constraints?" research monograph, January 2000, www.cob.ohio-state.edu/fin/dice/papers/2000-5.pdf.

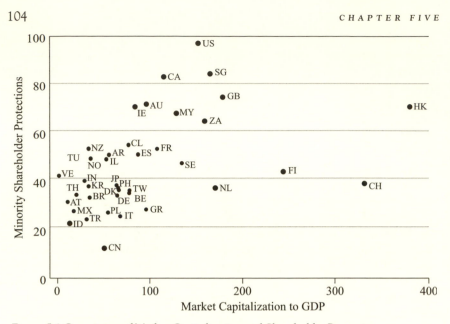

Figure 5.1 Covariance of Market Capitalization and Shareholder Protections

Accurate data for many of the countries in our sample is incomplete or, in some cases, unobtainable. Indeed, given the importance of the issue, we are surprised at how incomplete the data is.

The mean weight of foreign penetration doubled for those countries for which data is available, from 12 percent in 1990 to 25.1 percent in 2000. For developed countries, the mean value grew from 15 percent in 1990 to 28.6 percent a decade later; for emerging countries, foreign penetration increased five times, from 2.3 percent in 1990 to 13 percent in 200.

For example, foreign penetration of the Korean stock market grew dramatically, expanding by 10 times between 1990 and 1995, and then almost tripling again by 1999, in effect moving from almost zero to more than 20 percent in ten years. The growth rate is striking not just for emerging markets, but also for several developed market countries with a large stock market value such as Japan, France, the United Kingdom, and Spain. Notably, foreign investors' penetration of the Swedish market capitalization quadrupled over the period in question.

Like the other data sets used in this book, these figures must be used with care. The IMF, the Federation Internationale des Bourses de Valeurs, and various country stock exchanges often use different methodologies to estimate the penetration figure. Moreover, many foreign investors own shares through local nominees or custodian accounts that mask the underlying foreign ownership, especially in emerging markets with foreign exchange controls, so these figures underestimate the true size of foreign investor penetration.

The bulk of these foreign investors are institutional investors, professional money-management firms such as pensions and mutual funds. Table 5.3 shows

TABLE 5.1
Penetration of Foreign Portfolio Investors

	1990	1991	1992	1993	1994	1995	1996	1997	1998	1999	2000
Argentina	6.5	10.3	23.3	27.4	30.7	30.7	32.2	31.5	10.0	2.2	
Australia	18.0	14.8	13.1	17.5	21.3	20.9	19.6	20.4	22.2	22.6	21.6
Austria	17.2	33.1	12.1	12.6	17.8	21.5	26.7	43.8	45.8	44.6	65.4
Belgium	8.6	8.4	9.3	10.6	11.6	9.5	9.3	8.8	7.3	8.4	7.8
Brazil								12.1	10.2	10.0	7.5
Canada	7.4	5.7	5.8	5.4	7.0	7.4	7.1	6.3	7.7	6.0	6.8
Chile							7.9	9.9	11.0	9.5	7.8
China	3.0									4.0	
Denmark		6.4	7.3	7.8	12.4	14.8	17.4	21.7	20.8	19.7	24.2
Finland	6.1	7.0	8.0	22.3	33.4	33.1	37.2	39.4	51.6	62.8	69.6
France	17.4	20.4	20.7	22.8	22.7	22.7	26.3	29.9	30.3	33.9	36.1
Germany	22.7	21.2	20.0	20.2	21.1	19.2	20.9	22.7	26.5	26.2	23.6
Greece									15.0	7.4	8.6
Hong Kong											22.1
India								10.6	13.4	7.1	10.6
Indonesia											
Ireland											
Israel					8.8	12.9	18.9	23.8	25.0	40.2	48.6
Italy	6.6	6.3	6.0	8.2	6.2	7.8	10.6	10.3	11.6	7.3	6.9
Japan	3.1	4.5	5.2	5.7	6.7	8.4	10.2	12.6	12.2	18.3	17.4
Malaysia	5.2	4.6	3.4	1.6	2.2						
Mexico											
Netherlands	46.7	48.8	48.9	50.8	37.2	36.5	47.4	47.9	51.2	52.3	54.7
New Zealand	10.2	7.2	3.1	5.2	3.0	4.6	0.7	3.4	0.8	0.8	24.6
Norway											19.9
Philippines											
Portugal				23.6	22.1	19.9	26.7	32.5	29.9	29.3	30.3
Singapore	5.0									10.0	
South Africa	2.7	2.9	5.2	3.5	4.1	4.5	5.5	5.7	10.3	10.1	11.0
South Korea	0.6	0.7	2.8	6.7	6.2	12	13	13.7	18	21.1	30.2
Spain			30.6	34.4	35.9	36.7	37.4	35.6	36.9	34.3	34.7
Sweden	6.8	10.4	16.7	20.3	27.4	27.0	28.4	29.1	33.7	34.7	32.5
Switzerland	49.3	49.4	46.5	51.2	47.4	41.3	43.9	42.8	47.0	44.7	48.2
Taiwan									8.7	7.4	7.2	8.8
Thailand											27.6
Turkey							10.3	9.9	11.0	13.6	10.6
United Kingdom	13.4	13.3	15.1	17.2	16.3	19.0	22.1	25.0	28.2	28.1	35.0
United States	8.0	7.3	7.3	7.3	7.8	8.0	7.9	8.4	9.3	9.7	10.8
Venezuela				11.4	28.8	29.0	24.7	26.6	21.8	28.8	21.3

Source: Country values from national stock exchanges or Federation International des Bourses en Valuer, fibv.com; Argentina from www.mecon.gov.ar/cuentas/internacionales/inversion00-01.doc; India from www.rbi.org.in/sec24/31825.xls; Norway from http://www.ssb.no/en/indicators/dsbb/.

TABLE 5.2
Foreign Investor Penetration Summary (%)

	1990	1995	2000
Observations	21	24	30
Mean	12.6	18.2	25.1
SD	13	12.6	17.6
Min	0.6	2.2	6.8
Max	49.3	47.4	69.6

TABLE 5.3
Institutional Investor Assets ($ billions)

	Assets 1993	Assets 1999	Equity %	Equity $	Equity Share
United States	8035	19279	0.51	9832	0.65
Japan	3012	5039	0.19	957	0.06
United Kingdom	1207	3264	0.68	2220	0.15
France	800	1695	0.42	712	0.05
Germany	665	1529	0.28	428	0.03
Italy	225	1078	0.22	237	0.02
Netherlands	427	799	0.43	344	0.02
Canada	376	748	0.27	202	0.01
Australia	176	375	0.5	188	0.01
South Korea	161	375	0.11	41	0.00
Total	15084	34181		15161	
Mean			0.36		

Source: Brancato 2000.

the dramatic scale of asset accumulation by these investors, which mirrors the growth in foreign market penetration shown above.

According to this table, institutional investors in the United States and the United Kingdom control two-thirds of the total assets in the 10-country sample, and allocate between two and three times the proportion of their assets invested in equities. Anglo-American investors account for 80 percent of total equity holdings among the 10 countries in this data sample. These U.S.- and U.K.-headquartered firms do manage funds on behalf of nonresidents, but by and large in both countries, most of the assets are held by residents of each. For our purposes what matters is fund managers' demand for minority shareholder protections, not the "nationality" of the original source of the capital.

THE GLOBAL PURSUIT OF RETURN AND DIVERSIFICATION

As the total assets in pension and mutual funds mushroomed during the 1980s and 1990s, fund managers began to diversify their portfolios away from their previously high proportion of government or private bonds. The largest shift was from fixed income to equities, and other high-return assets. The equity shift was accelerated by the findings of scholars who consistently demonstrated that the long-term return of U.S. equities exceeded the bond market between 1926 and 1960.[13]

By the same token, due to the gradual acceptance of the capital asset pricing model in portfolio evaluation, investors realized that they could reduce the risk of their portfolio without sacrificing return if they could place their equity "bets" in stock markets that fluctuated according to different cycles. Not only did many foreign (especially emerging) markets promise higher growth rates in underlying profitability, they also reduced the overall volatility of the portfolio, insofar as most foreign equity markets fluctuated on a different cycle than the United States.[14]

As a result of these two profound changes in investment strategy, U.S.-based investment managers shifted the weight of equities in their portfolio composition from 26.5 percent of total assets in 1988 to a ratio of 47.4 percent at the beginning of 1999, while dramatically increasing their exposure to international equities.[15] The spillover effect of this large shift to equities explains why U.S.- and U.K.-based investors became such big players in global equity markets, providing the backdrop for the "global competition for capital" rationale of agreements such as the OECD Corporate Governance Principles.

TEPID EMBRACE BY BLOCKHOLDERS

Sifting through the country cases in our sample, there is no discernable pattern of informal changes leading to formal changes in corporate governance practice, as the investor model would predict. To the contrary, in cases such as France, Germany, Italy, Japan, Korea, Malaysia, and Singapore, formal changes *preceded* informal changes, with the government imposing higher standards of accounting and disclosure, or mandating the use of one-share, one-vote control practices, over the objections of blockholders. Indeed, in Korea and several other of our countries, the governance reforms were imposed by the state over the objection of the private blockholders. And in the long-term cases of blockholder diffusion that took place in the United Kingdom and the United States, which we explore in more detail in chapter 7, diffusion appeared to have taken place in the context of private bonding schemes between blockholders and other shareholders in historical periods before the introduction of regulatory-based MSPs.

[13] Lawrence Fisher and James H. Lorie, "Rates of Return on Investment in Common Stocks: The Year-by-Year Record, 1926–1965," *Journal of Business* 41 (1968): 291–316; Torben Ibbotson and Rex Sinquefield found similar conclusions in an updated study of data from 1926 through 1974, "Stocks Bonds, Bills, and Inflation: Year by Year Historical Returns (1926–1974)," *Journal of Business* 49 (1976): 11–47.

[14] In other words, foreign equity markets did not perfectly covary with the U.S. or other major equity markets, and thus provided a way to reduce the overall variability (and thus risk coefficient) of an equity portfolio.

[15] Michael S. Clowes, *The Money Flood: How Pension Funds Revolutionized Investing* (New York: Wiley, 2000).

Overall, there has been no race by private blockholders to appoint NEDs to their boards, or put in place incentive option schemes for their managers that shift their allegiance to all the stockholders, rather than the blockholder. Contrary to the prediction about private bonding mechanisms of the investor model, it is more often the case that the state has forced blockholders' hand to adopt minority shareholder protections, such as imposing a minimum percentage of NEDs as part of changes in the company law or rules controlling stock exchange listings. The case of Korea which we explore below is a good example of that process.

Against this backdrop of a flood of foreign portfolio investors applying a governance premium and discount around the world, did firms and governments change their behavior and their rules as the investor model would predict? Although we have ample evidence of demand for minority shareholder protections from foreign portfolio investors, there is little corresponding evidence on the other side that private blockholders stepped up to supply these enhanced protections. According to the script of the "good-governance deal," private blockholders should adopt informal practices that provide greater minority shareholder protections where they can, and lobby their governments for formal changes that create stronger protections.

Nor do we find many examples of private blockholders lobbying the state for governance changes, either individually or on a collective basis. Most countries in this sample have a business federation that engages in collective lobbying of their governments, such as the Federation of Korean Industry (FKI), Brazil's ABRASCA, Germany's Bundesverband der Deutscher Industrie (BDI), Spain's Circulo de Empresarios, and Japan's Keizaidantai-rengokai (or Keidanren for short). Curiously, in most of our sample countries, these collective business entities have been either passive or hostile with regard to corporate governance reforms, despite active lobbying across a wide range of other regulatory issues. Business federations have been actively hostile to governance reforms in several countries with a high concentration of private blockholders, and where "old money" blockholders had the tightest control over the political agenda of these federations. Brazil, Italy, Sweden, and Taiwan all provide examples of resistance by private blockholders to minority shareholder protections, but the Korean case reveals the political tensions of the investor model in particularly rich detail.[16]

---

[16] In Brazil, for example, "The concentrated ownership structure of Brazilian family-owned business groups and the warding-off of strategies that involve a dilution of control are clear indicators of the significant private benefits of control. It might therefore be expected that controlling shareholders would oppose any measures that meant a reduction in their control rents. This opposition was in fact very effective in the debates in Congress in 2001 about the new corporate law. The public position of these shareholders towards governance matters, usually voiced by the Brazilian Association of Public Companies (ABRASCA), a traditional representative of the business elite, does in fact reveal their tendency to oppose some measures that might improve governance in the country." Luciano Coutinho and Flavio Rabelo, "Brazil: Keeping It in the Family," in *Corporate Governance in Development: The Experience of Brazil, Chile, India, and South Africa*, Charles P. Oman, ed. (Washington, D.C.: OECD Development Center, 2003), 49.

LIMITED LIQUIDATION?

The investment model of change predicts that private blockholders should incrementally liquidate their concentrated holdings to take advantage of the foreign portfolio investors' premium for good governance. The evidence for this is mixed. There is scattered evidence of a modest sell-down of blockholdings in some countries, such as France, Argentina, and the Scandinavian markets, and also evidence of an increase of blockholder concentration in other countries such as Korea, Chile, and Brazil. Until we have another set of reliable data points on ownership concentration akin to the index presented in chapter 3, we cannot dependably test this prediction of the investor model. Meanwhile, scattered and anecdotal evidence for this country sample suggests no trend of liquidation of control by private blockholders.

In many markets where blockholding dipped, the reduction in the weight of firms held by blockholders is traceable to two factors. One is the rapid increase in floatation of state-owned enterprises, such as telecom operators, transportation, and other utilities, in most of these countries. The sheer size of these firms often made them the largest, or among the largest, firms in terms of stock market capitalization, thereby causing the weight of blockholders to fall—but not because the blockholders sold down. The second factor is also traceable to new issues in those markets. The clearest evidence of block sell-down was undertaken by "new money" entrepreneurs, who sold portions of their blockholdings to portfolio investors on local parallel exchanges such as the Neuer Markt, or by cross-listing their shares in the U.S. or U.K. markets, which we discuss more below.[17]

In contrast, it appears that the "old money" blockholders in these sample countries did not rush to the altar to embrace foreign portfolio investors and the good-governance deal. For example, in Korea, the top 30 chaebol blockholders have *increased* their concentration within affiliated groups in recent years, in the face of intense pressure from the state to reduce these holdings.[18] A study by Hasung Jang shows that the controlling families of Korea's big chaebol firms increased their total blockholdings of group firms from 17.9 percent in 1996 to 33.3 percent in 2001, almost doubling their control during a period that spanned the Korean financial crisis of 1997–98, largely by means of pyramid holdings through equity affiliates.[19] Nonchaebol families also increased their holdings during the same period, from 24.7 percent in 1996 to 30.3 percent in 2001.

Data compiled by the Federation of European Stock Exchanges (FESE) suggests that family holdings have also increased over the past five years in Italy and

---

[17] The ownership pattern data presented in table 2.1 is static, essentially a snapshot, drawn for this sample from the first wave of ownership disclosure in Europe and Asia that began in the mid-1990s. Until this analysis is repeated to provide at least a second set of more recent data points, it will not be clear how much ownership concentration has changed overall, and thus whether liquidation has taken place.

[18] Myeong-Hyeon Cho, "Corporate Governance in Korea," paper presented for the Conference on Corporate Restructuring in Korea, University of California, San Diego, October 2000.

[19] Hasung Jang, "Corporate Restructuring in Korea after the Economic Crisis," *Joint U.S.-Korea Academic Studies* (2003): 147–84, table 10.

Spain. Individuals and families increased their ownership of the Borsa Italiana from 21 percent to 25 percent and of the Bolsa de Madrid from 22 percent to 31 percent.[20] The same FESE data shows individual and family holdings falling in France (18 percent to 8 percent), Norway (9 percent to 6 percent), and Sweden (15 percent in 1998 to 13 percent in 2000). Individual and family ownership figures were basically flat for Germany and Portugal. This data is suspect insofar as it does not pierce the corporate veil to track ultimate control and thus conflates "retail" individual investors with private blockholders, but it is indicative of a broader trend.

In Asia, anecdotal evidence from Taiwan, Malaysia, and Singapore shows no signs of large private blockholders reducing their holdings in order to profit from higher valuation by foreign portfolio investors; on the contrary, as in Korea, many owner-families have been concentrating their ownership holdings, although some have sold portions of the family "empire" directly to multinational corporations (which then appears as foreign direct investment rather than foreign portfolio investment) or to international private equity funds.[21] In other emerging markets, there is evidence of some reduction in blockholdings in South Africa and Argentina, with increases in Chile and possibly Brazil.

OBSTACLES TO THE INVESTOR "BARGAIN": COLLECTIVE ACTION HURDLES

Why the tepid reaction by blockholders to the good-governance deal on the "supply side" of minority shareholder protections—contrary to the predictions of the investor model? Surveying our country cases, it appears that there are several roadblocks on the way to the good-governance deal.

For example, stock market valuation can motivate blockholders with money, but it may not compensate blockholders for the psychological benefits of control. These benefits include garden-variety prestige, nationalism, as in the case of the chaebol founder-chairmen whose firms built the Korean "economic miracle," or the satisfaction of placing children into jobs in the family firm. Other private benefits may include the gratification of owning an "old-fashioned family-style firm" that "takes care of the employees" and "gives back to the community." For example, Agnblad et al. argue that concerns for "social standing" by blockholders in Sweden such as the Wallenbergs are an impediment to expropriation costs, as well as profit-maximizing behavior of selling down to foreign portfolio investors.[22]

---

[20] Federation of European Stock Exchanges, *Share Ownership Structure in Europe*, 2002, http://www.fese.org/statistics/share_ownership/share_ownership.pdf. This data is not adjusted for ultimate control, so it may not provide an accurate picture, especially for big family holdings.

[21] Private equity funds provide a large potential circuit for private blockholders to sell down to foreign portfolio investors. Private equity funds purchase control from private blockholders in private transactions, and then may repackage or relist parts of these firms on local exchanges or even on global equity exchanges. These funds are largely subscribed by the same Anglo-American institutional investors who also hold large amounts of foreign equities directly, but there is virtually no reliable public-domain data on the activities of these private equity funds.

[22] "Social prestige is an important, even dominant, part of the total benefits associated with control of large corporations in Sweden. Many owner families try to build a legacy around themselves as good citizens and project themselves onto the public arena as important contributors to socially worthy

The good-governance deal also involves a good deal of uncertainty. Stock markets can be capricious, and private blockholders observed the rapid run-up and abrupt crash of emerging market valuations during the latter half of the 1990s. In contrast to these market uncertainties, although the private blockholder is exposed to high risk because of his concentrated holdings, he also has the benefit of insider knowledge and (usually) accumulated expertise in his industrial sector. Moreover, since many old-money blockholders control a horizontally diversified group of firms—with some family firms in Asia holding horizontal interests in industries including flour milling, semiconductors, and banks—the portfolio gains from the good-governance deal may be limited.

There is another concern about information, namely that accepting the good-governance deal from investors also exposes the private blockholder to the tax collector. In contrast, private benefits of control can be hidden or routed through offshore tax havens. Anecdotal evidence suggests that several countries with the high private blockholder weights exhibit patterns of capricious taxation by the authorities and (allegedly) widespread tax evasion by blockholder business owners, in Argentina, Brazil, Italy, Korea, Spain, and Taiwan.

If these payout and information problems can be circumvented, private blockholders may still face a formidable problem in selling off ownership in small increments to foreign portfolio investors. For a smooth transition to take place, the blockholder must issue a credible promise not to steal from the firm, and the foreign portfolio investors must promise to compensate the blockholder for giving up those private benefits of control—in effect, paying a premium over the current value of traded minority shares in that firm.

If the sale of the firm is done in small increments, the marginal transaction that transfers control from the blockholder to the new minority investor must carry a price that embodies all the private benefits of control—a big price tag. No rational minority investor will enter this transaction, since all the previous shares were acquired at the lower traded price. Yet without such a price premium, no rational blockholder will sell enough stock to threaten his control. Unless this transaction problem is solved, blockholders' support for the good-governance deal may grind to a halt at the transfer of the 51st percent of control, leaving the private blockholder in charge and minority shareholders still exposed.[23]

Even if blockholders are motivated to accept the good-governance deal and find a way around the problem with transactions that decide control, they encounter a collective action problem themselves. In a market dominated by other blockholders and with weak protections for minority shareholders, what blockholder will be brave enough to go first, adopting good-governance institutions that limit

---

causes like philanthropy, endowments, and research. . . . We believe that significant control benefits, which are provided and protected by the corporate law, but restrained by informal social constraints, has [sic] been one of the pivotal elements of the Swedish corporate governance model." Jonas Agnblad, Erik Berglöf, Peter Högfeldt, and Helena Svancar, "Ownership and Control in Sweden: Strong Owners, Weak Minorities, and Social Control," in Barca and Becht 2001, 252.

[23] This is one reason why private equity transactions may be more appealing to these blockholders.

his own private benefits, and exposing himself to expropriation as a trusting minority shareholder at the hands of other buccaneering blockholders?

Blockholding and the dense network of relationships associated with it may carry some economic advantages that owners may be reluctant to give up. They allow production strategies that involve reciprocal commitments, extensive information sharing, and reduction of transactions costs that arm's-length market relations inhibit. Firms may invest in interdependencies, for which the blockholding and cross-shareholding are buffers. The concept of agency costs of cash flow assumes no benefit to the system; that may be erroneous, and may not indeed be perceived by blockholders. Blockholding, moreover, does allow owners to directly monitor their agents, as the other systems do not; here again change may seem quite risky.

FREE-RIDING ON A TRUSTED BLOCKHOLDER

Contracterian theory exaggerates investors' attraction to diffusion rather than blockholding. Several countries in our sample have solid shareholder protections but high concentration, Sweden and Chile, for example. Blockholding may have advantages even in a high-MSP environment, and high-quality corporate law is, in incentive terms, compatible with alternative forms of corporate governance. Rather than promote diffusion, better corporate law may simply make distant shareholders more confident in blockholders.[24]

For example, the securities regulatory regime in the United States focuses primarily on personal abuse by insiders. In particular, it seeks to prevent the diversion of shareholder resources for insiders' personal gain—looting the firm through loans and gifts, improper assignment of resources, and padding the payroll, to name a few. But shareholders can lose as much or more money from bad management, argues Mark Roe, and about that American law of fiduciary duties is silent. The business judgment rule[25] shields directors and managers from legal inquiries regarding the quality of management. Judges have rejected efforts to punish bad decisions, rather than abuse for personal gain. One case that supported such a suit, *Smith v. Van Gorkom*,[26] was "a decision excoriated by managers and their lawyers, and promptly overturned by the state legislature."[27] Thus American corporate law does not make managers liable for decisions on those areas that have the biggest impact on shareholders.[28]

It is just here that the blockholder system may provide advantages. Large blockholders have the incentive and the means to deal with "shirking, mistakes, and bad business decisions that squander shareholder value."[29] With big stakes, they have the power to replace or discipline managers.[30] In the Berle-Means firm, collective

---

[24] Roe, 2003b, and Mark Roe "Delaware's Competition," *Harvard Law Review* 117 (2003): 588–646.

[25] Roe 2003b, 172.

[26] Smith v. Van Gorkom, 488 A.2d 858 (Delaware 1985).

[27] Roe, 2003b, 172.

[28] Roe 2003b, 171–72.

[29] Roe 2003b, 172.

[30] For a discussion on the attractions of blockholding, see Shleifer and Vishny 1997. Tax evasion may also motivate the reluctance to list shares in order to avoid scrutiny by tax authorities.

action problems face diffuse shareholders; they have little incentive to pay the transactions costs of organizing pressure on directors to move against managers. Shareholders can sell, though this depresses stock prices. The major mechanism for managerial discipline in the U.S. system is the market for corporate control: a badly run firm becomes a target for takeover. But this will happen only after considerable loss of shareholder value creates the target. Mergers appear to be costly to the shareholders of the acquiring firm, so mergers and acquisitions may themselves become vulnerable to costs of managerial agency, with the dealmakers, not the shareholders, making the money.

Deductively, then, an argument based on the quality of shareholder protection cannot specify which set of incentives—the fear of managerial agency costs from personal corruption versus the fear of managerial agency costs from poor management—will determine the form of corporate governance. The former may encourage shareholder diffusion models, but the latter may encourage concentrated blockholding.[31]

Finally, blockholders and investors alike may worry about the political stability of strong MSP. To be politically sustainable, corporate governance practices need to serve not only owners' preferences but to have a firm political foundation. Credibility—or at least predictability—is the coin of the realm in finance. Blockholding may be preferred when uncertainty is high.

ENTREPRENEURIAL NEW MONEY

The lack of enthusiasm by blockholders for the investor model's good-governance deal is not monolithic, however. It provides an example of the actor fragmentation discussed in chapter 4, and an insight into the potential fluidity of coalitional formation and change in the politics of corporate governance.

There appears to be a big difference in the corporate governance preferences of "old money" blockholders and "new" entrepreneurs. The pattern of resisting enhanced minority shareholder protections and increased concentration by old-money blockholders contrasts sharply with the behavior of many new-money entrepreneurs in many of these same markets during the same period, who participated in domestic "new markets" that offered greater shareholder protections than the first-tier exchanges, and cross-listed in the United States (usually the NASDAQ) with stricter conformance to the full set of U.S. protections.[32] This confirms the need to disaggregate the categories used in finance theory: we don't have simply "investors" or "owners," but types of them, having different incentives, thus different interests in MSP.

---

[31] See Hall and Soskice 2001. The book's introductory essay, "An Introduction to Varieties of Capitalism," provides an excellent statement of the varieties-of-capitalism approach, and various other chapters provide access to American, German, and British research. For extension of the concept of "institutional complementarities," see Hall and Gingerich 2001.

[32] Gerald F. Davis and Christopher Marquis, "The Globalization of Stock Markets and Convergence in Corporate Governance," in The Economic Sociology of Capitalism, Victor Nee and Richard Swedberg, eds. (Princeton: Princeton University Press, 2005).

Anecdotal evidence suggests that, unlike the old-money blockholders in these markets, the founder-entrepreneurs of these new firms embraced the good-governance deal in order to raise capital for their growing firms, as well as to partially cash in themselves, selling down part of their blockholdings to diversify their portfolio by means of an offering on the new parallel exchanges (discussed immediately below). They did not need to create a broad-based political coalition to lobby for these changes insofar as the changes were handed to them prepackaged, as it were, by the financial markets, insulated from the governance practices that prevailed in the rest of the country.

Nonetheless, these entrepreneurs were often allies of center-left political coalitions that pressed for governance reforms more broadly, and they provided a useful counterweight to old-money businessmen for politicians seeking to convince voters that reforms in governance were progrowth rather than antibusiness. For example, in Korea even as the Kim Dae Jung government pilloried the old-money chaebol, it vigorously championed a class of new-money entrepreneurs, particularly from high technology. State agencies leaned over backwards to accommodate the KOSDAQ, analogous to the NASDAQ, with corporate governance practices superior to those of the first-tier Korean Stock Exchange (KSE), which was dominated by old-money chaebol and former SOE firms.

Thus the politics of governance reform do not reduce in a simple way to investors all on one side: they turn out to be heterogeneous in their preferences and to lobby for contrasting policies.

NO ADR VENUE-SHOPPING

If the investor model is correct, firms controlled by private blockholders should be the most enthusiastic issuers of American Depository Receipt cross-listings in New York or London as a way to "opt out" of their domestic regulatory regime and provide the enhanced protections for minority shareholders associated with conformance with the corporate governance rules of the NYSE, NASDAQ, or London Stock Exchange (LSE).

Contrary to this prediction, blockholding firms have not been the most enthusiastic users of cross-listing, as measured by the pattern of foreign firms that have tapped the U.S. ADR market. To the contrary, SOEs (state-owned enterprises) were the most aggressive users of ADRs from most foreign markets, rather than firms controlled by private blockholders. The database of international listings on both the NYSE and the NASDAQ suggests that for a sample of countries whose private blockholders might care to cross-list in the United States in order to reap a venue-shopping valuation premium, the percentage of U.S. cross-listers is weighted towards government-owned firms, to an extent far larger than the weight of state-controlled firms in their domestic stock markets: 50 percent of the Argentinean issues, 60 percent of those from Brazil, 35 percent from Chile, 60 percent from France, and 60 percent from Italy.[33]

---

[33] William L. Megginson, "Appendix Detailing Share Issue Privatization Offerings, 1961–2000," http://faculty-staff.ou.edu/M/William.L.Megginson-1/; NYSE ADR listings, 2003; NASDAQ international company listings, 2003.

Consistent with the previous story of chaebol resistance to the investor model, fully 80 percent of Korean firms issuing ADRs were government-owned; only a handful were blockholder-controlled chaebol. Of course, larger firms find it easier to cross-list, given the bias towards large-cap investments by portfolio investors, and so we await a more definite test of the ownership of cross-listing firms that controls for size and other sectoral variables.

A stronger piece of evidence against the hypothesis that blockholders found a way to embrace the good-governance deal by means of cross-listing is based on a close examination of corporate governance behavior by these firms before and after cross-listing. It appears that firms engaged in ADR cross-listing rarely (if ever) adopted the full set of U.S. minority shareholder protections, regardless of their underlying pattern of blockholder ownership. A study of 210 firms with NYSE and NASDAQ cross-listings (from the United Kingdom, France, Germany, Israel, Chile, and Japan) by Davis and Marquis showed remarkably little change in nondisclosure aspects of corporate governance by these firms: "At this time, the choice to list on a U.S. securities market may be intended as a signal of shareholder-friendly governance, but it is evidently not followed by other substantial structural changes."[34]

The corporate governance requirements on foreign issuers in the United States have long been exempted by the SEC under so-called carve outs, whereby foreign issuers must restate their financial figures in GAAP and use an external auditor, but are otherwise exempted from almost all U.S. rules of oversight, control, and executive compensation. Foreign issuers are free to adopt other protections for minority shareholders, but few do so. The comparatively rare exceptions were high-technology firms (mostly from Israel, a smaller number from China and elsewhere in East Asia) that deliberately fashioned their corporate governance structure on the U.S. model from the beginning with an eye on a NASDAQ initial public offering as their exit strategy. These firms were controlled by new-money entrepreneur blockholders, whose preferences in corporate governance differ from those of old-money blockholders on several important points, which we explore elsewhere in this chapter.

CHEERLEADING BY THE "NEW EXCHANGES"

The investor model predicts that the reputational intermediaries and stock exchanges will take an active part in lobbying governments to provide greater protections for minority shareholders. There is some evidence for this practice during the early 1990s, when financial services firms in many of our sample countries encouraged their governments to approve a parallel exchange for start-ups modeled after the NASDAQ in the United States, with higher standards of corporate governance than those of the major exchanges. Examples include Germany's Neuer Markt, Brazil's Novo Mercado, Korea's KOSDAQ, and Italy's Nuovo Mercato. In

---

[34] "On average, the foreign firms we studied organize their boards in the same ways as their domestic counterparts. Few make their financial statements available electronically. They typically attract few equity analysts and receive very little interest from institutional investors (a median of under 2%). And the lack of transparency of their ownership suggests that the SEC's enforcement does not extend beyond U.S. borders." Davis and Marquis 2005.

these lobbying efforts, the financial services firms often invoked the language of the broad benefits of enhanced protections for minority shareholders in provid-ing deeper capital markets—as well as pointing out the undesirable consequences of having promising domestic firms "defect" to the NASDAQ or NYSE if the local environment did not improve.

These parallel "new" exchanges distinguished themselves from the first-tier exchange by offering (they claimed) greater protections for minority shareholders particularly in the areas of disclosure. By opting into these parallel new exchanges, blockholders who decided to engage in the good-governance deal with foreign investors and list their shares with higher shareholder protections had an opportu-nity to "opt out" of their own native governance environment.

The bust of the high-tech bubble in the late 1990s tarnished the glow of these parallel exchanges and weakens the argument that they are able to create the trans-formative effect claimed on their behalf. Politically, they are interesting because their advocates were vocal members of reformist governments among many of the countries in our sample. In principle these markets remain a strong mecha-nism for making the investor/private bonding mechanism work. They have not provided evidence that bonding cannot by itself overcome regulatory and politi-cal obstacles. Again, the state matters.

THE AMBIGUOUS REPUTATIONAL INTERMEDIARIES: CROSS-PRESSURED

The same diversity of purposes can be discovered among reputational interme-diaries—accounting, law, bond-rating agencies, finance houses. They do not appear to have acted as a monolith in terms of corporate governance prefer-ences. They have not acted the way the investor theory suggests—as the objec-tive intermediary providing the key information needed for shareholder monitoring to work. Some intermediaries tilted towards the investor side and toward MSP, others toward the blockholders' side or the managers' side of the equation, and did so at different points in time, in different countries. They lent their considerable political weight and technical expertise to coalitions on both sides of the divide. When the scandals of the late 1990s broke, reputational intermediaries were part of the problem: accounting firms and others collabo-rated with managers and blockholders to cook the books; they lobbied hard, and still do, against regulations that would separate their various business functions of earlier period.

The income of investment bankers and accountants, their slice of the "fran-chise value" of their firms, stems from their role as reputational intermediaries in securities markets. There is an asymmetry of information between the firms that issue stocks and the investors who buy them, and a temptation for firms to mis-lead investors, as they only issue stock from time to time, sometimes only once.

In game theory terms, accounting and securities firms turn this one-time game of stock issuing into an iterative game, by performing "due diligence" on issuing firms. They work in tandem to render a professional opinion on equity securities, in effect "renting" their reputation to issuers for a fee. They perform the same role in their ongoing scrutiny of publicly traded firms, the accountants auditing the financial statements with an opinion letter, and the securities firms rendering a buy or sell opinion. Investors are the customers for these professional opinions, and they deal with the accountants and the securities firms day in and day out. These investors have long memories and punish accounting or securities firms who breach this professional reputation.

Nonetheless, breakdowns in the functioning of this "objective" private bonding role occurred in many firms in many of our sample countries—including Korea.

There is anecdotal evidence that the stock exchanges in many countries have tilted towards the side of issuing firms. In the United States, a series of suits brought by the attorney general of the State of New York in 2002–3 against Wall Street firms accused of kickbacks and misleading advice were settled when the firms paid large penalties and several individuals were prosecuted criminally. The Securities and Exchange Commission fined Deutsche Asset Management, a subsidiary of Deutsche Bank, $750,000 for a "disclosure lapse" over its voting of proxies at the 2002 merger of Hewlett-Packard and Compaq, a transaction in which the parent firm's investment-banking arm was an advisor. "Regulators found that Deutsche—which switched 17 million votes at the last minute to favor the deal—had failed to tell clients about its parent bank's lucrative ties to HP."[35]

Similar doubts about the corporate governance integrity of the exchanges surfaced in September 2003 when the chairman of the New York Stock Exchange revealed his deferred compensation of $139.5 million, awarded by a compensation committee that he had hand-picked, representing firms that were nominally "regulated" by the NYSE.[36]

In accounting, as well as finance and the exchanges, global consolidation in the audit and accounting industry presented the Big Six accounting firms with a structural conflict of interest. The accounting and audit industry went through a rapid consolidation during the latter half of the 1980s and all through the 1990s. The Big Six (soon to become the Big Five, and then the Big Four in 2001) firms competed to absorb firms in all the major developed economies, assembling a network of global firms.[37] Interviews with accounting professionals suggest that the Big Five doubled their market share in the countries in this sample between 1980 and 2000. They aggressively marketed not only their accounting and audit skills, but particularly their consulting expertise in a wide range of financial specialties,

[35] Davis Global Advisors, "Conflict Patrol," *Global Proxy Watch*, September 5, 2003, 2.

[36] "The NYSE describes itself as 'a private entity with a public purpose.' But it operates like a wholly owned subsidiary of Wall Street. It is a self-perpetuating entity that is neither accountable through the political process nor the market. That is the worst of both worlds for its most important constituency, the investor community." Nell Minow, "When Does a Pay Package Become Too Outrageous?" *Chicago Tribune*, September 14, 2003.

[37] The Big Five consisted of Arthur Andersen, Price Waterhouse Coopers, Deloitte Touche Tohmatsu, Ernst & Young, and KPMG Peat Marwick. Andersen crashed with the Enron debacle.

including tax management, information systems, personnel policies, and risk management.[38]

The accounting firms in the United States understood well the political framework of their business. They lobbied extensively against efforts by the SEC in the 1990s to separate consulting from accounting. Passage of Sarbanes-Oxley in 2002 represented a political defeat for them—but implementation remains to be determined. In any case, the ambiguous role of the reputational intermediaries with regard to enhanced MSPs—sometimes in favor, sometimes against—does not comport with the predictions of the investor model, and points to a possible alignment of interest between these firms and managers, rather than on the side of blockholders, diffuse investor-owners, or workers at large. We explore these politics in more detail in the following two chapters.

THE IFOS WEIGH IN

The more elaborate versions of the investor model predict that international financial institutions (IFOs) also play a role in lobbying for enhanced shareholder protections.

How can international financial institutions influence policy outputs on corporate governance, which remain, still, policies set at the nation-state level? This influence may come from several sources: funding and widely publishing economic research on corporate governance, embracing the notion of deep capital markets as a concomitant of economic growth, arm-twisting national regulatory

---

[38] As the Big Five consolidated around the globe, the value of the global partnerships' professional franchise became hostage to the often mixed quality of these newly acquired country practices. All of the Big Five found themselves embroiled in extensive and expensive lawsuits on three continents—North America, Europe, and Asia—during the 1990s, accused of sloppy accounting and poor auditing. This triggered a decade-long struggle by the Big Five to institute uniform internal professional discipline throughout their global practices, and to create common accounting systems, audit procedures, and interpretations of standards inside their firms, and a common accounting and audit framework by authorities on a country level.

In the late 1980s, the accountancy profession began a 10-year effort to forge a set of global accounting and audit standards, in close cooperation with international financial organizations. The consolidating Big Five firms, who played a dominant role in both the International Accounting Standards Board and International Federation of Accountants, spearheaded this effort. In 1995 the IASC and International Organization of Securities Commissions agreed on a work plan whereby the IASC would create a set of core accounting standards that would be acceptable for cross-border capital raising. The IASC was reorganized in May 2000 with a new constitution and regulatory structure that enhanced its autonomy in setting accounting standards. Through IFAC, the Big Five also began work on a common set of auditing practices, paralleling these firms' internal efforts to forge a consistent set of professional practices within their global networks. IFAC was reorganized in early 2000 to enhance its autonomy in setting international standards for auditing (ISA) procedures.

For example, working through IFAC, the Big Five hammered out a collective agreement on the language they would use in their audit opinion letters for clients. This agreement specified the precise language used in these letters, including an explicit description of the differences between IAS and country-level accounting standards. This language explicitly alerted investors that audited figures from "nonstandard" countries do not conform to global standards. This program, termed the Legends Program, was first introduced in four East Asian countries, Japan, Thailand, Indonesia, and—where it prominently figured—Korea.

authorities to adopt governance reforms, and imposing microeconomic governance reforms as part of the quid pro quo of macroeconomic bailouts. This kind of influence has been modeled analytically as "epistemic"[39] and as "soft power."[40] It is noted particularly by the economic sociologists interested in "scripts"—the idea that countries conform to norms of appropriate behavior, rather than purely instrumental or "consequentialist" behavior.[41]

There is considerable evidence supporting the prediction of cheerleading by the IFOs, through promoting research on the economic benefits of enhanced shareholder protections. For example, the World Bank and OECD jointly created the Global Corporate Governance Forum (GCGF) that explicitly funded research and seminars in regional emerging markets touting the benefits of these reforms and proposing specific policy solutions.[42] But there is little evidence of arm-twisting or imposing corporate governance quid pro quos by the IFOs in their direct dealings with national authorities.

For example, in the wake of the Asian financial crisis, the IMF was criticized for attempts at microeconomic reformism (including corporate governance) and encouraged to "stick to the adjustment basics." Many of the corporate governance reforms adopted by the Korean government after the crisis were attributed to pressure from the IMF, but that may have been a convenient rationale used by the Kim Dae Jung government to justify restraints on the chaebol that it desired for political reasons.[43]

COVARIANCE OF CONCENTRATION AND INVESTOR PROTECTIONS

The overall prediction of the investor model connects the basic cause of the preferences of portfolio investors with the effect of enhanced governance by firms. The end result of this connection should be a high covariance between the weight of portfolio investors in each market—particularly foreign portfolio investors—and the supply of enhanced shareholder protections by that market.

---

[39] Emanuel Adler and Peter Haas, "Conclusion: Epistemic Communities, World Order, and the Creation of a Reflective Research Program," *International Organization* 46 (1992): 367–90; Peter Haas, "Introduction: Epistemic Communities and International Policy Coordination," *International Organization* 46 (1992): 367–90.

[40] Joseph S. Nye, *Soft Power: The Means to Success in World Politics* (New York: Public Affairs Press, 2004).

[41] March and Olsen 1998.

[42] In language echoing the demand for regulation model, the GCGF argues, "In an increasingly globalized economy, firms need to tap domestic and international capital markets for investment. But capital providers have choice—and the quality of corporate governance is increasingly becoming a criterion for investment and lending. Expanding and deepening the capital pool for developing and transition economies requires full attention to corporate governance standards. This sets the imperative for reform." Global Corporate Governance Forum, "Mission Statement and Charter," May 2002, http://www.gcgf.org/about.htm.

[43] Stephan Haggard, *The Political Economy of the Asian Financial Crisis* (Washington, D.C.: Institute for International Economics, 2000); Stephan Haggard, Wonhyuk Lim, and Euysung Kim, *Economic Crisis and Corporate Restructuring in Korea: Reforming the Chaebol* (Cambridge: Cambridge Univesity Press, 2003).

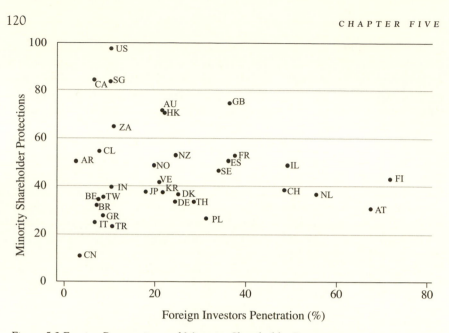

Figure 5.2 Foreign Penetration and Minority Shareholder Protections

Our country sample provides no significant positive correlation between foreign portfolio penetration of equity markets and the level of minority shareholder protections, as shown by the scatter plot in figure 5.2 (in which the correlation is −.08). This lack of correlation holds for the developed countries, the emerging countries, and the sample as a whole.

We do not have data on the penetration ratio of all *institutional* investors, including domestic investors, in each country market, but we do have data on the relative weight of retirement assets in each market.

We will explore this more thoroughly in chapter 7, on the transparency coalition; there is a positive correlation of .56 between the ratio of retirement assets to GDP in each country and the shareholder protections index for this sample, and a fitted OLS line suggests a statistically significant relationship for the sample, as indicated by figure 5.3. (See also appendix table A.12.)

BUT INVESTORS AREN'T THE ONLY PLAYERS

As discussed earlier in this chapter, there is ample evidence that pressures for enhanced minority shareholder protections are growing on the demand side; money flows toward firms and countries that provide such protections. And yet there is little evidence on the supply side that blockholders worked to change the system to provide these enhanced protections.

For several of the country cases developed below and in subsequent chapters, there is no paper trail of blockholders lobbying for enhanced protections for minority shareholders; if anything, there is more evidence of blockholders

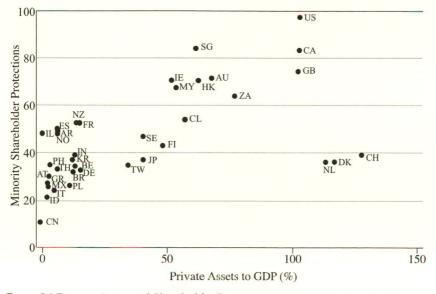

Figure 5.3 Pension Assets and Shareholder Protections

resisting these reforms. The private behavior of firms controlled by blockholders is, in the absence of regulatory changes, not what the private bonding argument would predict.

The investor model does capture something important: the vast expansion in investment funds, in the flow of money, the mobilization of many individual savers' accounts into increasingly global pension funds. These have an impact on the politics of corporate governance reform, but it is not well captured by the investor model. The basic idea of political pressure as a driver of public policy on corporate governance makes a great deal of sense. External investors do want enhanced minority protections, and will pay a premium or assign a discount accordingly. By the same token, some (but not all) blockholders will respond positively to this price signal.

The power of capital to mold corporate governance outcomes on both a country and international level is a widely held view. Much has been written about the "Washington consensus" concerning the neoliberal prescription of free markets, limited government, and deregulation. Competition among countries to satisfy capital is commonly invoked as the engine of global convergence in governance, echoing the global political triumph of liberal democracy and the "end of history" argument. As Hansman and Kraakman argue,

> A principal reason for convergence is a widespread normative consensus that corporate managers should act exclusively in the economic interests of shareholders, including non-controlling shareholders. This consensus on a shareholder-oriented model of the corporation results in part from the failure of alternative models of the corporation,

including the manager-oriented model that evolved in the U.S. in the 1950s and 1960s, the labor-oriented model that reached its apogee in German co-determination, and the state-oriented model that until recently was dominant in France and much of Asia. . . . Since the dominant corporate ideology of shareholder primacy is unlikely to be undone, its success represents that "end of history" for corporate law.[44]

In a globalized open economy, what Cheffins characterized as a "Darwinian victory of the U.S. model" will displace alternative approaches to corporate governance; what investors want, they will eventually get, or they will take their money elsewhere, across borders if need be, to find a set of governance practices that protect their investment from both agency and expropriation costs.[45]

This competition for capital was one of the principal rationales for a worldwide standard of good governance invoked in the preamble of the *Principles of Corporate Governance* issued by the OECD. "International flows of capital allow companies to access financing from a much larger pool of investors. If countries are to reap the full benefits of the global capital market, and if they are to attract long term 'patient' capital, corporate governance arrangements must be credible, and well understood across national borders."[46] The OECD principles explicitly connect the dots between capital mobility, governance discounts, and political outcomes concerning regulation.

Theorists of varying political colorations have noted the special power of capital in determining political outcomes.[47] Politicians are judged by the health of the economy. If investors at home are unhappy with policy, they stop investing or export their capital abroad, leading to recession and unhappy voters. If investors abroad (including domestic capital taken flight) are unhappy with policy, they assign a risk premium to investing at home, or simply don't come at all. No other group can have quite this direct an effect on the economy; thus the economic vote of investors counts greatly against the mass of votes in elections.

In this sense, the investor model puts minority shareholder protections in the same category as the ratings for government debt or fixed-income securities. International bond markets monitor governments' behavior in terms of fiscal balance and reporting; they assign a premium or discount thereupon. International investors also require high standards of reporting and honoring of instruments such as covenants from private issuers of bonds; they assign a premium or discount thereupon. These hard market realities of investors' preferences for government and firms' bonds are indeed "credible, and well understood across borders," as the OECD report suggests, and corporate governance practices are becoming another hard reality that countries must deal with.

---

[44] Hansmann and Kraakman 2000, 1.

[45] Cheffins 2002a.

[46] *OECD Principles of Corporate Governance* (Washington, D.C.: OECD, 1999), 9; see also *OECD Principles of Corporate Governance*, 2004, found at http://www.oecd.org/dataoecd/32/18/ 31557724.pdf.

[47] Charles E. Lindblom, *Politics and Markets: The World's Political Economic Systems* (New York: Basic Books, 1977).

There are, however, many ways to "deal with" global market expectations, including expectations regarding corporate governance, as there are many ways to deal with global bond markets. Political leaders around the world have struggled to convince domestic political forces to accept the sacrifices required by international bond markets; not surprisingly, it is often a very hard sell.

Analytic Narrative

KOREA: CHANGING INSTITUTIONS, SHIFTING PREFERENCES

Korea illustrates the speed with which a country can shift governance patterns if both preferences and political institutions are changing quickly. Institutional change alters the political balance. It empowers some groups and constrains others. Over the past decades Korea has gone from military dictatorship, to modified authoritarianism, to constitutional democracy: from presidential rule by decree in the 1950s, to the generals' junta of the 1960s and 1970s, through the democratic elections in the 1990s of Kim Young Sam, Kim Dae Jung, and Rho Moo Hyun during the last decade. It has shifted from hard authoritarian—not totalitarian, but strong military rule—to moderate authoritarian, with limited freedoms, and some autonomy for civil society especially in the economy, to transitional democracy, with free elections, competitive political parties, and a change of leadership from one party to another, the classic indicator of true democratization.

Over these same years, Korea's corporate governance system has also been dramatically transformed, as has the ownership pattern of listed firms. Korea has gone from 100 percent blockholder control with effectively zero shareholder protections, to a concentration rate of 32 percent in 2000, which is lower than the mean of our country sample as a whole, and a shareholder protections index of 37, close to the sample mean.[48]

The two transformations are fused: Korea began as a classical example of oligarchic dominance by owner-blockholders in early industrialization, drawing on close connections to authoritarian political power to obtain what they wanted in many policy arenas, from corporate governance regulation, to labor, lending, sheltered trade laws, and so on. As the scale of firms stretched the ability of founders' capital and retained earnings to fund growth, the owners and managers then began to selectively extend minority shareholder protections to outside investors, principally global portfolio investors, in a slow-motion version of the investor model. But then in the 1990s, Korean politics changed dramatically, giving voice to other interests and resulting in altered political power alignments. Labor unions, smaller businesses, civil servants—a coalition of groups previously excluded from political power—were able to demand accountability from the

---

[48] This figure underestimates the true current level of shareholder protections in Korea, since many of Korea's reforms are so recent that they are not yet reflected in the underlying indices that we and La Porta et al. used, especially the accounting and disclosure index. As noted above, Korea's shareholder reforms were adopted rapidly in a narrow window of time in the aftermath of the Asian financial crisis.

government. Through the government, they demanded accountability from firms as well, specifically the chaebol firms dominated by owner-blockholders in league with professional managers. The resulting triumphant coalition (at least temporarily) of Korean domestic actors imposed a set of corporate governance reforms on the chaebol firms by fiat, by political choice—not by market adjustment, not by a mutual "good-governance deal" between owners and outside investors, but by executive and legislative writ.

A governance policy that took almost 150 years in the United Kingdom and at least a century in the United States to develop, Korea compressed into four decades. Korea's dramatic economic growth since 1960 compressed into a mere 40 years many of the shifting preferences and governance changes that required far longer to develop in other countries.

The Korean trajectory shows vividly how political power and preferences interact. Constitutional change altered political power in ways that had bearing on government policy and regulation of great consequence for corporate governance. Governance issues were by no means the sole or primary driver of change—but they had some connection to it: the demand for democratization was fueled in part by resentment toward the privileged insiders of the chaebol system and its cozy connection to the authoritarian regime.

The Korean case shows the importance of tension between labor and capital—or at least a part of labor and part of capital—in shaping outcomes in corporate governance. But the coalitional pattern is more complex and more fluid over time than either the investor or labor model conveys. We use it as our first country case because it so graphically shows the consequences of political change on governance outcomes.

From Oligarchy to the Investor Model? The Korea case begins in the 1960s as a clear-cut example of oligarchy. Chung Ju Yung of Hyundai, Lee Byung Chul of Samsung, Koo In Hwoi of Lucky-Goldstar (LG), and Kim Woo Choong of Daewoo were the founders of the largest chaebol. They were in a sense the Andrew Carnegies and John D. Rockefellers of Korea's rapid industrialization, an analogy they frequently made themselves. They built their initial fortunes in the heavy manufacturing sectors that powered Korea's rapid economic growth in the 1950s and 1960s—shipbuilding, transportation, and chemicals—and they did so with ample funding through "directed lending" by Korea's government-controlled banking system (rather than through equity markets). Below them in the corporate food-chain were dozens of other lesser chaebol, also created by a founder-entrepreneur who similarly called the shots.

Chaebol owners and Korea's ruling generals (most notably Park Chung Hee) struck a political bargain that left the chaebol blockholder a free hand in most issues of firm management, including corporate governance. Political repression ensured that managers and workers were effectively excluded from voice in this management—as were smaller capitalists, regional interests, and religious and other groups. Foreign entry was severely restricted; antitrust protection of domestic competition was nonexistent. The chaebol owners called all corporate governance shots, such as there were; with concentrated ownership and few minority shareholders, either domestic or foreign, the chaebol founders had enormous latitude.

As a result, Korea's blockholder concentration ratio of listed firms was high in the 1980s and much of the 1990s, close to 80 percent. Chaebol family owners controlled a horizontal network of firms in diverse industries through a classic pyramid structure. These networks functioned like the original Japanese *zaibatsu* system, on which it was modeled, rather than the current Japanese *keiretsu* system of interlocking networks without a clear controlling party. Indeed, the Chinese character compounds in the Korean language for *chaebol* are the Japanese kanji compounds for *zaibatsu*, not *keiretsu*.

The chaebol played a key role in Korea's rapid economic growth, when Korea was one of the four Asian tigers. The Federation of Korean Industry (FKI) served as a classic instrument of top-down economic planning; it was an intermediary organization between the government and blockholders, not a "peak bargaining organization" with which business engaged labor unions. Moreover, the instructions went generally one-way, from ministry to firm; the FKI was largely staffed by former bureaucrats and retired military officers.

The chaebol owners cooperated with Korea's military government, and the development script transmitted by the FKI, by providing high levels of fixed investment and aggressive exports, in return for rents in the form of preferential capital access and protection from product-market competition.

As a function of increasing scale and technical complexity—"Chandler variables"—the great chaebol owners began to rely more and more on the skills of professional managers, just like prototypical oligarchs in other industrial histories, and struck an alignment of convenience with Korea's professional classes. During Korea's slow-motion political democratization, the chaebol blockholders gradually brought a cadre of professional managers and former government officials "into the tent." The criteria for hiring and firing remained opaque; top chaebol managers were hand-picked by the chaebol chairman's office, to which they remained beholden, rather than by the board of directors.[49]

As a result, Korea experienced, however briefly, a transition from initial owner blockholding to the early managerial pattern—blockholders who hire professional managers. With the authoritarian politics, other voices could be excluded. Blockholders and managers were thus on the same side of a class divide, clashing with unions, often violently.

As Korea began its process of democratization under Rho Tae Woo, the governance pattern shifted. Chaebol blockholders gradually wrested control of the FKI away from the state, to the point that by the late 1990s the FKI was known as the "private club" of the top six chaebol families—to the exclusion of the interests of the private blockholders of the so-called "6 to 66 chaebol," as well as the interests of new entrepreneurs.

[49] Anecdotal evidence suggests that incompetent managers were rarely left in place long, unless they happened to be sons or other relatives of the founder-chairman.

Concentration fell somewhat during this period, but not because of a good-governance deal with external investors; the weight of family-controlled chaebol firms on the Korean Stock Exchange (KSE) was reduced by several share issues by big SOEs such as Pohang Iron and Steel, and by an influx of foreign portfolio investors who viewed Korea—despite numerous barriers to direct investment—as one of Asia's "hottest emerging markets." These foreign investors generally relied on an implicit sovereign risk guarantee from "Korea Inc." rather than financial transparency or shareholder protections. Far from striking a good-governance deal with the chaebol owners, who in any case could obtain most of their needed external funding from the domestic banking sector, the foreign port-folio investors accepted the slim shareholder protections extended by the chae-bol oligarchs as the price of admission to a high-growth market opportunity, on the hope that a rising Korean GDP tide would lift all ships, including theirs. Lit-tle change took place in terms of minority shareholder protections during the 1980s and most of the 1990s.

Thus, complete oligarchic dominance was modified to allow some external shareholder participation, and the state receded as a controlling force. This was not a full shift to the diffusion model, however, as minority shareholders remained subservient to blockholding concentration, and the managers, while growing in importance, remained monitored by blockholders.

There were several reasons for the shallow effect of this alignment on gover-nance outcomes. First, the chaebol blockholders did not need to bend to the gov-ernance demands of external investors in order to fund their growth. Throughout the 1980s and 1990s, they managed to retain loan funding from the domestic banking sector (taking advantage, among other things, of both the "too big to fail" syndrome and systematic corruption). The chaebol also acquired their own financial intermediaries, the so-called merchant banks, also known as "nonbank financial intermediaries." The NBFIs channeled funds from domestic savings and foreign capital markets into the chaebol to finance the high levels of fixed investment that drove the economy.

By the second half of the 1990s, Korea's financial sector had bifurcated, with the chaebol-controlled NBFIs' assets rivaling those of the state-controlled com-mercial banking sector. Almost all of the NBFIs became insolvent during the Asian financial crisis in 1997–98, and 33 were closed in the wake of the crisis. The unhedged foreign exchange liabilities of these NBFIs were one of the prime causes of the crisis in the first place.

Second, the highly concentrated nature of Korean industry obviated the path of buying out other founder-owners in the same industry during its consolidation phase, the process that diluted the blockholdings of founder-blockholders in the United States and Europe, as chronicled by Alfred Chandler. Barriers to entry, direct bank lending, and other forms of state favoritism had allowed the chaebol to dominate the economic landscape without a lot of competitors.

Third, the sheer size of the chaebol, as well as their horizontal diversification, reduced the incentives of the founder-blockholders to engage in a good-governance deal of any kind with external investors. By the second generation, these families were extremely wealthy, with ample funds at their disposal even without selling down their blockholdings. They may also have acquired the "psychic income" of sustained blockholding—a nonmonetary private benefit of control—like the Wallenbergs in Sweden.

Korean Struggles over Job Security and Governance. During the 1990s Korea's labor unions were emerging from decades of repression by the state and took an increasingly assertive voice in national politics—during roughly the same period that the chaebol blockholders and foreign investors were striking their own halting accommodation over minority shareholder protections. The chaebol owners were tough customers on both counts.

As happened in Europe, notably Germany, concentrated industrial ownership helped generate concentrated labor organizations, intensified further by the political anger at collaboration between the chaebol owners and the generals' junta. The history of business-labor relations in Korea between 1960 and 2000 was one of harsh conflict punctuated by temporary bargains. The pattern of wage gains, which is supposed to be smooth in classic corporatist countries, was characterized by long periods of suppression punctuated by short bursts of rapid growth.

As unions asserted their right to exist and conducted a series of massive strikes in the 1980s (despite official repression), the chaebol owners worked out a temporary bargain with organized labor. The chaebol were tacitly allowed to extract private benefits of control in exchange for a no-layoff policy at the big firms, a policy that was reflected in labor laws that made layoffs difficult and expensive. Rapid economic growth (despite lagging labor productivity), restrictive competition policy, and barriers to foreign entry insulated this convenient arrangement from the chill winds of market forces. This was a highly unstable arrangement: there were few institutional arrangements involving both owners and workers to stabilize this agreement, given the backdrop of deep mutual distrust.

As Korea democratized under Kim Young Sam and then Kim Dae Jung, government policy shifted against the closed world of the chaebol. A change in political institutions led to a change in power relations, in turn causing a shift in policy, which in turn led to changing patterns of corporate governance.

The chaebol were widely portrayed as complicit with the generals during the long years of repression. Elections brought to power governments reflecting voter concerns with corruption and efficiency. There was substantial political tension between Kim Dae Jung and his center-left support base and the chaebol families, especially the Daewoo owners, as well as the attempt by the Chung family to use their control of Hyundai to enter Korean electoral politics.

During the 1990s, with constant media attention and a president in the Blue House seeking to consolidate a new political power base, many of the special deals between the chaebol and the banking sector became public. Instances of private benefits of control, outright asset stripping, and high-profile feuds between second-generation members of the chaebol family kept corporate governance on the front pages.

In parallel with movement towards democratization in the 1990s, Korea adopted a policy of privatizing (or corporatizing) SOE utilities and state-sponsored heavy industrial firms such as Pohang Iron and Steel, Korea Electric Power (KEPCO), Korea Telecom, and Korea Tobacco. These firms accounted for a growing percentage of the total market capitalization of the Korea Stock Exchange, driving the percentage weight of blockholder-controlled chaebol down. SOE SIPOs were particular favorites of foreign portfolio investors wanting to buy into the "Korean Miracle" (or simply diversify their global portfolio) but who continued to doubt the chaebol blockholders' commitment to minority shareholder protections. Although equally opaque and dominated by government objectives, at least these firms had an implicit sovereign guarantee as part of Korea Inc.; no one believed the Korean government would openly loot Pohang or KEPCO, much less allow them to go down the drain.

Thus, privatization increased shareholding, and open politics undermined the special deals with chaebol families. At the same time, blockholders used the Asian financial crisis to attack employee protection policies, arguing that the government had to eliminate the job protections as a matter of national emergency. Once these rules were lifted by executive fiat, they engaged in rapid and massive layoffs.

Although the first move in Korea's financial crisis went to the chaebol, this was quickly followed by a string of corporate governance reforms passed by a new government led by Kim Dae Jung, elected during the financial crisis. Kim had strong support from all the groups left out of the previous regimes—labor unions, regional groups from Cholla, small owners excluded from the chaebol system, civil servants, reformers of various kinds, grouped within Kim's reformist Millennium Democracy Party. The coalition of support resonates with those found in other countries.

Korea's corporate governance reforms were imposed on the chaebol by changes in political institutions, which allowed these new forces to upset the governance policies that had been in place for decades. The Millennium Democracy Party had strong ties to organized labor, and the political language of its governance reforms was initially tinged with "labor versus capital" rhetoric. But there was a solid cross-class coalition in favor of punishing the great chaebol, whose moral hazard flaws had been revealed by the crisis, and the costs of which were ultimately borne by the employees and the taxpayers—the former losing their jobs, the latter picking up the vast tab for bailing out the NBFIs and propping up the tottering chaebol after 1998. Korea's shifting political institutions thus provided an opportunity for a voice for actors with preferences for shareholder protections—or who opposed the preferences of the chaebol blockholders.

Close process-tracing of the burst of reforms in Korean corporate governance institutions in 1998 indicates that these reforms were adopted by the newly elected Kim Dae Jung government—with a thin veneer of consultation with the blockholders, but essentially imposed upon them by political choices of the governmental process. This was not a private bargain between owners and external investors, as a simple version of the investor model would predict, but politically determined by rules and regulations. In the importance of formal rules, it resembles, in a much shortened time period, the process in the United States.

In 1998 Korea's newly launched Financial Supervisory Commission (FSC)— which was struggling to deal with foreign skepticism about Korea's country risk premium—radically overhauled Korean Financial Accounting Standards (KFAS) to bring them in line with the IAS. External auditors were made mandatory for use by listed firms. An independent institution for accounting standards, the Korean Accounting Standards Board (KASB), was created in June 1999, separating it from the Ministry of Finance and Economy.[50]

At the same time, new regulations were written to require detailed disclosure of insider financial transactions between chaebol blockholders and public firms. Korea's informal institutions of third-party financial analysis—consisting of the Seoul affiliates of international securities firms—went into overdrive as a result of better financial disclosure and more reliable accounting data, as well as a panicked concern by global investors that they had miscalculated the underlying business risk in Korea and overestimated the good-faith corporate governance of the chaebol owners—along with a sinking realization that the implicit state guarantee by Korea Inc. did not extend to all foreign investors in all firms.

In 1998 the Kim Dae Jung government moved to force the chaebol to replace their family-dominated boards, which generally rubber-stamped the orders of the founding blockholders, with increasing numbers of NEDs. The top five chaebol of Hyundai, Samsung, Lucky-Goldstar (LG), Sunkyong (SK), and Daewoo (now bankrupt) were the special target of these reforms.[51] These firms were required to obtain 50 percent of their directors from outside, with a strict definition of independence.

At the same time, the legal obstacles to filing a derivative suit against a firm were reduced, from 1 percent to .01 percent of the stockholding, which made it much easier for small shareholders to bring such suits. A flurry of derivative suits was filed, of which several were won by the plaintiffs. Efforts to make class action suits easier were rejected by the National Assembly, allegedly due to counterlobbying by the chaebol.

Similarly, Korean regulations that limited hostile takeovers by capping such acquisitions at 10 percent of the target firm were removed. The requirement to obtain government approval for merger and acquisition (M&A) transactions was eliminated, and voting procedures and tendering rules were changed to enhance the protection of minority shareholders. Nonetheless, there have been no hostile takeovers, even in the wake of the financial crisis in 1997–98.

Some changes in Korean regulations made it easier to use stock options, but in actual practice their use remained low; as a result the ratio of performance-based

[50] Il-Sup Kim, "Financial Crisis and Its Impact on the Accounting System in Korea," Korea Accounting Standards Board Manuscript, 2000.

[51] All of these firms were controlled by their founding blockholders or their immediate families. These founder-blockholders include Chung Ju Yung of Hyundai, Lee Byung Chul of Samsung, Koo In Hwoi of LG, and Kim Woo Choong of Daewoo (now a fugitive).

compensation to total compensation in Korea is well below the mean. Senior chaebol managers had been promoted and rotated largely within the group during the 1980s and 1990s, but there were many anecdotes of increasing managerial mobility in the aftermath of the crisis, prompted by a string of crises, new foreign investment, and the appearance of international managerial placement (aka headhunter) firms.

In parallel with its governance reforms, the Korean state stage-managed a series of corporate governance deliberation commissions: one managed by the Ministry of Finance and Economy (MOFE) and the Financial Services Authority (FSA), which endorsed the 1998 reforms despite vehement opposition by chaebol representatives, and another managed by the Ministry of Justice, which hired a team of technical professionals from international accounting, law, and securities firms to come up with a detailed series of regulatory reforms for Korea in line with global governance standards.

But there were limits to these corporate governance reforms, limits traceable to the preferences of the underlying political coalition, which supported the government's efforts to impose enhanced MSPs from above. Push came to shove when many of the overextended chaebol firms attempted to renegotiate their loans with Korean banks, since foreign investors had largely headed for the exits and the Korean Stock Exchange had cratered in 1998. The government effectively nationalized most of the Korean banks during the financial crisis. But rather than go through liquidation—which would have entailed even more massive layoffs—the vast majority of the chaebol remained on "life support" loans from the FSA through government-controlled banks, which in turn meant they were effectively under the thumb of the Ministry of Finance. During a long, troubled work-out period, the Korean state attempted to reform these enterprises while minimizing layoffs; many a compromise was struck on corporate governance principles when the consequence of strict fidelity would have been loss of jobs by the well-organized—and politically militant—labor unions. Korean workers cared about corporate governance, but they cared about their jobs even more.

This is a crucial lesson of the Korean case. The foreign-investor-driven model of governance reform, no matter what the asset class, bond or equity, has a thin domestic political base. The greater mass of Korean citizens stands to benefit little from these reforms, which rebound largely to foreign investors. Koreans do not have the pension savings that could go into the reorganized firms. Thus the case lacks one of the key components of the transparency coalition—the uniting of workers with pension funds to protect with the mass of small external shareholders. The reasons have to do with prior decisions taken in the areas of pension funding and, to a lesser degree, the role of financial intermediaries in Korea. We treat this issue in more detail in chapter 7, but to keep the Korea case an integrated whole, we signal the story here.

Although the data in table 5.3 shows that Korean institutional investors have accumulated almost $400 billion in assets, the equity portion of these holdings is only about 10 percent. South Korea's total pension assets as a percentage of GDP are about 13 percent, well below the mean for OECD and developing countries in our sample. Moreover, this asset figure masks the severely underfunded nature of the Seoul governments' pension obligations to its citizens.

Many Korean workers lost their company pension benefits when their employers went bankrupt during the financial crisis; severance benefits from the chaebol firms were funded from current operations, rather than funded with external financial assets. When these firms went under, workers' claims on the firms' future cash flow were written down, along with those of stockholders and external lenders. Failed or tottering firms acquired by foreign direct investors also wrote down or eliminated entirely much of their pension obligations to workers.

Compounding this firm-specific loss, many workers' individually funded pension plans were devastated by huge losses in the postcrisis period. Several pension funds were bankrupted by ill-advised investments in equity markets urged on them by the finance ministries. In one notable case, several private pension funds made large purchases of securities in Daewoo group companies as part of a government-organized bailout of the struggling firm, a bailout that ultimately failed, wiping out several of the pension funds.

Adding fiscal insult to these economic injuries, the Korean government was so burdened by the mammoth cost of the bailout that its ability to cushion workers' personal losses with a national welfare safety net was severely limited. The Korean government, and every Korean taxpayer by implication, had become an expropriated minority shareholder in the failed chaebol.

As a result, Korean workers and, more broadly, Korean voters widely attributed these losses to moral hazard failures in the corporate governance of chaebol firms—a sentiment echoed by the Kim Dae Jung government as it pushed through these reforms over the objections of the chaebol blockholders. This gave many of Korea's corporate governance reforms a punitive tone. The measures often appeared to be adopted more to damage the chaebol blockholders than to enhance the interests of minority shareholders—in which Korean workers often had little remaining positive stake, having incurred a negative liability instead. Minority shareholders meant "foreign" shareholders, not Koreans themselves. Thus in Korea, transparency reforms arrived in a political context that mixed labor power elements and cross-class coalitional features but very little of an investor model.[52]

[52] Sea-Jin Chang and Jung-Ho Kim, "The Chaebol Reforms," paper presented at the Joint International Conference of the Weatherhead Center for International Affairs and Korea University, March 2000, in Cambridge, Massachusetts; Lee-Jay Cho and Yoon-Hyung Kim, eds., *Korea's Choices in Emerging Global Competition and Cooperation* (Seoul: Korea Development Institute, 1998); Cho 2000; Yoon-Je Cho and Joon Kyung Kim, *Credit Policies and the Industrialization of Korea* (Seoul: Korea Development Institute, 1997); Seong-Min Yoo, "Corporate Restructuring in Korea: Policy Issues before and during the Crisis," Korea Development Institute Working Paper No. 9903, 1999; Seong-Min Yoo, "Evolution of Government-Business Interface in Korea: Progress to Date and Reform Agenda Ahead," Korea Development Institute Working Paper No. 9711, 1997; Seong-Min Yoo and Young-Jae Lin, "Big Business in Korea: New Learning and Policy Issues," Korea Development Institute Working Paper No. 9901, 1999; Youngmo Yoon, "Chaebol Reform: The Missing Agenda in 'Corporate Governance,'" paper presented to the Conference on Corporate Governance in Asia: A Comparative Perspective, March 3–5, 1999, Seoul.

SECTION 2: WORKERS DOMINATE OWNERS AND MANAGERS

The Labor Power Model

The focus of finance theory on agency costs and investors neglects other players in the firm, as well as other players in the political system—the employees. We turn next to what happens when the other side of the coalitional alignment of owners plus managers versus workers wins. The logic of the investor model suggests the possibility of class conflict on issues of governance: workers defend their interests by resisting the goals of owners. But in the labor power model, workers have different interests, different ideas, and different institutions (parties and trade unions) with which to influence policy. Workers in this model are far from passive observers of blockholder and investor arrangements; they are active players inside the firm and in the political system at large.

The counterpart to the investor model is the same cleavage with the opposite outcome: In the investor model, governance patterns are shaped by the political victory of the capital. In the labor model, the workers prevail. The investor model presumes what capital wants, capital gets, and this is minority shareholder protection. The labor model assumes workers fight for income, job protection, and other goals, and that they regard the highly competitive aspects of a diffusion model to be inimical to those goals. To the extent they succeed, their policy goals become law and regulation, and thus structure corporate governance.

PREFERENCES AND POLITICAL INFLUENCE

In democracies, workers vote; as regulations are made by political systems, voter preferences need to be integrated into a model of policy outcomes. Workers have two forms of power to bring to bear on the governance issues: market power (the ability to withhold work through a strike, or slowdown) and political power. These can be potent forces. We need to think about workers' preferences and how they use their forms of power to get them. Labor influence and left versus right political cleavage has been examined to explain a variety of outcomes in the field of political economy, from trade to social welfare.[53]

Workers compete with owners for income share, directly in wages, indirectly in taxes and social welfare. The labor model assumes workers also have different preferences than owners in terms of corporate governance. They favor corporate governance practices that will preserve jobs and maximize labor's share of the firm's income, even at the expense of shareholder value.

This is the point of departure of the labor-left argument that purports to explain variations in minority shareholder protections and concentration. Mark Roe calls this the "Social Democracy model," after the political party most noted

---

[53] On the Philips curve trade-offs, see Douglas A. Hibbs Jr., "Political Parties and Macroeconomic Policy," *American Political Science Review* 71 (1977): 1467–87; Hibbs, "Industrial Conflict in Advanced Industrial Societies," *American Political Science Review* 70 (1976): 1033–58; Garrett and Lange 1996.

for articulating workers' goals in the twentieth century.[54] We find the label somewhat confusing because social democratic parties are coalitions, not purely labor in composition—a point to which we return in looking at cross-class coalitions in the next chapter. We prefer to use the term *labor power model*, and reserve the term *social democratic* to political movements, one of whose components is labor. The labor power model argues that corporate governance outcomes are driven by electoral outcomes, and assumes labor is closely aligned with the political left. The more politics tilts to the left, the less we observe shareholder diffusion.

According to this model, two mechanisms sustain ownership concentration. The first mechanism is the impact of left power on the economic situation of the firm. Left strength gives voice to claims on the firm in addition to those of shareholders. Workers seek job security and push for laws that make it difficult to discharge employees; they seek a greater income share of the firms' profits, so they push for equalizing income taxes and policies of wage compression; they want social insurance and so push for health care, unemployment and disability insurance; they want stability and push for laws that make it difficult to close factories. Faced with pressures from stakeholders influenced by labor power, blockholders will resist diffusion of ownership. Blockholders seek to retain their leverage in the boardroom to resist labor-driven political pressures on the firm. Outside minority investors also shy away from this system. Blockholding is the result.

The second mechanism from labor power to blockholding passes through the mechanism of minority shareholder protections. Left political parties are assumed to oppose shareholder rights in order to maintain the blockholding relations that promote stability and other values they seek.[55]

We explore both mechanisms in this chapter. The power balance of left versus right should therefore be tested as an explanation of the provision of minority shareholder protection, in comparison with other predictors (legal family, for example, or the power of investors). At the same time, we should also explore the more systemic argument about left power: that it is not the provision of shareholder protections (or their absence) that causes blockholding, but the incentives for concentration produced by other policies.

Overall, the evidence supports the relevance of class conflict in influencing corporate governance outcomes, as the power balance between left and right does have a bearing on corporate policy and practice. But as we argue here and in the next two chapters, we think the channel of labor influences is cross-class coalitions.

Labor rarely wins elections on its own. It mobilizes the support of other groups, with other goals. In the most famous labor-oriented case, Sweden, the Social

[54] Roe 2003b. Roe is fully aware of the labels problem: he uses *social democratic* to stand for antimarket criticism, whatever its source. There is a valid distinction. Our goal is to explore the owner-labor tension suggested by various theories, and for that the distinction between broad social criticism of the market and labor power specifically is important.

[55] We note that this is not Roe's argument directly. Roe stresses the broader impact of left power on power relations in the boardroom and claims on the firm. He notes that quality of corporate law in its strict definition is not something labor necessarily opposes, and can be found where the Left is strong.

Democrats came to power in alliance with a farmers' party, the Agrarians. Groups with other goals—community and regional development, religious views, environment, nationalism—may join in these coalitions, but these other goals and their proponents are not strictly speaking from the side of labor. Labor and its claims are one part of these coalitions, an important, essential player, but still only one coalition partner.

We explore this problem and propose an alternative solution in the next two chapters. In this chapter, we lay out the labor argument and evaluate it in detail.

PREDICTIONS OF THE LABOR POWER MODEL

The labor power model predicts that where labor is politically strong, shareholder concentration is high.[56] The argument has two channels. One focuses on the supply of MSP. Where labor is weak, MSP will be high, and therefore shareholder concentration is low. The other channel focuses on capitalist economic policy: where labor is strong, competition and liberal economic patterns will be weak, and therefore blockholding will be high. Labor strength is in this way the driving force behind the politics that inhibits both MSP and competitive economic policies.

The prediction of a negative correlation between shareholder protections and concentration is similar to that of the investor model. In this regard it is in the same family as all the arguments that stress the importance of MSP, or more traditionally, the quality of corporate law, QCL, but it differs from the La Porta et al. school in the *cause* of legal quality. The labor power model places the root cause of high or low MSP not in deep historical legal families, but in country-level political processes.

We note that Roe's argumentation in his recent *Political Determinants of Corporate Governance* is not directly what we call the labor model. Many readers will associate it with him because he has been the most vigorous researcher looking at the power of labor. He certainly does argue that where labor is strong, blockholding is greater. But his channel of causality is not MSP. Blockholding happens because of other consequences of labor power besides MSP or QCL—labor rules, tax policy, and the like. We agree with him on this point, on the insufficiency of MSP, and on the greater power of political variables other than legal family. We try here to examine the labor model as an explanation of MSP and the capitalist structure variables. Our disagreement with Roe lies with the adequacy of labor power, of left-right cleavage, in explaining the politics that produce these policies. We think that MSP does matter (Roe does not wholly dissent), that capitalist structure variables matter (as does Roe), and that politics explains both. We think cross-class cleavages do better than left versus right in modeling those politics.

---

[56] Roe 2003b.

In this chapter we explore the left versus right evidence, continuing the mirror image of the discussion from the first part of the chapter.

The predictions of the model are

- A strong Left will produce lower levels of shareholder diffusion.
- A strong Left produces lower MSP.
- Both higher levels of employment protection and greater income equality correlate with lower levels of shareholder diffusion.

We test the predictions of the effects of left political power on governance outcomes for our sample countries with three indicators of labor political strength: the partisan composition of government, employment protections in law, and income inequality. These tests are similar in type to those employed by Roe in *Political Determinants of Corporate Governance*, but we repeat his tests with expanded and in some cases more recent data.

LEFT-RIGHT PARTISAN POLITICAL STRENGTH

Roe examined ownership concentration calculated by La Porta et al. at the 20 percent control threshold for 16 countries, regressed against an index of left-right political party control of governments between 1980 and 1991, based on data created by Cusack.[57] The correlation is weak at .305, though significant at $t = 3.62$, supporting one of the predictions of the labor model.

We believe that a political window of only a decade is brief when searching for the political roots of corporate governance decisions. We note that after 1991 a number of governments in this sample switched sides politically, including several countries that moved to the left. Margaret Thatcher and John Major were replaced by Tony Blair in 1997, Ronald Reagan and George H. W. Bush by Bill Clinton in 1993, Helmut Kohl by Gerhardt Schröder in 1998, and the Liberal Democrats in Japan by more complex coalition politics.

But at the same time, Italy moved to the right with Silvio Berlusconi (briefly in 1994 and again since 2001), as did Spain with José María Aznar (in 1996 and again since 2002), France with conservatives gaining control of both the presidency and the National Assembly in 2002, and the United States with George W. Bush winning the presidency in 2000 and the Republican Party controlling both houses of Congress in 2003.

Table 5.4 shows that Roe's results are not robust to model specification. If we take a larger political window, for instance, when we regress the same index of concentration/diffusion that Roe uses on government orientation for 1960–96, significance of the coefficient drops. We then repeat Roe's test using our data on concentration. Roe uses La Porta et al.'s index of diffusion for midsized firms, which is the inverse to our measure of concentration. Both measures are negatively correlated ($r = -.6208$). Even though the models return opposite signs on

[57] Thomas R. Cusack, "Partisan Politics and Public Spending: Changes in Public Spending in the Industrialized Democracies, 1955–1989," *Public Choice* 91 (1997): 375–95; and "Partisan Politics and Fiscal Policy," *Comparative Political Studies* 32 (1999): 464–86.

Table 5.4
Left-Right Political Strength and Concentration/Diffusion Tests

Dependent Variable	Roe Diffusion Index[a]	Roe Diffusion Index[a]	Ownership Concentration (G-S Data)	Minority Shareholder Protections
Partisanship[b] (1980–91)	0.28*** (0.09)			
Partisanship (1960–96)		0.29** (0.12)	−17.83* (9.30)	17.88 (11.12)
Constant	−0.60 (0.27)	−0.62 (0.39)	94.04*** (28.81)	−5.90 (34.44)
Observations	16	16	16	16
F(1,14)	10.46	5.53	3.67	2.58
Prob. > F	0.0060	0.0338	0.0630	0.1302
R^2	0.4276	0.2832	0.2077	0.1558
Adj. R^2	0.3867 0.2011	0.2320	0.1511	0.0955
Root MSE	9	0.22514	16.803	20.09

[a] Portion of midsized firms without a 20 percent blockholder in 1995.
[b] From Cusack.
*$p < .10$ **$p < .05$ ***$p < .01$.

the coefficients on partisanship, both seem to point in the same direction: concentration (diffusion) is higher (lower) under left governments. Yet the coefficient is weaker when the dependent variable is our measure of concentration, and significance levels are lower (see table 5.5).[58]

EMPLOYMENT SECURITY

Roe looks for other indicators of labor (in his vocabulary, social democratic) strength besides votes per se. First, he looks at employment security, regulations that restrict the firing of workers. Where labor is strong, employment protection should be high, he predicts. In the labor power channel of causality, that would increase claims on the firm, which minority shareholders would dislike; thus ownership would remain concentrated. Roe's empirical data support this expectation. The United States has the weakest employment protection and the highest diffusion; Italy has the strongest labor protections and is also among the countries with the least diffusion.[59]

Using our ownership data and the same index of employment security employed by Roe, we find a similar positive and significant correlation between concentration

[58] Note that our measure ranges from 0 to 100, while the diffusion measure is a 0 to 1 ratio. Note that results also vary when we use La Porta et al.'s measure of diffusion for the largest firms.
[59] Roe 2003b, 52, graph 6.2.

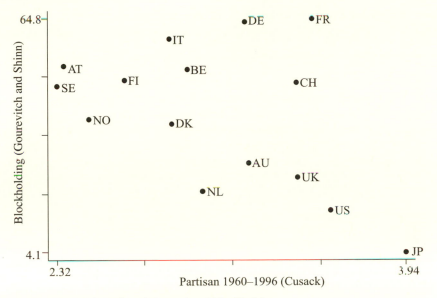

Figure 5.4 Left-Right Political Control and Blockholding

TABLE 5.5
Summary of Political Control and Concentration Tests

Data Set	Blockholding		Shareholder Protections	
Daa Set	t	R^2	t	R^2
Cusack 80-91, LLSV	3.62	0.446		
Cusack 60-96, LLSV	2.35	0.232		
Cusack 60-96, our data	−1.92	0.151	1.61	0.096

and employment security practices, with correlation of .69 and t = 3.6, as shown in figure 5.5.

Turning to the channel of shareholder protections, we find similarly strong negative relationship between our index of shareholder protections and job security practices, −.65 with t = 3.21. (See also appendix tables A.13 and A.14.)

These findings support the job security prediction of the labor power model. That is, where job security is strong, diffusion is weak and minority shareholder protections are weak. This does not prove, however, that job security is the direct result of labor partisan strength.

Job security does influence governance because investors are affected by it. While the presence of job security rules could reflect left power, it may also reflect cross-class coalitions.

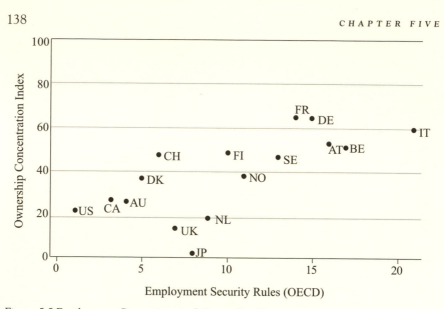

Figure 5.5 Employment Protections and Ownership Concentration

INCOME INEQUALITY

As a third possible indicator of labor power (or social democracy), Roe examined income inequality. The distribution of income reflects political choices concerning income tax, social welfare provisions, job promotion, training programs, and other policies that shape the distribution of income. Thus income inequality is another proxy for labor strength. Presumably, the stronger the left political control, the lower the income inequality (as measured by the traditional Gini coefficient). Roe finds that the greater the income equality (the lower the Gini coefficient), the more concentrated the ownership. Conversely, the more unequal the income (the higher the Gini coefficient), the more diffused is ownership.[60]

We repeat this test using the same country set and Gini coefficients, but with our ownership concentration data. In our test, the signs are the same as in Roe's results, but the statistical relationship is looser. Blockholding has a negative correlation of −.45 with income inequality (the higher the Gini coefficient), with $t = 1.83$, below the level of significance at .05. On the other hand, shareholder protections do have a positive correlation of .60 with income inequality, with $t = 2.73$, consistent with Roe's view. (See also appendix table A.15.)

RIGHT EMPHASIS, WRONG MODEL

We agree with the labor power model's stress on politics, the importance of party competition, and the importance of left versus right cleavages in the political system. As noted in the previous chapter, we share Roe's criticism of the legal family interpretation for neglecting the role of these political variables in shaping

---

[60] Roe 2003b, 54, graph 6.3.

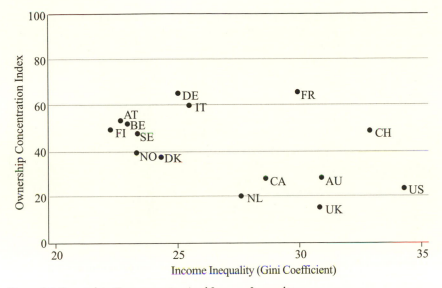

Figure 5.6 Ownership Concentration and Income Inequality

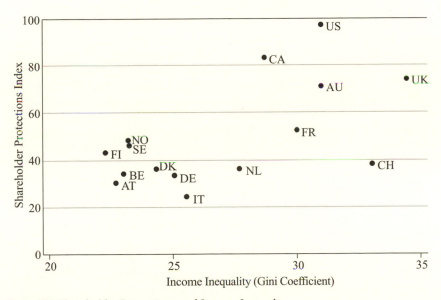

Figure 5.7 Shareholder Protections and Income Inequality

governance outcomes and the way law operates. We also share Roe's concern that MSP (and its component of quality corporate law [QCL]) taps only part of the drivers of governance: economic policy of other kinds, such as economic competition, labor markets, and welfare, also impacts the incentives that influence diffusion.

Where we disagree is with the labor power model's account of the politics at work. Left versus right is one of several cleavage lines in politics. It may be decisive. The shift rightward in French politics accounts in part for the greater neoliberal character of economic policy that in turn contributes to the decline of the state's role in governance. Yet other coalitional patterns can and do occur: cross-class coalitions are also established and in many circumstances, we believe, may be more powerful as explanations. Political institutions also play a role in shaping the structure of cleavages and the winners of political competitions.

If we focus on owners and workers alone as coherent political groups, in conflict with each other, we will not get to an understanding of the politics that leads to the Berle-Means firm. Owners and managers and workers fight each other and among themselves. They seek allies from labor, farmers, or other groups. Which coalition of owners, workers, or managers and their related "intermediaries" prevails can only be explained by relating the struggle between them to other conflicts and processes, to which we turn in the next chapter.

LABOR AND CAPITAL: BOTH MATTER, BUT HOW?

The labor power model reminds us that employees matter in a firm, and they matter very much in society at large, where the rules are set that influence corporate governance. The investor model emphasizes the very great importance of capital, of investors, in shaping economic outcomes.

Analytic Narrative

SWEDEN: THE EXEMPLAR OF THE LABOR POWER MODEL?

Sweden is for many students of comparative political economy the paradigmatic case of labor power in a democracy. For critics of social democracy it is the paradigmatic villain of the welfare state, for supporters the exemplar. Yet Sweden does not fit either stereotype. It is hardly a pure case of socialism because most of the economy, 80 percent is in private hands, a high figure in Europe. State ownership is quite limited, and state planning nonexistent. There is no equivalent of the Japanese Ministry of International Trade and Industry (MITI), for example. Sweden is far from the Soviet model politically, as it has had solidly implanted democratic institutions for over a century. At the same time, Sweden has had a vigorous labor movement, overwhelming single-party dominance by the Social Democratic Party since 1933, a highly developed welfare state with extensive social services, high taxes, and considerable income equality. Thus Sweden fits many images of labor power in a democratic market economy.

The power of labor does matter. Sweden evolved as it has because labor is influential. Sweden could not crush an autonomous labor movement as Korea did for a time, or as the fascists did in Italy and Germany, or as the Communists did in the Soviet model. The way labor is incorporated into the political system— repressed or accepted, autonomous and influential or autonomous and marginal—does matter for public policy. And it matters for corporate governance.

Strong labor obtains goals that influence managerial choices and constrain own-ers. Sweden does exemplify the bargain that Roe so clearly analyzes. What we question is whether the focus on labor obscures the other elements of the bargain.

Recent scholarship on the welfare state in general has shifted the framing of its origins from battles between Left (pushing the welfare state) and Right (opposing it) to a more complex cross-class pattern. Mares, Hall and Soskice, Streeck, Swenson, Thelen, Martin, and Estevez-Abe among others explore the ways in which some elements of business supported various provisions of a regulated capitalism seeking stable, better-trained, healthier employees in whom they could invest.

If Sweden does not perfectly fit the labor power model, it also does not fit the investor model's trade-off between concentration and minority shareholder protec-tions, both of which are high, at 46.9 percent blockholding and 54 on the 100-point minority shareholder protection index, respectively. Foreign portfolio investors are pouring into Sweden, now accounting for 32.5 percent of the market, well above the mean, and the ratio of market capitalization to GDP is fairly high, at 137 percent. But there are few signs of blockholders accepting a "good-governance deal." We see little sell-down of blocks in the biggest families such as the Wallenbergs, and periodic resistance to specific reform measures on their part. A relatively small group of blockholding families continues to exercise voting con-trol over large portions of the public market by virtue of complex pyramids and sharply skewed ratios of voting to cash flow rights; 55 percent of listed companies have such differentiated rights (as in voting A shares and nonvoting B shares).

In Sweden, workers and managers (on one side) and blockholding owners (on the other) struck a long-term accord on corporate governance as part of a broad corporatist agreement on wage determination and employment conditions, granting job security to the former group in exchange for allowing blockholders substantial latitude on the other. Agency costs have been kept in check by Swe-den's relatively open economy and its consequent exposure to product-market competition from abroad.

By the same token, private benefits of control extracted by blockholders at the expense of minority shareholders appear to be limited; indirect attempts at mea-suring the control premium suggest that it is small, a few percent, and there are few anecdotes of blockholders ruthlessly expropriating minority shareholders.

Historical Roots of the Bargain: Interest Groups and Institutions. Like other coun-tries, Sweden's industrialization began with founder oligarchs. Primarily agrarian and extractive before the 1870s, Sweden, relatively poor compared to the larger west European countries, was quite involved in international trade, exporting timber, grain, and ores. Industrialization began with materials connected to these origins, high-quality engineering items such as ball bearings, electricity genera-tors (related to substantial water power), motors, and telephones. With a small and relatively poor population base, Sweden continued to be export oriented. Industrial leadership came from various elites, well connected to the Crown, and the aristoc-racy. Corporate governance there, as was the case everywhere, was "oligarchic"—controlled by founder insiders with strong banking connections.

In World War I, the landowning-industrial elite pursued a pro-German policy, protectionist economic policy, and conservative social policies. The British blockade made life difficult. Then toward the end of the war, a political shift changed things dramatically: export-oriented industry and agriculture plus labor overthrew the government democratically, switched to the British and French side in the war, and brought in universal suffrage.

This foreshadowed the political response to the Great Depression of 1929. At first Sweden pursued the same orthodox policy response as everyone else: cutting spending to balance the budget. In early 1933, another dramatic political shift brought a "break with orthodoxy."[61] Sweden, like Denmark at the same time, and Norway a few years later, and the United States, created the "cow trade"—a bargain between farmers (middle holders who broke with the big estate owners), who got price supports, and labor, who got unemployment compensation. The political surprise came from the farmer-labor alliance, as these two were thought to be at loggerheads.

The deal set the stage for what became known as Keynesian economic policy, deliberate deficit spending for demand stimulus. When this new coalition won the general elections of 1936, the "capitalists" agreed to make a bargain. They would accept labor unions in the workplace and a welfare state in public policy, in exchange for owner-manager control of the firm's strategy and practice and agreement by labor not to strike. Formulas were established to have wage increases linked to productivity increases. The bargain was explicitly worked out at a specific time and place, Saltsjobaden near Stockholm in 1938. Similar policies and bargains evolved elsewhere, including the United States, but not so explicitly and directly. Usually it happened through a process over time. Direct "social pacts" were agreed to in other places, for example, France at the time of the Matignon Accords (creating the 40-hour workweek, paid vacations, and the beginning of some democratic aspects of the workplace relationships), but they were and are relatively unusual, most social bargains come from a process, not a "smoking gun" at a particular moment.

The industrial groups involved in the Swedish bargain were the large, highly developed industrial groups, engaged in export, interested in world trade, and concerned about social peace. Indeed, industries of that type have been among the leaders in bargains with labor. The small democracies of Europe have long been known for free trade, high taxes, extensive welfare state arrangement, and vigorous trade unions. The logic is to have social peace at home so as to protect an economy dependent on foreign trade. But not all "capitalists" were willing to effect such a bargain, only those particularly concerned about trade, high technology, and trained, skilled workers.

This bargain is what we call the corporatist compromise, which we analyze in greater detail in the next chapter. We note it here both to develop the labor model and to indicate its shortcomings. Without strong labor, the bargain would not occur, or at least not on these terms. The industrialists would certainly have wanted labor peace, trained workers, and economic prosperity through demand

---

[61] Gourevitch 1986, chaps. 3 and 4; Peter Hall, ed., *The Political Power of Economic Ideas: Keynesianism across Nations* (Princeton: Princeton University Press, 1989).

stimulus. But getting these policies through the corporatist bargain was not their first preference. They came to accept it out of circumstance, and not every industrialist did so. Those in a particular position in the economy were more likely to accept it because they held more of the goals, we have mentioned than did industrialists. Thus, we see this social pact as a bargain among strong labor, smaller farmers, and particular kinds of industrialists. It is partly due to strong labor, but that explanation is incomplete.

The Swedish story since the period of depression, war, and readjustment was for many years a continuation of the Keynesian welfare state approach. An expanding welfare state, wage compression through a social solidarity pact, full employment, and retraining workers to handle economic adjustment made Sweden a society with full employment and equality. Esping-Anderson and others note the distinctive features of the Scandinavian model, different from the Christian Democratic one (see the next chapter and discussion of Germany), which has higher unemployment, less equality, and less participation of women in the workforce. Sweden exemplified the "third way"—not planning, state control, and authoritarianism of the Soviet model, nor the freewheeling capitalism and inequality of the pure market model, but some compromise, widely sought after the intense social blows of the depression, the world wars, fascism, and communism.

By the 1990s, though, the Swedish model faced problems. Rapid growth in the world economy and considerable technological change eroded the bargains from within. Not only did management seek more freedom in shifting production and workforce allocation, but also workers' agreement about wage equality began to erode. Workers in the advanced, export-oriented sector resented the loss of income opportunities to those in nontradables or weaker sectors. Social policies for jobs and equality stressed budget limits. An aging population threatened social services and retirement schemes.

A recent study of governance summarizes the issues succinctly:

> The specifically Swedish model of corporate ownership and control has emerged out of a close interaction between high finance, the political authorities, and the trade union movement—the "iron triangle," as it is sometimes called. The mutual purpose has been stable, long-term ownership in exchange for looking after certain interests that are of importance to the economy and the trade unions when making decisions. For a quarter of a century following the Second World War, this model appeared to function well. It delivered a high rate of growth combined with a high, stable level of employment. In the closing decades of the twentieth century, the down sides of the model became apparent. They lie in the difficulty faced by new entrepreneurs and owners in asserting their interests under the present regulatory framework, so as to be able to challenge the existing owners' control over companies and markets. This has undermined the regenerative power of the business sector. There is thus an inherent danger in the consensus between the political authorities, the owners of capital, and the trade union movement.[62]

[62] Hans Söderström, Erik Berglöf, Bengt Holmström, Peter Högfeldt, and Eva Milgrom, "Corporate Governance and Structural Change," Studieförbundet Näringsliv och Samhälle Economic Policy Group Report, 2003, 29–30.

Pressures for change developed, and processes of change began. Some of them hint at a transparency coalition. Voices are heard calling for an end to the historic bargain, but resistance remains strong from blockholders, some workers, and some employees. The balance lies with what politics gets the "political authorities" to do.

Change: Glasses Half Full, Half Empty. We see change in Sweden: foreign money is being invested, the labor force is changing, codes delineating shareholder rights are being discussed, but blockholding remains. Sweden has considerable concentration of power: *Ägarna Och Makten.*

At 47 percent, Sweden has a relatively high ratio of blockholding, about average for the total country sample, highest among the Scandinavian countries, but below that of the continental European countries. The data on Swedish ownership is fairly accurate; both La Porta et al. and Faccio and Lang agree on this concentration number, while Barca and Becht place it somewhat higher.[63]

The Swedish National Pension Insurance Funds (the Fourth and Fifth Boards) are major owners of Swedish shares (they hold about 4 percent of the total market capitalization value), while Swedish investment funds hold 4.8 percent more. In 1998 figures, foreign shareholders owned over 31 percent of total market value of the Stockholm exchange, and that percentage is likely higher now.[64]

The 50 largest shareholders account for 43.2 percent of the total market capitalization value. All other shareholders include about 3 million individuals. Among the 50 largest shareholders we find three private families (Persson, Douglas, and Lundberg); the rest are categorized as institutions.[65] It is interesting to note that the Wallenberg-owned investment company Investor has lost its ranking as the number one owner. The strong position of the Wallenbergs has weakened, as institutional investors sold shares in Scania to its main rival, Volvo, expressing dissatisfaction with the Wallenberg's handling of potential merging candidates for Scania. However, the Wallenbergs still have major influence over Swedish industry. For another group of large companies, owner control is lacking, as the firms are protected by cross-shareholding and limits on voting rights that make prohibitive the cost of acquiring voting rights.

There may have been some minor reduction in blockholders of large firms, as the by-product of larger merger-and-acquisition activity, not by a deliberate sell-down of control positions to foreign investors. There may be some undisclosed sales of

---

[63] Petra Adolfsson, Urban Ask, Ulrika Holmberg, and Sten Jönsson, "Corporate Governance in Sweden: A Literature Review," Report Submitted to the European Commission DGIV, May 1999. Classification from Anneli Sundin and Sven-Ivan Sundqvist, *Owners and Power in Sweden's Listed Companies,* 1997 (Stockholm: SIS Agarservice AB, 1998).

In the financial press this sale of Scania shares to Volvo was seen as an active demonstration of ownership control from the institutions. They were said to be dissatisfied with how the main owner-investor (the Wallenberg-owned Investment Company) handled (stalled, according to some commentators in the press) discussions with potential merging candidates for Scania.

[64] Sundin and Sundqvist 1998, 20.

[65] Sundin and Sundqvist 1998.

control blocks through private equity transactions. There were relatively few IPOs, and few cross-listings on the NYSE or NASDAQ—there was only one Swedish listing on the NYSE as of 2001—reflecting the high degree of industrial concentration and relatively small SME sector in Sweden. In effect, there was relatively little "new money" to support a transparency coalition.

Minority Shareholder Protections. High blockholding is all the more interesting in this country case, because Sweden has fairly high minority shareholder protections, 54 on our 100-point index, above the mean for the whole sample and for the European countries. Standards of financial accounting and control are, on whole, favorable for minority shareholders, despite the widespread skewing of control to cash flow rights, and the de facto barriers to takeovers; these rights are buttressed by Sweden's reliable rule of law, which is not captured by this index. In addition, "Many companies have differentiated voting rights for "A" and "B" shares (or the equivalent). This is the case for 19 out of the 35 most traded companies."[66] Standards of financial disclosure are medium to low, as are the ratio of NEDs, and the relatively conservative use of stock options as an alignment device.

There are several anecdotes of Swedish blockholders pushing back on attempts to impose higher standards of disclosure and more equitable control procedures to defend minority shareholders.

Pensions. In terms of the transparency coalition model, certain elements of the reform mechanism are emerging. Workers are gradually becoming owners. Sweden has a high IPD ratio of 132 percent, the legacy of the fabled postwar Swedish welfare state, and a medium ratio of private pension assets, at 33 percent of GDP. This is starting to change: a series of pension reforms in the Allmänna Tilläggspension (ATP) national social insurance system has trimmed benefits for the first pillar, switched to a quasi-defined benefit system, and transferred some portion of the payroll tax to private accounts in the second and third pillars, in a miniature version of the Chilean approach.

This reform was the result of a tortuous political compromise through Sweden's highly consensual (and multiple veto-player) political process. The change was spread out over 15 years of consultation and legislative negotiation, and the effects in terms of private pension asset accumulation will be gradual. Consensual political institutions retard change, placing a sea anchor on the transformation of governance practices towards a transparency coalition. But such institutions do not prevent change, and may sometimes add additional impetus in that direction by providing a voice to all players and allowing a collective sharing of blames as well as credit. Pension reforms are costly and unpopular. If all the parties are involved, actors in a consensual political system can make a credible commitment not to blame each other for the cost. Actors in majoritarian systems have trouble making such deals and sticking to them.

[66] Sundin and Sundqvist 1998.

Sweden's expanding second- and third-pillar assets are being concentrated in a few large institutional investors whose own governance structure resembles CalPERS more than, say, Fidelity Investments. It is unclear how aggressive Sweden's new giant pension funds will be in terms of disciplining firms in which they invest. This doubt draws forward forcefully the point that the sheer size of pension fund accumulation does not by itself tell us whether we will observe activism on behalf of shareholders' interests. We need to know as well the micro-institutions of the pension fund management: do the funds have autonomy from the interests of management or from inside blockholders?

The goal of this reform was to make Sweden's pillar 1 scheme more of a funded defined contribution plan, with payout more precisely depending upon pay-in, and to divorce the income transfer effects ("social policy") of the pension scheme from its retirement effects. Consensus was built gradually, as the existing system came to be regarded as "unfair, perverse, and depleted," compounded by alarm over structural lags in the Swedish macroeconomy, and deep recessions (1992–93 and 1997–98).[67]

These reforms were endorsed by both the Social Democrat and Center Parties with the Greens and the Communists objecting. The labor unions were generally in favor of reform—the white-collar unions (Tjänstemannen Centralorganisation) more so, the blue-collar unions (Landsorganisationen) less so—while business organizations (the Svenska Arbetgivarförening, or SAF) acceded to the relatively high levels of sustained payroll tax in exchange for creating the transfers to private accounts.[68]

Understanding the politics of the reform requires deeper knowledge of the incentives of the various groups. Ideological issues are at play: commitment to equality versus growth, for example, But so are differences in economic position in the international and domestic economy. Swedish labor, a key player, has faced strains within its commitment to wage compression, or equal pay across categories of work. Skilled workers in export industries conflict with unskilled workers or service sector workers not benefiting from rising productivity. This weakens the commitment to uniformity of a labor position, and draws such workers into concerns for productivity—and even for corporate governance.

Sweden thus represents a good case for tracking the role of preferences as they slowly change, against a backdrop of stable consensual political institutions. With a relatively small number of big pension funds on one side and a smaller number of blockholders on the other, negotiations over corporate governance could proceed very quickly—or be blocked entirely. In Sweden, as in the Netherlands, minority shareholders may ultimately exit if they are not given voice.

[67] Edward Palmer, "Swedish Pension Reform: How Did It Evolve, and What Does It Mean for the Future?" in *Social Security Pension Reform in Europe*, Martin Feldstein and Horst Siebert, eds. (Chicago: University of Chicago Press, 2002), 184.

[68] Palmer 2002.

CONCLUSION

This chapter has explored the two poles of the class conflict political model for explaining corporate governance. The investor model derives from the law-and-economics tradition of identifying the goals of owners. It makes explicit what much of that literature suggests but does not bring forward. The argument rests on the ability of owners to prevail in politics. The investor model assumes a unified view by all owners on behalf of an external diffusion model with strong shareholder protections. It assumes investors will want firms that provide them. Firms that fail to provide such protections will lose investors, as the market forces change—the purely private ordering version. If bonding is not adequate, investors, managers, and owners will want the political system to provide legislation and regulation that produce MSP. It is assumed the political system will provide it.

We critique that model on theory and facts. In theory, it is doubtful all owners have uniform preferences. Blockholders like their privileged position and may resist changes. In fact they do resist them. In theory, it is doubtful politicians will just provide MSP. They have many constituencies to integrate, and MSP does not just happen.

The obverse of the investor model is the labor model. It is the logical next step from the finance theory version of the investor model. What capital wants, labor will not. Thus, strong labor means low MSP. It also means policies in the economy that inhibit diffusion—what we called in the previous chapter the capitalist economic policy pattern. Weak economic competition, weak antitrust, extensive labor market regulation, managed prices, all inhibit the market for control and diffusion.

The politics of the labor model suggest that strong labor power produces anti-diffusion policies. It does do that, but not without assistance. Labor power rarely gets its way without striking a bargain with other groups.

Korea shows the impact of political power on policy: Blockholders privileged in the authoritarian regime did not have to take other groups' demands seriously, but did have to accommodate to state power. As democratization began, state power weakened, leaving the chaebol freer, thus leading to oligarchical owner power with little constraint. Further democratization brought forth other voices, which demanded transparency in public finance and public affairs generally. This ended the chaebol's privileged access to the state, then encouraged new regulations about corporate governance. Shareholding has risen, albeit mostly foreign, and managers and owners alike are more influenced by market factors. Changing political balance meant changing governance practices. In the changed coalitions, labor, excluded entrepreneurs, and other groups had more voice.

In Sweden policy change expresses shifting power within a stable constitutional framework. Major changes in party coalitions, in particular the Social Democratic–Agrarian Party alignment in the 1930s, set the stage for an accommodation with certain business groups. That produced the policy environment that provides employment protection and high wages, combined with substantial managerial autonomy and protection of the special pyramidal control mechanisms in the governance system—the corporatist compromise. Sweden ranks high in labor power indicators, yet at the same time, the Social Democratic governments operate as a coalition. Despite substantial changes in many aspects of Swedish life, that system remains in place.

The labor power model balances the omissions of the investor model in neglecting labor. No account of the politics of corporate governance can do without paying serious attention to both investors and labor. But that account is not sufficient. Class conflict, left versus right, capital versus labor, is one model of cleavage, but not the only one and does not necessarily predict the victor in terms of outcomes. We turn to examine other dynamics—situations that put managers with workers against the interests of inside owner-blockholders. Sweden and Korea both show strengths and limits of the investor and labor power models. In both cases we see cross-class coalitions at work. We turn now to a more direct examination of these cross-class coalition models.

CHAPTER 6

Preference Cleavages 2: Sectoral Conflict

SECTION I: CROSS-CLASS COALITIONS

The previous chapter explored political cleavages along the class divide between capital and labor to explain variation in corporate governance across countries. In so doing, we identified several cleavages that cut across class. We found different kinds of owners: blockholders and external minority shareholders ("insiders" and "outsiders"), as well as institutional investors with strong links to management and others whose primary allegiance was to their beneficiary shareholders. We found workers with preferences similar to shareholders, and those less sympathetic. In this sense, both the investor and the labor models are flawed, in our view, by their oversimplification of the preferences of owners, managers, and labor and their mapping of those preferences in society at large. Other cleavages besides the labor-capital divide manifest themselves in politics.

In this chapter we group these observations together into an alternative model of cleavages. In this cross-class pattern, managers and workers join together in a broad bargain providing job security, stability, and regularity: workers cede authority to managers in exchange for stable jobs and pay increases; managers preside over a large organization secure from hostile takeover. Blockholders, too, are drawn into this bargain: they keep some benefits of control, but have to share authority and rewards with workers and managers. We call this bargain *corporatism* after the label most often used to describe the broad institutional pattern that makes it work.[1]

This cross-class bargain was struck during a historical period sometimes termed the Historical Compromise, beginning in most countries during the interwar years, in others, such as Japan, shortly after World War II. Responding to the intense social conflicts during World War I, the hyperinflation of the 1920s, the Great Depression of the 1930s, and the cataclysm of World War II, efforts were made to forge a framework for social peace: to reconcile management and labor, repress class conflict, build a welfare state, develop corporatist institutions of representation, and constrain several competitive market forces while still preserving the basic structures of a private economy, all in the framework of constitutional democracy. Corporate governance outcomes were rooted in labor-management cooperation; minority shareholder preferences took a backseat, and blockholders accommodated this new alignment—some out of choice, others out of necessity, but all at the expense of outside shareholders.

---

[1] Some Japanese observers use the term *kaisha-shugi* or "companyism" for governance outcomes in which the preferences of managers and workers take precedence over the suppliers of capital. Our term is *managerism*.

On the other hand, if the other side of the owners versus managers plus workers alignment triumphs, we have oligarchy: owners set the corporate governance rules with few if any constraints. This result has historical referents everywhere: in the United States during the robber baron period after the Civil War (i.e., after 1865); in Russia today after the collapse of the Soviet Union, whose owners are called oligarchs; in some Asian countries after World War II, as one aspect of so-called crony capitalism, and in a small number of Latin American countries as well.

Thus in both corporatism and oligarchy, the ownership concentration and MSP outcomes are the same as in the labor power model, but the political routes are different. The political road to oligarchy is rather short; owner-entrepreneurs exercised preponderant political influence in early stages of industrialization—the late nineteenth century in the United States, in Meiji and Taisho Japan, in Korea from 1960 through 1990, and, arguably, in Russia today. These owner-oligarchs dominated policy, politics, and the boardroom, able to wheel and deal as they desire, with little constraint from managers, workers, or minority owners.

The political road to corporatism is longer and more indirect; rather than corporate governance outcomes reflecting labor's political strength, we see corporatist governance as a complex bargain across classes, with managers and workers aligned against owners—concentrated owners, because minority owners have little or no means to protect their interests. For the country sample as a whole, corporatism is associated with relatively high owner concentration (see appendix table A.16).

The Corporatist Model: Workers and Managers Dominate Owners

The social categories used in the class-based models derived from traditional finance theory fail to differentiate cleavages within the groups they analyze.[2] On some issues, capital and labor do capture the conflict cleavage, but on other issues they do not. There are many forms of capital and many forms of labor, each forming subgroups within the whole. Sometimes these subgroups cooperate with their class neighbors, but other times they may clash with them, reaching across class lines to find common ground on other principles of cleavage. This provides the elements for a more complex political explanation of policy outcomes in fields as varied as trade, welfare, labor, and competition; in this chapter, we extend the logic of such explanations to corporate governance as well.

We have already noted the inescapable point of fragmentation in earlier chapters. In chapter 5 we observed that capital breaks not only into owners and managers—the principal distinction in finance theory—but also into different sorts of owners. There are blockholders and dispersed minority shareholders; among blockholders, there are founder-entrepreneurs, their families, and their trusts; among minority shareholders, there are "rentiers," who earn their livelihood from investment income, small savers planning retirement, and a host of sizes in between.

---

[2] As Zingales (2000) notes, different theories of the firm will lead to a different understanding of interests and policy preferences: that suppliers and workers contribute to firm value and thus have grounds for "voice" fits into this cross-class approach.

These different varieties of capital holdings can be blended and aggregated in quite different ways: held by individuals through individual share purchases in separate companies; or aggregated into blocks by pension funds and investment houses, each of which have their own incentives and relationship to the investor and the firm whose assets are purchased. These investors have different risk and time horizons—well known to finance theory—as well as different capacities for collective action and political lobbying.

Owners of capital differ substantially in their positions concerning trade, competition, regulation, and labor.[3] Firms with strong export capacity support open economic policies; firms vulnerable to acute competitive pressures do not. Firms in high-technology markets support public research and education; firms at the low-tech end do not. Borrowers fight with lenders, big capital with small, banks in small towns with large financial institutions. Firms that rely on skilled labor may invest heavily in worker training and long-term commitments to employees, while others will seek the shortest obligations and the lowest training costs.[4]

On the side of labor we find significant cleavages as well.[5] Workers in highly competitive industries are in tension with workers in protected and inefficient ones; the former tend to support open trade, the latter oppose it. Demands for wage equality may be resisted by "elite" or highly skilled workers. Workers may support the industry or the firm of which they are a part, so all the variance among owners of capital reappears among workers as well. Farmers often have policy goals quite different from their urban or industrial capitalist counterparts, and are available for political coalitions dealing with trade, finance, transportation, taxes, and other issues that can have an impact on corporate governance.

STOLPER-SAMUELSON OR RICARDO-VINER?

We draw these threads together by relying on ideas about sectoral conflicts and specific assets developed by specialists in the politics of international trade policy. The class conflict assumptions of the investor and labor power models stem from the Stolper-Samuelson theory (or Karl Marx). Economies are composed of land, labor, and capital in each country, which are either abundant or scarce compared to other countries. Owners of abundant factors in a given economy tend to gain higher returns from factor mobility across countries, and thus (other things

---

[3] Rogowski 1989; Gourevitch 1986; Michael Hiscox, *International Trade and Political Conflict: Commerce, Coalitions, and Mobility* (Princeton: Princeton University Press, 2002).

[4] Zingales 2000 stresses the role of labor's importance on the authority system of the firm.

[5] Zingales 2000; and Gøsta Esping-Anderson, "The Three Political Economies of the Welfare State," *Canadian Review of Sociology and Anthropology* 26 (1989): 10–36; Espring-Anderson, *The Three Worlds of Welfare Capitalism* (Cambridge: Polity Press, 1990); Torben Iversen and David Soskice, "An Asset Theory of Social Policy Preferences," *American Political Science Review* 95 (2001): 875–93; David Soskice and Torben Iversen, "Multiple Wage-Bargaining Systems in the Single European Currency Area," *Oxford Review of Economic Policy* 14 (1998): 110–24; Soskice and Iversen, "The Nonneutrality of Monetary Policy with Large Price or Wage Setters," *Quarterly Journal of Economics* 115 (2000): 265–84; Margarita Estevez-Abe, Torben Iversen, and David Soskice, "Social Protection and the Formation of Skills: A Reinterpretation of the Welfare State," in Hall and Soskice 2001; Torben Iversen and Thomas R. Cusack, "The Causes of Welfare State Expansion: Deindustrialization or Globalization?" *World Politics* 52 (2000): 313–49.

equal) prefer free trade. Conversely, owners of scarce factors prefer protection from factor mobility, which reduces their relative returns. This approach has been used by researchers to explain the politics of trade preferences around the world[6] and continues as one type of interpretation in vigorous debates over issues public policy caused by economic globalization.[7]

An alternative economic theory looks at sectoral conflict between industries, rather than class conflict within them. In trade politics, this approach is represented by the Ricardo-Viner theory. Whereas Stolper-Samuelson assumes factor mobility between sectors as well as countries, Ricardo-Viner asks what happens if factors are "sticky" and sector-specific ("specific assets").[8] Under those conditions, workers and owners are both concerned about protecting the specific assets of their investment—owners in their physical capital, workers in their human capital. Workers may join their bosses and owners in political efforts to shelter "their" sector and "their" firm. For example, steelworkers in importing countries often join shareholders in resisting free trade in steel, lobbying for tariffs instead, a political coalition that cuts across class.

Similar lines of reasoning have been applied to a number of other areas. Specialists in the welfare state and social policy, for example, see substantial cooperation between some business groups and labor in building systems that stabilize labor markets. Mares argues that the introduction of employment insurance in France and Germany was supported by large firms. Swenson shows that the development of centralized wage-bargaining institutions in Denmark and Sweden came not from class struggle but from a cross-class alliance in the sectors most exposed to trade and competition. Manow explores the engagement of employers in the development of the German and Japanese welfare state.[9] Thelen traces labor-employee relations

---

[6] It was also used to explain the politics of the Philips curve: in a trade-off between employment and inflation, workers prefer low unemployment at the cost of some inflation, while the owners of capital prefer the reverse. Thus where the Left was strong, unemployment would be low and vice versa. See, e.g., John H. Goldthorpe, ed., *Order and Conflict in Contemporary Capitalism* (New York: Oxford University Press, 1984); Dani Rodrik, *Has Globalization Gone Too Far?* (Washington, D.C.: Institute for International Economics, 1997); Hibbs 1977.

[7] See, e.g., Garrett 1998; Garrett and Lange 1996.

[8] Either the class conflict (Stolper-Samuelson) or the cross-class (Ricardo-Viner) cleavage line is analytically possible. Which one prevails depends, as Hiscox 2001 argues through studying the politics of international trade disputes, on historical circumstances.

[9] Isabella Mares, *The Politics of Social Risk: Business and Welfare State Development* (Cambridge: Cambridge University Press, 2003); Peter A. Swenson, *Capitalists and Markets: The Making of Labor Markets and Welfare States in the United States and Sweden* (New York: Oxford University Press, 2002); Swenson, *Fair Shares: Unions, Pay, and Politics in Sweden and West Germany* (Ithaca, N.Y.: Cornell University Press, 1989); Philip Manow, "Welfare State Building and Coordinated Capitalism in Japan and Germany," in *The Origins of Nonliberal Capitalism: Germany and Japan in Comparison*, Wolfgang Streeck and Kozo Yamamura, eds. (Ithaca, N.Y.: Cornell University Press, 2001); Manow, "Business Coordination, Collective Dares, Bargaining, and the Welfare State: Germany and Japan in Historical Comparative Perspective," in *Comparing Welfare Capitalism: Social Policy and Political Economy in Europe, Japan, and the USA*, Bernhard Ebbinghaus and Philip Manow, eds. (London: Routledge, 2001); Philip Manow and Bernhard Ebbinghaus, "Introduction: Studying Varieties of Welfare Capitalism," in Ebbinghaus and Manow 2001; Höpner 2003b provides a concise summary of some of these issues, as does Hall and Gingerich 2001.

today back to decisions made before World War I to define how artisanal associations, trade unions, and firms interacted to shape the system of skill development and production strategies.[10]

FROM RICARDO-VINER TO THE VARIETIES OF CAPITALISM

The literature on the cross-class bargains underlying a wide range of capitalist institutions can be aggregated into comparative analysis of market economies—the Varieties-of-Capitalism material discussed in chapters 3 and 4. Corporate governance, we argued there, cannot be explained only by looking at MSP. The incentives that shape the organization of the firm are greatly influenced by the regulatory regime in industrial relations, price setting, competition, and the relationships among firms, and finance, the regimes we referred to as coordinated market economies (CMEs) and the liberal market economies (LMEs).

These systems in turn influence the structure of debate over economic policy in general and corporate governance in particular. Countries with relationship network systems reward cross-class cooperation. Countries with arm's-length contracts encourage class conflict. A positive feedback loop is at work. Cross-class cooperation produces policies that shape production strategies that in turn induce the cooperation that sustains them. If countries develop a "coordination" pattern, they are more likely to sustain it, as the policies and institutions involved become self-reinforcing.

PREDICTIONS AND TESTING

The overall prediction of the corporatist compromise model for our sample countries is that corporatism is positively correlated with concentration and negatively correlated with MSP. The logic is that the corporatist compromise between workers and managers lies in preserving the firm from the whiplash of forces favored by external shareholders in breaking the "agency costs of cash flow" that retain assets in the company. A high degree of corporatism "protects" firms from that process and is therefore an indicator of a labor-manager–inside owner bargain.

As noted in chapter 2, we use as our measure of corporatism the Hicks-Kenworthy composite index of the 18 OECD countries. This index was created by scoring each country between 0 and 1 on seven measures of economic cooperation, including business centralization, wage-setting coordination, and cooperation between labor and management. There is quite a bit of variation on this index within the OECD, as shown in table 6.1. Sweden is at the top; the United States, not surprisingly, at the bottom.

For these 18 countries, the mean value is .51, the standard deviation is .34, the minimum value is .023 and the maximum is .973.

The data from the 18 countries from our sample for which we have a useful index of corporatism supports the prediction that patterns of corporate governance are associated with the corporatist compromise. The correlation between

---

[10] Kathleen Thelen, *How Institutions Evolve: The Political Economy of Skills in Comparative-Historical Perspective* (New York: Cambridge University Press, 2004).

TABLE 6.1
Corporatism Values for the OECD

Sweden	0.973	SE
Austria	0.96	AT
Norway	0.955	NO
Finland	0.878	FI
Germany	0.795	DE
Japan	0.774	JP
Denmark	0.723	DK
Belgium	0.669	BE
Netherlands	0.578	NL
Switzerland	0.55	CH
Italy	0.439	IT
France	0.395	FR
Australia	0.165	AU
New Zealand	0.136	NZ
United Kingdom	0.096	GB
Ireland	0.066	IE
Canada	0.043	CA
United States	0.023	US

corporatism and concentration is +.44, whereas the sign is reversed between corporatism and MSP, at −.76. This is shown graphically in figures 6.1 and 6.2.

As we probe more deeply into the institutional components of corporatism, the predictions of the corporatist compromise model continue to hold. Tables A.17 and A.18 in the data appendix reproduce correlation coefficients of minority shareholder protection and ownership concentration with variables associated with corporatism, labor and business organization, and influence.[11]

Ownership concentration is positively correlated with the corporatist score, and with the indices of labor and business influence. The coefficients on the

[11] The measure of corporatism used in this section is the Hicks-Kenworthy index. Lane Kenworthy and Alexander Hicks, "Cooperation and Political Economic Performance in Affluent Democratic Capitalism," *American Journal of Sociology* 103 (1998): 631–72. Data on labor and business influence was obtained from Duane Swank and Cathie Jo Martin, "Employers and the Welfare State: The Political Economic Organization of Firms and Social Policy in Contemporary Capitalist Democracies," *Comparative Political Studies* 34 (2001): 889–923, and reflects averages for the decade. The data is available in year intervals for most countries, yet we decided to use averages due to data restrictions on the dependent variables, especially on the index of concentration. Employer centralization is an index constructed by looking at national employers' federation and the peak federation's powers over members (i.e., appointment power, veto power over collective bargains and lockouts, own conflict funds). Employer coordination is a standardized score of the coordination of employers in collective bargaining. Enterprise cooperation is a standard score index of cooperation among competitive firms in research and development, training, standard setting, production, and so forth. Union power is an index constructed from measures of union density and union peak association power. Collective bargaining is a standard score index for the level of collective bargaining among employers and employees.

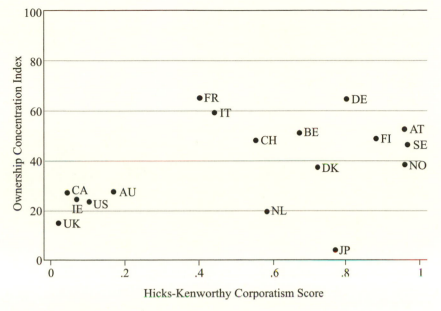

Figure 6.1 Corporatism and Owner Concentration

Hicks-Kenworthy index of corporatism and on those variables that capture the influence of owners tend to be larger. The association between corporatism and minority shareholder protection appears to be stronger. On the other hand, shareholder protection is negatively correlated with measures of corporatism. Correlation is also strong with measures of labor and business power. Correlation coefficients with those measures traditionally associated with the organization and influence of employers seem to be larger.

To test the significance of these relationships we conduct additional tests of the corporatist hypotheses by running bivariate regressions of each of the two measures of corporate governance on each of the variables associated with labor and business organization influence. We reproduce these results in appendix tables A.17–A.25.[12]

In all models corporatism returns a negative coefficient when the dependent variable is minority shareholder protection, and a positive coefficient when the regression

[12] Data availability forces us to limit our analysis to 18 developed countries, a very small sample that may render the estimates suspect in terms of efficiency (larger variance) and bias due to a relative departure from the asymptotic properties of the OLS estimator. Nonetheless, we think that the results from these bivariate regressions help estimate confidence intervals around the correlations between variables. In practical terms they are also quite telling: they seem to uncover a trend that survives even in a small-n sample. We have run additional models using a limited number of additional controls such as GDP per capita, openness, and market capitalization, which can be construed as belonging in the models. Results remained basically the same. We decided not to report them here because the additional variables included in the right-hand side of the estimating model constrain the degrees of freedom, making the estimates inefficient.

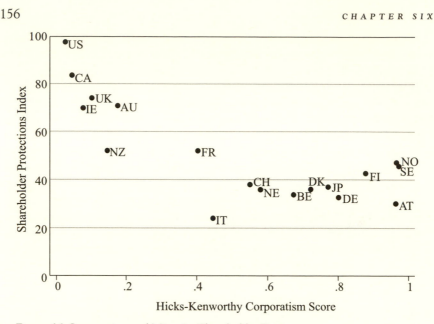

Figure 6.2 Corporatism and Minority Shareholder Protections

is our measure of concentration of ownership.[13] The variables that measure organizational features of groups—employer concentration, employer centralization, and enterprise cooperation—also relate negatively with the index of minority shareholder protections. These results are statistically significant beyond conventional levels, and capture a substantive effect: going from the lowest to the highest level of corporatism in the sample, for instance, would result in a 43-point fall in the minority shareholder scale, and a 20-point increase in the index of blockholding.[14]

The relationships between the two measures of corporate governance and those indices associated with organizational features of labor—union density/concentration—are in the right direction, but hardly significant at conventional levels. Regressing shareholder protection on union density returns a negative sign, while the sign on blockholding is positive.[15] Another test uses centralization of

[13] The coefficient on the index of corporatism becomes stronger and the level of significance remains high even when controlling for labor and business influence.

[14] A full-range movement from lowest to highest level in the employer centralization index is associated with a 48-point decrease in the index of shareholder protection, and a 32-point increase in the index of ownership concentration.

[15] Note that even when significant, the relationship seems to disappear when controlling for business influence (see table 7.4). However, these results should be interpreted with even more caution. Labor and business organizations have reciprocal feedback effects: when labor is strong, business tends to respond by organizing around peak organizations to counterbalance labor's influence. The reverse trend is also true. Including both terms in the right-hand side of the estimating equation introduces the problem of multi-collinearity, a difficulty that cannot be solved easily with the data at hand due to the limited number of observations.

collective bargaining as the explanatory variable. Centralization of organizational structure on the side of business and labor may be considered one of the necessary, though not sufficient, conditions for the emergence of the corporatist compromise. Centralization may facilitate bargaining between the two groups, enabling them to make credible commitments to corporatist arrangements. The test results give support to the predictions of this chapter: minority shareholder protection tends to be lower in countries where collective bargaining is centralized, while ownership tends to be more concentrated in these countries.[16]

The Politics of Grand Bargains

The data presented above show that corporatist structures correlate strongly with blockholding outcomes. We use this as evidence that cross-class processes are at work in producing this outcome, for corporatism is by its nature an institutionalization of a bargain among groups to ensure that all have a voice. It is a politically created bargain. That is, corporatism itself is an expression for the desire to strike a bargain. As such it reflects the influence of preferences and political institutions.

We noted in chapter 3 that political institutions influence preference aggregation. That matters greatly in this part of the discussion because consensus institutions are more likely to produce corporatist bargains than are majoritarian ones. This suggests that class conflict preferences alone will not tell us what happens. Knowing the prevalence of left versus right governments tells us something, but omits the impact of the bargaining among groups induced by institutions: electoral law, legislative executive relations, and other elements of the system.

As noted in chapter 3, consensus political institutions correlate with blockholding patterns of outcomes. They also correlate with the policy instruments of the CEP policy cluster we examine. Political arrangements such as proportional representation and coalitional cabinet government have the effect of encouraging compromise across producer group lines. They allow groups to invest in a bargain with some confidence that the bargain will be kept.

The structures of corporatism influence the outcome. Highly centralized "peak associations" of employers and employees indicates cross-class coalitions. The previous point stressed formal political institutions—electoral law and national constitutions that shape the way voting and lobbying impact the political process. Another set of structures matter: the professional associations of business, labor, and other groups, and the way they interact with each other.

Corporatism is the inclusion of economic and social groups in the process of policy formation. The type and degree of inclusion is generated by the formal political process: governments decide, for example, to require workers to have representatives on boards, though firms may do so on their own. Government policy decides who administers training programs, social insurance plans, and the like. The origins of codetermination in Germany, for example, go back to the Bismarckian

---

[16] These results are statistically significant for shareholder protection at the 95 percent level of confidence, though not for the blockholding variable.

social insurance system of the 1880s, in which worker representatives sat on the boards that administered it.

Employer and employee associations form part of a corporatist system as well. Countries differ substantially in the degree of centralization of the employer federations, some quite decentralized, some the opposite. This affects strongly the process of price determination, in products and wages. CME countries are highly centralized, while LME countries are not.

The presence of such structures is therefore evidence of a bargain across social groups: it reflects a bargain in the past, and its presence indicates the continuation of that bargain in the present. We do not use corporatism to explain the cross-class bargain, but rather as evidence that it has taken place. Corporatism is itself an instrument of commitment by partners in a bargain to sustain it. If corporatism unravels, we expect the underlying bargain to unravel, because the demise of corporatist arrangements would be a symptom the parties no longer support the bargain, that it is no longer self-enforcing.

For those countries in our sample for which data of this type in available, we find a strong effect of institutional centralization among business groups, and a weak one for centralization among unions. This is what we would expect from a corporatist argument, but not a labor power one. Corporatism consists of cross-class bargains and their institutionalization in a set of relationships in civil society, authorized or acknowledged by the state. Business groups work through professional associations to coordinate prices, production, technology, education, and assistance from the state. Business, labor and other "social partners" work through various structures to bargain issues of wages, work, and other elements of "class tension."[17] Where corporatism is well developed, we are likely to find institutional centralization. What is more plausibly independent of the political agreement to construct the bargain is the character of the associations of unions and industry, the fact that the employer and labor centralizations are highly centralized. That may help induce the bargain.[18]

And where corporatism is strong, we are likely to find blockholding, not diffusion. Corporatism reflects a left-right bargain, so that its presence means a

---

[17] On social mechanisms of coordination, see the treatments of Jonah Levy, *Tocqueville's Revenge: State, Society, and Economy in Contemporary France* (Cambridge: Harvard University Press, 1999); Pepper Culpepper, *Creating Cooperation: How States Develop Human Capital in Europe* (Ithaca, N.Y.: Cornell University Press, 2003); Nick Zeigler, *Governing Ideas: Strategies for Innovation in France and Germany* (Ithaca, N.Y.: Cornell University Press, 1997); Gary Herrigel, *Industrial Constructions: The Source of German Industrial Power* (Cambridge: Cambridge University Press, 1996); Locke 1995; Iversen and Soskice 2001; Soskice and Iversen 2000; Hall and Soskice 2001.

[18] Roe sees this point quite well. In the interests of parsimony, his statistics focus on left versus right. His country narratives and general observations show cross-class alignments, path dependence, and covariation. "One might argue that the analysis here gets the structural sequence backwards. Blockholding came first and resisted change. Hence, blockholding plausibly induced codetermination, and not codetermination that initially induced blockholders." "But a focus on the historical sequence misses the point. Once the two were in place, neither could change easily without changing the other. . . . Evolution was harder, and maybe still is because the two complementary institutions must move in unison." Roe 2003b.

different sort of politics than left versus right.[19] In our view, the presence of strong job security protections and low income inequality counts as evidence of a cross-class bargain, not just of labor power. Without the ability to attract political allies into a coalition, labor is unlikely to prevail on its own.

Vital to the formation of these bargains was the existence of party organizations that reached across class lines. In some countries such as Sweden and Denmark, this bargain was struck before World War II. In most countries, including Japan, there were elements of the political Right who preferred some kind of regulated economy and some elements of welfare, while some elements of the Left preferred a market economy to extensive state regulation, especially in countries that had gone through Fascist statism in World War II.

In Europe, religion had a major impact on these debates. On the right, Christian Democrats strongly supported state assistance to families, expansion of the welfare state, trade unions and market stabilization. On the left, Christian Democracy organized workers into non-Marxian unions, critical of markets, but supportive of capitalism.[20]

These ideas, parties, and union and business structures provided an important foundation for the construction of the cross-class bargains. They marked part of a debate within the Left and the Right over which subgroup defined the interests of the "class" as a whole. As we have noted elsewhere, collapsing this debate into a bifurcated labor-versus-capital divide provides theoretical parsimony at the expense of reality.[21]

Analytic Narratives

To illustrate the dynamics of cross-class coalitions and the corporatist bargain we use narratives on Germany, Netherlands, and Japan. Germany has high blockholding, high corporatism, and middle to low MSP. Japan has low blockholding

---

[19] Historians find the roots of these bargains in older arrangements such as labor relations and banking systems before World War I. But the post-1945 period is the most visible and dramatic, with the *compromesso historico* in Italy, the *Soziale Marktwirtschaft* in Germany, and *kyōtō keizai* in Japan, all terms used to describe the cross-class bargains in those countries following the bitter experiences of Fascism, Communism, the Great Depression of the 1930s and World War II.

[20] Torben Iverson and Ann Wren (1998) note some strong differences in policy and outcomes among "Christian democratic," "social democratic," and "neoliberal" advanced industrial countries: Christian democratic governments stress equality and budgetary restraint over growth, social democratic governments pick equality and growth over budgetary restraint, and neoliberal governments pick high employment and budgetary restraint over equality.

[21] A classic analysis of party cleavages is Seymour Martin Lipset and Stein Rokkan, eds., *Party Systems and Voter Alignments: Cross-National Perspectives* (New York: Free Press, 1967); Samuel H. Beer, *British Politics in the Collectivist Age* (New York: Knopf, 1965); Louis Hartz, *The Liberal Tradition in America: An Interpretation of American Political Thought since the Revolution* (New York: Harcourt, Brace, 1955). Hartz's view is itself contested. In the South and elsewhere, traditions were far from liberal. Some Southerners imagined a slave empire including much of the Caribbean basin; see James M. McPherson, *Battle Cry of Freedom: The Civil War Era* (New York: Oxford University Press, 1988), chap. 3, esp. 115–16, and George M. Fredrickson, *The Black Image in the White Mind: The Debate on Afro-American Character and Destiny, 1817–1914* (Scranton, Pa.: Harper and Row, 1971), chap. 11.

but extensive cross-shareholding that produces a similar result; it has low MSP and a particular form of corporatism, with labor incorporation, but not fully autonomous unions. The Netherlands has low blockholding, high corporatism, and low MSP.

All three countries represent important examples of a social bargain type of politics after World War II. They did not get there in exactly the same way—the Netherlands had no powerful domestic fascism—but their policy and political arrangements had some similarity. All are experiencing stress on this "high corporatist" bargain. Germany and Netherlands show the most signs of stirrings in the direction of a transparency coalition.

GERMANY: FROM CORPORATIST BARGAIN TO A TRANSPARENCY COALITION

We argue that Germany is a case of a corporatist compromise accommodating pressures towards a transparency coalition. The preferences of workers and managers are changing, against a backdrop of constant consensual political institutions. The fabric that bound the coalition of managers and workers is fraying, some blockholders are defecting from their accommodation to this alignment, and new strategies by the banking sector (reputational intermediaries) are putting severe pressures on the status quo. These changes are being led by a Social Democratic government, in the blockholding heartland of continental Europe, in a country traditionally rooted in a corporatist compromise. With a series of measures that provide greater protections to minority shareholders, Germany has modified the web of regulations that sustained what Michel Albert called "Rhenish capitalism."

Germany thus shows some signs of an emerging transparency coalition but with dynamics different from those in the United States. Pension funds play a small role in altering workers' preferences. Instead, workers and their unions are in alignment with financial and neoliberal interests in the Free Democratic Party to oppose the "traditionalists" in the Christian Democratic Union so as to forge a new bargain on corporate governance rules more in line with the preferences of shareholders and employees, but leaning towards the preferences of employees. This emerging coalition and its governance goals are obstructed by some unions, some blockholders, the overhang of the underfunded pension system, and the mixed motives of Germany's largest money managers.

The corporatist bargain emerged in Germany out of the midcentury traumas of depression, Fascism, Communism, and war. The major groups of German society bargained explicitly after World War II to create structures that would institutionalize democracy and create the kind of economic and social security whose absence many blamed for Hitler's rise to power in 1933. Codetermination, the welfare state, institutionalized wage and price bargaining—all of these were directly negotiated while the new constitution was written.

While the bargain was recent, its roots go back to the nineteenth century. Co-determination emerged out of the social insurance plans brought forth by Bismarck, an authoritarian conservative, to neutralize labor agitation. Worker representatives were placed on the governing boards to manage the retirement and unemployment insurance plans.[22] Germany is classified as a "late developer," entering the game in the mid–nineteenth century at the iron-steel stage of economic development, when capital requirements were large and when Britain already dominated the scene. It embodied the features Gerschenkron ascribed to it:[23] an important role for banks and for the state, and interlocking relationships among firms—"organized capitalism," as it was called.[24] Here lay the origins of the CME analyzed by Hall and Soskice. Agriculture was an important player and mostly sided with the conservative or authoritarian parties, unlike in Scandinavia. Authoritarian militarism favored the concentrated domestic industries with protectionism, and not the export orientation favored by newer industries like electrical equipment. Blockholding dominated the scene. While Germany grew rapidly, equities markets did not flourish in comparison with the United States, the United Kingdom, or France.

Wartime governments, both in 1914 and 1939, increased the authority of the state, and the Nazis extended it even further. During the Weimar Republic years, the Social Democrats and unions entered governments, but as coalition partners, and accepted the market economy. During those years, there was no challenge to the insider/management control of the firm. After 1933, the Nazis crushed labor organizations completely as they destroyed all autonomous political and economic life. They left private property in place, but under extensive state supervision and planning.

After 1945, the reconstruction of Germany was led politically by the Christian Democrats led by Adenauer and the Social Democrats—two parties whose opposition to the Nazis gave them legitimacy and personnel experienced with democratic politics. The Nazis and the Communists were excluded from public life, with the support and supervision of the Allied occupation of West Germany. The Social and Christian Democrats worked out the "social market" economy: private ownership, union representation on boards, high levels of social services, and the institutions of the coordinated market economy. The system of corporate governance continued: blockholding, dense interlocking networks, deference to trade associations in managing competition, a highly structured labor market, and training methods linking workers, public educational institutions, and employers.

This "German" model expresses the bargain of the specific political conditions of the postwar era. Unlike the U.S. experience described by Roe, there was no sustained movement of populism against financial centralization and centralized control. Organized, cartel-like competition prevailed among business groups; labor was incorporated into the system, given strong protections in job security, in social welfare, voice on the boards, and a strong political party in the national democracy.

It is thus interesting that current changes in Germany reflect a potential break with the past: political support for change comes from a coalition of the Social Democrats and the neoliberal Free Democrats against the opposition of the traditional business party, the Christian Democrats. This fits well with our model

[22] Philip Manow, *Social Protection, Capitalist Production: The Bismarckian Welfare State and the German Political Economy, 1880–1990*, forthcoming; Thelen 2004.

[23] Gerschenkron 1962.

[24] Gourevitch 1986.

of blockholder resistance to the "good governance" bargain proposed by outside investors and the emergence of new alliances in a transparency coalition.

Slow-Motion Change in Blockholding and Shareholder Protections. As the corporatist compromise model predicts, Germany has high levels of ownership concentration, 65 percent according to Faccio and Lang, slightly above both the European and total sample mean. While several of Germany's largest industrial firms such as BASF and Bayer are widely held, with no ultimate blockholder in the web of cross-holdings with Deutsche Bank, the vast majority of the so-called *Mittelstandt* firms are family controlled, and there are many of these on the Frankfurt Stock Exchange. As that model also predicts, Germany has low minority shareholder protections, a score of 33 overall, below both the European and total sample mean.[25]

During the 1990s Germany modified its system. In 1998 the Bundestag modified the company law (Aktiengesetz) with two comprehensive reforms, the Law on Facilitating Raising Capital (Kapitalaufnahmerleichterungsgesetz, or KapAEG) and the Law on Control and Transparency of Corporations (Gesetz zur Kontrolle und Transparenz im Unternehmensbereich, or KonTraG). The KapAEG permits German firms to use IAS for their consolidated financial reporting rather than the rules set by the old Handelsgesetzbuch (HGB, or Commercial Code), thereby avoiding the cost of maintaining two sets of accounting records; it also allows German firms to publish US-GAAP, which the NYSE requires as a precondition for listing. The KonTraG legalized share buybacks, facilitated the introduction of stock options, and abolished unequal voting rights. The Ministry of Justice's commentary on the KonTraG replaced the historic "stakeholder" view of the firm (written down in the Stock Corporation Act of 1937 and approved by the Constitutional Court in 1979) with a shareholder-oriented perspective.[26] These laws were all passed by a CDU-led government; the government changed hands in 1998, and, under SPD leadership, passed even more important reforms.

The Corporate Sector Transparency and Publicity Act (TransPuG) of 2002 obligates firms to publish a yearly statement as to whether and why they do or do not accept the corporate governance code of the proshareholder Cromme Commission. A widely publicized step was the Tax Reduction Act of 2000, which abolished the tax on the sale of shares. This eliminated a major support of the interlocking ownership system among firms and banks, encouraged capital mobility, and thus increased pressure to reward shareholder value. The law was taken up and passed by the SPD-led government, which came into office in 1998, thus

[25] Germany's MSP score is dragged down by the low score on control rules and the large percentage of insiders on the *Aufsichsrat*. Germany's low score on information rules reflects the fact that La Porta et al.'s accounting quality index is quite old; many of Germany's recent reforms, including the widespread use of IAS, are not reflected in this figure. Indices such as the Davis Global Advisors evaluation that reflect these recent reforms show a significant rate of change in Germany's minority shareholder protections.

[26] Höpner 2003a, 13.

between the KonTraG and the TransPuG. In 2001, the government took up the takeover codes, after their failure at the level of the European Union, making hostile takeovers easier than they had been before.

These measures do not transform Germany, but they are steps that move it away from its past practices. On all of these measures, the Social Democrats favored liberalization and were closer to the FDP than was the CDU; Höpner finds a distinct pattern "inconsistent with the ideological affiliation thesis. The CDU, not the SPD turned out to be the party of 'Rhenish' capitalism."[27] Höpner explains this by a mixture of employee mistrust of management and self-interest. Managers have, in the view of workers, too much discretion and too great a capacity to promote their interests ahead of those of workers and the firm. "If shareholder value helps to limit this risk [of managerial agency—our words] this must be in the interest of employees."[28]

This political coalition's newfound interest in "shareholder value" as a counterweight to potentially risky managerial defection from the corporatist compromise was reflected in regulatory changes that slowly boosted MSP in Germany. Among other things, the KonTraG created an independent Deutscher Standardisierungrat (DSR), through which private-sector accounting experts on the Deutscher Rechnungslegungs standards committee (DRSC) debate and set new accounting systems, implicitly based on the IAS.[29] This improved the informational protections for minority shareholders by forcing firms to reveal financial figures in a standard accounting format that had heretofore been available only to blockholders, management, and labor board insiders.

Significantly, the insider board rules remained intact. Germany's two-tier board system of managerial *Vorstand* and supervisory board *Aufsichsrat* remains intact, with the principle of 49 percent employee representation on the Aufsichsrat. Employee representation on supervisory boards was enshrined as an element of *Mitbestimmung* (codetermination) in a series of laws passed in the 1950s and expanded in the mid-1970s.[30] In each of the committees composed of outside experts that reviewed and then endorsed specific corporate governance reforms in Germany, the Mitbestimmung practice remained off-limits—especially under the SPD.

Despite some minor trimming back, bank representatives continue to sit on the Aufsichsrat of major German firms, although this has been reduced by the KonTraG, which has limited the ability of banks to vote proxies for shares deposited with them. Along with tax changes that make it more attractive for the

---

[27] Höpner 2003a, 18.

[28] Höpner 2003a, 24.

[29] With this improved financial data, third-party analysis of German public firms expanded in both scope and sophistication. Notably, the Deutsche Vereinigung für Finanzanalyse und Asset Management issued formal guidelines. Deutsche Vereinigung für Finanzanalyse und Asset Management, "Scorecard for German Corporate Governance," July 2000, www.dvfa.de.

[30] In postwar Germany, the American Occupation authorities kept most of the giant industrial holding companies intact, but put worker-employees on their boards of directors to "democratize" oversight; in postwar Japan, the American Occupation authorities dissolved all of the giant zaibatsu holding companies, but left manager-employees in charge of the boards of directors.

big banks to unwind their equity portfolio, the unwinding of bank blockholdings, as well as the German banks' pursuit of a new strategy as international investment banks, opened the window to contests for control. The dramatic Vodafone-Mannesmann takeover may mark a turning point in this regard.[31]

Although large German firms such as Siemens and Daimler-Chrysler resemble Japanese firms in terms of their promote-from-within recruiting, the market for managers is now competitive by world standards, and incentive stock options are being more widely used.

Germany's Conflicted Financial Intermediaries. Money management and pension firms, financial analysts, and the shareholders' association have been vocal proponents of funding second and third pillars, as well as corporate governance reforms. As in France, extensive lobbying by the financial sector resulted in some incremental pension reform legislation adopted in May 2001 that scaled back the benefits of the state-sponsored retirement system and introduced a supplementary private pension scheme.[32] But these reforms are modest compared to the scale of underfunded pensions in Germany. Reflecting the history of its pension system, Germany has primarily a first-pillar pension system, with low levels of the second and third. This means relatively low employee pressure on the governance system from the standpoint of protecting pension assets, so the German mechanism in the transparency coalition is different than in the United States.

Germany is facing a major pension squeeze, the legacy of relatively generous benefits, a low funding percentage, and the same unfavorable demographic transition as much of the rest of Europe, with an IPD of between 68 and 138. The ratio of pensioners to workers will more than double in the next three decades, from 25:100 to 55:100 by 2035. Based on this prospect, "the range of possibilities open to the politicians for 2035 is between doubling the contribution rates for the same pensions and halving the pensions with the same contribution rates.

---

[31] The "Mannesmann case was unprecedented in post-war Germany as a successful hostile bid made on the open market." Martin Höpner and Gregory Jackson, "An Emerging Market for Corporate Control? The Mannesmann Takeover and German Corporate Governance," Max-Planck-Institute for the Study of Socities Discussion Paper 01/4, 2001, 22. Other hostile takeovers were settled by small coalitions of blockholders; this one was fought out and decided by a larger number of dispersed shareholders, thus representing the "new" mechanism of control typical of the other model. At the time of the takeover, German funds controlled only 13 percent of Mannesmann, while U.S./U.K. funds owned 19 percent. The 10 shareholders holding stakes of 1 percent or more totaled 25.7 percent of all shares, and the 63 holding 0.1 percent or more had a total of 44.3 percent, or 34.1 percent if the single largest shareholder, Hutchison Whampoa, holding 10.2 percent, is excluded; thus shareholding was quite dispersed.

In October 1999, Mannesmann made a move to take over a U.K. firm, Orange, threatening Vodafone's home base, which then led Vodafone to take over Mannesmann. While Mannesmann's dispersal of shares was unusual, it is not isolated. Among the 100 largest companies in Germany, 11 have 75 percent dispersal, with a majority of dispersal in 23. New laws may increase fragmentation further.

[32] Marc A. Stern, "Pension Reform and Global Equity Markets," Birinyi Associates Inc., Topical Study No. 17, Westport, Connecticut, June 2001, 36.

The politicians can choose some point within this range but they cannot perform miracles."[33]

The German guild of financial analysts, the Deutsche Vereinigung für Finanzanalyse und Asset Management, which represents 1,000 professionals in 400 investment banks and asset management firms in Germany, issued a set of formal guidelines that "scorecard" the accounting, auditing, and disclosure practices of listed firms.[34]

But Germany's financial firms have not been universally enthusiastic about the effort to reform corporate governance. Deutsche Bank, for example, also manages Germany's largest private-sector money management firm. With a broad set of services and a close relationship with Germany's biggest industrial firms—with a Deutsche Bank representative sitting on the board of most large listed firms—Deutsche Bank is conflicted in pressing for strong corporate governance discipline.

The successful hostile takeover of Mannesmann by Vodafone in 1999–2000 was an unusual move in the German context. It strengthens the notion that change is under way that erodes the "institutional complementarity" concepts used to describe the standard German model. German banks are reorienting from "house" bank to investment bank, a significant segment of German business may become subject to a market for corporate control, German firms are increasingly under pressure to achieve higher market valuations, and, as a result, the distributional compromises of the German model are under pressure.[35]

At the same time, other debates on corporate governance, more specifically regarding the institutions regulating contests for control, have taken place both within Germany and in the European Union, suggesting that the Mannesmann takeover may have been an anomaly, not a marker of a sea change in German attitudes towards takeovers.[36]

---

[33] As in many other countries, a committee of economists working for the Federal Ministry of Economics and Research recommended switching as much as possible from the first pillar towards second- and third-pillar schemes instead, rather than raising taxes to fully fund the first pillar, because of "the covetousness with which the politicians would look at a capital stock accumulated by the pension insurance system. It is hard to imagine a future federal Minister who wants to win the next election, resisting the pensioners' desire to use the capital stock prematurely. Public money is a great temptation." Hans-Werner Sinn, "The Crisis of Germany's Pension Insurance System and How It Can Be Resolved," NBER Working Paper No. 7304, 1999, 17.

[34] Deutsche Vereinigung für Finanzanalyse und Asset Management, "Scorecard for German Corporate Governance," July 2000, www.dvfa.de.

[35] This would mark a shift from a historical pattern of low rate of return but low valuation. Höpner and Jackson argue this is now unstable, as lower market-to-book ratios leave a greater scope of takeover premiums through restructuring and as lower relative valuations make corporations vulnerable to takeover from share swaps. Höpner and Jackson 2001.

[36] Bank ties at Mannesmann were not strong, and job loss fears appear to have been low, perhaps because this was an expanding sector, telecommunications. Labor appears to have accepted the importance of the firm's strategy over its class interest, and did not use codetermination to inhibit the outcome. It sought some protections, which do not appear to have been followed after the merger. Some worker-owners sold shares to Vodafone to get a good price. Regulatory powers were not used to stop the process.

More revealing about the politics of governance in German debates is the case of discussion in the European Parliament of Article 9 concerning rules on mergers and the market for control. As the European Community seeks common standards, Article 9 required shareholder approvals in advance of defensive measures by the target company in the case of a hostile takeover.[37] The opponents wanted more protection for the target firms, the supporters less. The measure was defeated on a tie vote on July 4, 2001.

Höpner's analysis of the voting shows that nationality and ideological affiliation mattered most and interacted in interesting ways. Ideology drives a correlation—the Left voted against a liberalized takeover rule. But Höpner shows the force of correlation is driven by the parties of green, liberal, far right and far left coloration. The more centrist parties, Social Democrats, Conservative and Christian Democratic, followed national lines, not ideological ones.[38] That is, Germany and other countries voted to defend their "national production model." The more LME (liberal market economy in the varieties-of-capitalism classification), the more likely a vote on the liberal side, the more OME, the more likely a vote against it. This evidence fits the corporatist explanation, cross-class voting in favor of a production system.[39]

This decision on Article 9 provides evidence for several arguments. The left versus right divide supports Roe's interpretation. The importance of national context (the defense of the "national production system") fits the corporatist argument and the logic of institutional complementarity of the varieties-of-capitalism authors. The intra-Germany pattern (Social Democrats more reformist than CDU) fits the transparency coalition logic. The business party more strongly favors the blockholders' status quo than does the labor party. The CDU relies heavily on firms deeply invested in the OME, in what Albert calls the Rhenish model of capitalism. Change appears quite costly to them. This does not fit the good-governance model which cannot explain the support by many owners of capital in Germany and elsewhere of blockholding and resistance to QCL.

Businesses more oriented toward markets and the "new economy" support the Free Democrats, the neoliberal party, who wish to dismantle the corporatist system and are not supporters of worker co-determination. This fits the corporatist model's predictions. The surprise lies with the SPD. There the leadership's position reflects the concern of many elements of the party and the union movement to adjust the economy to new conditions and find ways of protecting workers in that transition. They fear the existing system gives the illusion of worker participation without the reality. Management has found ways of concealing information, of layering decisions to exclude workers' representatives. Unions, therefore, demand greater transparency as a way of assuring their ability to participate in decisions and monitor management. In so doing, they also articulate the concerns of outside investors about management autonomy.

[37] Höpner 2003a, 3.
[38] Höpner 2003a, 8.
[39] Höpner 2003a, 10.

Privatization of firms contributes to the development of public traded shares. Capitalization of the economy deepens. More shares are available for trade. This generates a lobby of investors (as our first model of corporate governance predicts) who become interested in regulatory reform for the sake of minority shareholder protection. We can see evidence of this effect in the behavior of prospective reputational intermediaries.

Change is also taking place among German business groups. Some question the older model. Firms heavily engaged in the world economy, in Europe, the United States, and elsewhere, see advantages to a more flexible system. Competition at the world level requires mergers and acquisitions; that need provides motive for higher capitalization of equity, as well as the capacity to shift funds toward higher rates of return. German banks and major firms want such flexibility. Smaller businesses interested in new technology, start-ups, and other aspects of the new economy similarly want access to more fluid capital. The Neuer Markt was formed in part to respond to those needs, but it failed when the stock market bubble burst in 2001.

We see, then, in Germany the struggle among alternative cleavages. In the framework of cross-class coalitions around corporatism, we see the possibility of a different coalition around transparency, at tension yet further with traditional left-right conflicts. This happens because there is movement within each of the major social categories—always a condition for a new political realignment. On the side of labor, we see rising concern with pension fund and other investment assets, and a demand for greater transparency in Mitbestimmung. On the side of capital and managers, we see motives for changing the system. Other players see business in a greater role for equity markets. More broadly, the politicians and their constituencies are under pressure to balance budgets and deal with pension issues.

These forces interact to make realignment of policy possible, the formation of a different policy majority. Can this happen in the same institutional framework? This is an interesting test of the role of different causal variables: if it does happen in the existing party and electoral system, that will tell us a lot about the greater role of preferences and underlying economic interests in driving policy. It would diminish the importance of formal institutions as an absolute constraint. New alliances are possibilities, but by no means inevitable. Politicians would have to construct these new alliances, as they are not automatic.

JAPAN: CONCENTRATION WITHOUT OWNERS

We argue that Japan is a case of a resilient corporatist compromise, grounded in a post–World War II historic compromise between managers and workers that is sustained by consensual political institutions. Since World War II there have been no broad changes in preferences towards governance, and only marginal changes in political institutions (a partial modification in electoral rules in 1996). As predicted by the corporatist compromise model, Japanese MSPs remain relatively low, although concentration is also low. This low level of concentration also has historical roots, when Japan's blockholding zaibatsu families were wiped out by the U.S. Occupation.

Workers' preferences towards corporate governance have not changed due to a largely unfunded pillar 1 pension system and a set of financial intermediaries with primary allegiance to firms and managers rather than to beneficiary shareholders. In the context of lingering keiretsu affiliations and the thumb of government bureaucrats, Japanese fund managers have been extremely cautious in flexing their corporate governance muscles. The Japanese Association of Pension Funds has made some modest noises suggesting that investors include asset return as well as "stakeholder values" in investment decisions, but has only tepidly endorsed the notion of corporate governance reform.[40]

Japan's consensual political institutions are sustained (and in turn sustain) a set of "peak" organizations such as the Keidanren and Nikkeiren, which, although atrophied from their height during the 1960s and 1970s, remain basically intact. Japan remains on the upper end of the corporatist scale, .77 according to the corporatist index. There is no explicit left-center coalition in Japan reflecting the manager plus worker alliance, as in the Netherlands; in fact, postwar Japanese politics have been dominated by a series of center-right Liberal Democratic Party (LDP) coalitions in the parliament (Diet). But the LDP ruling coalitions operate within a highly consensual institutional framework with multiple veto points—veto points within the LDP itself, its shifting coalition parties within the Diet majority, and finally with the opposition parties.

A Japanese-Style Great Reversal In the late nineteenth century, Japanese founder-oligarchs and an equity market grew together. In this sense, Japan's pattern resembled Germany as a late developer: strong state involvement, benefits to those with privileged access to the new imperial Meiji system, the growth of large economic combines in Japan called *zaibatsu*, with interlocking firms containing a bank and several related industries. The founders of the great zaibatsu firms in Taishō and Meiji Japan, like Iwasaki Yotaro of Mitsubishi, built their vast industrial empires under the modernizing political umbrella of the Meiji political oligarchs—figures such as Ito Hirobumi and Yamagata Aritomo, who were generals before they became statesmen—with a single-mindedness to industrialize that presaged the Korean generals by 100 years, but more skill at grafting a facade of democracy and national legitimacy on their industrializing program.

At the same time, a Japanese stock market also began to emerge, as Rajan and Zingales observe, more prominent than the classic view of Japan normally allows. Labor was weak, though unions and left parties emerged around the turn of the century—along with other social institutions such as rudimentary welfare and educational organs borrowed from Bismarck's Germany, thereby laying the

---

[40] Ministry of Welfare, Pension Fund Management Bureau, "Regarding Basic Asset Management Policy for National Pension and Retirement Savings Accounts," paper presented to the International Corporate Governance Forum in Tokyo, July 2001; Tomomi Yano, "Nenkinshikin unyō kara mita corporate governance," paper for the International Corporate Governance Forum, July 2001, Tokyo.

groundwork for corporatism far in the future.[41] But democratic political institutions were weak and collapsed in the interwar years.

War and militarism made the system even more centralized. State elites constrained the autonomy of the zaibatsu, and a variety of structures of state supervision of the economy developed. Japan's military junta of the 1930s (whose ideology incorporated populist, even leftist ideas, mixed with nativism and far-right nationalism) despised their homegrown "great capitalists" as profiteers from the high-growth period of the Taishō era and fostered a group of competitive, essentially state-controlled "new zaibatsu" such as Nissan and Furukawa. The economy was in private hands technically, but state directed in many respects. Many of the instruments of state supervision that became famous in the 1960s with Japan's great boom were forged and refined during the 1930s and 1940s by the military government.

Then the U.S. Occupation expropriated the old zaibatsu blockholders (such families as Iwasaki and Mitsui) after World War II. The American occupation wiped out the families who owned these zaibatsu and pushed through land reform that expelled the landowning aristocrats (in Germany, similarly, the landowning aristocratic Junkers lost their estates as well). While the owners were removed, the firms remained intact. The U.S. Occupation proscribed the zaibatsu and imposed antitrust laws and free unions. But the firms undermined those rules by developing extensive cross-shareholding. This left managers in charge, free from any effective market for control.

Labor was incorporated into the system, but in a subordinate position. After 1945, labor militancy was high with many strikes. Forcible repression was forbidden by the U.S. authorities. Management and workers settled on a "deal," job security in exchange for managerial control—the same deal we see in many parts of Europe. Unlike most European countries, the unions lost their autonomy; they became company unions, under managerial tutelage. Union-affiliated political parties were not able to form a coherent political opposition, alternating in office or sharing power. Lifetime employment developed for some percentage of workers in this period; it was not, as often misunderstood, a permanent eternal feature of the Japanese economy.

Japanese professional managers worked hard during the postwar decades to foster the notion that managers and workers were in the same boat.[42] This was an explicit goal of both the Nikkeiren and the Keidanren, the powerful business organizations who served as the voice of business in Japan's corporatist negotiations. Unions were organized on a company basis, rather than on a trade basis, further cementing the coalition of mutual interest between workers and managers on one side and "capital" on the other. With institutions such as lifetime employment (at least for large, usually listed firms), job security became extremely important to the average worker and to the manager alike.

[41] Andrew Gordon, *The Evolution of Labor Relations in Japan: Heavy Industry, 1835–1955* (Cambridge: Harvard University Press, 1985); Gordon, *Labor and Imperial Democracy in Prewar Japan* (Berkeley and Los Angeles: University of California Press, 1991).

[42] Bi Gao, *Economic Ideology and Japanese Industrial Policy: Developmentalism from 1931 to 1965* (Cambridge: Cambridge University Press, 1997), chaps. 2 and 3.

Profit-maximizing capitalists were few and far between on the other side of the coalitional divide. The few postwar entrepreneurial blockholders such as Honda and Morita who survived Japan's restrictive administrative, competitive, and financial policies (by relying on export markets in new product areas) were themselves gradually absorbed into the corporatist system and their family blockholdings diluted over time, until family "control" of vast firms such as Toyota Motors and Matsushita was in name only: the professional managers were in the saddle.

"Active capital" usually meant foreign capital, which was also held at bay by the state for most of the postwar period. In contrast, domestic capital flowed through a heavily regulated and state-supervised banking system, which also held, through cross-shareholdings, a sufficiently large block of equity in industrial firms (and each other) so as to neutralize the market for corporate control.

Japanese managers had, in effect, created a set of synthetic blockholders, though not with an interest in maximizing shareholder value. Nonetheless, the interlocking network of fellow-keiretsu managers and "main banks" was alleged to provide a substitute mechanism of monitoring and discipline for managers.[43] Whether this system of synthetic discipline by keiretsu affiliates worked well or worked at all is a matter of continuing debate. Japan did grow prodigiously after World War II, well enough to challenge for a time the ideological hegemony of the U.S. model and generate serious evaluation of other models.[44]

At its height, pundits and not a few scholars celebrated the system's virtues in contrast to the arm's-length relationships of the U.S. model: cross-subsidizers able to make a longer-range evaluation of product development; the interlocking supplier-producer-distributor relationship able to make continuous marginal improvements and low-defect production through incentives for information sharing; labor relations giving management an incentive to train workers and workers the incentive to acquire firm-specific skills; "patient capital" able to take the long view; and so forth.

Between 1985 and 1995, the bloom of Japan's economic miracle started to fade. Japanese listed firms gradually reduced their reliance on external bank financing. This meant bank discipline weakened, leaving Japanese managers in a monitoring vacuum and opening up the door to the agency costs of free cash flow.[45] Punditry

[43] Carl Kester, *Japanese Takeovers: The Global Contest for Corporate Control* (Boston: Harvard Business School Press, 1991); Kester 1996; Masahiko Aoki and Hugh Patrick, *The Japanese Main Bank System: Its Relevance for Developing and Transforming Economies* (New York: Oxford University Press, 1995); Eusuke Sakakibara, *Shihon shugi o koeta Nihon: Nihon-gata shijo keizai taisei no seiritsu to tenkai* (Tokyo: Toyo Keizai, 1990); Porter 1990.

[44] Aoki 2001; and World Bank, *The East Asian Miracle: Economic Growth and Public Policy* (New York: Oxford University Press, 1993).

[45] Miyajima demonstrated that the turnover of Japanese senior managers as a function of financial performance has been steadily declining over the five periods of his study (from 1959 through 1993), which the author attributes to the declining ability of Japanese banks to monitor these firms. According to Miyajima's database of 100 leading publicly traded Japanese firms, the correlation between turnover and financial performance began to disappear in the period 1984–88. Miyajima's more recent findings override earlier studies by Kaplan, which argued that Japanese executive turnover was little different from U.S. or European turnover. Hideyaki Miyajima, "The Impact of Deregulation on

shifted from celebrating the superiority of the Japanese system in the 1980s to decrying its shortcomings in the 1990s.

Japan's macroeconomy showed all the signs of inattention to return on equity, with slumping productivity and extremely high capital intensity during the late 1970s and through the 1980s. The Tokyo stock market imploded in 1989, yet few industrial firms were allowed to go under. And despite a decade of slow-motion crisis, especially in the banking sector, cross-shareholdings unwound only very slowly, from 21.2 percent at their peak in 1990 to 18.2 percent in 1997.[46] This gradual liquidation was propelled chiefly by the banks' need to bulk up their capital in order to meet the Basle criteria for financial leverage.

A Slow March on MSPs Despite these financial pressures, shareholder protections changed only slowly in Japan. For example, Japanese institutions of accounting and audit remained well below global standards for decades. Until 1999 Japanese firms continued to report on an unconsolidated basis, thereby allowing firms to "park" losses at unconsolidated affiliates. Japanese accounting practices also allowed Japanese firms to carry assets at book rather than market value, permitting managers to avoid recognizing losses on deflated real estate or securities holdings—a serious issue in the aftermath of Japan's post-bubble asset collapse. As of fiscal year 2001 (after many slips and compromises) most Japanese firms began to report figures on a consolidated basis, use a mark-to-market basis for asset valuation, and recognize unfunded pension liabilities on their balance sheets—although the government continued to issue special reporting dispensation for some financial sector firms.[47] The net effect of these lags in accounting and audit is that only insiders knew the true extent of a firm's financial performance and risk.

Japanese company law and the listing rules of the major exchanges even allowed firms to use internal rather than external auditors to validate financial figures to the outside. Some cosmetic changes were made to the role of the internal auditor, or *kansayaku*, in company law changes in 2002, but the kansayaku position as defined by Japanese law fell far short of independent external audit. It remained an insider job, a sinecure for former employees or retired bank executives.

Corporate Governance and Finance," in *Is Japan Really Changing Its Ways? Regulatory Reform and the Japanese Economy*, Lonny E. Carlile and Mark C. Tilton, eds. (Washington, D.C.: Brooking Institution Press, 1998), 68; Steven Kaplan, "Corporate Governance and Corporate Performance: A Comparison of Germany, Japan, and the U.S.," *Journal of Applied Corporate Finance* 9 (1997): 86–93.

[46] Megumi Suto, "New Developments in the Japanese Corporate Governance in the 1990's: The Role of Pension Funds," *Hamburgische Welt-Wirtschafts-Archiv*, July 1999, 13.

[47] *Nihon Keizai Shimbun*, Nikkei Weekly, "Accounting Standards to Be Set by Private Institution," April 3, 2000, 13. Japan's standards-setting institution, the Kigyō Kaikei Shingikai (Business Accounting Discussion Council, or BADC), formerly under the thumb of the Ministry of Finance (MOF, now Zaimusho), has recently been shifted to the new Financial Supervisory Agency (FSA). The FSA, JICPA, and Keidanren have agreed to replace the BADC with a new standards-setting organ, independent of the ministry, at least in principle, with a full-time staff and budget.

There was also little movement towards independent outside boards of directors. Employee-managers dominated the boards of listed firms: 80 percent of
Japanese corporations had no outside board members at all. The small number of
"outside" directors came from affiliated firms or the main bank: in the limit, insiders all, just like the nominally independent kansayaku.[48]

Under the pretense of corporate governance "reform," in 2001–3, a handful of
prominent Japanese firms announced reductions in the size of their boards, split-
ting the board into a supervisory board on top in charge of strategy, and an executive board below in charge of operations, in a widely publicized reorganization
known as the "operating executive system," or *shikkō yakuinsei*. A handful of
prominent academics, retired public officials, and a few token foreigners were
appointed to these boards by the insider chairman, but they served the function
of similar trophy directors in the West: to go through the motions, offer sage
advice to the insiders, but otherwise stay out of really monitoring, much less compensating, the insider managers. The notion of a majority of outside directors
holding insider management teams to account, on behalf of the stockholders, was
beyond the pale.

Some changes in Japan's standards of fiduciary duty of directors and accounting practices that took place in the late 1990s and were heralded as evidence of
a new wave of corporate governance reform were instead, we argue, the unintended by-product of moral hazard losses and gross managerial incompetence
stemming from Japan's so-called Bubble Period of 1985–89.[49]

The managers of large Japanese public firms continued to be either promoted
from within, meaning selected by their predecessors and chairmen, or in some
cases from a senior government post, as an *amakudari* official, usually if the firm
were highly regulated or government-controlled.

Japanese top managers have few long-term incentives to align their interests with
shareholder value. The use of stock options spread only slowly despite regulatory
changes in 1997 that made it easier for firms to issue options, and despite Japan's

---

[48] Robert Monks and Nell Minow, *Corporate Governance* (Cambridge, Mass.: Blackwell, 1995),
272–73.

[49] It is unlikely that the Keidanren or the Ministry of Justice anticipated the number of financial
scandals that would result from the bank bailout and subsequent Diet hearings, nor did they foresee
the emergence of fee-seeking lawyers willing to pursue such shareholder claims in Japan's historically
unlitigious business culture. The bulk of the shareholder lawsuits in Japan have been filed by a quasi-
populist legal organization, the Kabunushi ("stockholder") Ombudsman, and by several small, politically active "gadfly" law firms in western Japan.

The tightening of the fiduciary responsibility of boards of directors towards shareholders was the
outcome of negotiations between the Keidanren and the Ministry of Justice regarding modifications of Japan's commercial code in 1992–93 that reduced the filing requirements for plaintiffs who
intended to bring suit against directors. Such suits had previously been deterred since plaintiffs
were required to file a fee corresponding to a fixed percentage of the total claim. This required
large sums to be deposited by the plaintiff for suits that could last five years or more. The new flat
fee of 8,200 yen (about $75) reduced the ante dramatically. Mark West, "The Pricing of Share-
holder Derivative Actions in Japan and the United States," *Northwestern University Law Review* 88
(1994): 1465.

remarkably favorable tax treatment for such options when they are exercised—the 26 percent capital gains rate is far below the marginal income tax rate for ordinary income for most managers.

There has been change in Japan, thus, but it has been gradual, and it has been generated by a public broadly unhappy with managerial incompetence and examples of fraud, not from altered public preferences towards corporate governance, or the emergence of a new transparency coalition.

In a recent book comparing Japanese and German corporate governance, Dore argues that change is taking place slowly, if at all, in most institutions of economic governance in Japan, including corporate governance, despite these slow-motion pressures for change in the financial system.[50] He posits a high degree of institutional continuity in Japan, including those that perpetuate the imagined community of manager-worker solidarity.

Yet this notion of continuity is disputed by scholars such as Curtis, who argue the institutional mechanisms of corporatist consultation in Japan have been steadily eroding since the peak years of joint dialogue and compromise on productivity and wage determination in the 1970s.[51] Labor union membership in Japan peaked in 1975, at 35 percent, declining to only 23 percent by 1997, and labor itself split into two groups, the left-oriented Sōhyō, with a stronghold in SOE unions, and private-sector unions, usually organized on a firm, rather than industry, basis. The overall Rengō labor federation is fractured and weak. By the same token, the Keidanren, Nikkeiren, and Keizaidoyukai have declined in coherence and influence over the years.

Nonetheless, these traditional organizations managed to slow down or entirely block changes in corporate governance rules in order to maintain the status quo. Employee-managers (rather than entrepreneurs) retained firm control of the corporatist entities speaking for business—the Keidanren, Nikkeiren, and Keizaidoyukai.

For example, in order to halt the unwinding of passive equity cross-holdings, which could open up the prospect of contests for control, given Japan's straightforward voting rules, the Keidanren pushed for a variety of methods employing tax changes and quasi-government entities to prop up stock prices and absorb these liquidated cross-holding shares.[52] Business managers who served on the accounting standards body tried to water down or delay the tighter accounting rules and enhanced disclosure, and were supported in this resistance by the Keidanren. In the face of calls for independent third-party audit, the Keidanren called for strengthening the role of the kansayaku, accepting a few cosmetic changes in the statutory qualifications of the kansayaku. In the face of calls for

[50] Dore 2000.

[51] Gerald Curtis, *The Logic of Japanese Politics: Leaders, Institutions, and the Limits of Change* (New York: Columbia University Press, 1999), 45–50.

[52] The Keidanren wanted tax changes that would allow firms to swap each other's mutual holdings without running the transactions through a market-clearing mechanism, thereby keeping stock prices high and keeping stock out of the hands of third parties. It also proposed a Securities Finance Corporation to manage equity cross-holdings from firms and then hold them in trust, using the shares as collateral for loans from the Bank of Japan.

independent outside directors, senior managers and the Keidanren used this as a justification to reduce board size, under the executive manager system, which further strengthened the hand of senior employee-managers rather than making them accountable to shareholders. Dore notes the deftness with which the trendy vocabulary of shareholder value was adopted from abroad and then stripped of most of its meaning in practice. In fact, Japanese managers showed skill in appropriating the language of corporate governance reform abroad by founding the Japan Corporate Governance Association.[53]

The rules in Japan's long-established commercial code that provide protection for the voting rights of minority shareholders conform to global standards, and are superior to those in many other markets.[54] But no change has occurred in Japan's informal control institutions that bar hostile takeovers, and make even friendly acquisitions difficult to execute. Japanese institutional investors, such as trust banks, insurance companies, and pension fund managers, do not tender their shares in hostile takeovers, and the high percentage of share cross-holdings, or *mochiai-kabu*, is unwinding only slowly. This inactive control market persists despite a large number of tempting targets on the Tokyo Stock Exchange with a market capitalization well below their asset book value.[55]

Political Institutions. How could this tightly knit insider system resist the corrosive effects of product-market and financial competition? We argue that the Japanese political system favored the corporatist cross-class bargain. Until the 1990s, Japan's electoral law had multi-seat districts. Candidates from the same party had an incentive to build specialized clienteles, an exchange of favors and regulation

[53] Noting the increasing discussion of reform abroad, and aware that the OECD was working on its own governance recommendations, they issued a set of recommendations for "reform," giving lip-service to the notion of shareholder value, but basically rejecting that approach in favor of a broad, "stakeholder" approach. They carefully divided their recommendations into those that should be implemented in short order ("step A principles") and those that "should be aimed for in the early twenty-first century or that require legal reforms on a grand scale ("step B principles"). The principle of a majority of outside independent directors was carefully designated as step B, meaning someday, but not now. In a stroke of irony, these Japan Corporate Governance Association recommendations managed to get the endorsement of CalPERS. Nihon Corporate Governance Forum, "Coporato Gabanansu gensoku: Atarashii nihongata kigyō tōchi o kangaeru," *Coporaato Gabanansu Gensoku Sakutei Iinkai*, May 26, 1998.

[54] Kester 1991, 97. Certain filing and prenotification requirements for undertaking a tender offer make it more difficult and expensive to engage in contests for control, but these requirements are comparatively less limiting than the U.S. state-level antitakeover statutes that were passed in the early 1990s.

[55] There are only a few other departures from this solid wall of indifference to the merits of (and financial gains available from) an active control market. Cable & Wireless managed to acquire a majority of the unlisted shares of International Digital Communications in 1999, to complete what was essentially a foreign direct investment (FDI) transaction, and M&A Consulting failed to obtain a majority of the listed (and steeply undervalued) shares of Shoei, a Canon affiliate. One has to go back more than a decade, to T. Boone Pickens's failed attempt to obtain a board seat after purchasing a sizable minority stake in Koito Manufacturing, to find another example of a hostile takeover attempt in Japan. Livedoor's hostile bid for Nippon Broadcasting in 2005 may indicate a sea-change; or, like Germany's Mannesmann deal, it may precipitate a new round of antitakeover regulations.

for votes and cash. This heavily favored producer interests rather than general-ized competition for the swing voter. Districting heavily overrepresented farmers and the countryside. Politics turned on jockeying among the LDP's internal po-litical coalitions, or *habatsu*, who competed for narrow segments of the electorate, but who could, once internal compromises had been forged, essentially dictate Diet legislation.

A partial electoral reform in 1996 created single-member, first-past-the-post electoral districts, equaling half of the Lower House seats, with a goal to create a stronger, disciplined competitive party system. This did not take place right away: instead of electoral districts the end of the LDP's decades-long Diet majority added several more veto players to the policy game, as coalition cabinets were cobbled together and the LDP further fragmented. According to a careful study by Tiberghien, the number of veto players rose from one in 1990 to a peak of seven in 1993–94 (under the Hosokawa and Hata cabinets), then fell to the two-to-three level for the balance of the decade—and currently is at three.[56] Change in formal institutions or in the party system has not caused any major shift in pol-icy outputs.[57]

Politics and Pensions. While the pension system in Japan had serious underfund-ing problems, it did not generate pressures toward transparency in the corporate governance system. Often referred to as the "third rail" of Japanese politics (indeed in most countries), Japan has difficult demographics, with a rapidly aging population and very low immigration. With a knife's edge majority in the Lower House and a minority in the Upper House, and with more veto players now in the game, the ruling LDP coalition was unwilling to antagonize any segment of vot-ers by cutting benefits or raising taxes.

Japanese law requires the Diet to revisit pension legislation every five years. There are many veto points along the way.[58] The Ministry of Health writes an assessment, which is pondered by the inevitable consultative *shingikai* including representatives of unions, employers, academics, and bureaucrats (in this case, the Pensions Advisory Committee), discussed by the policy affairs committee of the LDP, debated at considerable length in the parliament, negotiated between the ruling LDP and its coalition partners, and then modified into law.[59]

The result was a slow, tinkering-at-the-edges approach to pension reform, with a slight trimming of pillar 1 benefits on one hand, and a modest attempt to encourage 401(k)-type third-pillar supplementary investments on the other. An

[56] Yves Tiberghien, "Veto Players, Financial Globalization, and Policy Making: A Political Analy-sis of the Pathway of Structural Reforms in Japan, 1993–2002," paper delivered at the Annual Meet-ings of the American Political Science Association, August 2003, 21–22.

[57] Tiberghien 2003, 21–22.

[58] Jon Choy, "Tokyo Hesitates on Pension Reform," *Japan Economic Institute Report*, January 28, 2000.

[59] Jean-François Estienne and Kiyoshi Murakami, "The Japanese Experience of Review and Reform of Public Pension Schemes," in *Social Dialogue and Pension Reform: United Kingdom, United States, Germany, Japan, Sweden, Italy, Spain,* Emmanuel Reynaud, ed. (Geneva: International Labor Organization, 2000).

ambitious parliamentary campaign to introduce 401(k) plans began in the late 1990s by several LDP political entrepreneurs.[60] These ambitious plans were cut back bit by bit as the proposal worked its way through the multiple veto gates. The final result, enacted into law in 2001, was extremely modest, leaving the existing three pillars intact.[61]

The net result is that the link between Japanese workers and the equity holdings of their retirement funds is attenuated. The size of pension funds alone does not by itself produce pressure for shareholder value, as we have seen in other cases, for that connection is mediated by the institutional relationship between the pensioners and the management.

Reputational Intermediaries. The Japanese case illustrates the critical role of financial intermediaries in enforcing corporate governance discipline on firms on behalf of the equity beneficiaries—or attenuating those pressures. As noted earlier in several chapters, financial intermediaries can put pressure on firms for enhanced protections of minority shareholders on behalf of the shareholding worker-beneficiaries. These institutions may also attenuate or even nullify that pressure completely. In Japan, the passivity of institutional investors plays a key role in maintaining the corporatist compromise status quo.

Domestic trust banks (*shinyō ginkō*) and insurance (*seimei hōken*) companies dominate the investment management business in Japan. Although the market share of foreign investment advisory firms grew from zero to 10 percent of Japan's pension market during the 1990s, the lion's share of the pension market—89 percent of all *kōsei nenkin kikin* funds, to be exact—remains in the hands of Japanese firms.[62]

Both trust banks and insurance firms come under the prudential supervision of the Financial Services Agency (FSA), the newest incarnation of the traditional Ministry of Finance, and are also subject to review by the Ministry of Health and Labor with regard to managing pension funds. Historically, these ministries imposed strict regulations on asset allocation percentages, such as the so-called 5-3-3-2 rule, which required 50 percent in secure fixed-income assets (usually government bonds), 30 percent in domestic equities, 30 percent in all foreign currency assets, and 20 percent in real estate. The supervisory ministries also discouraged competition among managing firms. Fees were set in a cartel-like fashion by the pension fund association, and were bundled into a total "relationship" that obscured true performance.[63] The legal trustee arrangements of these

[60] Yasuhisa Shiozaki is an LDP Diet member from Ehime Prefecture and an outspoken supporter of corporate governance and accounting reform in Japan. See Y. Shiozaki, "Corporate Governance Standards and Capital Markets," speech presented to the Symposium on Building the Financial System of the 21st Century, October 4, 2003, Tokyo, available at http://www.y-shiozaki.or.jp/en/speech.

[61] For employed workers, the maximum tax deductible amount was limited to 17,000 yen per month, paid entirely by the employer, with no additional matching by the employee. For the self-employed, this was capped at 86,000 yen per month.

[62] Suto 1999, 21.

[63] Norio Nishi, "The Transformation of the Japanese Pension Market," *National Bureau of Asian Research Publications: Executive Insight*, No. 14, December 1998, 13.

pension funds effectively severed the link between the control rights of stock ownership and the ultimate beneficiaries.[64]

Moreover, the largest trust banks and life insurance companies were also central members of the keiretsu, with little incentive to oppose the management of fellow keiretsu firms—whose corporate governance practices generally mirrored their own.[65]

Whither Japan? Among the major industrial countries, Japan seems the least responsive to the supposed Darwinian pressure of international capital flows in forcing governance reform toward the shareholder value model. Ronald Dore concludes that "for the moment, the redistribution of labor income through payroll and other taxes and PAYGO pensions seems likely to continue to be the mainstream. Japanese savings are going to remain more modest in proportion and to find their way into the global economy through bank lending, rather than through asset managers operating in secondary markets all over the globe. The number of votes with a direct interest in global financial markets . . . is thereby limited. As far as pensions go, the state-market balance has not tipped decisively in favor of the market and there are no immediate signs that it will soon do so."[66]

NETHERLANDS: THE EVOLUTION OF "POLDERMODEL" CORPORATISM

Casual readers may be taken aback by the juxtaposition of Japan and the Netherlands as corporate governance cases—though it is a striking historical footnote that the world's first large corporation, the Dutch East India Company (or VOC, described in this book's preface) spent a good part of two and a half centuries negotiating with the Japanese government on the terms of its operations and its trading monopoly halfway around the world.[67]

[64] "In sum, in the Japanese pension funds scheme ownership and control rights to control the companies are separated. In any contracts, legal shareholders are trustee bodies such as trust banks and life insurance companies, though actual shareholders are pension funds. In the existing regulatory framework, there are no distinct rules for pension funds to exercise their rights as shareholders. All shareholders' rights are passed through to their trustee bodies." Suto 1999, 26–27.

[65] "[T]he constraints derived from relations with sponsoring companies [of pension plans] on the behavior of corporate pension funds might be stronger in Japan than the U.S. If the Japanese corporate pension funds had an explicit route to execute voting rights it could be more difficult for them to use it in practice than in the U.S., because of stronger relationships between business companies and financial institutions." Suto 1999, 30.

[66] Ronald Dore, "Globalization and the Possibility of National Opt-Outs," in *Pensioners to the Casino*, forthcoming.

[67] The VOC established a permanent trading foothold in Japan at its "factory" in Dejima, near Nagasaki, and was granted a 250-year trading monopoly, from the Tokugawa shogunate, as part of very extended commercial and diplomatic negotiations. So central was the VOC lens to the Japanese government, which otherwise adopted a policy of rigid isolation from the outside world (*sakoku*) that the Tokugawa government depended upon Japanese translations of VOC dispatches and reports for its view of the world from roughly 1600 until the Meiji restoration in 1868—so much so that Japanese experts on foreign affairs and science for two centuries all studied Dutch and were known collectively as *rangakusha*, or "Netherlands scholars."

The pairing of Japan and the Netherlands, however, is less surprising to two rather dissimilar groups—equity portfolio managers and comparative political scientists. The former group is used to investing in "world scale" Dutch and Japanese firms as part of their global portfolios and, indeed, regularly must select listed firms from the Amsterdam and Tokyo stock exchanges in order to construct a balanced global portfolio; Netherlands accounts for about 2.5 percent of the MSCI index and Japan for almost 10 percent.

Comparative political scientists find much in common between the two countries, despite their remote geographical and historical roots—both late developers in a Gerschenkronian sense, both with a corporatist solution to social pressures hammered out in the period following World War II (after different experiences between the wars), both with consensual political systems, and both with low MSP and low concentration—nominally "outliers" in the standard view of corporate governance.

The shareholder concentration and MSP levels of the Netherlands and Japan pose a puzzle for corporate governance scholars. The Netherlands' level of shareholder protections is 34 on our 100-point minority shareholder protection index. This is below the mean of the total sample and in the lower third of European countries. This low level of shareholder protections is combined with low blockholder concentration of 20 percent—a level of broadly diffused ownership exceeded by very few countries, despite this low level of shareholder protections.[68]

Equally anomalous is the high ratio of market capitalization to GDP, at 170 percent, and the high penetration of the Amsterdam Bourse by foreign portfolio investors, around 55 percent. More striking, and puzzling at first glance, is the Netherlands' high ratio of accumulated private pension assets, at 113 percent of GDP. This is consistent with a low IPD of the pillar 1 scheme, at only 55 percent of GDP, low by European standards. But this is inconsistent with the prediction that high private pension assets will enhance workers' preferences and activism for enhanced shareholder protections—which is distinctly not yet the case in the Netherlands.

How can these points be squared? In our taxonomy, we argue that the Netherlands is, like Japan, a particularly resilient example of a corporatist compromise, defying economic pressures that would otherwise move it towards a transparency coalition. Managers and employees of large incorporate firms (Naamloze Vennootschap, or NV) have effectively insulated listed companies from the pursuit of shareholder value, and instead continue to wholeheartedly embrace the ideology of stakeholding. There are few private blockholders in the picture. To keep it this way, managers and the Netherlands' self-appointing boards of directors have surrounded firms with a thicket of antitakeover measures, among the most complex and sophisticated in the world, to ensure that a profit-seeking blockholder does not emerge to enforce accountability or maximize shareholder value.

---

[68] Abe de Jong, Rezaul Kabir, Teye Marra, and Ailsa Röell, "Ownership and Control in the Netherlands," in *The Control of Corporate Europe*, Fabrizio Barca and Marco Becht, eds. (New York: Oxford University Press, 2001).

And although workers have accumulated large pension "stakes" through their funds, these funds have largely exited from the Netherlands' equity markets in favor of foreign investments—a case of exit, not voice—thereby attenuating what would otherwise be pressures for enhanced minority shareholder protections in Holland.

Despite the low level of concentration, there are virtually no contests for control. Boards of directors essentially appoint themselves: shareholders have virtually no vote. Managers and employees of large listed firms in the Netherlands have created a set of governance rules, sometimes referred to as the *structuur regeling* (structural regime), that effectively insulate listed companies from the pursuit of shareholder value.

As Go-Feij sums it up, "the Dutch corporate governance system protects—or has hitherto protected—firms from the domination of 'outsiders.' . . . As such, it is by definition an 'insider-dominated' system. However this does not mean that control over management is directly exercised by individual (or groups of) shareholders (as for example in Italy largely by families, or in France during the 1980s by the central state). On the contrary, what appears to happen in the Netherlands in the larger firms is that the protective measures are used to allow management (using the term broadly to include non-executive directors) to find its own preferred balance among the interests of the various stakeholders. . . . What appears to result is a clear-cut case of broad stakeholder coalition, with strong influence of workers on the larger firms affected by the structural law, and scope for influence of suppliers, customers, creditors etc."[69]

This set of governance rules is embedded in a consensual political system and a well-developed set of corporatist institutions.[70] According to de Jong and Röell, "The corporatist model of centralized, consensual economic decision-making, known as the Poldermodel, was very successful in the reconstruction of the Dutch economy after World War II. . . . This means that corporate decision-making has a direct public interest dimension."[71]

The Dutch have privatized pensions more than other corporatist countries. As one result, the Netherlands has a high ratio of accumulated private pension assets, 113 percent of GDP. As private pension funds accumulated assets, they did not accumulate influence to discipline these firms from a governance standpoint. This is partly because their inclination to do so is attenuated by their conflicted motives—the financial services industry has rapidly consolidated, mixing commercial banking with investment banking with money management.[72] In

---

[69] Denise Go-Feij, "Corporate Governance and Technical Innovation in the Netherlands," Report to the European Commission, May 1999.

[70] The Netherlands score on the Hicks-Kenworthy index is 58: above the mean of that sample, but still well below that of the Scandinavian countries, Germany, and even Japan.

[71] De Jong and Röell, forthcoming.

[72] "The Dutch financial regulators allowed financial intermediaries to become financial conglomerates over the last 15 years. This led to a wave of mergers and acquisitions among commercial banks, insurance companies and investment banks, and in the emergence of financial conglomerates." Go-Feij 1999.

Holland, public employee pension funds became the most forceful advocate for corporate governance reforms, even as their private-sector colleagues shied away.

Moreover, existing Dutch governance practices served in a real way to effectively divorce cash flow rights from voting rights—the "wedge" between ownership and control is extremely high in the Netherlands. This made it difficult for even large institutional investors to use their votes as a cudgel with which to discipline errant managers and directors.

Overall, the Netherlands demonstrates the "stickiness" of corporate governance practices, the reinforcing nature of institutional complementarity, and the sustained effects of consensual political institutions that created and sustain these practices.

In its historical evolution, the Netherlands resembles Sweden in many respects, with democratic development of a corporatist compromise in corporate governance, along with a broad set of parallel institutions in other aspects of the economy that sustained a manager-plus-worker coalition in an alignment against owners.

The dynamics that led to this precede World War II. As a relatively small state in a competitive world economy, the Dutch learned in politics the virtues of social accommodation, including a sustained period of wage restraint, job-training programs, and other management-labor consultative mechanisms that help rebuild the economy after World War II. The virtues of this bargain were institutionalized on the political side as well. For example, Holland adopted proportional representation in the Parliament, one of the cases Rogowski cites to show how institutions were changed to achieve substantive outcomes.[73]

From early foundations in blockholding, the economy continued in this path, reinforced in a desire to limit market forces from disrupting domestic society and social peace, yet still disciplined by the need to compete in an open economy—Holland has a high dependency on foreign trade—and within the European Union. In the postwar years, the compromises of social peace were extended by welfare state provisions. Politically, the Netherlands exhibits extensive institutional development of power sharing across the various lines of cleavage. It is a classic and core case of Lijphart's ideas about consociational democracy and the institutions that embody it.[74]

Concentration, Industrialization, and Dilution. As noted above, most listed firms in the Netherlands are now widely held. Founding individuals and blockholding families of listed firms have largely sold out or been diluted.[75] In a long-term study of Holland's listed firms, based on three detailed snapshots in 1923, 1958, and 1993, de Jong and Röell use several proxies for family control to track blockholder control over time. One proxy shows family-controlled firms dropping from

---

[73] Rogowski and Kayser 2002.

[74] Lijphart 1999.

[75] There remain many privately owned small and medium enterprises, employing 57 percent of the private workforce and accounting for 15 percent of trade.

16.4 percent to 16.2 percent to 1.3 percent over those periods; a second proxy shows a similar downward trajectory, from 43.2 percent to 40.5 percent to 10.4 percent.[76]

The Netherlands went through relatively late industrialization, more akin to Germany than the United Kingdom in the European experience, but these early firms were funded largely by equity markets rather than bank lending. Moreover, these equity markets relied heavily on private bonding mechanisms rather than formal regulation.[77] After World War II, many blockheld firms delisted from the exchanges, tilting the markets towards more diffusely held firms with professional managers in the saddle.

As may be expected in a small open economy, large firms now dominate foreign trade with a distinct multinational caste to them, headquartered and listed in the Netherlands but doing the bulk of their business overseas. This is true of the so-called Big Five in Holland—Philips, Shell, AKZO, DSM, and Unilever—especially for Royal Dutch Shell, which is colisted in the United Kingdom and which alone accounts for 20 percent of the market capitalization of the Amsterdam Bourse. Shell and the next 14 firms cumulatively account for 75 percent of the total market capitalization in the Netherlands.

As blockholders were gradually retiring from the picture (especially in the 1960s), managers and workers were putting in place a set of governance rules to inhibit contests for control and the possible emergence of a profit-focused blockholder.[78] Indeed, despite its reputation as a "globalized" economy, corporate governance institutions in the Netherlands remained surprisingly unattractive from the standpoint of minority investors.[79]

The most important rules favoring managers and workers over owners in terms of corporate governance were embedded in the landmark 1971 *structuur-regeling* laws, which combined rules for corporate governance with rules for management-labor consultation (including the creation of works councils) in one overarching legislative package.

---

[76] De Jong and Röell, forthcoming, table 1, p. 31. Historical ownership registries did not provide data to directly calculate control, so they constructed two proxies based on the percentage of firms with the founder or two family names on the board.

[77] De Jong and Röell, forthcoming, 9–10.

[78] According to one survey, "The Netherlands now lags Euronext markets in tolerating governance features considered by institutional investors as contrary to their interests. It has more takeover defenses, fewer voting rights, and less truly independent boards than other surveyed countries, with the exception of Japan." Davis Global Advisors, *Leading Corporate Governance Indicators, 2000*, December 2000, 75.

[79] For example, PricewaterhouseCoopers surveyed 40 institutional investors on their attitudes towards the corporate governance of Netherlands firms: "Two thirds of the respondents felt that Dutch corporate governance does not allow for sufficient investor influence on corporate policy. 55 percent of the analysts felt that the shareholders of Dutch companies have less voting rights and less influence on management than shareholders in their international peers. More than half the survey respondents attributed discounts of up to 25 percent in the valuation of Dutch companies to their poorly-regarded corporate governance systems." Jos Nijhuis and Jaap van Manen, "Competing for Capital: Analysts' Perceptions of the Competitive Position of Dutch Companies," *PricewaterhouseCoopers Netherlands*, 2002, 23. But despite these unfavorable MSP levels, Holland retained a high and steady level of foreign portfolio penetration; foreign investors accounted for about 55 percent of the Netherlands stock market. By the same token, the ratio of market capitalization to GDP is fairly high, at 170 percent, among our sample of countries.

The *structuur* regime had little effect on accounting, for by international standards, accounting and audit protections in Holland have always been rather high. The majority of Netherlands listed firms use International Financial Reporting Standards (IFRS) of the International Accounting Standards Board (IASB), among other reasons because a significant amount of their business is abroad, and global firms generally prefer global standards for internal control reasons.[80] Requirements for financial disclosure are set by Title 9, Book 2 of the Civil Code, and the Amsterdam Stock Exchange mandates third-party audit of financial statements for listed firms.[81]

Oversight protections for minority investors, in contrast to Holland's generally good information rules, are remarkably low. The *structuur* regime mandates a two-tier board: the Supervisory Board, or Raad van Comissarissen, and the Management Board, or Raad van Bestuur. The former is nominally composed of 100 percent NEDs; the latter is 100 percent inside managers. The Supervisory Board is unaccountable to shareholders, and reelects itself by a process known as "co-optation."

By a simple calculation of the percentage of NEDs on boards, the Netherlands would rate high in terms of oversight protections.[82] But as a practical matter, the board of directors is unresponsive to all shareholders. In our index of MSP we follow the Leading Corporate Governance Indicators judgment in assessing the oversight protections afforded by Netherlands boards of directors as low from the standpoint of outside shareholders—who have virtually no say in selecting or removing the board.

Netherlands public firms have a set of control institutions that effectively disconnect cash flow rights from voting rights. The managers of listed firms hide behind a thicket of antitakeover devices, making it almost impossible to mount a hostile takeover of a Netherlands-listed firm. So effective are Netherlands control institutions in frustrating takeovers that some European firms have reincorporated themselves in Amsterdam in order to avail themselves of these complex antitakeover devices.[83]

---

[80] In an interesting corporatist twist on standards-setting, the Council on Annual Reporting is the arbiter of accounting and disclosure standards in Holland, based on wide consultation with professional accountants, firms, investors, and unions. Nijhuis and van Manen 2002, 23.

[81] Laurence van Lent, "Pressure and Politics in Financial Accounting Regulations," University of Tilburg, January 1995, 10.

[82] "According to Netherlands Company Law, the supervisory board has to look after the interests of the company as a whole, thereby accounting for the various subsidiary interests in a well-balanced way. No single subsidiary interest should prevail over the interest of the company as a whole." Pieter Moerland, "Corporate Supervision in the Netherlands," paper for the Conference on Convergence and Diversity in Corporate Governance Regimes and Capital Markets, Tilburg University, November 1999, 14.

[83] "The Netherlands is a popular place to incorporate for tax and corporate governance reasons. Shareholders can benefit financially but generally have to accept a regime that restricts their rights in comparison with other European systems. . . . Many investors, however, are less concerned about voting rights than about short-term financial gains. The Netherlands does not tax dividends paid to companies incorporated in the country, nor capital gains on sales of shares in subsidiaries." "A Firm's Home May Not Be Sweet for Shareholders," *International Herald Tribune*, June 12, 1999, 17.

Approximately 25 percent of firms use priority shares, which skew voting and cash flow rights; 35 percent use voting certificates, held by an insider trustee, rather than the external shareholder; and 50 percent have protective preferred shares.[84] "The enduring popularity of non-voting shares, preference shares and priority shares still strip shareholders of any say."[85]

"In diluting shareholder rights, firms frequently rely on take-over defenses that limit the number of votes of shareholders. As a consequence many firms violate the one-share one-vote principle and the voting structure of firms differs substantially from the ownership structure derived from looking at the shares. Whenever the firm strips the voting rights from the cash flow, it controls the votes."[86] These takeover barriers come in four flavors, including preferred shares, priority shares, binding appointments, and voting caps.

In effect, Netherlands managers have arranged to create a synthetic block-holder as in Japan, by setting up an administrative or so-called trust office—an *administratiekantoor*—and transferring voting rights to these offices, which strip the voting rights from the cash flow rights and then pass-through the shares with the cash flow rights onto the stock market.[87] The net effect is similar to keiretsu cross-holdings. "Trust offices, which own major voting blocks are used widely by Dutch listed companies as antitakeover measures. These concentrations of voting rights explain partly the absence of hostile take-overs in the Netherlands."[88]

It is important to note that these antitakeover devices were put in place by managers and workers, not by blockholders. De Jong and Röell note that takeover defenses and blockholding are negatively correlated in their sample of firms in the 1993 snapshot.[89] In other words, the boards of widely held firms in the Netherlands, controlled by insiders whose primary allegiance is to the managers and workers of the firm, are more likely to employ antitakeover devices than firms that have a blockholder.

[84] "Firm's Home" 1999, 6.

[85] Go-Feij 1999.

[86] "Preferred shares are first issued to foundations controlled by the firm that then place them, detached from voting rights with investors. They are the most widely adopted antitakeover devices in the Netherlands. These shares are issued in the name of the holder (usually friendly partners) because of their control function, with only 25 per cent of par value to be paid up. . . . A company can curb the voting power of ordinary shares, by issuing priority shares. The articles of a company can assign special rights to holders of priority shares, like proposing or preventing the appointment of particular new members of the management and the supervisory board, approving the issue of ordinary shares, liquidation of the company or changing the articles. . . . Binding appointments of new supervisory board members by the management board strengthen their own control. Ordinary shareholders are deprived of the possibility to appoint their own supervisory board members. Only a two-thirds majority at the general meeting of shareholders can overrule the binding appointment." Go-Feij 1999.

[87] "A company can deposit its share capital at a trust office, which instead trades depository receipts on the stock market. Even if a raider obtains the majority of these depository receipts, voting power at the general meeting still rests with the trust office." Go-Feij 1999.

[88] Go-Feij 1999.

[89] De Jong and Röell, forthcoming, table 8.

In terms of executive compensation and incentive schemes, the "hire from within" personnel systems and corporate culture of large Netherlands firms resemble those of large manager-controlled firms in Japan. Long-term incentives as a percentage of total compensation are around 8 percent, rather low for Europe, although this is hard to measure precisely, insofar as the disclosure of executive compensation in the Netherlands is relatively limited.

Continuity and Consultation. The Netherlands' political institutions, both party structure and parliamentary procedures, have sustained a high degree of continuity of fiscal and social policies, with an emphasis on consultative, marginal reforms rather than radical changes, and with a high degree of confidence in the *structuur* regime. This is the style with which the Netherlands tackled its own looming pension crisis—a decision to gradually trim back benefits, while encouraging the growth of pillar 2 and pillar 3 schemes to compensate for the pillar 1 IPD hole.

Aware that its social security taxes were among the highest in Europe, and facing resistance from labor on trimming of benefits, the Netherlands chose to privatize its state pension scheme in 1990, seeking higher returns from the pool of pension assets that had hitherto earned low returns under state management. It also removed the caps on equity exposure and international exposure from these funds—a decision that was consistent with the Netherlands' adherence to the European Monetary Union, but which had probably unintended consequences for corporate governance monitoring at the end of the decade.

The pillar 1 pension scheme, the Algemene Oudermans Wet (AOW) is a PAYGO system with high coverage and replacement ratios, and unfunded, as most PAYGO systems are, with an IPD estimated at between 54 percent and 104 percent of GDP. After a series of reforms, the AOW's IPD deficit is more than offset on a country basis by the large private and firm-level pension funds, estimated at 113 percent of GDP—one of the largest percentages in the sample. Firm-level pensions are collected and managed largely on an industry-wide rather than firm-level basis, with representation by labor unions on the boards.[90]

Several powerhouse public employee pension funds emerged from this reform. The civil servants' pillar 2 funds were rolled into the Stichting Pensioen Fonds ABP, now the second biggest pension fund in the world, just behind CalPERS, and number 55 among all global money managers, with the equivalent of $130 billion under management at the end of 2001, with about 40 percent allocated to the equities portfolio. Health care workers' pensions were rolled into the Stichting Pensioenfonds voor de Gezondheid, Geestelijke en Maatschappelijke Belangen (PGGM).

ABP and PGGM became vocal critics of the inattention paid to shareholder value by listed Netherlands firms, and mounted a vigorous campaign of reform

---

[90] Jeroen Kremers, "Pension Reform: Issues in the Netherlands," in *Social Security Pension Reform in Europe*, Martin Feldstein and Horst Siebert, eds. (Chicago: University of Chicago Press, 2002).

within the country, resembling CalPERS in many respects. Along with the pension funds of workers in the national railway (Spoorwegpensioenfonds), telephone company (KPN), and airline (KLM), ABP and PGGM banded together to establish the Stichting Corporate Governance Onderzoek voor Pensioenfondsen (SCGOP) to press a code of shareholder-focused corporate governance, and began to delicately but firmly confront poorly performing Netherlands companies at annual meetings.[91]

In sum, the public employees pension funds began to challenge the *structuur* regime on several fronts, but they encountered resistance to enhanced minority shareholder protections from managers, from labor unions, and from the political parties, as well as a distinct lack of enthusiasm on the part of the Netherlands' large financial conglomerates.[92]

Pension Funds and Politics: Voice or Exit. The pension funds' campaign for enhanced minority shareholder protections ran into roadblocks imposed by the Netherlands's highly consensual political institutions—the same political institutions that had engineered the pension reforms in the first place.

For example, after the release of the Peters Commission Corporate Governance Report in 1997, the pension funds supported a draft proposal to the Netherlands Parliament to reduce the use of antitakeover devices by listed firms, which included the provision that management boards should consider lifting their defenses in the event that a third party acquires over 70 percent of the outstanding equity and holds it for a full year. This was opposed by management organizations and labor unions through the consultative tripartite Social and Economic Council (Sociaal Economische Raad, or SER) on which they have representatives.[93]

A watered-down version of this bill permitted the owners of 70 percent of the control rights to actually have their voice heard by the board, if the firm's works council concurs, and if the Enterprise Chamber of the Amsterdam Court of Justice agrees that allowing the majority shareholders to exercise these rights has no deleterious consequences for stakeholders and the public at large. Managers reacted to this mild measure by spinning stronger webs of synthetic blockholders.[94]

---

[91] The pension funds of Phillips, Unilever, and Shell also joined SCGOP later on (http://www.scgop.nl). SCGOP also collectively hired Déminor, a third-party governance consultant, to subject large Netherlands companies to close scrutiny.

[92] ING Group is the largest pension fund manager in Holland, with $347 billion in assets (dollar equivalent) under management, which is one of its three core businesses—the others being commercial banking and insurance. AEGON Nederland is the second biggest manager ($260 billion in assets), combining pension management with its core business of insurance. ABP is third in rank among Netherlands firms, followed by ABN AMRO ($113 billion), another "integrated financial services firm."

[93] Robbert van het Kaar, "Pensions and Pension Funds Become Major Issue in Dutch Industrial Relations," August 1998, *European Industrial Relations Observatory Online*, www.eiro.eurofond.ie.

[94] "The new legislation has already provoked reactions from several interested parties. In reaction to the bill, several larger firms such as Hoogovens, Ahold and DSM issued preferred stock and placed it in the hands of friendly stockholders. These companies are apparently trying to install a group of friendly shareholders in order to discourage or hinder third parties in trying to acquire a 70 percent share in the company." Go-Feij 1999.

Blocked by the thicket of governance practices that protect incumbent managers and boards of directors that elect themselves, and by the broad political
opposition to any changes in the *structuur* regime, ABP and several other private
pension funds began to place a rapidly increasing percentage of their investment
portfolio abroad—in effect, defecting from the Netherlands' corporatist compromise. Stripped of voice, they exited. In 1990, Netherlands pension funds held $15
billion in domestic equities and $12.5 billion in foreign equities; by 2000, they
held $75 billion of domestic equities and almost $100 billion of foreign equities.
As one example, ABP rapidly expanded its global exposure and with a sharp governance edge, including a $2 billion investment joint venture with State Street
Investments of the United States.

Unstable Equilibrium. The Netherlands captures the complexities of a moving
target and the shifting equilibrium of a manager-plus-worker coalition, even one
with a relatively stable political foundation. The rise of pension funds' assets
held in equities has led to a demand for greater transparency and weakening of
the networks' grip. But the pension fund lobby has not been able to overcome
the opposition of adherents to the corporatist regime—including the same corporatist peak institutions who oversee the collection and investment of many
industries' pillar 2 pension funds.

The employers' business federation is controlled by the managers of big firms,
too, and private blockholders have virtually no voice—this is just like the BDI
and the Keidanren. The employers' federation supports the *structuur* regime
against calls for reform, as do the big unions. Both of them worked together on
the SER to block reforms pushed by the pension funds. We have thus another
complex struggle among competing cross-class coalitions: managers and union
officials, some segments of industrial labor, and large banks on one side; with
blockholders, pension funds, and service sector and government employees on
the other.

The triumph of the Netherlands' managers-plus-workers insider coalition is
no guarantee of permanent equilibrium between the coalition partners. On the
contrary, some experts on Dutch corporate governance see the results as skewed
in favor of entrenched, autonomous managers—managers who are themselves
tempted by the sizable increases in both income and autonomy that accrue to
managers in a different alignment, including both outcomes of the alternative
transparency coalition and managerism.

Indeed, the notable Jaap Winter, chair of one of the mainstream corporate
governance committees in Holland, referred to this outcome as a "cynical"
rather than "corporatist" compromise: "The starting point was the idea that
labor and capital were equally valuable, and both should have equal power.
In reality a cynical compromise was reached; the heart of their powers has
been taken away from the shareholders, while little more was received by
employees."[95]

---

[95] Jaap de Winter, FEM *Business*, September 13, 2004, quoted in de Jong and Röell, forthcoming, 21.

What happens when preferences change, as pension assets accumulate, but political institutions block change? In the case of the Netherlands, the pension assets flowed abroad, pulled by opportunities for portfolio diversification and the lower exchange rate risks of the expanded Euro zone, but also pulled by better minority shareholder protections abroad. This was an example of "voice or exit," the usual alternatives faced by outside investors on a micro scale, but on a macro country scale instead.

Section 2: Building Coalitions in Authoritarian Systems

The Oligarchy Model: Owners Dominate Workers and Managers

Most countries pass through oligarchy at one period, usually the first period of industrialization, in their development. It is, in a sense, the primal model of corporate governance, the way most firms in the purely private sectors begin: some founder owners invest capital in a firm they wholly control and whose managers they supervise directly. They then have to decide when and how to diversify ownership and control. It is the default model when a political framework is left out, when there is no political context that shapes the bargains that develop.

This default model, which excludes politics, does not account for the many occurrences of state-led control in the governance bargain, in which firms rise to power and wealth through privileged access to state power. Examples include Korea, as we have seen in the authoritarian period, in Meiji Japan, in Brazilian firms that flourished behind trade barriers of so-called import substitution growth, in Malaysia's *bumiputra* firms, in modern Russia, in the German and French mercantilist beneficiaries of state-led contracts for growth, and even the special deals some American firms got from the state for railroad building, aviation, health, and defense.

Where workers have little voice in politics—because the regimes are authoritarian or the democracies weak and corrupt, or merely new—they have little ability to contain owners in politics and the workplace. Where owners have great resources in the political arena, managers have little autonomous voice. Where there are weak intermediate institutions of finance, investment, pensions, and stock markets, there is little voice for shareholder rights.

This is the classic dilemma of the governance problem in this alignment—getting the owners to yield power to others, not getting the managers to obey the owners (the classic Berle-Means dilemma).

PREDICTIONS AND HISTORICAL EVIDENCE

We do not test the predictions of the oligarchy model against our country sample because our data set is a mid- to late-1990s snapshot, when most countries had already passed through the oligarchy stage—some a century or more ago, others just a few decades ago. Instead, we look at a few country examples from the past, and at the Russian case today, to extract the core features of this model in terms of preferences and political institutions.

Politics are central to this argument. In long-lived democracies in western Europe, Japan, and North America, strong owners exercised disproportionate political influence during industrialization.

The political power exercised by British industrialists in the late eighteenth and entire nineteenth centuries—running for Parliament, opposing the protectionist tendencies of the landed aristocracy, and fending off intrusive regulation from London on an array of issues, ranging from labor law to corporate governance—is well documented.[96] Across the Atlantic, through skillful control of state legislatures, some American "robber barons" in the late nineteenth century obtained monopolistic regulations and various subsidies, such vast grants of land to the railroads from the state on very favorable terms. Others pursued concentration within industrial sectors while fending off labor regulations and antitrust behavior at the federal level. It was the antitrust laws of 1890 that first breached the autonomy of founder-entrepreneurs to set the terms of corporate governance on the basis of private bonding.

On the other side of the Pacific, we noted in the previous discussion of Japan in this chapter how the great zaibatsu families managed to ride out the transition from the post-Restoration junta to embryonic Meiji democratization and its full flower in the early-twentieth-century Taishō era—and the even rougher slide back into political authoritarianism of the 1930s and 1940s. Throughout this period, for example, the founding Iwasaki family of Mitsubishi accommodated a wide range of regulatory innovations by the government in Tokyo—including a set of labor and social welfare rules borrowed from Bismarck and Wilhelmine Germany—while retaining a high degree of autonomy in setting the terms of corporate governance.

Elsewhere in Asia and Latin America in the twentieth century, during their high-growth periods of economic development, strong owners and political authoritarianism often arose together. Economic power can concentrate because politicians need resources, and the economic actors need political favors, particularly in early stages of industrialization. There is little surprise that this marriage of convenience between authoritarian rulers and wealthy capitalists has included the rules for corporate governance as well—or the lack of rules to constrain oligarchs.

For example, the previous chapter described how the chaebol founder-blockholders negotiated a deal of mutual convenience with the Korean generals, beginning with Park Chung Hee all the up to Rho Tae Woo. A host of local crony-capitalists worked out similar deals with autocrats in Indonesia and the Philippines, such as Liem Soe Liong of the Salim Group and Lippo Group's Mochtar Riady with Suharto, and a similar cast of protocapitalists under the protection of Ferdinand Marcos. There is a long list of private blockholders accommodating juntas in Brazil, Argentina, and Chile.

[96] Moore 1966; Paul Smith, *Disraelian Conservatism and Social Reform* (London: Routledge and Kegan Paul, 1967); F.M.L. Thompson, *English Landed Society in the Nineteenth Century* (London: Routledge and Kegan Paul, 1963); Eric J. Hobsbawm, *Industry and Empire: An Economic History of Britain since 1750* (London: Weidenfeld and Nicolson, 1968); P. F. Clarke, *Lancashire and the New Liberalism* (Cambridge: Cambridge University Press, 1971); Stasavage 2002.

The influence of blockholders in politics did not necessarily end with the removal of their autocrat-patrons. Indeed, in Korea's fractious first decade of democracy after the generals were removed, the chaebol owners played a pivotal role in electoral politics. Chaebol money filled (and continues to fill) the coffers of political parties on both sides of the spectrum in Korea. Chung Ju Yung of Hyundai even ran for president in the late 1990s. So did entrepreneur Thaksin Shinawatra in Thailand's on-again, off-again democracy—and he won.

For our purposes, the oligarchy model highlights the importance of countervailing power in society, of groups with the resources able to compete effectively for power, at least in terms of creating corporate governance practices with broad political support. They show as well the importance of political institutions. Oligarchs need access to power but not too much centralized power: enough to prevent other groups from limiting them with protection of minority shareholders and labor rights, not so much as to make them a threat to politicians and tempt the government to expropriate them.

Analytic Narratives

Russia, China, and Singapore present the problem of "weak democratic" or "soft authoritarian" governments making credible commitments to investors worried about shareholder protections. The weakness or absence of democracy, as we noted in chapter 4, leaves investors with a grave predicament: even if they can get governments to provide the sort of shareholder protections they want, and these governments have the authority and the institutional capacity to provide those protections, that very same authority also raises to investors the risk of predatory action by the government. It is indeed the frying pan or the fire: the strength to protect is also the strength to predate.

In stable democracies, the balance of political forces in the context of stable means of political succession sustains the rule of law, the enforcement of contracts and codes, the reality of protection. In nondemocracies or weak democracies, this is always problematic. This is one of the reasons why countries with authoritarian government or weak democracies tend to generate blockholding. Private bonding occurs as a substitute for weak law, but it takes the form of internal supervision mechanisms, ones that exclude a market for control; it does not operate as a replacement for formalized MSP to allow protection of external shareholders, but to exclude them altogether.

The three cases of Russia, China, and Singapore differ considerably in their politics. Some readers will be surprised at our grouping them together. We do so to explore the issues of substantial government involvement in the life of the firm and the impact this has on governance. If these three countries move further down a democratization path, that will affect their governance patterns in profound ways. Singapore is an example of a nondemocratic country making strong commitments of property rights to investors; China and Russia, to varying degrees and in various ways, have been doing the same.

RUSSIA: OLIGARCHS AND POLITICS

In Russia a handful of oligarchs (many former apparatchiki) with access to political power obtained assets cheaply in the great wave of "privatization" under Yelstin and then Putin in the early days of Russian democracy.[97] The result has been a colossal concentration of wealth in a few hands, limited competition, minimal shareholder protections, and few worker rights.[98]

In some respects contemporary Russia resembles the United States during its rapid industrialization from 1865 to World War I, though the origins of the sudden creation of wealth by the Russian oligarchs are different. The so-called robber barons created immense wealth by exploiting rapidly growing markets, economies of scale, rapid technical innovation, and an open "political" market that granted them leeway in building and controlling large firms.

In post-USSR Russia the origins of wealth creation by the oligarchs lay more with the state, in the transition from public ownership and total planning to private ownership and quasi-competitive markets. Political leaders cooperated with the "barons," as they needed their support to manage the elections in an unstable democratic process. As in Korea, the oligarchs played a pivotal role in electoral politics, providing political funding, buying media outlets to parry with each other (and the state), and even starting political parties in the Duma. Mikhail Khordokovsky of Lukoil considered running for president himself, which hardly endeared him to Vladimir Putin and the other former apparatchiki who staffed senior positions in the Russian government. It is no small irony, though an excellent example for our purposes, that he was jailed and tried by the Putin government for alleged tax avoidance and, in effect, poor corporate governance.

Large portions of what had been publicly owned assets were privatized at low prices in ways that allowed blockholders to assume effective control. While

---

[97] Thanks to Christopher Backemeyer for research assistance on the Russian case. Among the sources consulted are Alexander Dyck, "The Hermitage Fund: Media and Corporate Governance in Russia," Harvard Business School Case 703-010, 2003; Dirk Willer, "Corporate Governance and Shareholder Rights in Russia," Centre for Economic Performance Research Discussion Paper No. 343; Eric Berglöf and Ernst-Ludwig von Thadden, "The Changing Corporate Governance Paradigm: Implications for Transition and Developing Countries," William Davidson Institute Working Paper Series No. 263, 1999; Jeffrey M. Hertzfeld, "Russian Corporate Governance: The Foreign Direct Investor's Perspective," paper presented to the OECD Conference on Corporate Governance in Russia, May 31–June 2, 1999, Moscow, and can be found at http://www.oecd.org/dataoecd/55/47/1921803.pdf; Luc Laeven, "Insider Lending and Bank Ownership: The Case of Russia," *Journal of Comparative Economics* 29 (2001): 207–29; Lucie Godeau, "Foreign Investors Shun Russia Despite Growth, BP Deal," *Baltic Times*, February 27, 2003; Malcolm S. Salter and Joshua N. Rosenbaum, "OAO Yukos Oil Company," Harvard Business School Case 902-021, 2002; Maxim Boycko, Andrei Shleifer, and Robert Vishny, *Privatizing Russia* (Cambridge: MIT Press, 1995); *The Economist* (U.S.), "Russia's Lousy Corporate Governance," July 24, 1999, 64; The Economist Intelligence Unit, Russia Country Report, 2003; United Press International, "Russia Launches Corporate Governance Reform," September 7, 2000; Yasheng Huang, Kirsten J. O'Neal-Massaro, and Anatoli Miliukov, "Unified Energy System of Russia," Harvard Business School Case 702-068, 2002.

[98] Is the general assessment of Russia too harsh? Shleifer and Treisman argue Russia is not all that different from other developing countries at comparable levels of wealth and growth. Andrei Shleifer and Daniel Treisman, "A Normal Country," *Foreign Affairs* 83 (2004): 20–38.

millions of Russian citizens were given shares in the new firms, shareholders had little confidence or knowledge about what they meant. Insiders were able either to buy shares cheaply, dilute them,[99] or even simply to erase shareholders from the registry[100]—a process familiar to countries at comparable periods in the development of their institutions.[101]

The data on ownership in Russia is fragmentary and still unreliable. Technically, in the 1990s there was widespread ownership, but in fact there was substantial concentration among manager-owners, and the obstacles to collective action by employee shareholders and other outsiders were even worse than normal.[102] Black notes that firms that have adopted governance principles have higher capitalization on the Russian stock market, which leads some optimists to hope this will induce a reform process.[103]

Russia illustrates vividly the pitfalls of looking at MSP without a political framework. Without enforcement, the codes and rules mean little. Enforcement turns on politics—on having actors with the political resources to pressure state actors to enforcement. Private citizens working through courts, suing malefactors, can only succeed if the courts rule with them. Courts only do that if they have political support or feel pressure.[104] Black and Tarassava note the "institutional complementarity" of the reform process: for rapid privatization to have worked effectively, the institutions of the market would have had to be in place. These would include, they note, anticorruption methods, the rule of law, tax reform, hard budget constraints on firms, competition and trade policy, banking reform, markets for land, and small business development.

Supplying these institutions of the market pushes the problem to a yet more fundamental level: what the political conditions are that would make it possible for Russia to create these institutions. Russia so far has lacked the capacity. Political parties are weak and unstable. Media resources are concentrated in the government. Civil society is weak. Oligarchs have great resources for action, but Putin and the state can still trump them.

---

[99] Carsten Sprenger, "Ownership and Corporate Governance in Russian Industry: A Survey," European Development Bank for Reconstruction and Development Working Paper No. 70, 2002.

[100] Joseph E. Stiglitz and Karla Hoff, "The Transition Process in Post-Communist Societies: Towards a Political Economy of Property Rights," paper presented to the Annual Meetings of the American Political Science Association, August 30, 2003, Philadelphia.

[101] Shleifer and Treisman 2004.

[102] Joseph Blasi, Maya Kroumova, and Douglas Kruse, *Kremlin Capitalism: The Privatization of the Russian Economy* (Ithaca, N.Y.: ILR Press/Cornell University Press, 1997).

[103] Bernard Black, "The Corporate Governance Behavior and Market Value of Russian Firms," *Emerging Markets Review* 2 (2001): 89–108.

[104] Bernard Black and Anna Tarassova, "Beyond Privatization: Institutional Reform in Transition: A Case Study of Russia," forthcoming in *The Ecology of Corporate Governance: The East Asian Experience*, Thomas Heller and Lawrence Liu, eds.; Bernard Black, "Does Corporate Governance Matter? A Crude Test Using Russian Data," *University of Pennsylvania Law Review* 149 (2001): 2131–50; Bernard Black, Reinier Kraakman, and Anna Tarassova, "Russian Privatization and Corporate Governance: What Went Wrong?" *Stanford Law Review* 52 (2000): 1731–1808; Simon Johnson, John McMillan, and Christopher Woodruff, "Entrepreneurs and the Ordering of Institutional Reform: Poland, Slovakia, Romania, Russia, and Ukraine Compared," *Economics of Transition* 8 (2000): 1–36.

Optimists think Russia is in the robber baron phase: the asset holders will realize they have more to gain by legitimating and standardizing their stakes, so they will push for legal enforcement. That is only a partial truth about the history of the United States. The reformers there had support from many other parts of the society and a well-functioning democracy, despite corruption in many places.

Shifts in political institutions can thereby cause shifts in patterns of corporate governance, as the case study of Korea has demonstrated. The Russian case seems unique because of its distinctive origins in the Soviet experience. But its current situation is not so unique. Indeed, argue Shleifer and Triesman, it resembles much of the world, looking very like other countries at its stage of development.[105] In most countries where politics are authoritarian or unstable, where inequality of political resources is substantial, we find something like Russian corporate government patterns.

China: "Selectorate–Electorate" Coalition

China presents the striking case of the state as oligarch, rather than private individuals as founder-blockholders. We argue that China is edging from this condition of state-as-oligarch towards a highly conditional (and risky) investor model as the state sells off minority equity holdings in "corporatized" SOEs to (mainly) foreign and (a few) domestic individual investors. This transition to the investor model is risky, given the thin political coalition on which it is built; China is showing signs of veering off instead into a unique form of insider kleptocracy, a sort of managerism with Chinese characteristics.

China's experiment with publicly traded firms and stock markets is only a decade old, and therefore the state is still the dominant blockholder. The state continues to hold, on average, 65 percent of the equity of traded SOEs, and only 35 percent of the equity is tradable as either A or B shares. Under the threshold-of-control rules used by various estimates of concentration, China has less than a 5 percent weight of private blockholders, and even this small number is of recent vintage, as several entrepreneurial firms from the booming east coast provinces have sought exchange listings in the past few years.

In parallel, the managers of these SOEs-in-transition, in league with other "interested parties" (usually local party politicians and bureaucrats who help to corporatize the SOEs) have been enriching themselves at the expense of both the nominal state blockholders and hapless minority investors. As a result, the state lacks the capacity and minority shareholders lack the means to monitor or discipline managers and their insider boards. In one sense, China resembles Russia, but without the private oligarchs.

How did this happen? Political institutions changed a little; preferences changed a lot—although the coalitional base of those whose preferences changed remains exceedingly narrow.

---

[105] Shleifer and Treisman 2004.

In terms of formal institutions, China remains a single-party autocracy, with the Communist Party defending its monopoly on political power, but slipping gradually into soft authoritarianism. The party has loosened its grip of general oppression (more selective now, though no less ferocious when challenged by new entrants such as Falun Gong) in a tacit deal with the Chinese people, who now have considerable latitude to organize their own affairs, including business affairs, as long as they leave organized politics to the party. As the party's ideological legitimacy has all but evaporated, its "right to rule" has increasingly turned on its ability to "deliver the goods," literally, in terms of providing the background conditions for sustained economic growth and improved living conditions for most Chinese citizens.

Within the party itself, leadership transitions have gradually depersonalized power (from Mao Tse-tung to Deng Xiaoping to Jiang Zemin, and now, Hu Jintao). This makes the leadership more accountable, in an indirect manner, to the preferences of what Shirk terms the "selectorate"—the few thousand party functionaries at the provincial, city, and national level; the central state organs (including the state security bureaus); and the People's Liberation Army.[106] The Chinese selectorate has strong preferences for social peace and high economic growth.

Corporatizing SOEs is one pillar of China's package of high-growth economic policies. Selling off minority shares in these firms serves several purposes, as least in principle: it provides some degree of outside discipline over the SOEs, who managed to lose billions of yuan (as most SOEs do, East or West); dilutes responsibility for layoffs from these firms when they do occur; and raises hard cash, as the Chinese government battles to raise revenue in the absence of a well-functioning tax system. Raising cash from outside minority investors (domestic or foreign) requires a modicum of MSP, starting from essentially zero. Thus the Chinese government began to wrestle with the paradox noted above: how to introduce MSPs, with one hand, by state fiat (in the absence of domestic political democracy), in order to reassure investors that they won't get expropriated with the other hand by the blockholding state oligarch.

Indeed, in the pursuit of its economic goals, the Chinese government must seek a credible commitment of self-restraint to reassure investors, both Chinese and foreign. Its domestic political challenge is formidable, with an incentive for market development to create wealth and jobs, and an incentive to regulate the economy to prevent job loss, social dislocation, and instability. It squares the circle by encouraging party members to promote growth, thus combining political loyalty with wealth creation. The government enables the formation of new firms with some autonomy from the party, but party cadres are wary of what happens to large firms in the "old economy" whose employees would be cut loose by true profit maximizers.

Thus China runs a number of systems in parallel: a core of state-controlled firms (with state as blockholder), another set under partial state control, yet

[106] Shirk 1993.

another set with a more distant state role, a very few almost private. The mechanisms of supervision are complex: ownership patterns and formal rules do not fully capture the role of party and centrally appointed officials, or the capacity of many forms of regulation outside the realm of corporate and securities law.[107]

The implications of this complex system for corporate governance are, however, rather straightforward. As Walter and Howie point out, "In China the markets are operated by the State, regulated by the State, legislated by the State, raise funds for the benefit of the State by selling shares in enterprises owned by the State. No doubt there is some self-conflict in this. In the entire system, the only things which do not belong to the State are the actual money, or capital, put up by predominantly individual investors and the market itself."[108]

This private capital was attracted by a number of changes in corporate governance pushed through in the 1990s by state (meaning, ultimately, Communist Party of China) fiat—not through democratic debate or coalition building.

For example, the newly formed China Securities Regulatory Commission (CSRC) took an early interest in improving Chinese accounting and disclosure rules. It required all listed Chinese firms to adopt Chinese Accounting Standards (CAS), nominally modeled on IAS. The Ministry of Finance issued the Provisional Accounting Regulations for Joint-Stock Limited Enterprises in 1992, which served as the foundation for CAS, with subsequent refinements and modifications. CAS resembles IAS but differs on key points such as the treatment of debt, asset valuation, and revenue recognition. CAS replaced an arcane and unwieldy accounting system originally developed for government monitoring of firms for tax-collection and state-planning purposes, rather than management decision-making or investment analysis.

The CSRC also mandated listed firms use a third-party auditor to verify financial statements—notoriously unreliable in the past, as Chinese firms had accumulated several decades of experience in manipulating financial figures in order to dodge the state tax-collector and planning auditor. In 1993 the Ministry of Finance issued a regulation on "Professional Qualifications of CPA Firms," which began establishing professional standards under the aegis of the China Institute of Certified Public Accountants (CICPA), and formal licensing by the ministry.[109]

---

[107] "[S]ome observers have dismissed China's two stock markets in Shanghai and Shenzhen as Potemkin villages. It is perhaps more accurate to refer to them as the tip of the iceberg, that is, as the shiny visible pyramid atop a huge murky mass of informal credit relations." Barry Naughton, "Financial Development and Macroeconomic Stability in China," in *Financial Market Reform in China: Progress, Problems, and Prospects*, Baizhu Chen, J. Kimball Dietrich, and Yi Fang, eds. (Boulder, Colo.: Westview Press, 2000), 158; Jean C. Oi and Andrew G. Walder, eds., *Property Rights and Economic Reform in China* (Stanford, Calif.: Stanford University Press, 1999).

[108] Carl Walter and Fraser J. T. Howie, *To Get Rich Is Glorious! China's Stock Markets in the '80's and '90's* (New York: Palgrave Macmillan, 2001), 10.

[109] The domestic market share of the Big Four rose from almost zero in 1990 to approximately 10 percent; all Chinese firms listing on the Hong Kong and New York exchanges use a Big Four auditor. China Securities and Regulatory Commission, "Information Disclosure and Corporate Governance in China," paper for the 2nd OECD/World Bank Asian Corporate Governance Roundtable, May 31–June 2, 2000, Hong Kong, 8–10.

The Ministry of Finance retained control over accounting standards setting and interpretation, based on inputs from a standing committee of the CICPA: "The Accounting Society of China (ASC) and the CICPA, both branches of MOF, serve as a bridge between the government and practicing accountants."[110]

Despite some hortatory language in various official regulations and listing requirements about directors' responsibility for protecting the rights of shareholders, in fact China's supervisory committee, similar in function to Germany's *Aufsichsrat*, continues to function as a rubber-stamp for the board of managing directors, and the managing directors are all insiders, appointed by the party. Between 80 percent and 90 percent of the board members of Chinese SOEs are nonexecutives (meaning nonemployees), but the majority are concurrently government employees.[111] In an analysis of 154 firms traded on the Shanghai and Shenzhen exchanges, Xu and Wang found that 50 percent of directors were state employees, and another 40 percent were employees of state-controlled "legal persons," an ambiguous category that includes other SOEs and state-owned banks.[112]

The CSRC adopted a number of rules on voting rights and contests of control that profess to protect minority investors and put these rights into Chinese company law. But disclosure, notification, and voting procedures make it difficult in practice for minority shareholders to exercise those nominal rights—even in the absence of a functioning court system to protect them. Moreover, minority shareholders are placed in a different class with regard to ownership rights than shares held by state entities. As a result, China has a bewildering variety of share types, which effectively nullifies the control rights of minority investors in general and foreign investors in particular.[113] In addition, external and foreign ownership caps effectively rule out the prospect of contests for control of SOEs.

There are some performance contracts for senior managers, but they are subject to political intervention. Steps have been taken towards incentive compensation for managers in some SOEs, but these are small, with little disclosure. Overwhelmingly, Chinese managers are compensated and selected in a manner that ensures loyalty to the state first (at least, their first loyalty after looking after

[110] "China has yet to establish an independent accounting standards regulatory body. In the absence of an independent authority, MOF is responsible for formulating, issuing, and administering accounting regulations in China." Martin Foley, "Accounting Adjustments," *China Business Review* 25 (1998): 23.

[111] Ironically, China's company law explicitly forbids government employees from serving as SOE directors.

[112] Xiaonian Xu and Yan Wang, "Ownership Structure, Corporate Governance, and Firms' Performance: The Case of Chinese Stock Companies," World Bank Working Paper, May 1997, 32.

[113] "[T]he regulations were imbued with the spirit of state planning, state control, and state interest. This is best seen in the very definition of shares which proceeded based on who owned them rather than on the particular economic rights they might represent in a company. Thus, if an agency of the government owned the shares, the shares were state shares, if a state enterprise with legal person status owned them they were legal person shares, and so on. Shares were given names based on the relationship of the particular owner to the State and it is absolutely amazing how many permutations of this relationship came to light over the next few years." Walter and Howie 2001, 42.

themselves and their families) and little loyalty, if any, to the interests of minority shareholders.

Approximately 2 percent of the compensation of Chinese senior managers is incentive based. These performance bonuses are swamped by the huge, across-the-board salary "bonuses" that are often awarded to the employees of SOEs, regardless of the performance of the firm. A survey of 680 SOEs between 1980 and 1994 "shows that among the profit-losing enterprises in the sample period, on average, more than 80 percent of them issued extra bonuses, i.e. bonuses at least 25 percent of the basic wage bill. . . . In other words, over one third of financial losses could be avoided had the insiders of those state enterprises been prevented from distributing extra bonuses for themselves."[114] But it is likely (though we have few ways of measuring it) that managers' enrichment at the expense of the state (and minority shareholders) has come overwhelmingly from insider transactions involving self-dealing, asset stripping, and the usual panoply of methods available to managers with poor supervision, corrupt government authorities, and the absence of a monitoring blockholder or institutional investor to keep them honest.

A Selectorate-Investor Coalition? Not all managers of Chinese firms, public or private, are corrupt; nor are their party and state overseers. The narrow "selectorate" coalition whose preferences ultimately underpin Chinese reforms in corporate governance has many cross-currents, though we hesitate to call them "cross-class" in a country whose official ideology is based on the "dictatorship of the proletariat." Many party officials (high and low) undoubtedly see corporatization of the SOEs, and corporate governance reforms associated with the corporatization process, as essential to maintenance of the current regime, as a way to gradually wean these firms from the state, and thus from corruption and mismanagement more generally.

For example, Ministry of Finance officials more immediately concerned with the solvency of the state banking system see governance reforms as a way to reduce the crushing burden of nonperforming loans from these SOEs, a burden that threatens to swamp the state budget (in the short run) or to even bring the financial system crashing down. Chinese officials in the State Council, the People's Bank of China, and related industrial ministries who subscribe to neoliberal economic measures, including many well-intentioned officials in the CSRC, see governance reforms and MSP more generally as a mechanism with which to replace the tottering state banking system with more efficient equity markets, free from the interference of party cadres and local officials with a more narrow axe to grind. Local party officials in Shenxen and Shanghai proudly point to their stock exchanges as a proxy for "investor friendly" rules and regulations that are important in attracting foreign direct investment to their regions—a slow-motion version of the

---

[114] David Li, "Insider Control, Corporate Governance, and the Soft Budget Constraint: Theory, Evidence, and Policy Implications," in *Financial Market Reform in China: Progress, Problems, and Prospects*, Baizhu Chen, J. Kimball Dietrich, and Yi Fang, eds. (Boulder, Colo.: Westview Press, 2000), 372.

competition for capital that is important in the performance rankings of senior officials in the provincial administrative and party ranks.[115] And many of the professional managers gradually ascending into the ranks of senior SOE management would rather deal with the notional discipline of capital markets, including the carping of foreign investors and the occasional fulminations of the *Financial Times* than the more pointed avaricious meddling of party and government officials.[116]

By the same token, the investors on the other side of the equity transaction have many motives. Individual Chinese investors with few alternative investment vehicles may well prefer shares in a corporatized SOE, no matter how poorly run, and with dubious MSPs, to their only alternatives—cash under the mattress, or deposits in the state-owned banking sector.

Foreign institutional investors may also be dubious of the MSPs protecting their investments in listed Chinese firms, but they also factor into the equation, as we have seen in Korea and in Malaysia, the upside of buying into a large economy whose growth prospects are widely believed to range between 8 and 10 percent per annum for the foreseeable future. Rapid growth in firms' aggregate revenues and in earnings can offset many sins, including an expropriation "tax" to corrupt officials and venal managers. These global investors can also reap the gains in portfolio diversification from holdings in stock markets whose correlation with the NYSE are far lower than Europe or Japan, and for most emerging markets, for that matter.[117]

Finally, we have the indispensable reputational intermediaries, conflicted in the case of China, as elsewhere. The Chinese banking sector is state-controlled and thus, by definition, conflicted in terms of its objectivity in representing Chinese firms to foreign investors. Many foreign investment firms (correctly) see themselves as agents of positive change in the capital market reforms propelled by the listing process of the SOEs. But all are under the incipient thumb of the Chinese government, which can grant them lucrative underwriting revenues, or exclude them entirely from the process.

Dealing with the government in Beijing is, literally, the only game in town for the major international investment banks operating in China. Beijing is the ultimate blockholder, and these intermediaries are extremely reluctant to impugn or

---

[115] Among other things, it was the success of local officials in Shanghai in attracting foreign capital that vaulted Jiang Zemin and his protégés, including Zeng Qinghong, to senior ranks in the Politburo.

[116] We have ignored the important role of Hong Kong's vibrant capital markets in this rather abbreviated description of China, for reasons of space and complexity. Although Hong Kong's autonomy is "guaranteed" by the Basic Law that established its Special Administrative Region, there have been considerable influences in institutional practices in both directions. It is an open question whether corporate governance practices in Shanghai will ultimately come more to resemble those in Hong Kong, or vice versa. Given the crucial role we assign to underlying political coalitions for the formation and preservation of corporate governance regimes in this book, we are inclined to the latter view.

[117] Some of the less conflicted international institutional investors, such as CalPERS, have declined to participate in the Chinese listed market.

otherwise criticize the corporate governance practices of "their" client companies, either when equities are issued or in the aftermarket. The government also controls the ability of the portfolio investment arms of these firms to trade in Chinese securities, by means of the "qualified foreign investor" rules, a regulatory tactic apparently borrowed from Taiwan.

Politics. The Chinese government thus has the capacity to expropriate investors, but to stoke the economy, it must restrain itself in its exercise of oligarchic powers. The party pays careful attention to public opinion, signs of unrest among workers and peasants, complaints from urban workers and SOE employees, and—finally, to some degree—the confidence of investors. It does these things in ways that do not look like an OECD democracy and cannot be measured by the same institutional indicators.

Nor is the pension issue at work in shifting the preferences of many Chinese workers in favor of some abstract notion of good corporate governance. China faces a massive challenge in pension funds and social services, both of which have traditionally been performed by SOEs rather than the government. As some SOEs go bankrupt or are privatized, the implicit pension commitments are vanishing. As these liabilities are picked up by the central and provincial governments, the IPD value continues to soar: the estimates of IPD range from one to four times annual GDP.[118] The Chinese government has attempted to plug this IPD hole by earmarking portions of the revenues from SOE IPOs to meet pension liabilities, but the management of those assets is murky in the extreme, as is their fiduciary obligation to the ultimate beneficiaries.

In any case, it is unlikely that the average SOE employee will attribute much weight to the notional benefits of corporate governance reform when faced with the more immediate threat of layoffs from his or her firm, which traditionally provided not merely salary, pension, and security, but a broad set of benefits including health care, housing, and education—the classic "iron rice bowl" of socialist employment.

In sum, China falls on a continuum: somewhat more commitment to the market than North Korea or Myanmar, and thus more concern for investors' confidence and for corporate governance, but fewer restraints on expropriation than in Russia. There is less institutional restraint on its powers than the advanced industrial democracies, and less than the mixed regimes of Malaysia, Indonesia, or the more democratized countries of South Korea and Taiwan.

The governance approach in China has often been likened to that of Singapore (or Singapore as a very small China), but the comparison stumbles on size and reliance on privatized pensions and deep capital markets. Singapore occupies one of the highest rungs in the ladder of shareholder protections, while China is near the bottom. Nonetheless, the governments in both countries face the same

---

[118] Nicholas Lardy, *Integrating China into the Global Economy* (Washington, D.C.: Brookings Institution Press, 2002).

dilemma with regard to corporate governance—how to credibly support MSPs in the absence of institutionalized democratic processes that locate shareholder protection in a wide popular coalition with both a stake, and a voice, in their provision.

SINGAPORE: SHAREHOLDER PROTECTIONS WITH "GUIDED" DEMOCRACY

Singapore is a fascinating case of average ownership concentration, very high MSP, and a soft authoritarian political system. How did this come about?

We argue that preferences for corporate governance have changed among the political elite in Singapore, and that the state has driven a set of top-down reforms that resulted in relatively high shareholder protections. Singapore's formal political institutions have changed very little, as in China, with Senior Minister Lee Kuan Yew (and now his son Lee Hsien Loong as the new prime minister) providing continuity and the People's Action Party (PAP) in control of the parliament, the judiciary, and the organs of executive government since 1959.

In Singapore, good governance, including economic good governance and especially good corporate governance, happens because the leadership elite chooses it as a policy. It is one of the keys to sustaining legitimacy for what remains essentially a one-party state—good corporate governance is one of the pillars of sound economic governance that have demonstrated the Singapore government's ability to "deliver the goods" and provide the highest income levels in Southeast Asia.

It is likely that the Singaporean elite (we say "likely" because we have no way to verify these preferences) also sees the mechanisms of corporate governance discipline as yet another tool by which to scrutinize managers and avoid the corruption and incumbent abuse that usually develops in one-party states. There is also a useful by-product of creating high MSP and a state-controlled institutional investor that supports increasingly diffuse ownership: it prevents the emergence of a potentially dangerous political challenger in the form of a successful and rich blockholder, such as Thaksin Shinawatra in Thailand, Chung Ju Yung in Korea, Silvio Berlusconi in Italy, or the hapless Mikhail Khordokovsky in Russia.

As in Malaysia, Singapore's pension system has created the potential for a transparency coalition in favor of good corporate governance. With growing pension assets, shareholders may want protections, but the democratic processes to translate demand into reality are missing, as Singapore's rubber-stamp parliament does not provide much direct accountability to the citizens. Nor is there a competitive market for financial services whereby money managers have an incentive to monitor and discipline listed firms in which they invest. The bulk of the Singaporean citizens' equity holdings are managed by the Central Provident Fund (CPF) and Temasek, both virtually branches of the Ministry of Finance.

As a result, the government itself is the principal watchdog for ensuring minority shareholder protections in Singaporean listed firms and, as such, encounters the conundrum of how strong states can credibly commit to minority protections. The problem is more difficult than in Malaysia, insofar as democracy in Singapore is more attenuated than in Kuala Lumpur. Strikingly, the results are similar and help explain why Singapore is an "outlier" from the investor model predictions (it has more blockholding than its MSP numbers would predict).

Concentration. Singapore's weight of private blockholders is 45 percent, similar to the mean of the sample overall, above the Asian mean, but typical of other Southeast Asian countries. These are typical *hua qiao*, family-controlled firms, usually diversified across industries and with deep roots in the Southeast Asian region. These blockheld firms exist side by side with large corporatized SOEs, the legacy of Singapore's rapid industrialization program, some of them world-scale listed enterprises, including Singapore Telecoms, Neptune Orient, PSA, Singapore Power, Singapore Airlines, Keppel, Singapore Technologies, Jurong Shipyard, and Sembawang (now SembCorp). As in Malaysia, these firms were privatized during the 1980s and 1990s, though without the agenda of bumiputra advancement; several became world-class, extremely well run firms.

The corporatized SOEs have led the way in adopting good-governance practices and enhanced protections for minority shareholders, with the family firms then complying, somewhat reluctantly, as they are poked and prodded by the regulatory authorities to follow suit. A large number of international high-tech firms have local operations or regional headquarters in Singapore and have provided a strong learning effect for governance practices.

Shareholder Protections. Singapore has high levels of minority shareholder protections, 89 on our index, almost double the mean value for the sample overall. Singapore's standards of accounting and audit account for its high score in terms of information institutions, among the highest in the sample. Singapore GAAP is functionally equivalent to IAS. The independent standards-setting committee, the Disclosure and Accounting Standards Committee (DASC) of the Institute of CPAs of Singapore (ICPAS) has recommended that Singapore adopt IAS in its entirety. All companies in Singapore are required by law to be audited by approved auditors, who in turn must hold a practicing certificate issued by the Public Accountants Board (the regulator) and join ICPAS. The Big Four have a large market share in Singapore, and their professional standards are, according to anecdotal evidence, among the highest in Asia.

Oversight institutions in Singapore are reasonably fair in protecting the interests of minority investors, and the listing rules of the Singapore Stock Exchange (SSE) require NEDs on all boards of public firms. The ratio of NEDs is estimated at 60 percent, although with the high proportion of private blockholders in listed companies, it is likely that many of these are nominees in practice. Like France, Singapore has a cadre of professional manager-bureaucrats that moves back and forth between the public and private sectors, and many of these individuals can be found on the boards of both private and privatized SOE firms on the SSE. Singapore law imposes a strong fiduciary duty on directors, and these rules are backed up by a court system that is generally fair and fast in the case of financial disputes.

By the same token, Singapore company law provides for a one-share, one-vote rule, and the Voluntary Code on Takeovers is similar in most respects to the U.K. City Code and is, by most accounts, reasonably effective in protecting minority rights during changes of control. Contests for control are rare, due to the remaining regulatory caps on foreign ownership (although they are in the process of being removed), the large presence of private blockholders (around 60 percent), the state's exercise of informal guidance regarding M&A transactions, and the state's preponderant position as an institutional investor through Temasek.

The market for managers in Singapore is competitive by international standards; the quality is generally high, with quite a bit of turnover and extensive use of incentive compensation, among the highest in the sample. Approximately half of the listed firms on the SSE have a stock option plan.

Pensions. As in Malaysia, the state-controlled pension funds are the largest single investor in the Singapore Stock Exchange. The Central Providence Fund is similar in function and coverage to Malaysia's Employees Provident Fund, funded by a compulsory surcharge of 20 percent of salary by the employee and 16 percent by the employing firm. There are now three million beneficiaries with claims on a total $50 billion in assets. In addition, the Ministry of Finance's investment arm, Temasek, holds an estimated 21 percent of the total Singapore equity market capitalization, including a controlling share in the large corporatized SOEs noted above. The state also holds an estimated $100 billion in offshore assets, including a large block of equity. Temasek's CEO, Ho Ching, is the wife of Prime Minister Lee Hsien Loong.

Singapore's large net external asset pool in effect transformed the state into a large foreign portfolio investor, with similar preferences for improved protections for minority investors around the world. Temasek professes a strong corporate governance policy, akin to those of activist institutional investors in the United States, with similar policies with regard to accounting and audit—including the use of so-called economic value added, or EVA, performance criteria, independent board oversight, and executive compensation. According to its chairman, "Temasek behaves no differently from any institutional investor, i.e. it seeks to maximize shareholder value. There is no divergence between Temasek's interests and those of other shareholders since its aim is to ensure that TLCs [Temasek listed companies] are well managed and create value for the benefit of all shareholders. Furthermore, it also continuously strives to institutionalize good corporate governance practices in TLCs to enhance their transparency and accountability."[119]

---

[119] S. Dhanabalan, speech to Asian Business Dialogue on Corporate Governance, October 2002, www.temasekholdings.sg.com.

Politics. Good corporate governance remains an important goal in Singapore, with a strong executive, competent judiciary (in commercial law), powerful investment organs such as the CPF and Temasek, and a compliant parliament. The PAP directly controls two-thirds of the elected seats in the 83-seat uni-cameral legislature, and strictly controls the rules for electioneering. It is no surprise therefore that efforts to enhance shareholder protections stem from the executive and not from the parliament; these are top-down, not bottom-up, reforms.

For example, in the wake of the Asian financial crisis, Singapore's Ministry of Finance launched a three-pronged effort to modify Singapore's governance insti-tutions by setting up a Committee on Company Legislation to reform the com-pany law and control issues, a Committee on Disclosure and Accounting Standards to review information institutions, and a Committee on Corporate Governance to focus on oversight, plus a new Singapore Institute of Directors, staffed by officers from government-linked C firms.[120]

Singapore provides a challenge for purely institutionalist interpretations. Investors want security against predation, from blockholders or other insid-ers in the firm, or from governments. Institutionalist political science assumes that this security from predation can only be provided by formal institutions that limit power. In the firm, that means quality law and regulation. In the polity, it means limited government—a set of institutions that restrains discre-tion and limits arbitrary power. This is the logic behind the design of the United States Constitution, with its checks and balances on the arbitrary executive.

Viewed in this context, Singapore has concentrated political power and weak formal limits on the government. But it uses that power with restraint so as to encourage economic development and investment. It curbs political freedoms but encourages economic freedom. To do so, it creates a voluntary restraint. It must credibly commit to investors not to act in ways they find arbi-trary.

In a sense, Singapore's government may be to politics what J. P. Morgan was to banking, an exercise of voluntary self-policing, a strategy of reputation building. It creates bonding as a public institution to private ones, it is able to foster credibility with investors by being consistent. Mr. Morgan built a reputation for probity—very useful in raising funds—by behaving differently from the other robber barons. By analogy, the Singapore government has built a reputation for probity and "virtuous management" by behaving differently from other autocratic and arbitrary governments in Southeast Asia, such as Ferdinand Marcos in the Philippines in the 1970s and 1980s, the Suharto fam-ily in Indonesia during the same period, the current junta in Myanmar, and the Leninist party leaders of Vietnam.

---

[120] "Move to Improve Corporate Governance," *Business Times Singapore*, December 1999, 2.

As with private bonding, there is the possibility of a breakdown. Institutions do not prevent this, only self-restraint. A government in Singapore has the power to interfere if ever it chooses to do so. Private investors, blockholders, even powerful foreign investors have no recourse at the end of the day.

Some economists and many political scientists think Singapore's is an unstable equilibrium. Countries with this model may go on for a while, they think, but in the long run, the lack of accountability and constraints on power results in corruption and arbitrary policy. This argument turns on how one imagines the alternatives.

Stable OECD democracies of Europe do have a longer track record. Where governments prefer to reassure investors, they seem able in some cases to make the kind of credible commitment to investors comparable to that provided elsewhere by constitutional, limited government.

Singapore is relatively small and specialized economically, as an entrepôt city-state. The model may not work for much larger countries or more heterogeneous economies. But in Singapore, as in China, political succession may ultimately attenuate the power of the central political oligarchs—of the PAP, as with the CCP. Prime Minister Lee Hsien Loong must sustain the approval of a broader selectorate than his founding father. If and when Singapore transforms into a truly pluralistic democracy, it is very likely that the current state commitment to MSPs by administrative fiat (and self-interest) will be smoothly adopted by a democratic commitment to the same values, since the prudent pension system of the CPF and Temasek have given every Singaporean citizen a direct pocketbook stake in good corporate governance.

Conclusion

These three countries highlight the direct relationship between political system and choices in corporate governance. Corporate governance presents autocrats with a fascinating conundrum.

The absence of orderly constitutional processes creates the potential for predation by centralized authority. It also weakens popular pressure to safeguard assets and rights. The overall effect is to favor blockholding models of control. At the same time, some countries, notably Singapore, are able to make credible commitments to investors that substantial property rights will be protected. They rule in ways that attract investment; this is credible because investors know the government does not want to disrupt the economy.

China and Russia have the disadvantage of size and natural resources. Russia especially has such wealth in oil that it could operate even without being very attractive to foreigners, China somewhat less so. Korea and Chile are good points of comparison, the former moving to democracy for the first time, the latter going back to democracy but a restructured political economy that changes the pattern of preferences.

This chapter has described one of the cross-class models that we develop as an alternative to the class conflict model of investors and labor. In this pattern, workers and managers join inside blockholders to resist the pressures of external investors for transparency.

In the next chapter we examine a different cross-class coalition, less familiar in the literature: the alliance of workers with external investors to fight against managers and blockholders.

CHAPTER 7

Preference Cleavages 3: Transparency, Voice, and Pensions

SECTION I: WORKERS AND OWNERS DOMINATE MANAGERS

In the investor model, workers are irrelevant. The labor, corporatist, and transparency models, in contrast, explicitly acknowledge the significance of workers as both employees within firms and voters within a polity. Employees are active players in the formation of corporate governance practices. Moreover, in the investor and labor models, workers' preferences are uniformly portrayed as antagonistic to those of "capital." But in the corporatist and transparency models, both labor and capital are internally divided, so that bargains across the class divide can, and do, occur.

That owners and workers can have conflicting goals surprises no one. That managers and workers can ally with insider blockholders to defend the firm is also a familiar theme in much literature on comparative political economy. But the idea of workers joining owners to oppose managers is nearly nonexistent either in the research literature or public discourse. And yet, politically the phenomenon is quite real.[1]

This chapter examines the theoretical basis and predictions of the transparency coalition, and then tests them with our country data set. As in previous models, we illustrate the interaction of preferences and politics in creating a transparency coalition—and its corporate governance outcomes—with an analytic narrative of a specific country, here Chile. Chile does not purely embody that model—indeed, none of our analytic narratives is a perfect example of the model it is paired with. In fact, some important changes, particularly in the privatization of social security, took place during the Pinochet period of labor repression and had a delayed effect. These changes then had an impact on the politics of regulation when democracy was restored.

After a description of Chile, we turn to the alternate possible outcome of the alignment of owners and workers versus managers, in which the governance outcomes favor the preferences of managers. We term this managerism, an awkward term, but less awkward than "managerial agency failure." We have narrated the cases of the United States, United Kingdom, and France to illustrate the dynamics that can lead to managerism.

---

[1] Martin Höpner has pioneered work in this direction. He stresses workers' interest in transparency to defend jobs, whereas we stress pension assets, thus workers as investors. Höpner, 2003a; and also John W. Cioffi and Martin Höpner, "The Political Paradox of Corporate Governance Reform: Why the Center-Left Is the Driving Force behind the Rise of Financial Capitalism," paper presented at the Annual Meetings of the American Political Science Association, September 2–5, 2004, Chicago. We note also a rich literature in the varieties-of-capitalism tradition exploring worker-owner bargains in other areas of policy.

The U.S. case fittingly illustrates the dynamic tension between a transparency coalition and managerism in contesting the terms of corporate governance, a contest that has very big stakes and thus is fought and fought again. The principals in this joust are institutional investors on one hand—whose power stems from accumulated pension funds, making them agents of owners and workers alike—and "professional" managers of public corporations on the other.

The U.S. case thus highlights the central role of reputational intermediaries in mediating the contest between the institutional investors and their managerial adversaries—an ambiguous role, a conflicted one, and deeply entangled in the politics of financial regulation. France illustrates another path to managerism, in which pension funds are relatively undeveloped as a countervailing power to managers seeking autonomy and personal enrichment.

From Class Conflict to Corporatist Compromise

To get from the class conflict model to the cross-class cooperation of the transparency coalition (or to managerism, its obverse), we challenge several of the simplifying assumptions of finance theory concerning preferences and the linkage between political activity and governance outcomes, and we include an explicit consideration of expropriation costs as well as agency costs. On the assumption that agency costs are the prime consideration, the finance literature implicitly assumes a shared interest between shareholders and managers on one side, in opposition to the interests of workers on the other side.

In the investor model, external investors favor companies with minority shareholder protections that buffer them from both agency and expropriation costs. The inverse of the investor preferences model is the labor model: workers seek protection from the market discipline of external shareholders that would, among other things, reduce the agency costs of above-market wages or excess employment. Both models assume a deep, unbridgeable chasm of interests between workers and owners.

But the investor model has difficulty modeling the way minority shareholder protections actually present themselves in the political system. It does not explain how preferences map onto political processes, or how the conflict between owners and managers is projected into politics. Nor can it explain the apparent failure of investor preferences alone to prevail. The labor model more clearly maps the preferences of workers onto policy outcomes, but it does not capture the cross-class pattern of political processes that deal with issues of governance policy.

From the labor and investment models we turned to the cross-class coalition model, the corporatist coalition between workers and managers, whose initial interests are opposed to those of shareholders, but who reach an accommodation with blockholding owners. These groups support a set of governance practices and regulations that increase both agency and expropriation costs, both at the expense of minority shareholders, in order to lower transaction costs and reap benefits of "relationship contracting."

The corporatist compromise shows that the interests of owners and workers are more complex than a simplistic confrontation of capital versus labor. These interests can cut in different directions. In some ways workers and owners do conflict, over wage share of income or job security, for example. In other ways, workers can have common cause with both internal owners and managers. Workers and managers can at times establish a bargain with blockholding owners (as in Germany and Sweden) or create synthetic blockholders (as in Japan's keiretsu), resulting in managerial dominance inside the firm and job protections for line workers.

Managers are not passive actors in this interpretation. They see alignment between their interests and those of the line employees to preserve the firm and employment within it. Minority shareholders face a "double whammy" under this model, with managers and workers draining agency costs away from minority shareholders, and blockholders extracting expropriation costs from the minority shareholders. Not surprisingly, minority shareholder protections remain low, and ownership concentration high.

The bargain struck by this compromise among the three inside players (workers, managers, and blockholders) is cemented by complementary institutions. These include practices such as lifetime employment and promote-from-within executive selection in Japan and, to some degree, in Germany; works councils in Germany or company unions in Japan; and barriers to hostile takeovers in both countries. The corporatist compromise is willing to mute product market competition in order to preserve steady rents for managers and workers to split among themselves—which coincidentally protects the private benefits of control for cooperative blockholders, too. It may provide some benefits in production strategy, for products for which relationship contracting has competitive advantages. The result is a system that privileges the rights of producers over the rights of consumers, the rights of concentrated capital over the many individual savers, the rights of insiders to those "outside."

THE CLOSED DOORS OF THE CORPORATIST COMPROMISE

It is important to note that the corporatist compromise takes place substantially behind closed doors. It is not predicated on transparency, for neither the blockholder owners nor the workers and managers wish to conduct their negotiations over corporate governance in a fishbowl. Instead, the overriding goal is mutual accommodation. Public accountability would expose practices and agreements that could be challenged by outsiders such as consumers, taxpayers, and minority shareholders. The mutual back-scratching among workers, managers, and blockholders is best conducted behind closed doors.

Blockholding systems do not function by providing financial information to the public at large. Standardized accounting practices are less important, insofar as blockholders (unlike pension investors) do not need to compare similar firms within an industry across national borders. Blockholders have direct access to the firm's internal financial statements and are motivated to dig as deeply as necessary to monitor the firm, both ex ante and ex post. And the higher the level of financial transparency, the more expensive it is for blockholders to extract the private benefits of control.

Blockholders don't want legal restrictions and duties imposed on the board of directors; they want to be able to nominate the directors themselves, tell them what to do, and replace them if they please. They don't like the whole idea of NEDs. Strict interpretations of independence would forbid the blockholders from serving on the board of "their" firm.

Concerning control practices, blockholders prefer to negotiate asset sales and other changes of control in private: who needs publicity, the press, the intrusive nose of the securities regulators, and bothersome minority shareholders who may clamor for an even deal? Blockholders rely on the "wedge" between control and cash flow rights to build and maintain their pyramids of control; the very notion of one-share, one-vote strikes at the heart of their ownership structure.

In the area of executive compensation, blockholders prefer to pay the managers in line with what the manager does for the blockholder. The blockholder does not want the managers thinking in terms of maximizing shareholder value for everybody.

As for workers and managers, they do not favor transparency in the corporatist compromise. Like the blockholders, they also have access to privileged financial information as insiders. In Germany, the Netherlands, some French boards, and many Scandinavian countries, workers have formal representation. And in Japan, instead of external auditors, listed firms rely on kansayaku, statutory auditors, to certify the quality of the financial figures. The kansayaku are retired members of the company's financial bureau or former main bankers—insiders all.

Blockholders and workers and managers prefer a system that sustains stability of employment and private benefits of control, rather than dividends and high share value. This may produce some social values in favor of stability and equality, and it may have some advantages in monitoring and in certain production strategies (see discussion in chapter 3 of the advantages of blockholding and the varieties-of-capitalism discussion in the previous chapter).

Whatever its other merits, the corporatist compromise is, from the standpoint of minority shareholders, a "bad governance deal." Systems that disfavor consumers in favor of producers also disfavor external stockholders in favor of insiders.

Under the corporatist compromise, minority shareholders are saddled with what Jensen called "the agency costs of cash flow." Capital is not allocated to the most efficient marginal return by the investor, choosing among a variety of investment options presented by market forces, but rather is allocated to investments preferred by the vested members of the firm, the insiders—blockholders, managers, and workers, in the case of the corporatist compromise. This discourages outside investors from becoming minority shareholders in the firm.

BRINGING THE WORKERS BACK IN

The transparency coalition challenges these arrangements by aligning workers with external owners to press for MSP. A key driver in this shift is the system of pension funding: as workers acquire pension assets, they become more concerned with returns on those assets and with protecting their minority shareholder stake. In certain conditions, workers may also seek transparency as a mechanism of job preservation. Our discussion explores the theoretical issues in this model, sets up several predictions of the transparency coalition, tests them against the country sample, and looks closely as the specific example of Chile—in which preferences and institutions interacted over time to create the political foundation of a transparency coalition in which workers play a role, emerging from an authoritarian regime that repressed unions.

In recent years three major developments have brought forward an owner-employee alliance on shareholder rights.[2] First, workers' equity ownership through pension funds has dramatically expanded over the past two decades, just as Drucker foretold, thus giving workers a direct property interest in corporate governance. Second, workers increasingly perceive good corporate governance as important to their job security, through practices that enhance transparency, promote good accounting, and reduce moral hazard by managers, and even—in some countries—providing them a voice in oversight. Third, managers in countries with diffused shareholdings such as the United States have frequently resisted accountability to shareholders while engaging in stock option and other compensation arrangements widely perceived as excessive by shareholders and workers alike.

At first blush, workers and shareholders are unlikely bedfellows. In many countries, managers and blockholders regularly invoke the principle of shareholder value to justify plant closings and firing workers. Stock markets frequently reward the firm's announcement of employee cutbacks with a brisk uptick in the share price, reflecting the market's vote of faith that management has the ability and resolve to "do the efficient thing." In this one-dimensional view of the world, workers are viewed primarily as costs. Wages and job security above the minimum competitive market requirements are considered pure "agency costs," costs that are expected to be trimmed back in the pursuit of shareholder value.

The classic law-and-economics literature on corporate governance historically focused on agency cost, presuming a conflict between managers and owners, and only secondarily on expropriation cost, based on the potential conflict between blockholders and minority shareholders. Throughout this literature, workers are assumed to view the firm from the bottom of the wage and power system. They are fighting for their share of what economists call *quasi rents* produced by the firm. Their overriding concerns are wage levels, job security, and insurance from the instability of competitive markets. These quasi rents are embedded in pay scales and work rules, protections against layoffs, and unemployment compensation, health insurance, and retirement pensions.

From the perspective of owners and managers, labor is viewed as another commodity, bought and sold on the market, at the lowest possible wage and with maximum flexibility in hiring and firing. From a nexus of contracts perspective,

---

[2] Labor votes were vital in creating the SEC, as part of New Deal coalition. Populist elements at times combine to attack concentration of finance and economic power.

workers and firms can enter into complete contracts; there is no issue of firm-specific investments by the worker that is not encompassed by these contracts; thus workers have no legitimate demand for a voice in the governance of the firm.

This bottom-of-the-pile perspective flows from neoclassical economics. Labor is a factor of production, but just one factor, that can be substituted or complemented by other factors of production—including capital and technology. Theorists of many political persuasions, from Marx on the left to market neoliberals and even conservatives on the right, highlight this potential for class conflict. It has continued to color much scholarly analysis of interest group conflicts concerning trade, taxes, and other distributional areas—including corporate governance.

FROM CORPORATISM TO TRANSPARENCY COALITION

Given the tempting appeal of the corporatist compromise for workers, under what conditions could workers have an interest in a transparency coalition instead? When would it make sense for them to pursue transparency in cooperation with owners, rather than—as assumed by the two coalitions examined so far—in competition with "capital"?

As we have seen throughout these chapters, the workers, owners, and managers are not unitary categories, with one deductively defined interest. They are large lumpy groupings, internally differentiated along several dimensions, with often divergent situations and goals, which can orient them in different directions concerning interests, ideology, and strategy of action.

The classical models of workers' behavior, as employees and as voters, impute to them a utility function in which only their wages and jobs matter. They worry about keeping their jobs and about the level of wages. These simple preferences lead toward the labor model or the corporatist compromise. But two shifts could cause behavior to change.

The first is a change in workers' utility function. The weight of relative goals shifts as workers acquire assets such as real estate, bank savings, pension entitlements, and mutual funds. Wages are a significant element in their calculation of wealth, but not the only element. If the weight of pension entitlements and securities holdings in their total wealth becomes large enough, their preferences can "tip" and workers increasingly align with owners around shareholder values, in conflict with managers.

This implies that Pagano and Volpin's elegant model of collusion among blockholders, owners, and workers that results in the corporatist compromise described in chapter 6 can be destabilized under some circumstances. With the same utility function but different asset weights, workers may defect from this bargain with managers and throw themselves into a cross-class coalition on the same side as shareholders.

The second possible source of a shift in workers' preferences for corporate governance practices is an adjustment in their strategy toward preserving jobs. In both the social democratic and corporatist compromise models, workers secure their jobs (and their slice of the quasi rents of the firm) as a junior partner of managers. In some countries, they have limited oversight institutions such as *Mitbestimmung* or other forms of employee consultation that provide a measure of insider information regarding the financial health of their firm. Mostly, workers and their unions rely on externally imposed governance rules that establish minimum requirements of disclosure on firms, while constraining owners and managers with regard to job flexibility, collective bargaining, and a range of requirements concerning social policy. In some places, labor sees advantages in greater public transparency to achieve the same goals. Disclosure and monitoring by institutional investors allow greater voice in debates over jobs, wages, and long-term strategy of the firm. This analysis makes labor available for the transparency coalition.

JOB SECURITY THROUGH TRANSPARENCY

So far this chapter has focused on workers' preferences for good governance deriving from their role as property owners through their pension funds and savings. In that regard, we model employees as shifting their interests from workers to shareholders, thus having dual and potentially conflicting interests between maximizing shareholder value and defending job security.

Another force generating a preference for transparency stems from workers' shifting views of what it takes to preserve their jobs in the long run. Managers make decisions with a substantial impact on workers. An alliance between managers and blockholders, sustained by a closed network of interlocking directors, can take many actions that negatively affect job security. This risk can push workers away from the corporatist compromise and towards a transparency coalition.

A striking indication of change in this direction can be found in Germany. Höpner makes this the key to explaining SPD and labor support of transparency: private pension participation remains low, Höpner argues, so it cannot be the driver.[3] Instead, it appears than some German labor unions have concluded that codetermination can only be effective if combined with full transparency; otherwise, they cannot know what is happening in the firm.

Höpner argues that German ideas about social democracy have changed: the postwar Left has become suspicious of the concentration of power in the economy as dangerous both to democracy (a cause of the collapse of the Weimar Republic and Hitler's rise to power) and to the interests of workers. They have in this respect become more sympathetic to neoliberal ideas about markets and competition instead of cartels and concentration. They believe the market can develop without necessarily undermining welfare systems, social services, and job protections.

LABOR SWORDS INTO INVESTOR PLOWSHARES

Pension plans are the most powerful countrywide mechanism through which workers can be turned into shareholders, more compelling than job security in some respects. Stock options and stock grants have attracted more public attention, and have had some effect. A study of stock and option grants in the United

---

[3] Höpner 2003a.

States contrasted the percentage of equity granted to nonexecutive employees in the top 100 technology firms and the top 100 Fortune firms. On a fully diluted basis, employees in the former group owned 19 percent of the equity, while employees in the latter group owned 2 percent of the equity.[4] Although some of the biggest firms with a broad-based option program have decided to trim back the wide distribution of these plans, such as Microsoft and Oracle, the option culture is alive and well in most high-tech sectors.

The practice of spreading stock options widely among the entire employee population (rather than on the top executives) has been largely confined to high-tech firms in the United States and the United Kingdom. It has been adopted on a limited basis by firms in high-technology enclaves in countries such as Singapore, Israel, and Taiwan. The option culture has also been adopted by several large European and Asian firms who acquired U.S. high-technology firms and decided to maintain these option plans intact in order to retain employees in competitive U.S. labor markets. Some of these firms (such as Alcatel) subsequently found themselves forced to offer versions of these U.S.-origin option plans to their European and Asian employees in order to maintain internal wage parity.[5]

In many countries retirement systems have become the biggest means for changing the patterns of shareholding. For workers in many countries, retirement benefits have become their most valuable asset. For many of these workers, particularly middle-aged and older workers, the net present value of their pension benefits rivals or exceeds the net present value of their future wage earnings.

We need to evaluate more thoroughly the implications this has for interests and politics around corporate governance practices and regulation. We need to understand the pension structure of employees. Two variables are salient for our purposes.

First is the nature of the pension plans themselves, the distribution of benefits and claims across the different "pillars" of pension plans. There are three such pillars, in the language of pension policymakers. The first pension pillar is government-run general retirement schemes, the second pension pillar occupational or firm-level retirement obligations, and the third pillar individuals' private pensions, also sometimes called supplementary pensions. The more workers' assets are accumulated in pillars 2 and 3, and the greater the allocation of these assets to equities, the more interested workers are in transparency and minority shareholder protections.

Second is the structure of the financial intermediaries that manage pension plans. The more autonomous the unit that controls pillar 2 and 3 investments is from company management, the more likely it is to articulate workers' concern for transparency and minority shareholder protections. We return to this point after a longish excursion into pension terminology and accounting; we provide

---

[4] Joseph Blasi, Douglas Kruse, and Aaron Bernstein, eds., *In the Company of Owners: The Truth about Stock Options (and Why Every Employee Should Have Them)* (New York: Basic Books, 2002).

[5] For example, Alcatel acquired U.S. telecom firms such as DSC and Xylan, but folded the employee option schemes of these firms into a broader Alcatel plan. As a result, 60 percent of Alcatel's U.S. employees and 25 percent of its European employees became participants in option plans. Mottis and Ponssard 2002, 5–7.

this detail in order to underscore the interaction of pension systems and corporate governance systems.

PENSION PATTERNS AND MOTIVES TO MONITOR THE MANAGERS

Countries vary substantially in the balance of assets among the three pillars of the pension system. These differences, based on decisions made in the past, impact greatly the way issues of pension reforms and corporate governance interact.

The Unfunded PAYGO Hole. The first pension pillar is government-run general retirement schemes. Pillar 1 schemes usually operate on a "pay as you go" (PAYGO) basis, which means that current benefits are paid by current contributions.[6] In most places, governments pay benefits above the level of per capita contributions.[7]

These pillar 1 plans are presented as "social insurance," with a presumed actuarial link between payments in and benefits out. This link is illusory for most places. Virtually all of these pillar 1 schemes are in an actuarial deep hole, in every country in our sample, with the net present value of future obligations far outstripping the value of assets accumulated. Nonetheless, most retirees view their pillar 1 claims as a quasi-contractual entitlement, and workers in a contributory scheme—no matter how imbalanced the relation between payments in and benefits out—tend to view these claims as a sort of deferred wage.

How big is this gap between claims and assets? Economists at the OECD and the World Bank have established a common terminology and method for converting this actuarially based future stream of benefits into a current debt equivalent, known as *implicit pension debt* (IPD), on a country basis.[8] The estimate of this net present value varies by the accounting method and the details of each country's unique benefits and classifications, and is sensitive to the assumptions made about future wage increases and the implicit discount rate for future benefits and asset returns.[9] Thus, although the figures from country to country are not precisely comparable, the overall pattern of unfunded first-pillar schemes is consistent, and heavily underfunded. Drawing on several different sources, we reproduce below an estimate of the IPD for 25 countries in our sample.

Although there is considerable variation in IPD among our country sample, the numbers are all large, and all negative (see also appendix table A.27)

For many countries in this sample, the IPD of their pillar 1 pension schemes exceeds the total national debt. In the case of Denmark, for example, in order to

---

[6] Bonoli 2000. Plans vary greatly in many dimensions, from the accumulation of assets versus dependence on current payments, to the qualifications for participation and the level of benefits.

[7] Bonoli 2000, 125.

[8] Robert Holzmann, Robert Palacios, and Asta Zviniene, *Reporting the Implicit Pension Debt in Low and Middle Income Countries* (Washington, D.C.: World Bank, 2002).

[9] The World Bank study proposes using a "termination liability" method of estimating IPD, which calculates the present value of the payment stream that the pension scheme will have to pay current participants and their survivors for contributions made to date, under current scheme rules." Holzmann, Palacios, and Zviniene 2002, 18.

TABLE 7.1
Implicit Pension Debt as Percentage of GDP

	OECD	Kune	World Bank	Siebert	Other	IPD Deficits
Argentina			85			85
Australia				97		97
Austria				93		93
Belgium		75		153		153
Brazil			330			330
Canada	121			101		101
Chile						
China						
Denmark		87		234		234
Finland		83		65		65
France	216			102		102
Germany		138		62		138
Greece		185			245	185
Hong Kong						
India						
Indonesia						
Ireland		55				55
Israel						
Italy		157		60		157
Japan				70		70
Malaysia						
Mexico					142	142
Netherlands	103			54		103
New Zealand				212		212
Norway						
Philippines		85				85
Portugal		93				93
Singapore						
South Africa						
South Korea		21				21
Spain		93		109		109
Sweden				132		132
Switzerland						
Taiwan						
Thailand						
Turkey			109			109
United Kingdom		68		24		24
United States				23		23
Venezuela						

Source: Feldstein and Siebert 2002; OECD; World Bank figures from Holzmann et al. 2002; Grandolini and Cerda 1998; Brooks and James 2001.

fully fund the currently promised stream of future benefits to its citizens, the government would have to levy on those same citizens a one-time tax equal to 230 percent of a whole year's economic activity—a staggering proposition. Social security reform is often referred to as the "third rail of politics" in the United States, suggesting that no politician can touch the problem and survive—in a country where the IPD is only 23 percent of GDP, one-tenth the level of IPD in Denmark.

These figures highlight the extraordinary political sensitivity of the pension issue in all the countries in this sample. As the World Bank pension forecasts conclude, "Since unfunded pension obligations are public debt, they co-determine the intertemporal budget constraint of the government. Keeping the government solvent requires future tax revenue, partial default on its pension commitments, or future lower public expenditure elsewhere."[10] One response to this deficit consists of funds based on private-sector assets, be these in pillar 1 or 2, and that in turn means that corporate governance is intertwined with the high politics of pension reform in every country in this sample.

Second-Pillar Assets. The second pension pillar present in most countries is occupational or firm-level retirement obligations, traditionally set up as defined benefit plans, but now increasingly converting to defined contribution plans.[11] Sometimes this takes the form of a lump-sum severance benefit, often the case in continental Europe, Japan, and Korea, in which case it is a liability on the books of the employing firm: it may or may not be funded. Second-pillar plans can be managed in a variety of ways: by the sponsoring firm, in-house or with an external money-manager; comanaged by firms and unions together, in what are called "Taft-Hartley" funds in the United States (this is the most common variety in Europe and Japan); or by government agencies, who often manage plans for special sectors such as farmers, self-employed, or health care workers, in addition to public employees.

A major subset of the second pillar is retirement schemes for civil servants, at both the local and national level. These usually bear a nominal resemblance to other second-pillar "occupational" schemes, but they are managed by a state agency, and they are funded with annual contributions from the government budget. In many countries in our sample, the terms of defined benefit civil service pension schemes are significantly higher than those for comparable jobs in the private sector—a perpetual political sore point.[12] Civil servant systems are usually PAYGO at the national level, although some municipal, state, and provincial units have partially funded systems.

Public employee pension funds turn out to be important for changing corporate governance practices. Where civil service pension schemes are partially or

---

[10] Holzmann, Palacios, and Zviniene 2002, 5.

[11] A defined benefit pension scheme promises to pay the beneficiary a fixed sum for a fixed period, regardless of contributions by that beneficiary; a defined contribution pension scheme promises to pay the beneficiary the variable future stream of earnings generated by the contributions paid in by the beneficiary (and the firm).

[12] For example, this is the case in France, Germany, Italy, Brazil, Argentina, Japan, Korea, Taiwan, and Malaysia.

fully funded, and those funds are held in private-sector equities or bonds, the institutional investors managing these funds have often been crusaders for minority shareholder protections (for reasons we explore later in this chapter), often with civil service labor unions enthusiastically supporting these reform efforts. In contrast, when civil service pension schemes are PAYGO with little or no asset accumulation, there are no institutional investors to articulate a preference for minority shareholder protections on their behalf, and instead the civil service labor unions focus their energies on fighting to maintain the share of the government's fiscal expenditure used to "pay as you go" for the civil service pensions.[13] In PAYGO systems corporate governance is largely irrelevant.

The Fully Funded Third Pillar. The third and final pillar consists of individuals' private pensions, sometimes called supplementary pensions, managed by private investment or insurance firms. By definition, they are always funded.

There are some hybrid second- and third-pillar schemes, such as 401(k) plans in the United States in which employer matches employee contributions, but the account is held in the name of the individual, not the firm.

Highly unionized "smokestack" industries in the United States were the most likely to retain defined benefit plans. These pension plans were the object of intense collective bargaining between management and organized labor. Managers resisted concessions to these plans because they were forced to recognize the net present value of pension obligations in the firm's financial statements; there was no way to hide the implicit liability, or to push it off into the future. As a result, many firms in the United States set up 401(k) plans as a replacement for defined benefit plans, which fell out of favor in the late 1980s and 1990s as the pension accounting and disclosure requirements on firms became increasingly onerous.

In contrast to these business firms, politicians were under no particular pressure to recognize the present value of pension concessions, there being no widely used equivalent of a consolidated financial statement for most cities, states, and national governments. Not surprisingly, politicians at all three levels in most of our sample countries were adept at making pension promises without funding these claims, in effect "kicking the can down the road" in the expectation that their term of office would expire before the pension claims came due.

Table 7.2 is an estimate of pillar 2 and 3 pension assets for the countries in our sample, as a percentage of current GDP.[14]

There are some differences in the values for given countries because of differences in classifying institutional investment accounts, such as those held by some banks and insurance companies. The variation among the countries is high for

---

[13] This struggle on the unions' part becomes increasingly bitter and absorbs greater amounts of their organizational energy since retirement benefits of civil servants chew up increasingly large percentages of government budgets, and the disparities between public and private benefit levels—an artifact of selective appeals to these unions by politicians in past wage negotiations—become more prominent.

[14] Stern 2001; Holzmann, Palacios, and Zviniene 2002; Martin Feldstein and Horst Siebert, eds., *Social Security Reform in Europe* (Chicago: University of Chicago Press, 2002).

TABLE 7.2
Private Pension Assets (% GDP)

	Stern	World Bank	Siebert
Argentina	7	3.3	
Australia	67	61	45
Austria	4	2.6	
Belgium	14	4.8	10
Brazil	13	14	
Canada	102	47.7	25
Chile	57	45	
China	0		
Denmark	116	23.9	21
Finland	49	40.8	1
France	16	5.6	3
Germany	16	5.8	6
Greece	3	12.7	
Hong Kong	62		
India	14		
Indonesia	3	2.5	
Ireland	52	45	
Israel	1		
Italy	6	3.2	4
Japan	41	41.8	18
Malaysia	54		
Mexico	3	2.7	
Netherlands	113	87.3	85
New Zealand	15		
Norway	7	7.3	
Philippines	4		
Portugal	12	12	
Singapore	61		
South Africa	76	57	
South Korea	13	4	
Spain	7	5.7	2
Sweden	41	32.6	16
Switzerland	127	117.1	70
Taiwan	35		
Thailand	7		
Turkey			
United Kingdom	102	83.7	82
United States	103	86.4	72
Venezuela			

this sample; the standard deviation equals the mean value of 38. See also appendix table A.28.

CROWDING OUT AND PATH DEPENDENCE

The distribution of benefits across these three pillars may have effects on workers' preferences towards savings, with some evidence of a "crowding-out effect" of IPD on private pension assets.[15] In other words, the higher the replacement rate of pillar 1 benefits, the less inclined the worker is to contribute to pillar 2 and 3 schemes. The magnitude of the trade-off between social security "wealth" and private wealth ranges between 0.1 and 0.5 in a variety of recent studies for several countries in our sample. For example, Feldstein estimates that personal savings rise by 0.5 for each unit decrease in IPD, and there are similar estimates for several European countries.[16]

The crowding-out effect is intuitively plausible. Attempts at pillar 1 reform, such as increasing the workers' mandatory contribution to these schemes (the so-called social security tax in the United States), leave less money for workers to set aside for supplemental schemes. Conversely, the higher the worker's pillar 2 and 3 benefits, the less inclined the worker is to support a strong pillar 1 system. This can make it very difficult for countries with a high IPD in their pillar 1 schemes to encourage their citizens to build a higher pillar 2 and pillar 3 "nest egg."

The replacement effect provides a striking example of path dependence and the long, lingering effects of institutional design. Once a country has gone down the path of a high ratio of pillar 1 benefits, personal savings adjust to the implicit "social security wealth," thereby reducing pillar 2 and pillar 3 contributions, and making it even harder for countries to offset their pillar 1 deficits by shifting to funded pillar 2 and pillar 3 schemes. But for countries that have gone down the other path, with lower pillar 1 and higher pillar 2 and pillar 3 proportions, personal savings go in the positive direction—and so do preferences for corporate governance.

LINKING PENSION PILLARS AND CORPORATE GOVERNANCE

The distribution of workers' pension benefits among these pillars has profound effects on their preferences for minority shareholder protections. The higher the ratio of pillar 1 benefits to total pension benefits, the lower the perceived interest in corporate governance and the transparency coalition; the higher the ratio of pillar 2 and pillar 3 benefits, the higher the perceived interest in minority shareholder protections.

---

[15] Brooks and James find a negative correlation between pillar 1 IPD and private pension savings in a sample of Latin American countries. Sarah Brooks and Estelle James, "The Political Economy of Structural Pension Reform," in *New Ideas about Old Age Security: Toward Sustainable Pension Systems in the 21st Century*, Robert Holzmann and Joseph Stiglitz, eds. (Washington, D.C.: World Bank, 2001).

[16] Martin Feldstein, "Social Security and Saving, New Times Series Evidence," *National Tax Journal* 49 (1996): 151–64; other studies summarized by Davis and Steil 2001, 289–91.

For example, if all the benefits will come from the first pillar, from a social security–style welfare plan, the workers correctly perceive no connection between corporate governance and their future stream of benefits if the pillar 1 scheme is thinly funded, or strictly PAYGO—as is the case in most countries in our sample. From the worker's standpoint, the ultimate payer of his pillar 1 pension is the government, which in turn has a potential (and prior) claim on the assets of all firms and individuals in the country. Corporate governance, good or ill, has nothing to do with the credibility of these claims.

Even if first-pillar schemes are partially funded, the government often imposes a firewall between the accumulated equity assets and the exercise of the associated equity voting rights. For example, in Japan, the government agencies holding equity assets on behalf of the Employee Welfare Pension Insurance Scheme are not allowed to influence how the proxy rights of those shares are voted. And in the United States, the voting rights for equity shares held by the civil servant beneficiaries of the Federal Employees Retirement fund are legally insulated from any input from the U.S. government agencies involved in managing the fund.

But if a higher proportion of total pension benefits come from second-pillar schemes, the worker perceives a direct connection between corporate governance and her future benefits. In a lump-sum scheme or firm-based annuity scheme, the worker hopes the firm will remain solvent long enough to pay her off, and so cares very much about the governance of her employing firm. In a funded diversified portfolio scheme, whether firm-based or occupationally based, the worker cares about the governance of all the firms in her portfolio.

THE 401(K) EFFECT

By the same token, when retirement benefits are accumulated in a third pillar of private investment, the worker also cares about corporate governance more broadly—sometimes known as the "401(k) effect" in the United States, where worker-controlled pension investment accounts became very popular. Workers may perceive the daily, incremental effect of good corporate governance on the portfolio returns of their 401(k) plans (which they often read monthly, and carefully), and they are intently aware of the effects of poor governance when a spectacular corporate scandal such as an Enron, Ahold, or Vivendi blows a big hole in their personal portfolio.

The scandals have a double effect: at one level they gut the assets of employees of the bankrupt firms whose pension commitments are often written down. At another level, the impact spreads to larger population groups when the losses hit the widely held pension funds such as the politically vocal public employee unions, at which point politicians quickly take notice. For example, in the Enron bankruptcy alone, the eight largest public employee pension funds in the United States lost almost $1 billion. These losses were quickly reported in the press and then repeated in the quarterly fund statements mailed to every plan beneficiary. Pension losses to poor governance were repeatedly cited in congressional hearings on Enron and WorldCom, as well as confirmation hearings for the SEC nominees

TABLE 7.3
Public Employee Pension Losses on Enron ($ millions)

Florida State Employees Board	$335
University of California Pension Fund	$144.9
Georgia State Employees Fund	$127
CalPERS	$105.2
Washington State Employees Fund	$103
Ohio Public Employees Retirement System	$59
New York State Common Retirement Fund	$58
California State Teachers Retirement Fund	$47.5

and in the months of debate in both the House and the Senate leading up to the Sarbanes-Oxley Act.[17]

Incidentally, these pension losses were a major issue in U.S. gubernatorial races in the states of California, New York, and Florida in 2000 and 2002. For example, H. Carl McCall was both trustee of the New York State Common Retirement Fund and the Democratic candidate for governor of the State of New York. His March 2002 announcement of the NYSCRF losses on Enron was widely trumpeted in the New York media and cost him dearly in the subsequent election.[18] The large losses in the NYSCRF were attributed to poor governance and laid at McCall's doorstep. In particular, this alienated many government employees, traditionally a key electoral constituency for Democratic (or liberal-left) candidates in the United States. McCall lost, and he went on to serve as chairman of the compensation committee that awarded NYSE president Richard Grasso a $139.1 million deferred compensation plan. Public outrage over this arrangement resulted in Grasso's termination and the resignation of the NYSE board—including McCall.

SHIFTING PREFERENCES OF WORKER-VOTERS

When the weights of the components of workers' wealth are rearranged in terms of wages and pension pillars, the worker-voters' utility function tips, and they begin to think like shareholders as well as employees. Recalling the Pagano and Volpin formulation, workers can become as much or more concerned with avoiding expropriation costs by blockholders than they are concerned with exacting agency costs

---

[17] Keith Perine, "Senate Accounting Industry Regulation Could Get New Legs after Recess," *Congressional Quarterly Weekly*, May 24, 2002; Keith Perine, "Senate Panel Approves Tighter Rules for Accounting Industry," *Congressional Quarterly Weekly*, June 21, 2002; Gebe Martinez and Keith Perine, "Corporate America Faces Shift in Legislative Landscape," *Congressional Quarterly Weekly*, July 5, 2002; "House GOP Opposition to Senate's Accounting Bill Vanishes," *National Journal's Congress Daily* July 18, 2002; Susan Crabtree, "Hastert Shoots Down GOP Attempt to Block Sarbanes Bill," *Congressional Roll Call*, July 18, 2002.

[18] "The Fund owned nearly 4 million shares of Enron through its index portfolio and active managers prior to the company's catastrophic downfall. Our losses are expected to exceed $58 million." New York State Comptroller H. Carl McCall, testimony before the Committee on Financial Services, U.S. House of Representatives, March 20, 2002.

themselves. In short, with these altered weights in their utility function, workers' preferences have shifted, including their preferences for corporate governance.

Workers now favor policy outcomes that result in greater minority shareholder protections. They still care about their current wages and their job security, but now they are not the only thing on workers' minds as they survey how their firm is managed, or corporate governance rules more broadly.

If the starting point was a country in a labor model, workers' interests are now conflicted. The labor versus capital, "us versus them" argument no longer looks so simple. If the starting point was a country in a corporatist compromise, workers don't think they are necessarily in the same boat as managers, and they no longer have an attractive "deal" with blockholders, swapping agency costs for expropriation costs; expropriation costs, the blockholder's private benefits of control, now come partly out of the workers' hide. As this new set of preferences sinks in, the corporatist bargain becomes unstable; workers are tempted to defect from their coalition with managers, and throw in their lot with shareholders.

The corporatist consensus could begin to unravel.

MANAGERIAL PREFERENCES AND AGENCY FAILURE

Confronted with the pressures for transparency and accountability of a shareholder-worker alliance, many managers recall the "closed doors" of the corporatist compromise with some fondness. As noted earlier, public accountability of management exposes practices and agreements that could be challenged by outsiders such as consumers, taxpayers, and minority shareholders.

Not surprisingly, managers generally prefer governance practices that minimize disclosure, independent oversight, and contests for control—and which maximize executive compensation, as discussed in chapter 3.

FROM CLOSED DOORS TO TRANSPARENCY: WORKERS' NEW PREFERENCES

What specific governance preferences do workers now have? These preferences will now be largely congruent, though not identical, with those of minority shareholders.

In terms of information institutions, they will favor more rigorous accounting, audit, and disclosure standards that allow both insiders and outsiders to monitor the health of their firm. Good accounting makes it harder for managers to hide losses or otherwise "manage" earnings, as well as reducing the surprise factor of sudden bankruptcies. Proper accounting and disclosure of revenues and assets on a line-of-business basis makes cross-subsidies clearly visible, thus highlighting managerial performance in more objective terms, which otherwise can be obscured by intrafirm transfers.

Proper accrual accounting for future benefits and unfunded liabilities, combined with accurate valuation of fund assets, allows workers to keep an eye on "their" slice of the firm's second-pillar pension fund. A firm's annual payments to a defined benefit pension fund are most sensitive to three values: the expected return of the plan's assets, the expected annual increases in compensation benefits, and the discount rate for future contributions. By arbitrarily adopting optimistic assumptions regarding these three values, a firm can dramatically reduce its annual contribution, or even take back overfunded cash from the fund. For example, a 1 percent change in the asset return and discount rate (they are usually set the same) will shift the liability up or down by about 12 percent.[19] Workers thus have a vital interest in corporate governance practices that ensure realistic estimation and tracking of these pension liabilities.

Workers also have a strong preference for financial reporting that is both accurate and timely. They want the board to have access to complete financial information on the firm and its lines of business, and not be "cut out of" the loop of sensitive information. When workers have representatives on the board of directors, they rely more on ex ante monitoring by the board to track or block errors by management, and this requires timely reporting of the consequences of key decisions. In contrast, outside shareholders rely more on ex post monitoring of results, usually long after the key decisions have been made.

In general, workers favor mechanisms of board oversight that make it tougher for managers to "capture" the board. They want board members whose prime duties are to the employees and the shareholders, rather than serving blockholders or managers. On these points, workers' interests diverge somewhat from those of minority shareholders, since workers prefer to have employee or union representation on the board, whereas outside shareholders prefer independent, nonexecutive directors.

Workers want a real board with real power; in this sense, oversight may be even more valuable from the standpoint of the workers, insofar as they can directly elect or select these board members, whereas the dispersed shareholders usually simply ratify a slate of directors proposed by the directors themselves. The risk for workers is that important discussions can take place among managers and blockholders in other settings. If so, the board on which workers' representatives sit can become a pro forma body, just going through the oversight motions with little real authority, or it can be bypassed entirely.

By the same token, if a firm is going through a transition from a concentrated blockholder towards greater dispersion, workers are concerned that the vacuum of monitoring, between blockholder oversight and dispersed market discipline, may leave managers unaccountable to anyone, with the latitude to entrench and enrich themselves at the expense of employees and shareholders alike.

Both workers and outside shareholders favor control rules that give shareholders visibility and a vote in major asset transfers that otherwise can jeopardize the health of the firm. Asset-stripping and self-dealing are the primary means by which blockholders extract private benefits of control at the expense of employees and shareholders alike. One-share, one-vote restricts the ability of blockholders to skew the ratio between control and cash flow rights, which in turn makes it more costly for a potential blockholder to extract private benefits of control.

Workers and outside shareholders part company on the rules for takeovers, however. Workers prefer rules of fiduciary responsibility for the board that give the board (and management) latitude to factor in the consequences on employment

---

[19] Michael Moran, "Pension Accounting and Funding: A Roadmap for Analysts and Investors," Goldman Sachs Global Strategy Research, December 2002.

of big decisions, including control transactions such as mergers or acquisitions. In contrast, outside shareholders prefer cut-and-dried rules for evaluating control transactions purely in terms of maximizing shareholder value.

Workers favor rules and standards for managerial compensation that reward competent performance. Workers do not necessarily object to performance-based compensation for senior managers, but they are sensitive to gross disparities between managerial and worker compensation. In contrast, outside shareholders are less sensitive to the absolute level of managerial incentive compensation, or the gap between managers' and workers' pay, as long as they perceive a connection between these incentives and maximizing shareholder value.

Both workers and shareholders object to incentive option plans that provide managers with a big upside should the firm do well, but have little downside if things go badly. To the degree that they understand how option plans work, these workers-as-shareholders object to options priced "at the money" rather than against a benchmark of similar firms. They want the terms and conditions of managers' and directors' compensation fully disclosed, to the firm, to the employees, and to the public.

But how will these monitoring and disciplining functions be performed by individual workers, the millions of beneficiaries of pension plans and mutual funds? It is crucial to note that workers are not direct owners of shares except in pillars 2 and 3 schemes—and even then, these shares are aggregated by pension or mutual funds ("unit trusts") that often register and vote the control rights associated with those shares. Where share ownership exists in the corporatist countries, financial institutions, not individuals, often control it. This leads to a crucial point: the connection between pension ownership and political action for minority shareholder protections is mediated by the structure of financial institutions and how workers relate to them. We will return to this point further in this chapter.

PREDICTIONS AND EVIDENCE

Given these changes in workers' corporate governance preferences, the transparency coalition model predicts the following:

- Workers are likely to increase their share of direct and indirect equity holdings by means of personal savings and retirement plans.
- Countries with a high proportion of pillar 1 IPD will correlate with lesser minority shareholder protections. Conversely, countries with a high proportion of pillar 2 and pillar 3 assets to GDP will correlate with greater minority shareholder protections.
- As workers' equity holdings increase, pension funds will press firms to improve their minority shareholder protections. Workers-as-voters will support corporate governance reforms.

Prediction 1: Workers are likely to increase their direct and indirect equity holdings through retirement plans and personal savings.

There is ample and striking evidence to support this prediction. Total financial assets of OECD pension funds grew from $3.7 trillion in 1990, about 30 percent of

TABLE 7.4
Institutional Investors ($ billions)

	Assets 1993	Assets 1999	Pension Funds	Pension (%)	Equity (%)	Equity ($)	Equity Share
United States	8,035	19,279	6,900	0.36	0.51	9,832	0.65
Japan	3,012	5,039	937	0.19	0.19	957	0.06
United Kingdom	1,207	3,264	1,226	0.38	0.68	2,220	0.15
France	800	1,695	0	0.00	0.42	712	0.05
Germany	665	1,529	63	0.04	0.28	428	0.03
Italy	225	1,078	33	0.03	0.22	237	0.02
Netherlands	427	799	448	0.56	0.43	344	0.02
Canada	376	748	310	0.41	0.27	202	0.01
Australia	176	375	253	0.67	0.5	188	0.01
South Korea	161	375	13	0.03	0.11	41	0.00
Total	15,084	34,181	10,183			15,161	
Mean				0.27	0.36		

Source: Brancato 2000.

GDP, to $16 trillion by 1999, about 40 percent of GDP, more than tripling in value terms. During this decade, the share of equities within the total asset port-folio of these funds increased from 35 percent to 51 percent, with the result that pension funds increased their total share of global equity holdings from 17 percent to 23 percent.[20]

When the pension funds of U.S. workers achieved similar levels of ownership of total U.S. equities in 1976, Peter Drucker published *The Unseen Revolution: How Pension Fund Socialism Came to America*. In that year, private noninsured pension assets had risen to $172 billion, of which $100 billion was held in equi-ties. Drucker claimed that employees effectively owned between 25 percent and 35 percent of the equity of listed American firms, granting them de facto control. The accumulation of equity ownership in listed firms is not a purely American phenomenon; it is OECD-wide. But the U.S. and U.K. component of this asset accumulation is very large.

As table 7.4 shows, U.S.- and U.K.-based pension and mutual funds continue to drive this worldwide accumulation of equity by workers.

According to this table, institutional investors in the United States and the United Kingdom control two-thirds of the total assets, and allocate a much higher proportion of their total portfolio to equities. As shown in the table, Anglo-American investors account for 80 percent of total equity holdings among the 10 countries in this data sample. Pillar 2 pension funds claim 36 per-cent and 38 percent of these assets in the United States and United Kingdom respectively; pillar 3 mutual funds probably account for a similar proportion in both cases.

[20] Stern 2001.

U.S.-based investment managers shifted the weight of equities in their portfo-lio composition from 26.5 percent of total assets in 1988 to a ratio of 47.4 percent at the beginning of 1999.[21] By 1998, the average beneficiary of a 401(k) plan in a U.S. firm held 64 percent of the portfolio in equities.[22] The spillover effect of this shift to equities explains why U.S.- and U.K.-based investors became such big proportional players in global equity markets. This portfolio shift is most appar-ent in the case of public employee pension funds in the United States, which tripled the proportion of equities in their portfolios, from 22 percent to 68 per-cent over this time period.

Ironically, politics initially blunted this wave of public employee investment in equities. In his postwar history of U.S. institutional investors, Clowes observes that "Public funds trailed corporate funds in moving to equities . . . [because] they were ultimately overseen by state or local legislators, or the state or local treasur-er, all of whom were concerned about political exposure if the funds lost money in investments."[23] A shift to greater equity exposure began at two U.S. state teach-ers' retirement funds, Ohio and Utah, in the pursuit of higher total yields, and then picked up steam across the country.[24] The public employee pension funds continued this more aggressive investment strategy by pioneering investment in international equities as well. As of 1997, 18 of the top 25 institutional holders of foreign equities were public employee pension funds.[25]

Prediction 2: Countries with a high proportion of pillar 1 IPD will correlate with lower minority shareholder protections. Conversely, countries with a high proportion of pillar 2 and pillar 3 assets to GDP will correlate with greater minority shareholder protections.

This prediction holds. As figure 7.1 suggests, the size of the pillar 1 IPD is neg-atively correlated with minority shareholder protections, at −.39. (See also appen-dix tables A.29 and A.30.) Though weak, this correlation is consistent with the third prediction of the transparency coalition model. Estimated with a fitted lin-ear regression, each one-unit increase in IPD results in a 0.1-unit decrease in shareholder protections, with a statistical significance at the .05 level ($t = 2.09$), for the 26 countries in the sample for which we have IPD estimates. For example,

[21] Brancato 2000, 22.

[22] "[L]arge and midsize companies devoted time and money to educating their employees about how to invest their 401k assets. Virtually all companies provided their employees with booklets out-lining the basics of investing: the power of compounding; the long term return histories of stocks, bonds, and cash; how risk and reward are related; how diversification can reduce risk without harm-ing long term return; how each employee should determine his or her own risk tolerance and build a portfolio appropriate for that risk tolerance. . . . The flood of assets into 401k plans, together with the investment education companies provided to their employees, changed the course of the debate about 'fixing' Social Security. . . . The 401k plan had thus provided one possible solution for the Social Security Crisis." Clowes 2000, 259–61.

[23] Clowes 2000, 134.

[24] Clowes 2000, 35.

[25] That would be 19 out of 25 if TIAA-CREF, a university teachers' pension fund, were classified as a public employee fund. Brancato 2000, 41.

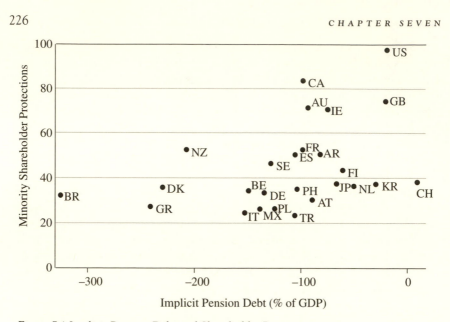

Figure 7.1 Implicit Pension Debt and Shareholder Protections

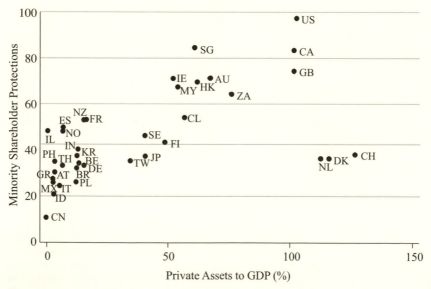

Figure 7.2 Private Pension Assets and Shareholder Protections

a 100-point increase in IPD debt roughly correlates with a reduction in minority shareholder protections from the level of Belgium to the level of Greece.

Conversely, as discussed in chapter 5, private pension assets in pillars 2 and 3 schemes are positively correlated with minority shareholder protections, at .56, as figure 7.2 reveals.

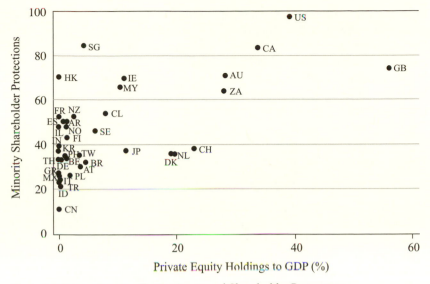

Figure 7.3 Private Pension Equity Assets and Shareholder Protections

There is some endogeneity in this relationship since investors provide a higher valuation for shares in countries with higher shareholder protections—the "good-governance premium." Nonetheless, estimated by a fitted OLS linear regression, each one-unit increase in private pension assets results in a .29 increase in shareholder protections, with a significance at the .005 level ($t = 4.05$, $r^2 = .31$) for the same sample. For example, a 50-point increase in pillars 2 and 3 assets per capita roughly correlates with an improvement of minority shareholder protections from the level of Korea to the level of Chile. (See also appendix tables A.31 and A.32.)

The fit between pillars 2 and 3 assets and shareholder protections is even tighter if we include the estimated percentage of these assets held in domestic equities and weight the total asset value by this allocation percentage. An OLS fitted line in the scatter plot shown in figure 7.3 is significant at .005 ($t = 4.64$, $r^2 = .37$).

Prediction 3: As workers' equity holdings increase, they press for corporate governance reforms that promote minority shareholder protections.

We established workers' interest in corporate governance as a function of their personal assets, especially pension assets, and we have tracked the growth of a sizable stake in pension funds. Has this translated into demands for minority shareholder protections? If all we needed to know was ownership, the answer would be yes. But this is the flaw of the investment model, which assumed that owners would automatically become lobbyists for minority shareholder protections. And we found this not to be the case.

As we examine the causal connection between pension asset accumulation and governance reforms, there are two potential pathways—one of pressure of these pension funds on firms to improve their governance, either by voting with their feet, or by directly voting their shareholder rights (proxies) and thereby forcing firms to observe their interests. In this pathway, it is critical how the institutions of pension investment actually are structured.

There is also an indirect pathway, whereby the equity holdings of workers in firms induce broad political support for "top down" corporate governance reforms that force firms to protect minority shareholders.

Analytic Narratives

CHILE: AUTHORITARIAN ROOTS OF THE TRANSPARENCY COALITION

Chile provides a fascinating case of authoritarian intervention, structural change in economic preferences, then political democratization. As with Korea, changes in political institutions altered the power balance, which had consequences for corporate governance. Chile moved from a stable, "bargained" constitutional government, to the left under Allende, then to right-wing dictatorship under Pinochet, and now to a constitutional democracy. Its corporate governance system reflected these changes: Allende toward state control, Pinochet toward a new liberal model that privatized firms and, important for our analysis, privatized social security. At the same time, some insider structures have been preserved: cross-shareholding has been prohibited, but pyramid control remains. The oligarchic pattern of the early years of industrialization shifted to a particularly statist version of labor power under Allende, then to a policy mixture under Pinochet of oligarchy and an investor model. Today, the politics and the pattern are mixed. Some features of a transparency coalition are noticeable. Privatized social security created the potential for pressures on the small blockholding elite. The Chilean citizen is a minority shareholder by virtue of the nation's privatized social security system; a bankrupt pillar 1 system was replaced with a funded pillars 2 and 3 system almost two decades ago.

Chile exhibits both high blockholding within firms and widespread shareholding in the population. Objectively, this creates tension between the blockholders and the individual owners, creating the possibility of change but not the inevitability of it. Private blockholders continue to control listed firms, with a concentration ratio of 90 percent. At the same time minority shareholder protections have been increasing slowly over time, among the highest in emerging markets. Pension funds and foreign portfolio investors own 10 percent of the equity market, and appear to be both monitoring and disciplining blockholders.

Pension reform was one of many neoliberal "Chicago school" economic policies adopted by the authoritarian Pinochet government, implemented with little opposition since political parties and trade unions had been crushed by the junta. Many years later, these changes, whatever their origin, acquired support by stakeholders now vested in them. That political support is strong enough to inhibit succeeding center-left coalition governments from doing anything to unwind the past. At the same time, the new structures that manage the privatized funds are controlled by the blockholding elite that dominates the rest of the economy with pyramid leveraging—while "the Chicago boys" pushed for neoliberal economic practices in the role of state ownership, they do not appear to have moved to break up elite control of firms.

This perspective on preferences and institutions helps solve the puzzle of Chile's position as an "outlier," with both high concentration and strong shareholder protections that drew it far away from the 45-degree line predicted by the investor model.

Controladores de los Conglomerados Chilenos. Closely held conglomerates dominate the field of listed firms in Chile. The so-called Big Five family groupings—the Angelini, Luksic, Matte, Pathfinder, and Sigdo Koppers—dominate the heights of corporate Chile.

In a careful study tracing ultimate controlling ownership, Lefort and Walker found that 73 percent of the firms listed with the Superindendencia de Seguros y Valores (SSV for short, the equivalent of the SEC) belonged to a conglomerate group, and that these groups were controlled with ownership pyramids by a small number of individuals and families.[26] This percentage has been increasing, from 66 percent in 1990 to 68 percent in 1994 to 73 percent of their sample in 1998. The average blockholding has been going up, too, from 52 percent in 1990 to 57 percent in 1998. The authors estimate that these blockheld groups account for 90 percent of the asset value of the Chilean stock exchange (plus ADRs), which roughly corresponds to a weighted blockholding figure for our purposes.

Reluctant Minority Protections. Chile was hardly a paradise for minority shareholder protections in its early stages of industrialization in the early 1900s, with the long history of oligarchic control of the economy typical of many Latin American economies. Blockholding provided shelter from insecure property rights, threats of predation from military governments or corrupt civilian politicians, and unruly labor activism. Chile had stronger rule of law than many countries and more political stability, but that did not translate into corporate governance greatly different from the other countries of the region.

Many of these oligarchs were dispossessed by the nationalizations of the Allende regime in the early 1970s. A strong swing to the left produced forced nationalization. With the Pinochet coup, a strong swing to the right produced privatization.

The influence of neoliberal thinking on the Pinochet regime, as theorized by the so-called Chicago boys, did not produce an immediate creation of neoliberal corporate governance practices. It is interesting that cross-shareholding was prohibited, but not pyramid leverage. That may reflect the ability of the old families to limit the extent of neoliberalization. This set up a constant tension between public authorities having a liberalization objective and the blockholders. Under substantial prodding and pushing from the securities regulator

---

[26] Fernado Lefort and Eduardo Walker, "Ownership and Capital Structure of Chilean Conglomerates: Facts and Hypotheses for Governance," *Revista Abante* 3 (1999): 3–27.

and other state agencies, accounting and auditing practices as well as control rules gradually improved during the 1980s and particularly in the 1990s. The family oligarchies retained tight control of the boards of directors; only about 10 percent of directors qualified as NEDs, and only after they were voted onto the boards over the objections of the blockholders by Chilean pension funds. The National Congress passed a broad reform law in October 2000, whose basic theme is the protection of minority shareholder rights in the area of control, by regulating the terms of tender offers, limiting self-dealing by block-holders, and granting equal rights to foreign portfolio investors who hold ADRs in listed Chilean firms. The pension funds themselves are vested in institutions, which are themselves part of firms controlled by blockholders.

AFPs on the Scene. The pension reform law of 1980 gave every worker the choice to opt out fully from the government-run first-pillar scheme and instead put the former payroll tax in a privately managed personal retirement account (PRA). Ninety-five percent of the labor force opted out of the pillar 1 scheme— widely understood to be insolvent—and into the PRA scheme, under which they chose one of five Administradora de Fondos de Pensiones (or AFPs) to manage their personal accounts.

As Jose Piñera, the Chicago school economist and architect of the AFP system, proudly noted, "Workers are free to change from one AFP company to another, and from one fund to another. There is then competition among the companies to provide a higher return on investment, better customer service, or a lower commission."[27]

The AFPs were carefully regulated (itself an interesting comment on the reluctance to believe fully that markets and private reputational mechanism provide adequate protection for a realm where controlling risk is an important goal), with portfolio limits of 30 percent maximum exposure to equities, 16 percent cap in foreign assets, and domestic caps of 7 percent of assets invested in any single firm.

Over a two-decade period, these funds gradually acquired 10 percent of the cash flow shares of listed Chilean firms. Agosin and Pasten document several anecdotes of AFPs monitoring Chilean public firms and taking collective action when threatened with expropriation by majority blockholders, such as the Enersis/Endesa and Téléfonica/Tera cases.[28] This is what we would expect from owner-controlled funds. In some ways the AFPs look more like TIAA-CREF,

[27] "Each worker is given a PRA passbook (if they want to update their balances visiting their AFP) and they receive a regular statement by mail every three months informing him how much money has been accumulated in his retirement account and how well his investment fund has performed. The account bears the worker's name, is his property, and will be used to pay his old age retirement benefit." See José Piñera, "Empowering the Workers: The Privatization of Social Security in Chile," *Cato Letter* No. 10, 1996, 2.

[28] Manuel Agosin and Ernesto Pastén, "Corporate Governance in Chile," paper for the OECD Development Center, April 1999; and "Corporate Governance in Chile," Central Bank of Chile Working Paper No. 209, 2003.

CalPERS, and various European labor-controlled pension funds than typical institutional investors in most capital markets, but in other ways they do look typical, in that the AFPs are not clearly independent of the private-sector institutions that supervise them. At the same time, the structure of the funds limits the "transparency effect" for corporate governance. The protection of savers continues to limit shareholding in the portfolio; lifting that limit would increase pressure for MSP, but expose savers to risk.

After two decades of experience with the PRA system (and the AFPs), Chile has a ratio of accumulated pension assets to GDP of between 45 and 60 percent, and zero IPD to GDP. It has had a vibrant IPO marketplace and has been one of the most attractive destinations for both FDI and foreign portfolio investment in Latin America.

The Politics of Transparency. What we have been calling the investor model for minority shareholder protection did not unfold in Chile according to the script of the investor model examined in chapter 5. There is no evidence that Chile's "old money" families supported the sequence of regulatory changes that enhanced minority shareholder protections, and some anecdotes suggesting that the Big Five opposed these changes. As democracy returned and deepened its roots after the generals had been removed from politics, many of the traditional blockholding families remained under a political cloud, residually tainted by their collusion with Pinochet and the junta—just as the great chaebol families in Korea remained tarred by their collusion with Park Chung Hee and his military successors.

In Chile, center-left governments, with fairly broad popular support, pressed the legislation enhancing minority shareholder protections. This in turn is traceable to the PRA and its pension-investing instruments, the AFPs, which have turned out to be politically durable. As Piñera observes, "It is not surprising that the PRA system has survived intact three center-Left governments in the last 12 years, since it really has become the 'third rail' of Chilean politics. Not only has it been untouched in its structural design, but technical adjustments have improved it allowing, for example, more competition in the management of voluntary retirement savings or enlarging the choices of funds from one to five."[29] At the same time, controversy has risen about rate of return in this plan, as people who joined the new plan claim they are doing less well than people who stayed in the government plan.[30]

Although tepidly greeted (or actively resisted) by the old-money blockholding families, Chile's new rules did receive support from many new-money entrepreneurs who emerged during the 1990s, a period that witnessed a flood of IPOs. In 1991–97, there were 44 IPOs valued at U.S.$1,157 million. IPOs represented almost 5 percent of all market turnover.[31]

The Chilean case reminds us that not all owners are identical, or necessarily with even similar preferences. If we disaggregate them by identifying their institutional

[29] Piñera 1996.

[30] Larry Rohter, "Chile's Retirees Find Shortfall in Private Plan," *New York Times*, 27 January 2005.

[31] Agosin and Pasten 1999.

positions—degree of blockholding, fragmentation of ownership, control over pension assets—we find a wide divergence of preferences. Those with stakes in big blocks want to hang on and resist minority shareholder protection. So do some institutional investors who collaborate with managers and blockholders. On the other side are minority investors, new-money entrepreneurs, and pension beneficiaries, many involved in the labor union system, who are able to solve collective action problems by having a responsive institution—their pension management group—fight on their behalf in the firm and, importantly, in the political arena.

MALAYSIA: ETHNICITY AND DEMOCRACY IN GOVERNANCE POLITICS

Malaysia is a striking case of shifting preferences for corporate governance, due to widespread equity ownership (the result of a deep pension pool) interacting with a set of political institutions that enable powerful and sometimes arbitrary governments. Malaysia resembles Chile in many respects, with strong shareholder protections and also substantial ownership concentration; in this sense it is also an outlier above the investor model's 45-degree line. There are similar factors at work; Malaysia has progressed along a similar trajectory resulting in a transparency coalition. Malaysia has broad popular support for shareholder protections and corporate governance reforms, stemming in part from Malaysia's high, 52 percent ratio of private pension assets to GDP, and also (unlike Chile) from the ethnic politics of Malaysia's fractious democracy—most private blockholders are also ethnic Chinese in a body politic controlled by ethnic Malays.

Like Chile, the large accumulation of domestic assets made foreign portfolio investors relatively less important in capital market development, and like Chile, domestic private blockholders have entered only slowly into an investor model deal with these external investors. For our purposes, Malaysia also exhibits the problem of credible commitment to shareholder protections when the government is a "hard democracy" with sometimes questionable allegiance to the rule of law.

Malaysia's weight of private blockholders in total market capitalization is 42.6, slightly below the mean of the sample as a whole though higher than the average emerging market. Most private blockholders in Malaysia are ethnic Chinese *hua qiao* families, with their roots in a wide variety of mining, trade, and financial activities, each with a classic founder-entrepreneur, and with active family participation in management. Over the last 50 years of Malaysia's rapid economic growth, some of these have grown into complex networks of firms, such as the Kwok family group, typically a diversified industrial group, sometimes with a "house" bank (controlled by the blockholder, often indirectly), with close ties across the ASEAN (Association of Southeast Asian Nations) region and investments in China. This reflected a classic oligarchical approach to corporate governance; outside investors were barely tolerated, used as a source of cash but kept largely in the dark. Hired-hand managers and employees were just that— employees—with no voice in governance.

As in many countries, the growth of these firms in terms of scale, complexity, and—importantly for a relatively small economy such as Malaysia—their international operations led to a gradual transition from oligarchy to investor model. Family members retained control and key management positions, but outsiders were brought inside the tent to help run the firm. Much has been made of this process of reluctant professionalization by firms in the so-called bamboo network. Despite their frequently opaque financial reporting and susceptibility to insider manipulation, many of these firms became the darlings of foreign portfolio investors, who saw them as an opportunity to participate in the high-growth opportunities provided by the "Four Tigers."

Shifting Domestic Preferences. Strikingly, Malaysia has zero IPD in its first-pillar pension scheme, due to the farsighted "forced savings" scheme of the Employees Provident Fund (EPF). The EPF was established in 1951, with a 90 percent coverage ratio and high salary replacement rate. Employees contribute 9 percent of salary, and employers kick in 12 percent of salary to the EPF. Beneficiaries of the EPF receive a detailed summary of their portfolio and the relative performance of the fund on a regular basis.

The EPF rapidly became the largest financial institution in Malaysia and continued to occupy that position throughout the high-growth period of the 1970s, 1980s, and 1990s. By 2002 the EPF had accumulated total assets of about $50 billion, accounted for 17 percent of national savings, and held two-thirds of the government's total fixed-income debt instruments. More important, the EPF also held 21 percent of its assets in equities, largely domestic, making EPF the biggest player in Malaysia's stock market. As in Chile, this density gave virtually all Malaysian workers a vital interest in the corporate governance of Malaysian firms.

The EPF was periodically tainted by scandals surrounding subsidies to bumiputra firms and other control transactions, which sometimes involved bribes and dubious political "contributions," but on the whole maintained a reputation for honest and reasonably competent investment management. It maintained a relatively passive approach to corporate governance of the firms in which it invested until the late 1990s, stimulated in part by large losses associated with the Asian financial crisis, which hit Malaysia's stock market quite hard—and rapidly engaged the Malaysian government.

Strong Institutions Meet Fragile Markets. Malaysia can be classified as a hard democracy with strong centralizing institutions. The Malaysian government has been controlled (but not ruled) by an ethnic Malay coalition since independence in the 1950s. This government pursued a policy of fostering ethnic Malay (or bumiputra) blockholders by means of preferential lending, transfers of SOE assets, and other subsidies.

Until his recent resignation, Prime Minister Dr. Mohammed Mohatir wielded effective control of the policy through his control over the United Malays National Organization (UMNO). With a coalition of smaller ethnic parties, the National Front (or Barisan Nasional), has a commanding majority of 148 out of 193 seats in the four-year-term parliament, the Dewan Rakyat.

Despite this superficial coalition structure, Malaysia has few veto points, in contrast with Thailand, with many veto points, and the Philippines—closer to Thailand in terms of the hurdles governments face in implementing policy reforms.[32] While Thailand also has a multiparty system, there the parties fight during the election and form volatile coalitions afterwards. In contrast, in Malaysia, "the parties divide the electoral map among themselves before the election to avoid competing with each other."[33]

The Barisan Nasional coalition is thus best understood as a unitary actor, or single party, where the crucial battles are fought not among the parties of the coalition but within the UMNO. If UMNO leaders favor a policy change, or the status quo, they get what they want, as there are no other veto players. Other groups exist and must be consulted by UMNO leaders. Technically, UMNO itself controls only 71 of the total Barisan Nasional seats, with 29 held by the Malaysian Chinese Association (MCA, or Persutuan China Malaysia) and therefore requires a measure of consultation and coordination before policies are implemented.

The Asian Crisis Meltdown. In the wake of the Asian financial crisis the Malaysian state began a renewed program to enhance minority shareholder protections, promoted as "top-down reforms." These reforms frequently pointed a finger at the governance sins of private blockholders, often a code word for "the Chinese." The Kuala Lumpur media (closely monitored by the state) reveled in lurid exposures of insider transactions and self-enrichment by (usually *hua qiao*) blockholders, which, it was implied, had led to the moral hazard losses associated with the Asian financial crisis. This reflected a conscious argument by the Malaysian government that it had been an example of fiscal rectitude during the late 1990s, and that therefore the crisis must be laid on the shoulders of evil blockholders and greedy foreign investors.

The top-down reform project began with a High Level Finance Committee on Corporate Governance established by the Ministry of Finance in March 1998, which unleashed a series of regulatory changes through the Securities Commission, the Kuala Lumpur Stock Exchange (KLSE), and the Registrar of Companies.[34]

These changes led to the creation of a Malaysian Corporate Governance Code, the Malaysian Institute of Corporate Governance, and the Minority Shareholder Watchdog Committee—each of which had strong participation by representatives from the EPF.[35] The motive for these changes was to reassure investors, both domestic and international, so as to hold and attract capital. Domestic groups had the usual response: blockholders did not like being challenged, yet domestic investors (including the EPF) wanted protections enforced.

---

[32] McIntyre 2001.

[33] McIntyre 2001.

[34] "Crusade for Better Governance," *New Straits Times*, May 4, 1999, 13.

[35] "Minority Shareholders Watchdog Group Looking for a Suitable Model," *Bernama News Agency*, August 16, 1999.

As a result, Malaysia's shareholder protections climbed to high levels, 67 on our index, placing it well above the total mean of 45, in the top 5 percent of the distribution.

Malaysian information institutions became robust in their protections for minority shareholders; Malaysia's generally accepted accounting principles were brought in line with IAS, with a few minor deviations. Reflecting the strong professional legacy of the Commonwealth, the accounting profession was well-organized through the Malaysian Institute of Accountants and the Malaysian Association of CPAs. The Malaysian Accounting Standards Board became relatively independent of the Ministry of Finance, with greater latitude in standards setting. The Companies Act mandated third-party audit, a requirement backstopped by new rules issued by the Kuala Lumpur Stock Exchange.

Oversight remained the toughest nut, not surprising when family members or nominees continued to control most boards. Recent studies suggest that 90 percent of listed companies have at least two NEDs, and the Malaysian Code of Corporate Governance has set a minimum of 30 percent independent NEDs on boards. The obligations of directors began to be monitored by the Government Minority Shareholder Watchdog Committee, created at the recommendation of the High Level Finance Committee on Corporate Governance. Malaysia's legal system imposes strong standards of fiduciary duty to minority shareholders, and the courts began to entertain derivative suits for breach of this duty, although class-action suits are not possible.

In contrast to the low score on oversight, Malaysia's control rules protect minority shareholders. The Watchdog Committee, the Securities Commission, and the KLSE enforced a one-share, one-vote rule, and ensured that minority shareholders have at least a nominal voice in key corporate decisions. Malaysia's Code of Takeovers and Mergers was revised in 1999 to resemble the City Code in most respects. In the 1990s the state imposed a 30 percent cap on foreign ownership of bumiputra firms and banks—although this cap was increased, removed, and reimposed over time—which inhibited foreign firms from engaging in competitive contests for listed Malaysian companies, but did promote a vigorous rough-and-tumble domestic M&A market.

Malaysia's market for managers came to adopt a fairly progressive use of stock options, reflecting in part the influence of foreign firms in Malaysia's high-tech corridors in Penang, Johore, and around Kuala Lumpur. There is some evidence that senior managers in large family-controlled groups continued to be compensated at the behest of the private blockholders rather than hired from a competitive outside market, similar in many respects to the practice of Korean chaebol.

Protection or Predation? Malaysia belongs in the "oligarchy" category of blockholder control, but its political basis is a complex cross-class coalition, relatively unstable, given the strong political institutions through which it must work to achieve results in corporate governance. Policies affecting corporate governance cut across party and ethnicity. Private blockholders, Chinese and bumiputra alike, fall on all sides of these political fault lines. Not all *bumi* entrepreneurs support UMNO, and not all Chinese blockholders support MCA.

As an added wrinkle, privatized SOEs account for a sizable portion of the KLSE market cap, thus lowering the weight of private blockholders. The government entered into a decade-long privatization program in the 1980s under the pressure of increasing capital budgets for the national air carrier, telecom provider, and petroleum company. These SOEs served as a vessel for implementing schemes for bumiputra advancement, as well as garden-variety corruption and a convenient money-pot through which to pursue industrial structure (such as the Proton "national car") or regional development goals that were important to politicians. The workers (especially bumiputra workers, who had hiring preferences in the SOEs) in these firms saw their interests aligned with those of managers— especially bumiputra managers—and not necessarily with those of faceless minority shareholders.

As a further complication, minority shareholder protections were also used as a weapon in UMNO and MCA intraparty factional disputes. Several cases were brought against blockholders and managers at the behest of the prime minister in order to punish party defectors or cut off financial backers in bitterly contested federal or state elections. For example, several prominent bumiputra backers of former finance minister Anwar Ibrahim were charged with corporate malfeasance when Anwar was jailed and his political supporters scattered. Domestic and foreign minority shareholders were not encouraged by these examples of the government's fidelity to good corporate governance, when the underlying motives were transparent—and worse behavior was tolerated by other owners and managers who stood (at least temporarily) in better political graces.

Strong States and "Permissive" Protections. Politically, the Malaysian state has the capacity to take decisive action to change policy, including reforms in corporate governance, if the leaders find it useful to do so. In this respect, Malaysia lies with the majoritarian countries of Europe, resembling that of the extremely majoritarian United Kingdom (no historical surprise, there). Policy changes can be sharp. This can be threatening to investors, as they cannot be sure of the stability of the policy regime, nor of even-handed application of governance rules. It can also mean strong response to problems and crises: McIntyre classifies Malaysia as having taken decisive action in response to the Asia financial crisis because its institutions allowed it to quickly implement steps that took years in Thailand and the Philippines.

Centralization of authority means reforms can be effective if the government pushes strongly behind them. It also means they can become window dressing, and they can be reversed if the government wishes to do so. Investors are likely to be cautious. Blockholders will only unwind their special advantages if they feel secure in protections. An interesting contrast with the European experience may be noted: there we found that majoritarian systems encouraged diffusion because they undermined the policy stability that the highly interlocked production systems of some blockholding countries required; volatility in these cases breaks the bonds among actors, leading to production strategies that prefer flexibility, in turn undermining the logic of blockholding. This may be an effect that happens only if there is substantial protection and confidence in the regulatory system.

In majoritarian countries such as Malaysia, however, the regulatory process may not be stable enough to provide those protections. There, volatility of policy may threaten the adequacy of shareholder protections and also the credibility of even-handed enforcement of these protections. If that is in question, blockholding remains an attractive option. Thus centralized institutions can be too powerful, leading to the opposite result of diffusion, which is sustained blockholding. This is consistent with McIntyre's insight on the U-shaped curve noted in chapter 3.

SECTION 2: MANAGERS DOMINATE OWNERS AND WORKERS

"Managerism"

There is a long and often bitter literature bemoaning the victory of managers over the owners and workers of firms, in the United States and elsewhere. The landmark corporate governance study of Berle and Means was predicated on the proposition that managerial agents had broken loose from the constraints of their owner-principals and were pursuing a different agenda. A series of more recent books such as those by Monks and Minow have echoed this theme.

Managerial compensation is one of the issues where the battle lines are most clearly drawn between owners and workers on one hand, and managers on the other. As Bebchuk argues, "The processes that produce compensation arrangements, and the various market forces and constraints that act on these processes, leave managers with considerable power to shape their own pay arrangements," suggesting that managers are indeed on the other side of a coalitional divide from owners and workers.[36]

As with our discussions of the roots of the transparency coalition, there are several ways in which managers as a member of a prior coalition, be it with owners or with workers, might begin to see their interests as benefiting from a different set of corporate governance practices.

According to the Chandlerian view, managers begin as very junior partners in their alliance with blockholder-owners, and gradually assert their independence on the basis of technical competence and superior "professional" judgment. These same preferences pull managers in the direction of enhanced autonomy—not to mention higher income—if they can practice their trade under the diffuse monitoring of capital markets, rather than intrusive (and sometimes arbitrary) blockholders. As firms continue to grow in scale and in international distribution, this trend towards independent managerism has a continual impetus.

[36] Lucian Bebchuk, Jesse M. Fried, and David I. Walker, "Managerial Power and Rent Extraction in the Design of Executive Compensation," NBER Working Paper No. 9068, 2002.

238

CHAPTER SEVEN

The same temptations of enhanced autonomy and income can easily lead managers to abandon the certitude of the corporatist compromise "solidarity" with workers. One striking mechanism is global market integration, whereby firms in "corporatist" countries expand their international reach (under the pressures of product-market competition) into markets such as the United States and United Kingdom, where indigenous managers are both independent and highly paid. Another perhaps equally powerful mechanism can be financial problems caused by cozy corporatist firms exposed to the same chill winds of global product-market competition; under the impetus of "crisis," managers can assert the need for autonomy (not to mention enhanced pay) in order to compete with these firms and cope with the pressures of "global capital markets."

We argue that global capital markets play a key role in enhancing the ability of managers to assert their independence from owners and workers alike. The following discussion explores the interlocking roles of pension funds and financial intermediaries in promoting managerism.

ACTIVE VERSUS PASSIVE PENSION FUNDS

Knowing the relative size of the three pension pillars is important in understanding workers' preferences, but not sufficient for understanding the likelihood of actually changing shareholder protections. We observe a striking divergence in shareholder activism among financial institutions, and contrasting degrees of responsiveness to the demands of owners and workers on one hand, and managers on the other.

Many other institutional investors with worker beneficiaries—indeed, most of them—remain on the sidelines while the public employee funds battle for enhanced minority shareholder protections in the United States and abroad. In the United States, Europe, and Japan, most money managers automatically vote with management on proxy issues and rarely contact firms directly or criticize management; if displeased, they "walk."

This distinction between activism and a passive stance in regard to minority shareholder protections and rights is important to the overall argument concerning the size and importance of employee ownership. If pension funds are to have weight in boardroom practice, then the share ownership has to be vocal. If it is passive, then it has no particular role. We have seen this before in looking at the investor model. That approach assumes that capital ownership translates automatically into minority shareholder protections by virtue of the governance premium or discount.

CONFLICTED MONEY MANAGERS

Why do some institutions press managers on behalf of their shareowners, while others cast their lot with managers? The critical variable appears to be the relationship of the financial institution to the managers of the firms in which they buy shares, and the connection between these financial institutions and their own beneficiaries.

Many institutional investors and reputational intermediaries have a strong economic interest in pleasing managers, or at least not antagonizing them. Managers decide who will manage the firm's defined benefit or 401(k) program. Managers select the auditors and pay the accountant's bill, not the shareholders. Managers employ the accountants as consultants as well as auditors. Arthur Andersen received more in consulting fees than in auditing fees from its client Enron. The temptations for institutional investors and reputational intermediaries to ally with managers against owners and employees are substantial, particularly if the managers as a group are skilled in pressing their goals.

Large integrated financial services firms that combine commercial banking, money management, merchant banking, and insurance are understandably reluctant to antagonize the corporate chieftains whose business they aggressively seek for many lines of business. Firms such as Deutsche Bank, Citicorp/Travelers, ING, Tokyo-Mitsubishi Bank, Hong Kong and Shanghai Bank, have relatively little to gain from pressing their client firms for enhanced minority shareholder protections and possibly much to lose.

There is little empirical evidence on how widespread this conflict is, nor any reliable estimate of its effect on corporate governance outcomes. These assertions of the institutional investors' conflict with regard to corporate governance monitoring are based on anecdotal evidence, but they are intuitively plausible.

In contrast to profit-driven institutional investors, employee-owned funds in the United States, Europe, and Asia cannot seek other business transactions from the managers of firms in which they invest. In theory they have only one mission, managing the assets of the pensioners.[37] They cannot compete to manage the pension funds of private firms (either by charter or choice) and thus are less solicitous of the tender feelings of CEOs.

As a result, pension funds controlled by employees or beneficiaries have been in the forefront of movements for enhanced shareholder protections and improved corporate governance in Chile, Malaysia, the Netherlands, Singapore, the United Kingdom, and the United States.

The largest single investor in Malaysian equity markets is the Employees Provident Fund (EPF), which also pools individual savings into a set of competing investment accounts, whose sole source of operating income is investment management. The EPF has often been accused of political interference in its investment choices, and in its sometimes selective support for governance reforms in general, but never of complicity with management, nor with the financial community at large.

---

[37] Of course, the money managers at public pension funds may have many other conflicts; they are often politically appointed, rather than recruited in competitive labor markets, and thus are often subject to pressure from politicians to make investment decisions on criteria other than pure return. Moreover, their salaries are often set at civil servant levels, thus well below competitive rates in financial markets, which leads to mediocre performance. As a result, there is some evidence that public pension systems have had below-market returns on their assets over the long run, suggesting poor judgment or political interference. Augusto Iglesias and Robert J. Palacios, "Managing Public Pension Reserves Part I: Evidence from the International Experience," World Bank Social Protection Discussion Paper No. 0003, January 2000.

In the Netherlands, civil servants' pillar 2 funds were rolled into the Stichting Pensioen Fonds ABP and health care workers' pensions were rolled into the Stichting Pensioenfonds voor de Gezondheid, Geestelijke en Maatschappelijke Belangen (PGGM). ABP and PGGM mounted a vigorous campaign in favor of corporate governance reform and helped establish the Stichting Corporate Governance Onderzoek voor Pensioenfondsen (SCGOP) to lobby for broad-based governance regulatory change—changes strongly resisted by managers in Netherlands firms and by several large financial institutions.

Singapore's Central Providence Fund is similar in function and coverage to Malaysia's EPF, and now has three million beneficiaries with claims on a total $50 billion in assets. CPF is a strong voice for corporate governance reform in Singapore and abroad. Even in Japan, where institutional investors have been fairly timid in advancing the rights of equity beneficiaries, the Public Employees Fund has finally broken with management to advocate better protections for minority shareholders.

In the United Kingdom, investment giant Hermes resembled the U.S.-based CalPERS in many respects. Hermes has its roots in the pension scheme for employees of British Telecom, and has broadened its investor base to manage sums for various entities, mostly public, union, or employee based. It has been remarkably aggressive in corporate governance issues.

In the United States, for example, CalPERS and TIAA-CREF have been the most vocal money managers pressing for enhanced shareholder protections. One of the pioneers in such activism was Jesse Unruh, then California state treasurer (in a liberal Democratic administration), who tired of "greenmail" payments to raiders by incumbent managers. The specific instance was a 1984 payment by Texaco to the Bass brothers of $1.3 billion for their 9.9 percent stake in the firm—at a $137 million premium of the current market price (at which CalPERS held its shares in Texaco).[38]

Unruh thought it important for pension funds to become interested both in the general rules that shape corporate governance regulation and in the activities of specific firms. As noted above, the CII was formed to achieve these goals. CalPERS took direct action at the 10 to 12 firms in its portfolio whose corporate governance practices were the most egregious. From 1985 through 1991, the pension fund pressed firms through shareholder proposals and proxy votes. Beginning in 1992, CalPERS began to hector poor performers in the press, as well.

Congressional testimony regarding U.S. corporate governance scandals in the late 1990s, as well as cases brought against these firms by the SEC and various state-level attorneys general (especially in New York) revealed a substantial blending of interests between firm managers, integrated financial services firms, accounting firms, and other financial intermediaries.

In the soberly stated opinion of the SEC, "the interests of a mutual fund's shareholders may conflict with those of its investment advisor with respect to

---

[38] Randy Chappel and Donald J. Roberts, "CalPERS and Institutional Shareholder Activism," Stanford Graduate School of Business Case S-BE-12, 1993, 5.

proxy voting. This may occur, for example, when a fund's advisor also manages or seeks to manage the retirement plan assets of a company whose securities are held by the fund. In these situations, a fund's advisor may have an incentive to support management recommendations to further its business interests."[39] As Monks observes, "the trustees of private pension plans are appointed by the plans' sponsoring companies, which are anxious to avoid a reputation for activism—as are the money managers to whom the trustees often delegate their buying decisions. In extreme cases activism invites reprisal; in more moderate circumstances it would tend to make them 'unclubbable' in a world where lucrative management contracts are available only to those who 'go along to get along.' "[40]

REPUTATIONS ON THE LINE

We see here the importance again of the reputational intermediaries in the system. Institutional investors as well as reputational intermediaries have a crucial role in transforming preferences for stronger protections for minority shareholders into pressure on firms and governments for policy change. Institutional investors are assumed to be agents, without an agenda of their own. But all agents also have a separate agenda—that is the logic of principal-agent theory.

As discussed in chapter 5, the U.S. securities regulation system assumes that institutional investors and reputational intermediaries are the agents of investors. One of the original architects of the SEC, Judge Landis, had the vision of a small efficient federal office overseeing complex capital markets with limited resources and intrusion. Instead of a vast federal police force, private actors such as the reputational intermediaries would provide the information that institutional investors need to evaluate managerial performance. The profit motive would provide the incentives for them to do so. The task of the SEC would be to prosecute managerial miscreants and also to monitor the intermediaries, to ensure they fulfilled their function.

This indirect, "light hand" approach to securities regulation assumed that the SEC would be successful in maintaining the laws and regulations that sustained the incentives for private actors to enforce good governance. Yet it has become increasingly clear to many observers that these private actors have multiple, complex incentives, not all of which are consistent with the original Landis view of regulation.

Analytic Narratives

THE UNITED STATES: A CONTESTED PATH FROM OLIGARCHY TO MSP

The United States is today regarded as the paradigmatic example of a corporate governance model of monitoring through a board by diffuse shareholders protected by a high level of MSP and disciplined by a vigorous market for control

---

[39] U.S. Securities and Exchange Commission, *Disclosure of Proxy Voting Policies and Proxy Voting Records by Registered Management Investment Companies*, September 20, 2002.

[40] Monks 1998, 153.

and highly competitive product markets. Only the United Kingdom shares a similar position among the large economies, and the United States got there first. (See appendix table A.26 for country descriptive statistics.) Like everyone else, the United States began with blockholding. Over time, it then traced what in retrospect seems a relatively smooth trajectory from primordial blockholding and minimal shareholder protections, to diffused share ownership and high shareholder protections over the last century. So smooth was this transition, at least in retrospect, that it bolstered the notion that this particular trajectory was more or less determined, intrinsic to industrial development and therefore inevitable for other countries.

We argue that the outcomes of high MSP and low ownership concentration were far from an automatic by-product of industrial development. Every step along the way involved intense political jockeying. Each step involved legislation, regulation, and enforcement, court cases that could have been reversed, rules that could have been ignored. Each step was danced across a political stage, to a tune called by the then-dominant political coalition. But the script was continually rewritten. Prospective winners and losers mobilized support or mounted opposition in state capitals and in Washington, D.C.

In the U.S. experience, each change in corporate governance, we argue, involved a shift in coalitions, pulling across the many divides of a large, complex society. Indeed, a hundred years into the battle, unlikely bedfellows and unexpected antagonists continue to tilt over the rules by which listed firms are governed.

The United States has relatively low private blockholding ratios, currently at 15 percent, at the lower end of the sample. There are still several old-line, family-controlled firms on U.S. exchanges, the American equivalent of Germany's *Mittelstandt*, and even a family-controlled industrial giant, Ford Motor, controlled by the eponymous family through the mechanism of closely held preferred voting shares just like the Quandt family at BMW. Aside from this handful of old-line, family-controlled firms, most current private blockheld firms in the United States are in relatively young high-tech firms with a large market cap such as Microsoft, Oracle, and Google, whose founder-entrepreneurs continue to hold a stake in the firm above the 10 percent control threshold (the criteria for blockholding in our data set).

These modern high-tech tycoons exercise great influence over the course of their industrial sectors and, to a much lesser degree, the way that competition policy is enforced and opposed. But unlike their fellow founder-entrepreneurs a hundred years ago, blockholders such as William Gates or Lawrence Ellison cannot call the shots in rules on corporate governance. In contrast, J. P. Morgan, Andrew Carnegie, and John Rockefeller exercised considerable latitude in structuring ownership and control in their firms, in their trusts, and in the functioning of financial intermediaries in America's capital markets, as they presided over— and forged their respective fortunes—waves of rapid investment and subsequent consolidation that swept through sector after sector.

The United States provides an excellent case demonstrating the limits of unitary categories like owners and managers, the growing importance of the pension fund issue, and the role of partisan maneuver within political institutions in shaping corporate governance outcomes. Over the past 20 years, sharp differences of interest and preferences have developed among owners and between various kinds of owners and various kinds of managers. Many of these differences and the opportunistic coalitions that emerged from these new calculations came to a head during the debate and lobbying run-up to the Sarbanes-Oxley Act of 2002.

The accumulation of money in pension funds did not translate automatically into a clear political push for higher MSPs, however. The growth of the pension funds, especially pillar 3 schemes such as 401(k)s, created a substantial economic interest in stocks and bonds among a wide range of the population, including groups not traditionally engaged in politics as investors. But as with the investor model examined in chapter 5, the translation of assets (a structural interest) into preferences and policies was not simple or direct. Sarbanes-Oxley illustrates the complex and often contingent process of translating these preferences into legislative and regulatory outcomes. In this chapter we trace the emergence of an owner-manager coalition from a blockholding foundation at the turn of the nineteenth century, the countervailing pressures that arose from various types of outsiders (farmers, small producers, labor) over time leading to regulations such as the SEC Act of 1934, the parallel emergence of Berle-Means managerism over the next 50 years, and the emergence of a new owner plus worker coalition—the transparency coalition—over the last two decades. The struggle among these coalitions over the shape of U.S. policy towards corporate governance remains alive, and the winner is far from certain.

In the Beginning, the Blockholders. Why does the United States have the most extensive Berle-Means firms in the advanced industrial world? At first blush, the class conflict model provides a simple answer. The United States has the weakest "social democratic" influence of any of the advanced industrial countries: unions with limited power; a moderate Democratic party strongly influenced by farmers and, until recently, by southern landowners, with strong ties to certain industries; and the least developed welfare state.

But weak labor cannot fully explain the U.S. pattern in two striking aspects: the decentralized character of financial institutions and the abandonment of the blockholder trust model since the end of the nineteenth century. Left entirely to themselves, conservative capitalist interests might well have developed strong instruments of private market control through strong concentrations of financial power, as they did in Europe. Indeed, there were signs this was happening. J. P. Morgan created a bank-trust system that made the United States look rather like Germany at the turn of the last century, and figures like Rockefeller and Carnegie exercised substantial blockholder control of their firms.

Diffusion of shareholding began in the United States through mergers and consolidations, prior to the establishment of government-mandated regulations on corporate governance. When they issued shares to the owners of firms they were acquiring, the nineteenth-century oligarchs adopted minority shareholder protections to the degree that it suited their private ordering interests, through reputation building and other bonding mechanisms. Law-based protections were few and far between. The leverage of great wealth and strong organizational capacity of the corporation translated into legislative power and influence. State legislatures were often quite corrupt; with indirect election of the Senate, oligarchs had a sustained ability to shape federal laws touching on the governance of corporations, private and listed. Thus a classic blockholder oligarchy dominance developed, keeping the government effectively at bay on many regulatory fronts: labor rules, taxation, competition policy, and corporate governance.

The oligarchs' power produced its own backlash. A complex coalition, mixing populism with economic rivalry among propertied interests, pushed through a set of regulatory steps. These included the Sherman Antitrust Act of 1890 (upheld by the Supreme Court against Standard Oil in 1906), railroad rate regulation, the Pure Food and Drug Act, the Insurance Act of New York prohibiting insurance firms from owning shares, the creation of the Federal Reserve, and the development of banking regulation. All of these, as Roe so ably analyzes,[41] served to limit financial power and constrain the ability of a blockholding system to corporate governance. Corporate and securities laws were formalized, significantly, at the state rather than the federal level, initially in Pennsylvania, New York, and New Jersey, then gradually shifting to Delaware, which became the leading corporate law court.

Still, shareholder rights were weak. Even as the populist alliance was reducing their operating latitude, the founder-owners began to forge the Chandlerian alliance with professional managers as their firms grew in scale and complexity. Their mutual interests intertwined, developing a managerial and professional class with similar views on corporate governance. This was the prototypical investor/blockholder alliance found in many other countries as well. It had not as yet, though, developed strong MSP.

As Chandler demonstrates in massive detail, during this transition the blockholders didn't simply promote a subset of hired hands into managerial equals; the process was more complex and the line between owner and manager was often fuzzy.[42] For example, the managerial team that Rockefeller assembled to build and run the Standard Oil Corporation was largely composed of founder-owners of smaller oil firms absorbed by Standard Oil during its rapid consolidation. Rockefeller kept the "best and the brightest" of the men he bought out, men who combined entrepreneurial energy with technical skills in petroleum mining, transportation, refining, or marketing, and forged them into a highly effective managerial team, arguably the first "professional" management group to head a major U.S. corporation. Standard Oil's transition from owner-managers at the top, to its progeny such as Exxon, which is managed entirely by professionals, took five decades.

Berle and Means were concerned by the effects of the progeny, not the parent. They described a world of managers with substantial and increasingly unfettered authority, a growth of diffuse shareholders with limited powers to monitor or discipline managers—the separation of ownership and control.

---

[41] Roe 1994.
[42] Chandler 1990.

Equity markets burst forward after World War I and the economy grew prodigiously. The collapse of the stock market in 1929 led to accusations of corruption, malfeasance, and instability. Against the backdrop of the Crash and the Great Depression, the political coalitions of the New Deal generated a number of laws and regulations with profound long-term consequences for corporate governance in the United States, including the creation of the SEC in 1934, the Glass-Steagall Act separating commercial from investment banking, regulation on accounting, on banking, on bond agencies—a great tissue of regulation and law that sought to prevent or dissolve concentrated corporate control, while strengthening MSP.[43]

What was the politics that produced this effort to curtail oligarchical power, a shift that may have allowed managers to dominate in the absence of effective monitoring by shareholders, despite the reforms? In his first book, Roe found the answer in populism. This answer would work if populism is integrated into a broader coalitional argument. Like the European social democrats of later years, the American populists got little of what they wanted unless they found allies. Farmers, free traders, workers, small businessmen, ethnic groups, regional tension, investors, and small savers all interacted to produce coalitions against the aggregation of economic power. Jim Fisk and Jay Gould made money by manipulating gold prices, while Morgan made money by reassuring investors.[44] But none of them wanted regulatory changes that led to the Berle-Means model. The lobby for that, instead, came from shareholders that were unwilling to rely on either type of titans.[45] This process was powerfully aided by the immense size of the U.S. economy, which helped create vigorous product and capital markets despite periods of tariff protection and regulation. Political institutions are relevant here: American federalism and the separation of powers gave populist voices and their allies a mechanism for influencing policy. The fragmentation of finance in the United States, Roe suggests, may have reduced the target for a labor reaction, in contrast to continental Europe.[46]

The process that gave birth to control of finance and strong MSP coincided with the development of a regulatory apparatus in other areas as well—the steps to an American version of the corporatist compromise. The creation of social security, the recognition of trade unions and a labor regulatory process, strong regulation of interstate shipping, airlines, oil, so-called fair trade retail pricing, extensive public works like the TVA, rural electrification, a large system of agricultural price supports and marketing boards—this all marked the development of what might be described as the embryonic American version of a coordinated market economy.[47] Corporate governance regulation was part and parcel of this

---

[43] See Roe, 1994, 51–101, 104–5.

[44] Jean Strouse, *Morgan: American Financier* (New York: Random House, 1999), shows Morgan's strategy of commitment to investors as a way of encouraging British capital exports to the United States.

[45] Coffee 2001.

[46] Roe 1994, 105.

[47] See discussion of degrees of coordination among LMEs vs. CMEs, chapter 4, and the varieties-of-capitalism literature noted there. Hall and Soskice 2001; Hall and Gingerich 2001; Gingerich and Hall 2002.

process and produced by the coalition that supported it: farmers and landowners, labor, industries of many kinds seeking help, thus another burst of populism mixed with owner interests that wanted a regulated economy—a corportist compromise coalition.

In that regulatory structure, the U.S. economy flourished. After World War II the United States dominated the world economy. Many firms faced what managers perceived to be a global market with huge potential economies of scale, and little competition from war-damaged rivals. Relations with labor unions, frequently bitter and violent before the war, gradually shifted to a more cooperative tone, or at least some institutionalized collective bargaining, the result of the National Labor Relations Act of 1935, often on an industry-wide basis (a consequence of the growth of the industry-based union, the CIO, alongside the craft-based AFL).

Market capitalization of firms grew substantially and stock ownership widened. While blockholding diminished steadily, shareholders faced the classic collective action problems in monitoring boards and managers. Product market competition was sluggish. Firms developed into conglomerates. Monitoring risks grew. The United States, with relatively high MSP, slid toward the managerial side of the balance: the Berle-Means account expressed the reality. Shareholder diffusion allowed substantial agency slack.

The Seeds of Contestation. In this context, the seeds were being laid for change. Complex cross-class alliances were developing: including "alignments of convenience" between managers and unions in some sectors (growing benefits and resisting contests for control); between managers, investment managers, and reputational intermediaries; between unions and other investment managers; between investment managers and some "new money" entrepreneurs (promoting contests for control); between these new entrepreneurs and their employees (through stock options); and a temporary alliance between new entrepreneurs and reputational intermediaries (against expensing stock options).

A major shift came from the growth of pension benefits, pension funding, and pension investments. In sectors characterized by oligopoly and limited (for a while) foreign competition, such as transportation, telecoms, and steel, professional managers established a comfortable adjustment with organized labor, passing on large wage and benefits costs to customers rather than risk labor unrest. The skill of unions in extracting greater pension benefits from managers during this period began the accumulation of pension funds that would ultimately help bring managers to heel decades later.

On another key preference item, both managers and workers (and, by extension, both firms and labor unions in their lobbying activities) agreed that defined benefit pension plans deserved the indirect, but very large, tax subsidy that was granted them by the Internal Revenue Code. By law, the IRS allowed firms to deduct pension expenditures from their income for tax purposes, and permitted beneficiaries to defer paying any taxes until the benefits were actually paid out—sometimes far into the future. This amount was calculated each year and defined as a "tax expenditure item," equal to the amount of forgone tax revenue that otherwise would have accrued to the Treasury. Beginning in the 1950s, the tax expenditure value of defined benefit plans began an inexorable climb, from about $17 billion in 1981 (even then, greater than the tax expenditure value associated by interest deductions on home mortgage loans, $15 billion), to $30 billion in 1982, and headed steadily upwards.

The roots of pension plan growth lay in a ruling by the National Labor Relations Board in 1948 specifying that employers and unions had to include the issue of providing pensions for all employees, not just white-collar employees, on the collective bargaining agenda, declaring that pensions "lie within the statutory scope of collective bargaining." "As a result, companies with unionized workforces were soon confronted with union demands that they offer pensions to their blue-collar workers, or if they already had such a pension plan, to improve the promised benefits and set aside money to guarantee them—that is, they were being asked to fund the pension plans."[48]

These pension plans were overwhelmingly of the defined benefit variety; the degree of actual funding of these liabilities, as well as their accounting treatment and disclosure, and the fiduciary obligations of these plans towards their beneficiaries, were left to the market. This ended during the bankruptcy of Studebaker Corporation in 1964, in which 4,000 employees received only 15 percent of their "vested" pensions, because of underfunding by the firm; another 3,000 employees received nothing at all. Labor unions were appalled by the Studebaker default, which demonstrated that the sizable pension benefits extracted by collective bargaining—one of labor's biggest postwar achievements—could be gutted by poor management and failures of corporate governance. Managers were equally appalled by labor union abuses of industry-wide pension plans, such as the Teamsters Union Central States Pension Fund, under the leadership of James Hoffa.

The Studebaker Roots of ERISA. In response to the Studebaker and Central States Pension Fund scandals, compounded by broad concerns about other underfunded pension plans—because of a bear stock market, many plans with assets had sustained sizable losses—the U.S. Congress passed the Employee Retirement Income Security Act (ERISA) in February 1974. The 500-page bill established new criteria for tax qualification of these plans; strict standards for plan fiduciaries (establishing the so-called Prudent Man Rule); participation and vesting rules, which made these plans more equitable across all ranks of employees; and guidelines for accounting treatment and disclosure in firms' financial statements. It created the Pension Benefits Guarantee Corporation (PBGC). "Because of its complexity, the law was nicknamed the Lawyers and Actuaries Full Employment Act of 1974."[49]

[48] Clowes 2000, 18.
[49] Clowes 2000, 95.

ERISA focused the attention of senior managers and boards of directors on their pillar 2 obligations in a dramatic way. "ERISA greatly increased pension costs in several ways. First it required funding of pension liabilities over 30 years. Some companies had not been funding, or had been doing so over 100 years. This change alone greatly increased costs for companies. Second, companies had to pay an insurance premium of $1.50 per year per employee to the PBGC. Third, costs for fund monitoring by consultants and actuaries increased. Fourth, ERISA called for more detailed (and hence more expensive) reporting by companies about their funds to the Labor Department and the IRS. Finally, ERISA made fiduciaries personally liable if something went wrong in the fund."[50]

Because of these enhanced obligations, firms began pouring cash and other assets into pillar 2 schemes; thus began the money flood into management firms and, ultimately, into Peter Drucker's Unseen Revolution of expanded equity ownership by U.S. workers. As the funds flowed in, Congress watched the growing costs of the implicit tax subsidy with growing alarm. When President Ronald Reagan attempted to slow the federal deficit by trimming back social security benefits, the Democratic-controlled Congress responded instead by cutting back on the tax deductibility of pension contributions by firms in the so-called Tax Equity and Fiscal Responsibility Act of 1982. TEFRA capped the income levels and therefore the pension contributions that qualified for tax deduction by firms at fairly moderate levels, thereby driving a wedge between managers and better-paid white-collar workers on one side, and lower-paid line employees (often union members) on the other.[51]

From Defined Benefit to Defined Contribution: The 401(k) Effect and Pillars 2 and 3. In 1985 Congressman Barber Conable (R-N.Y.) added a small modification to the language of the Internal Revenue Code that opened up the opportunity for firms to replace increasingly expensive defined benefit second-pillar plans with defined contribution third-pillar plans—the famous 401(k). Under this interpretation, the IRS would allow a tax deduction of up to $30,000 per year (or 15 percent of salary) in a qualified plan. Companies recapturing surplus defined benefit funding rapidly replaced them with employee stock option plans, profit sharing, or 401(k)s. By 1998, the average 401(k) participant in company plans had boosted the equity weight to 64 percent of their total portfolio. "The flood of assets into 401(k) plans . . . thus provided one possible solution for the Social Security Crisis." U.S. worker-voters had begun to acquire a substantial stake as minority shareholders.

Despite the sometimes hysterical tone of public debate over the "insolvent" U.S. social security system, the estimated IPD of the United States pillar 1 system is low, at 23, far below the sample mean and all of Europe. Pillars 2 and 3 assets

---

[50] Clowes 2000, 98.

[51] Sylvester Schieber, "The Employees Retirement Income Security Act: Motivations, Provisions, and Implications for Retirement Security," paper presented to the Conference on ERISA after 25 Years: A Framework for Evaluating Pension Reform, September 17, 1999, Washington, D.C., 25–27.

are correspondingly large, amounting to 70 percent of GDP—a big number, though still below the accumulated pension assets percentages for the United Kingdom, Netherlands, and Switzerland. In 1945 the United States had $14 billion in total pension assets: 30 percent in insurance company annuities, 20 percent USG bonds, 20 percent fixed income, and 5 percent equities. By 1999, this had grown to $7 trillion in assets, 30 percent fixed income and 60 percent equities.

This large pool of funds to stoke equity markets spawned a class of money managers independent from the traditional Wall Street banks, including the public pension funds such as CalPERS, hybrids such as TIAA-CREF, Taft-Hartley union funds, and mutual funds such as Fidelity. This vast asset accumulation set in motion the machinery of widespread equity ownership among American citizens that Peter Drucker had described as "pension fund socialism."

Although exempted from ERISA, public employee pension obligations at the local, state, and federal level came under increased scrutiny by elected officials, and especially by the public bond markets, who imposed a risk premium on borrowing costs for jurisdictions with an unfunded liability. This kicked off a similar flood of cash into public employee pension funds, which rapidly became the largest single institutional investors in the financial landscape.

This river of money in new channels created new possibilities. The pension funds could become targets for social activist or political objectives, and they could become instruments for corporate governance concerns, including a more aggressive market for control (hostile takeovers), executive compensation, and other issues.

From "Social Investing" to Rates of Return and Corporate Governance. The initial impetus for the involvement of public pension funds in corporate governance was political, not economic. Because the public pension funds became so large so quickly, they became tempting targets for political entrepreneurs and social activists with concerns other than rates of return and corporate governance, more typical of "left-labor" political coalitions.

One element of "social investing" was job preservation, as the pension funds considered how governance affected factory closings and openings, wage levels, and benefits. Soon it expanded to include international causes such as divesting South African assets in protest against apartheid, and local causes such as urban renewal and local industrial development. Such issues entered the political arena at times; in-state investing by pension funds was discussed in 1982 gubernatorial races from Pennsylvania to Illinois to California. Pension funds began to look more closely at the governance of the firms in which they were holding larger and larger equity positions—not to see how well the managers were protecting the interests of the beneficiary shareholders, but how the terms of governance affected other corporate decisions, such as factory openings and closings.

Rather soon, though, the focus began to shift. The funds became more concerned with a narrower, technical focus on corporate governance and rates of return. As that happened, fund managers became less conservative in the instruments they chose.

Initially almost all pension funds were conservative investors, especially the public employee funds.[52] After the state teachers' retirement funds of Ohio and Utah led the way toward greater equity investment,[53] equity index funds became particularly popular with these administrators (and their political overseers) since index funds did not require active stock picking or much administrative overhead.

Public employee funds accelerated their investment in equities as they took big losses in bond portfolios as the Federal Reserve hiked interest rates in the late 1970s and early 1980s to squeeze out inflation. Regional trust banks were shoved aside by new money-market managers from Wall Street, using more advanced financial engineering and "niche" investment strategies, including small-cap stocks, hedge funds, buyout funds, venture capital funds, derivatives, and interest-rate anticipation strategies. As this process developed, worker-based funds began to see themselves as allies of shareholders rather than as notional victims, and elements of a new cross-class alliance—minority share-holders and worker pension funds—began to emerge around arguments over corporate governance.

The Sea Change of Hostile Takeovers: Challenging Managerism. As institutional investing grew, so did the foundations for challenging managerism. The world of conglomerates, regulated markets, the primacy of the firm, and managerial autonomy came under attack in the 1980s from a new hybrid group of owner-entrepreneurs, the frequently vilified, hostile-takeover and leveraged-buyout specialists. Though often decried in the press as greedy buccaneers, such as Carl Icahn and T. Boone Pickens, these entrepreneurs built new markets (especially in services) or consolidated older industries in sectors from broadcasting (Ted Turner's CNN) and telecoms (Craig McCaw's national cellular network) to health care (Columbia) and banking (Wachovia)—reaping considerable wealth from the same cycle of consolidation that had enriched John Rockefeller in oil and Andrew Carnegie in steel. Pension funds, not banks, provided the bulk of the financing for the wave of hostile takeovers by this new class of entrepreneurs. Takeover financiers such as Michael Milken of Drexel Burnham Lambert provided huge returns to his pension fund investors.

Few professional managers were happy with this new world of contests for control and consolidation. Managers began to push back. In particular, the Conference Board, an organization dominated by professional managers, became a vocal opponent of hostile takeovers. Executives in target companies across the country lobbied their states for antitakeover rules, portraying the raiders as heartless outsiders intent upon shuttering local firms. Some labor unions were enthusiastic

---

[52] "Public funds trailed corporate funds in moving to equities . . . [because] they were ultimately overseen by state or local legislators, or the state or local treasurer, all of whom were concerned about political exposure if the funds lost money in investments." Clowes 2000, 134.

[53] Once they had developed a taste for the higher returns provided by equity as opposed to fixed-income portfolios, they extended their new investment strategy abroad. Clowes 2000, 35; and Brancato 2000, 41.

allies in these lobbying efforts, though the pensions arm of labor was at tension with the jobs arm. The combined forces of managers (with their lobbying dollars) and unions (with their lobbying muscle and "feet on the street") were irresistible to state legislatures across the country: a host of states imposed antitakeover rules between the late 1980s and 1995.[54]

Managers also attempted to use their influence over the investing activities of their own firms' pension plans to resist these hostile takeovers. This took place at Grumman, A&P, and Harper & Rowe.[55] Having discovered that workers were increasingly owners in their firms, due to the accumulation of benefits over the years, managers realized that the rules concerning how this ownership was voted became increasingly vital to their incumbency. Managers also began to pressure commercial money managers to support them in resisting hostile takeovers. Such tactics were used by the CEOs of Rockwell, GTE, International Paper, NCR Corp., Anheuser-Busch, American Airlines, and Colgate Palmolive in a series of contested takeover transactions.

And when they failed to foil hostile takeovers by invoking the votes of captive or externally managed pension funds, many incumbents simply bought off the raiders, in the controversial process termed "greenmail." Incumbent CEOs would agree to purchase back large blocks of shares accumulated by would-be raiders at a premium to the market—thereby retaining their jobs, at the expense of the existing diffuse shareholders. This practice brought to a head the latent difference between the preferences of managers and shareholders and precipitated the wave of investor activism that led, through many twists and turns, to new regulations such as Sarbanes-Oxley. In cooperation with a dozen other public employee pension funds, CalPERS launched the Council of Institutional Investors to present a collective voice in favor of better corporate governance in the United States. The CII grew over the years to become the most influential voice for corporate governance reform and enhanced minority shareholder protections in the United States. Losses in public employee funds in the string of corporate collapses in the late 1990s (listed in table 7.3) raised the issue of corporate governance high on the agenda of the CII and its members. These losses also provided a key argument with which to convince Congress to engage in the pivotal governance reform of the Sarbanes-Oxley Act of 2002.

A striking example of this simmering conflict among money managers and of an emerging tendency for workers to make common cause with shareholders in the United States, occurred during the SEC's 2002 deliberations regarding mandatory disclosure of proxy voting by mutual funds. The AFL-CIO labor

[54] Davis 1991a, 1991b.

[55] In response to the Grumman transaction, the U.S. Department of Labor grumbled that turning down a lucrative takeover deal might violate the fiduciary duty of the trustee towards pension beneficiaries In 1985, the Department of Labor issued the so-called Avon Letter, in which it advised Avon's pension trustees that they had a prior fiduciary duty to beneficiaries of the pension plan and could not vote with management automatically to repel a legitimate takeover offer. Notably, this was a unilateral executive action taken without legislative support or even senior-level support within the Reagan administration.

federation was a strong supporter of this proposed rule. Several commercial money managers, including giant Fidelity, opposed mandatory disclosure, preferring "candid conversations with managers behind closed doors" to proxy fights.

In a letter to the SEC, the AFL-CIO took strong issue with this position, claiming that "mutual fund investors have no way of knowing whether these closed door conversations are good faith efforts by their fund companies to represent shareholder interests, or schemes to trade proxy votes in order to win business managing the company's 401(k) plan. . . . This is exactly the conflict that Fidelity confronted at Tyco International in 1998, when it cast its proxy votes against a shareholder proposal calling for a majority of independent directors on Tyco's board. Fidelity's vote may have furthered its own interests, as Fidelity earned $2 million in 1999 administering Tyco's employee benefit plans. But we do not believe that this vote was in the best interests of Fidelity's mutual fund shareholders, particularly in light of subsequent events at Tyco."[56]

There is conflicting evidence whether "activist" pension funds generate a higher return than passive or indexed funds, or whether such superior returns offset both the activist transactions costs and liquidity costs.[57] Since the managers of these funds are often politically appointed or elected by their beneficiaries, rather than forced to compete on portfolio return with other commercial investment firms, they have the latitude to take an activist role regardless of the effects on portfolio returns.[58] In any case, the beneficiaries of these public pension funds have little choice and incur significant "switching costs" if they transfer to another money manager, so these funds can take a longer investment horizon and, indeed, sacrifice short-term investment returns in exchange for longer-term rewards. Pension investors are not subject to the liquidity constraints of mutual funds, which must always be prepared for large redemptions, and which therefore often cannot take a "long view" even if their managers wish to.[59] On the other hand, the private investment funds often have conflicts of interest with their depositors, in seeking contracts from managers for other services, inhibiting them from challenging the executives.

For example, in 2003 the SEC circulated a set of proposed rules to ensure that shareholders be given greater rights to nominate and elect directors, and to submit resolutions to shareholder vote, rather than the "approve this slate" method currently in use at all public companies that are not engaged in an active proxy fight. The Business Roundtable took this as a dual challenge, possibly leading to both greater director oversight and more likely contests for control.

In a letter from the vice chair of the Roundtable's Corporate Governance Task Force, the Roundtable formally objected across the board to any rules that

---

[56] Letter from Richard L. Trumka of the AFL-CIO to the SEC, "Comments on the SEC's Proposal S7-36-02 to Require Mutual Funds to Disclose Their Proxy Voting Policies," December 6, 2002, 4–8.

[57] Steven L. Nesbitt, "Long-Term Rewards from Shareholder Activism: A Study of the 'CalPERS Effect,'" *Journal of Applied Corporate Finance* 6 (winter 1994): Steven L. Nesbitt, "The 'CalPERS Effect': A Corporate Governance update," Wilshire & Associates, 19 July 1995.

[58] To sort this out thoroughly we need more research on these institutional details.

[59] Brancato 2000 examines the varying investment horizons of different institutional investors.

TABLE 7.5
Shareholder Proposal Adoption

Year	Proposals	Adopted	%
1999	394	55	14
2000	395	64	16
2001	406	66	16
2002	439	99	22.5
2003	560	153	27 (to date)

enhanced shareholder power in public firms. The letter argued that a director should still take a board seat even if half the shareholders objected and withheld their votes: "a percentage equal to 50% or greater withhold votes for a director who is subsequently renominated is appropriate in order to target companies where the proxy process is ineffective."[60] In the same letter, the managers noted with alarm the rising percentage of shareholder proposals that had received a majority vote (see table 7.5).

Consequently the Business Roundtable objected to rules that might require management to adopt resolutions supported by a majority vote of the shareholders: "we believe that triggering shareholder access using a majority vote on a shareholder access proposal is inappropriate."[61]

The managers also objected to allowing minority shareholders nominate directors for election to the board, suggesting instead an ownership threshold of 25 percent "in order to justify the cost and substantial disruption borne by all shareholders resulting from contested director elections."[62]

Through the Business Roundtable, managers opposed regulations that would give shareholders more control over the proxy agenda, resisted requirements for shareholders' approval for option plans, blocked election of directors by the shareholders through cumulative voting, and argued against measures for enhanced disclosure of compensation and benefit plans.

As hostile takeovers tailed off in the late 1980s, due in large part to the new state-level regulatory barriers, the boom in executive compensation was taking off. Even more than lavish cash compensation and bonuses, stock options were the most common means of enriching managers. By some estimates, as much as 10 percent of the total ownership of U.S. public firms was transferred from the existing stockholders to senior managers through stock option grants between 1990 and 2000.[63] As the magnitude of cash and option compensation began to filter into the

[60] Henry McKinnell, chairman of the Board and CEO of Pfizer Inc, Vice-Chairman of the Corporate Governance Task Force and Chairman of the SEC Subcommittee, The Business Roundtable, letter of October 1 2003 to the Securities and Exchange Commission, 2, http://www.brtable.org/document. cfm/1011.

[61] McKinnell 2003, 4

[62] McKinnell 2003, 5.

[63] Monks 1998.

mass media—against the backdrop of plant closings and layoffs in many sectors, itself the result of technical innovation and foreign compensation—workers were reminded that managerial incumbency was not necessarily a "good thing" for them, too. As Sarbanes-Oxley is being implemented, these battles over shareholder and institutional investor powers in proxy fights and election of managers continue quite vividly in the SEC, as many of the key votes are divided three to two.

Conflicted High Techies. "New money" blockholders, especially venture capitalists (who were largely funded by pension funds) and high-tech entrepreneurs, were initially important constituents of the transparency coalition because of their need for a liquidity "exit strategy." The widespread use of stock option plans for *all* employees, not just incumbent senior managers, built another bridge between workers' interests and minority shareholder protections in a politically influential segment of the U.S. workforce. Firms controlled by entrepreneur-blockholders were far more progressive in sharing stock options down through the employee ranks than widely diffused firms, whose managers tended to restrict options to the upper ranks of managers alone.

But the stock option issue that reinforced the notion of worker-shareholder common interests also created an issue on which new-money entrepreneurs (and some workers) opposed reform. Stock options receive favorable tax treatment under U.S. law, with firms being allowed to deduct the notional value of option grants against their taxable income. Options also receive curious accounting treatment: according to GAAP, stock options are not expensed on the firm's profit and loss statement and are treated as balance sheet "dilution" instead. Critics have long charged that this militates against good corporate governance, by reducing transparency and encouraging option grants, at the expense of minority shareholders.

High-tech entrepreneurs fought long and hard to retain the status quo treatment of options, insofar as their own wealth was created through stock options, and their ability to attract and retain talented employees also relied heavily on stock option programs. On this score they were firmly in bed with managers of most public firms, who also relied on stock options and their relative lack of transparency and public accountability

Senior executives from Silicon Valley regularly lobbied their congressmen and testified repeatedly that changing the treatment of options would negatively impact both technical innovation and capital formation. High-tech lobbyists stymied efforts by SEC chairman Arthur Levitt to alter the accounting treatment of options, a decision nominally in the hands of the quasi-independent FASB.[64] For example, they managed to have Michael Oxley, chairman of the House Committee on Financial Services, send a letter to FASB discouraging any revision of option accounting with a veiled threat of tighter congressional oversight on the FASB and its budget.

Wall Street on Both Sides. As mentioned earlier, the reputational intermediaries had huge and conflicted stakes in corporate governance. The pension funds were

---

[64] Arthur Levitt and Paula Dwyer, *Take on the Street: What Wall Street and Corporate America Don't Want You to Know: What You Can Do to Fight Back* (New York: Pantheon, 2002).

among their biggest customers on the "buy side"; the fixed income and equity income from selling to these funds were the bread and butter of daily transactional income for most Wall Street firms. On the other hand, incumbent managers were also becoming big customers to the reputational intermediaries on the "sell side." Transactional income from equity and bond floatation, as well as the M&A market, became increasingly important to these same firms throughout the 1980s and 1990s, and this fee income—immensely profitable—was largely in the hands of incumbent professional managers.

Wall Street became understandably reluctant to bite the hands that fed it such largesse. This conflicted position was not limited to investment banks; other reputational intermediaries such as the Big Six (then Five, then Four) accounting firms followed suit. They were also opposed on general principle to strong regulation by the U.S. government, either directly by the SEC, or indirectly through "delegated" overseers such as the NYSE or the FASB.

The U.S. system of corporate governance turns on the ability of the SEC to sustain a set of incentives for private actors to provide information and monitoring of managers, rather than directly supervise firms and markets. But during the last three decades of the twentieth century, the political center of gravity in U.S. politics shifted against regulation, including the SEC's relatively "light hand" and emphasis on private enforcement. Deregulation was launched under the Carter administration in the 1970s and accelerated by the Reagan administration in the 1980s, especially in financial services. The structure of the 1930s, the firewalls created by Judge Landis, was criticized as inhibiting financial markets from innovation. Law-and-economics critics of regulation, arguing the capacity for private bonding to solve most problems of market risk, made the case.

Politically, these arguments were pushed by the financial community, the securities industry, the reputational intermediaries, many professional managers, and by academic proponents of deregulation. Wall Street wanted to end the strict definitions of banking boundaries (such as commerce versus investment, interstate, brokerage, insurance), which had provided barriers to entry and rents for incumbents. The procompetitive goals of the financial sector resonated with the Republican Party's traditional commitment to competition and deregulation. The result was the long-debated Gramm-Leach-Bliley Act of 1999, which broke down these barriers and stimulated competition across a host of financial sector markets, in the United States and abroad.

As a result, financial services firms, insurance companies, and accounting firms were among the biggest corporate contributors to congressional races, for both parties, during the 1980s and 1990s. Republican congressman Michael Oxley and Democratic senator Joseph Lieberman were both persuaded by the Business Roundtable and an alliance of high-tech firms to pressure the SEC and FASB against accounting reforms regarding stock option treatment.[65]

[65] For example, letter from Michael G. Oxley, chairman, House Committee on Financial Services, and John A. Boehner, chairman, House Committee on Education and the Workforce, addressed to Harvey Pitt, chairman of the SEC, copied to Paul Volcker and the trustees of the International Accounting Standards Board, on the topic of employee stock option accounting, October 12, 2001.

Fragmented Alignments Meet on Capital Hill. In the run-up to Sarbanes-Oxley, reputational intermediaries proved themselves important political players, able to influence the regulatory process in significant ways. Many traditional elements of the Republican Party worried about the effects of governance abuses on financial markets—the traditional "Main Street" elements of the party—as well as private investors and retirees.[66] On the other side of this argument stood free-market advocates (who feared rent-seeking opportunities from regulation in Washington, D.C.) corporate chieftains, small businessmen, Wall Street, the accounting profession (the reputational intermediaries again), and—strikingly—"new money" entrepreneurs.

By the same token, the Democratic Party was also internally divided on corporate governance. Two major groups of business with substantial voice in the Democratic Party had mixed positions on various aspects of governance reforms: financial interests in New York (Wall Street is adept at working both sides of the aisle), and high-tech business symbolized by Silicon Valley.

Although moderately majoritarian, the U.S. political system exhibits permeability to highly organized particularistic interests. This fragmentation creates multiple points of entry for focused groups. This is in contrast with the United Kingdom or Canada, where parliamentary and strong parties provide a comprehensive policy integration, under the umbrella of encompassing coalitions, rather than partial ones.

Sarbanes-Oxley: Private Ordering or Public Scrutiny? Even after the Enron, Tyco, and WorldCom scandals, corporate governance reform was resisted by many Republican members in Congress and ignored, at least initially, by the Bush administration.[67] When it appeared that an accounting and governance reform bill was going to emerge from Congress, the Bush administration argued that stronger penalties against "wrongdoers" was sufficient, essentially a version of the private ordering and tort law argument. Because of the permeability of the U.S. political system, there were several potential veto points at which the legislation could have been watered down, blocked, or vetoed: in the Senate Banking Committee, chaired by Paul Sarbanes, with a thin Democratic majority; in the House Financial Services Committee, chaired by Michael Oxley, with a slight Republican majority; in conference between the two chambers; or when the bill reached the White House for signature. In fact the bill was passed rather fast, due to pressures from a falling stock market and the exploding revelations of corporate malfeasance.[68]

The original House bill reflected the private ordering preferences of the Bush administration and largely deferred to the SEC rather than impose any new

[66] The venerable Robert Monks, a pioneering corporate governance activist, for example, was a longtime Republican and Reagan administration appointed official.

[67] Our account here can only suggest the richness of the politics involved in passage of the Sarbanes-Oxley bill.

[68] David Hilzenrath, "How Congress Rode a 'Storm' to Corporate Reform," *Washington Post*, July 28, 2002.

regulations. According to political observers, on the Senate side, recent governance scandals energized two pivotal members and neutralized a third. On the committee, Georgia Senator Zell Miller was stung by huge Enron losses incurred by the Georgia state employees and teachers pension funds—$43 million and $79 million respectively. Wyoming senator Michael Enzi, a former accountant (a sole practitioner, not a Big Five executive) was appalled by the apparent breaches of professional standards. Texas senator Phil Gramm, a vocal opponent of the bill, was neutralized by his association with Enron. The committee ultimately voted the bill to the Senate in late May with a slim majority, whereupon it risked lingering and not coming to a vote by the Senate as a whole. On June 26, the WorldCom scandal hit the media, inducing the Senate on July 15 to vote the bill into law, 97 to 0.

The House Financial Services Committee chairman was hostile to the Senate bill and intended to water it down in conference. A number of Republican freshmen, fresh from their districts where they had heard constituents' complaints about the corporate scandals, threatened to end-run the chairman with a petition directly to the House leadership unless the House accepted the Senate version.[69]

Meanwhile, the White House essentially stood on the sidelines. Treasury secretary Paul O'Neill was hostile to the Senate bill, but his own standing with the president was already in decline. SEC chairman Harvey Pitt was widely viewed as a political liability. Wall Street had the jitters from the stock market fallout of the scandals; several prominent executives quietly urged the president to support reform, quickly. The high-tech lobby brought in Andrew Grove of Intel to oppose the bill; the Conference Board brought in IMB chairman Louis Gerstner and CSX chairman John Snow to oppose the Senate version, too. Compromise legislation largely resembling the Senate version was voted out by the conference with broad support at the end of July.

Sarbanes-Oxley resulted in some strengthening of the traditional regulatory system, especially rebuilding the objectivity and reliability of the reputational intermediaries.[70] The bill authorized the formation of a new Public Accounting Oversight Board, responsible to and appointed by the SEC in consultation with the Federal Reserve and the Treasury Department, which would develop and enforce standards for the industry. This would in principle strengthen shareholder protection by taking away self-monitoring from the industry.

The bill also made managers squarely responsible for the accuracy and timeliness of financial disclosure. It established a code of ethics for chief financial officers, and required chief executive officers to personally certify financial statements and make a series of disclosures to board audit committees and external auditors—with criminal penalties for failures to do so. It tightened insider trading rules, forced managers to keep an arm's-length relationship with auditors, and forfeited bonuses and option grants in cases of breach. It also empowered the SEC to adopt rules addressing

---

[69] With WorldCom's woes and other unsavory corporate stories dominating the news, Republican congressmen such as Foley and Rogers feared their party was "about to get clobbered politically" and that it could be political suicide to fight it out in a House-Senate Conference. Hilzenrath 2002, 2.

[70] *Sarbanes-Oxley Act of 2002*, H.R. Report No. 107-610 (2002).

conflicts of interest for securities analysts, and reformed pension fund "blackout periods" to put both managerial and employee equity holdings on the same footing.

Passage of the law did not determine how it would be implemented. The SEC has been subject to strong lobbying by all the players, from reputational intermediaries to shareholder groups and managers. U.S. politics and its associated regulatory regime still provided many access and veto points for both managers and reputational intermediaries to push back at efforts to translate the 2002 law into enhanced minority shareholder protections.

For example, the accounting industry lobbied SEC chairman Harvey Pitt to block appointment of the TIAA-CREF's John Biggs as head of the new accounting oversight organization. When Pitt's next choice, Judge Webster, turned out to have ethics problems, Pitt was himself forced to resign. Meanwhile, CSX chairman Snow was appointed by the White House to replace Paul O'Neill as Treasury secretary, and William Donaldson was appointed to head the SEC, where he presides over a deeply split commission.

Lessons from the U.S. Case. The United States has a highly articulated system of rules and an enforcing agency, the SEC, with potentially extensive power. The federal nature of the U.S. system allows a means both of escaping regulation and of enforcing it. Legal scholars continue to debate whether competition between states over corporate law makes possible a race to the bottom, as managers are able to lobby states to protect them from the market for control or adopt other antishareholder practices, or a race to the top, as states compete to attract investors.[71] State attorneys general can be proactive if the SEC is not. Attorney General Elliot Spitzer in New York successfully prosecuted Wall Street's financial intermediaries for conflicts of interest.

In the case of the United States, the La Porta et al. legal family argument, the legacy of U.S. common law in allegedly protecting minority shareholders, did not function as expected. Political preferences among major players allowed regulatory agencies to be captured and shareholder protections to be incrementally trimmed. In parallel, the incipient political power of worker-owners created the possibility of a new political alignment in favor of minority shareholder protection.

The American pattern reveals the importance of preferences: broad support for minority shareholder protections, driven largely by the pension system and by sectors such as high technology, opposed by narrower interests and issue-specific bargains among other actors. At the same time new interests emerged demanding reform, against the backdrop of several high-profile corporate governance scandals. The struggle of these opposing preferences takes place against a backdrop of majoritarian politics, albeit with multiple veto points.

---

[71] Roberta Romano, "The State Competition Debate in Corporate Law," in *Corporate Law and Economic Analysis*, Lucien Bebchuk, ed. (Cambridge: Cambridge University Press, 1990); see also Roe 2003a, which argues federal law is overshadowing the traditional assumption that states regulate corporate governance.

The combination of managerial excess, flawed performance by reputational intermediaries, and Drucker's pension fund socialism generated political momentum for enhanced minority shareholder protections. But the triumph of a transparency coalition is no sure thing. Resistance from managers, from some reputational intermediaries and some financial groups remains strong. The passage of Sarbanes-Oxley did not signal the end of tension and jockeying back and forth across the transparency/managerism divide but another marker in the ongoing political battle over law, regulation, and implementation.

The rules of corporate governance remain, fundamentally, a permanently contested issue in the United States.

UNITED KINGDOM: THE POWER OF MAJORITARIAN POLITICAL INSTITUTIONS?

The United Kingdom provides an interesting contrast with the United States and its continental neighbors. It ranks among countries with the most diffusion in shareholding, the highest MSP, and high LME characteristics. Indeed in the judgment of many observers it has better shareholder protections in practice than the United States despite its lower score on the MSP index (74 for the United Kingdom versus 97 for the United States). The United Kingdom has more vigorous markets for control, shareholder rights (for proxy fights, as an example, where takeover decisions reside with target shareholders, not managers),[72] codes of corporate responsibility on financial and social standards, and active financial intermediaries who press managers.[73] It has transformed its regulatory system, from an informal "club" reliant on private mechanisms, to a formalized system, with more enforcement teeth than the United States.

The United Kingdom came to this position through choices made by a combination of private bonding mechanisms mixed with law and regulation. In the late nineteenth century, family founder blockholding prevailed there, as elsewhere. Then several waves of mergers occurred, leading to dilution of shareholding. Families yielded controlling blocks but for a time held important seats on boards. Formal law and court behavior did not provide shareholder protections. The London Stock Exchange did have standards that some historians believe provided protection via private bonding.[74] For a time diffusion remained limited; Cheffins suggests this reflected norms among financial interests that thought buying shares was too risky.[75]

---

[72] Franks, Mayer, and Rossi, forthcoming, 8.

[73] Monks 1998.

[74] Cheffins 2001, 472–76, argues that shareholding in the United Kingdom developed from assurances given by the London Stock Exchange and financial intermediaries like banks and brokerage, not by law and regulation.

[75] See Brian Cheffins, "Putting Britain on the Roe Map: The Emergence of the Berle-Means Corporation in the United Kingdom," in *Corporate Governance Regimes: Convergence and Diversity*, Joseph A. McCahery, Piet Moerland, Theo Raaijmakers, and Luc Renneboog, eds. (Oxford: Oxford University Press, 2002), 158–60.

In the years after World War II, the United Kingdom appeared to have a mixed system and to be, Frank, Mayer, and Rossi suggest,[76] at a crossroads. Some trends suggested a move toward continental patterns of blockholding and restricted markets for control. Dual class shares, strategic blockholding, partial acquisitions or pyramids insulated managers and insiders from effective supervision. Britain could have moved down this road, reinforced by other corporatist arrangements in labor, competition policy, and elsewhere.

Then financial institutions and the London Stock Exchange pressed to dismantle these arrangements. They objected to these managerial protections, arguing for greater shareholder protection. Financial institutions worked through the Bank of England to generate a working group that led to the Panel on Takeovers and Mergers by 1967: "the political process was not at the end of the day guided by the interests of the corporate sector which sought to limit hostile bids and to erect takeover defenses but by those of the financial institutions."[77] The Financial Services Act of 1986 and the big-bang deregulation of the City continued this process. Self-regulation (SROs, self-regulatory organizations) remained important; they were given monopoly control of their various markets: members had to obey. These in turn were subject to control by the Securities and Investment Board (SIB). The language was self-regulation, but not only did this involve a great increase in codification, so that rule books became ever more detailed and effectively legal, but the powers of the SIB were also extended.

Based on statute, the SIB's own constitution was prescribed in law, its leading officers were publicly appointed, and it was required to report to Parliament and to the central state in Whitehall. Eventually this self-regulatory corporatism did not endure. A decade of instability, regulatory crisis, and scandal led to more controls and more formalization, culminating in the Financial Services and Markets Act of 2000 and the formation of the Financial Services Authority (FSA; established in 1997, but empowered by statute in 2000).

Compared to the United States, the new system is remarkably centralized. What is dispersed in the United States among states and federal authority is concentrated in the United Kingdom in the FSA. The Treasury appoints the board; it reports annually to the Treasury and the House of Commons and is required to give testimony to the Commons Select Treasury Committee.

What are the politics that led to this process, that led the United Kingdom away from the continental model toward the diffuse shareholder one? Frank et al. note the influence of institutional investors and the stock exchange but do not fully explain just how that mechanism operates. Comparing the United Kingdom to the Continent makes this plausible, but the United States has important versions of both without the identical results. And why does the United Kingdom have both important financial institutions and a strong stock market?

Roe looks at the particular balance of left versus right in the United Kingdom: the Left was strong enough to inhibit diffusion, though not so strong as to prevent

---

[76] Franks, Mayer, and Rossi, forthcoming.
[77] Franks, Mayer, and Rossi, forthcoming, 25.

the adoption of MSP.[78] Cheffins also challenges the social democracy thesis by noting that diffusion did increase during the strongest years of labor influence, from 1945 to 1979. Roe counters by noting that the rate of diffusion increased even more dramatically after U.K. politics shifted rightward under Margaret Thatcher. The historical development of British patterns of "economic coordination," its version of the liberal market economy, helps clarify the failure of the corporatist pattern to emerge. As Alexander Gerschenkron noted in his famous discussion of early and late development, the United Kingdom had a unique trajectory as the first industrial nation. Its firms were small, its banking system was decentralized, and its labor movement was weak. It developed securities markets and shareholder protection early on.[79] Finance became a vital economic sector and a politically influential one. Securities markets and shareholder protection emerged early in the development process, when British politics favored property and markets. Private bonding mechanisms appear to have developed to support shareholder protections. Markets were small enough, relationships personal, frequent, and direct, so that individuals would accept positions in each other's firms as part of a merger process, or diversification generally. Thus shareholding produced the demand for legal protections, which came afterward.

Britain was also the first country to turn to free trade, as well as the first to expose agriculture to world-market forces. It developed strong product-market competition in both industry and agriculture. It developed an important financial sector, for a time the world's center before New York overtook it. The industry was an important force in lobbying, and its orientation was not that of the commercial banks and bond lending, not the German industrial bank approach. Overall, the economic situation of a wide range of British groups favored a decentralized market economy. High MSP locked in early in the interest group and party structure of the country.

When politics turned leftward in 1945, this policy area was not challenged. Institutions were built and they persisted. Then, as Roe, notes, in the Thatcher years the turn to the right accelerated the process.

Political institutions may facilitate this coalition and the policy approach that goes with it. The United Kingdom is the archetypal majoritarian system. Once the elements of corporatism weakened (never as strong in the United Kingdom as in Germany), they eroded quickly—small vote shifts produced big effects. Privatization of firms and a comprehensive contribution-based pension helped generate the constituency.

Moreover, the strong centralized features of the United Kingdom political system insulated the FSA from the lobbying influence of specialized actors, including the powerful financial sector firms in the City of London. Managers cannot get state and local governments to generate protections from the market for control or reward accountants who lobby the regulators or legislation to weaken their obligations.

[78] Roe 2003b.
[79] Gerschenkron 1962.

Circumstances and the United Kingdom's majoritarian political institutions accelerated the process: the Thatcher government had significant power because the opposition split, labor and the center allowed long years of neoliberal government, which never got a majority of the popular vote. The power of unions and labor-market-centered politics declined. The country's economic rationalizers and modernizers who sought to position the United Kingdom in the European and global economy by liberalizing the economy had ideological influence. To bring labor back in power, Blair positioned himself as leader of the "New Labour" position. He accepted rather than challenged the institutional reforms of the Thatcher years.

The pension structures of the United Kingdom seem to provide stronger support for transparency than elsewhere as well. Britain has an extensive pillars 2 and 3 pension profile. Its pension funds are quite well developed, organized, and active. Hermes resembles CalPERS in many respects. Hermes has its roots in the pension scheme for employees of British Telecom and has broadened its investor base to manage sums for various entities mostly public, union, or employee based. It has been remarkably aggressive in corporate governance issues. The Frank et al. research underscores the importance of understanding how financial institutions differ among each other in being vigorous defenders of shareholder interests or passive participants in a joint game with managers.

While the United States has deeper capital markets, the United Kingdom has gone farther in formalizing shareholder protections. One comparison is with the blockholding countries. Both the United Kingdom and the United States are majoritarian compared to the coalition systems, and have the expected policy outcome. The United Kingdom is more majoritarian than the United States. When politics and preferences shift, British institutions allow change to go faster. At the same time, Britain's structures encourage aggregation toward public goods, toward a more general bargain and the common goals, more than the U.S. model, which gives plenty of space to particularistic interests.

FRANCE: WITHOUT THE STATE, WHO IS IN CONTROL?

France is changing. It no longer fits the paradigm of state leadership of a market economy, a label it gave to the world with Colbertism in the seventeenth century. It has gone through several periods, from private blockholding to a growing equities market (the years before World War I), to strong state-led blockholding (from 1914 to the 1980s), and now, to a decline in both state blockholding and cross-shareholding, a rise in foreign investment, the growth of equities holding, and some growth of MSP. But if the old system has faded, it is far from clear what is emerging and where it will go. Transparency pressures are weak: the pension system remains largely pillar 2, with low private assets relative to GDP. Labor is weak in numbers and organizationally divided but has a strong capacity to mobilize public sympathy through strikes. Managers, no longer monitored by the state or blockholders, have substantial leeway as they face imperfectly organized shareholders and weak labor and a confused situation where the new rules are not clear. Thus, investor participation is growing, class tensions remain politically alive, managerism is significant, and a transparency coalition is not well formed. All these changes occurred in a stable political system, with significant changes toward market liberalization taken under a Socialist president and important Socialist majorities in parliament. How did these changes come about?

Concentration and State Leadership. As it developed among Europe's leading industrial economies, France mixed private blockholding with state activism. Charters, monopolies, public work projects (from transportation to military spending) had influenced growth before the Revolution and continued to do so afterward. In comparison with Britain, it was always a more regulated economy. At the same time, compared to the rest of Europe and indeed the world, it had vigorous markets, entrepreneurs, technological innovation, and steady if not spectacular growth. It developed a legal framework for the limited liability company and in some ways had more organizational options for investors than the United States.[80] High private savings fueled overseas loans, notably to Russia, and a strong equities market; Rajan and Zingales mark it as one of the strongest before World War I. French politics were conservative towards the economy, and "radical" in its politics, in the sense of aimed at promoting the Republic against the monarchy, secularism against the church, individualism and equality against traditional hierarchy and social caste. Antimarket ideas lay largely among property owners, who wanted protection from instability; labor was weak. The rules favored owners. Institutions like the Bank of France were controlled by a small number of families.

With World War I, state engagement increased substantially, banks expanded their role, and equity ownership dropped. Economic adjustment to postwar conditions was difficult. Then came the depression, another war, German occupation, intense conflict in the postwar Liberation period, and a second rebuilding period. Firms were nationalized, banking brought under public control, unions recognized and institutionalized in labor relations, the welfare state extended—the French version of the corporatist compromise. Politically, the basis of support for this set of adjustments is by now familiar to us: a deeply distressed private sector seeking state aid, strong labor activism, unhappy farmers, Christian Democratic criticism of free markets joining a Marxist critique, a large public employee sector whose employees vote on the left—a cross-class coalition.

Compared to other industrial countries, France had a powerful state sector. As such, it has never fit very well with the drive for dichotomous classification by varieties-of-capitalism authors[81] of either the corporate governance systems or the national production systems. France is not an LME (liberal market economy) because of a strong state role in the economy, substantial blockholding, low capitalization, regulations on competition, an important role for banks and other

---

[80] Naomi R. Lamoreaux and Jean-Laurent Rosenthal, "Legal Regime and Business's Organizational Choice: A Comparison of France and the United States during the Mid–Nineteenth Century," *American Law and Economic Review* (forthcoming).

[81] Hall and Soskice 2001 treat France, along with Italy, Spain, etc. as intermediate cases, neither an LME nor an OME.

coordinating networks, extensive regulations on labor markets, and welfare. It is conversely not a CME (coordinated market economy) because corporatism is quite limited, there are few institutions for labor-management common action and coordination, and labor and price market mechanisms are not well structured.

Some authors have treated France as an intermediate case, while others have seen it as the exemplar of a distinctive model: state-led coordination rather than blockholder-led.[82] In place of banks or large blockholders as in Sweden or Germany, in France, the state, most notably through the Ministry of Finance, coordinates the allocation of credit, market structure, technology development, prices, welfare and labor markets, and foreign economic relations. France does have a substantial private sector, an active market economy, so that the active state role does not put it in the camp of a planned or socialist economy. Leaders of the economy come substantially from the civil service elite, who go from their public-sector job to managing the great firms—a similarity with Japan's *amakaduri* practices. To varying degrees Spain, Italy, and Portugal are generally thought to resemble this statist model.

This characterization of the French system seems accurate for France up until the end of the twentieth century. But in recent years, since the early 1980s, the role of the state has been substantially curtailed by a wave of privatizations and elimination of regulations.[83] The Banking Act of 1984 ended the separation of investment and commercial banking; this was followed by the creation of commercial paper and treasury bills, allowing large firms to access money markets, the creation of a futures market for bonds, and the ending of brokers' monopoly on paper. In 1990, capital controls were abolished, following the requirements for the Single European Act of 1986. Foreign direct investment was liberalized when the requirement of prior approval by the prime minister was abolished. Substantial privatization took place in three waves (1986–87, 1993–96, and 1997–2002); this cut employment in the public sector dramatically, down to the level of 5 percent of total French jobs in public-sector tradables by 2000 (while employment in civil servant positions like teachers and civil servants has grown). Employment protections have been weakened by legislation starting in 1986. The Bank of France was made independent in 1993.

---

[82] Schmidt 2002.

[83] Culpepper 2003, Pepper Culpepper, "Institutional Change in Contemporary Capitalism: Coordination and Change in Finance during the 1990s," paper presented to the 14th International Conference of Europeanists, Chicago, March 11–13, 2004. See also Mottis and Ponssard 2002; Plihon, Ponssard, and Zarlowski 2001; Gerard Charreaux, "Au-dela de l'approche juridico-financiere: Le role cognitive des actionnaires et ses consequences sur l'analyse de la structure de propriete et de la gouvernance," Université de Bourgogne Research Center in Finance, Organizational Architecture, and Governance Working Paper 020701; Dominique Plihon and Jean-Pierre Ponssard, *La montée en puissance des fonds d'investissement*, la Documentation Francaise, 2002; Michel Boutillier and Patrice Geoffron, "*Vers une convergence des systèmes de douvernement d'entreprises en Europe?*" Final Report Commissariat Général du Plan, December 2001; Frédéric Lordon, *La politique du capital* (Paris: Odile Jacob, 2002); Claude Bébéar and Philippe Manière, *Ils vont tuer le capitalisme* (Paris: Plon, 2003).

Corporate governance was directly addressed in the New Economic Regulations bill passed in 2001. It allows separation of CEO and chairman; limits to five the number of boards on which directors can sit, so as to reduce interlocking directorates; requires higher transparency on the management report including all payment to directors, lessening the threshold for shareholder suits; and requires more open voting methods.[84]

Specialists now question whether the notion of "state enhanced"[85] any longer applies to France, or even whether the "character of state intervention" matters rather than its extent.[86] In education and training, the French state used to manage a system for the low skilled, but is increasingly not able to do so. At the elite level, increasing numbers of students seek private-sector jobs, so that the channeling through the state's ability to select the best and brightest via the civil service is declining. In industrial relations, the government has tried to regulate less and turn more functions over to associations of firms and to unions. Some of these organizations turn out to have weak capacity for action, so the state is drawn back to help them perform the intended function.[87]

In the first decade after this privatization, no clear mechanism of monitoring replaced the state, and employee-managers (of the former SOEs) had substantial autonomy. Privatization resulted in a sort of synthetic keiretsu, with many firms protected from private blockholders and takeovers by a hard core (*noyau dur*) of other corporate shareholders. The state (with Mitterrand as Socialist president and Chirac as center-right prime minister) encouraged these *noyaux durs* to shelter firms from competition. Many of the largest firms belonged to cross-shareholdings centered around two groups, each with a large commercial bank and insurance company at the core: UAP-BNP (Unions des Assurances de Paris and Banque Nationale de Paris) and AGF-Paribas (Assurances Générales de France and Paribas).

This stage did not last to the degree expected. The state no longer had the levers to control the process. The managers of former SOEs were aggressive in seeking external capital in order to finance investment in R & D and equipment required to compete in a consolidating European and global market. Hanké notes, "As a result of the cross-shareholdings, a lot of the capital to cover such investments was simply not available."[88] By the mid-1990s, the *noyaux durs* had broken up.

[84] Yves Tiberghien, "Political Mediation of Global Economic Forces: The Politics of Corporate Restructuring in Japan, France, and South Korea," Ph.D. diss., Stanford University, 2002, 215, provides careful analysis of this legislation and the process by which it came about.

[85] Schmidt 2002.

[86] Levy 1999; Culpepper 2004, 18.

[87] Culpepper 2004.

[88] Bob Hanké, "Restructuring in French Industry," in Hall and Soskice 2001, 330–31. In some cases, as much as 40 percent of the market capitalization of the top 40 firms listed on the Paris Bourse was tied up in these cross-shareholdings in the late 1990s. These funds were badly needed at a time when competition heated up again and the fastest way to have access to it, and assure a steady flow in the future, was by opening up the capital structure of the companies since the volume of shares floated after the privatization of the early 1990s was simply too large to be absorbed by French capital alone. Schmidt 2002; Michael Goyer, "Corporate Governance under Stress: An Institutional Perspective on the Transformation of Corporate Governance in France and Germany." Ph.D. diss., Department of

In the 1990s, French companies used equity markets heavily to raise money, and interlocking share ownership had begun to fall. By the late 1990s, average cross-shareholding of the 40 largest firms dropped dramatically. In place of French-owned interlocking patterns came foreign institutional investors, largely British and American, which by the first years of the new century owned over 40 percent of outstanding shares in the CAC-40 companies.[89]

Large, former SOEs appear to have been in the vanguard of tapping foreign capital markets, and we do not have data on how many private blockholders engaged in this type of transaction. The large percentage of IPOs suggests that "new money" as well as "old money" and former SOEs were attracted by the good-governance deal. There is also anecdotal evidence that a number of small and midsized French firms controlled by family blockholders delisted from the bourse to engage in private equity transactions, which reappeared on the Paris Bourse (and other international equity exchanges) as an IPO later down the road.

With the change in business-state relations came substantial change in French firms. An extensive rationalization of production took place: factories closed, workers were laid off, and new product lines developed. Firms developed supplier networks resembling patterns in other countries. Unlike Germany, French CEOs dismantled conglomerate structures in order to focus on core competences.[90] Militant labor unions were neutralized, and new forms of relationships were developed with a core workforce, involved in participative management techniques and worker training. Firms used state resources and structures, such as regional governments, to generate regional production networks. Overall, French managers have become more active in shaping their institutional context, and less passive responders to state direction.[91]

In the process, French managers appear quite free to set their strategies. If the state does not constrain them as before, neither do shareholders or blockholders. Firms use unequal voting measures mechanisms to concentrate power. More than 90 percent of big firms have used stock options to reward top executives, a higher percentage than in the supposedly more liberal United Kingdom[92] ("with strong

---

Political Science, MIT, 2003; "Core Competencies and Labor: An Institutionalist Perspective on Corporate Governance in France and Germany," in *Global Markets, Domestic Institutions: Corporate Law and Governance in a New Era of Cross-Border Deals*, Curtis Milhaupt, ed. (New York: Columbia University Press, 2003); and "The Growth of Stock Markets in France and Germany, 1995–2002: The Importance of Work Organization Institutions." Paper presented to the American Political Science Association, Chicago, August–September 2004. Francois Morin, "A Transformation in the French Model of Shareholding and Management," *Economy and Society* 29 (2000): 36–53.

[89] Goyer 2003a, 2.

[90] Goyer 2003a, 8.

[91] Hancké, 2002. 190.

[92] A high marginal tax rate and social security levies on options make these arrangements relatively less attractive for managers. Gunnar Trumbull, "Divergent Paths of Product Market Regulation in France and Germany, 1970–1990," in *Handbook of Global Economic Policy*, Stuart S. Nagel, ed. (New York: Marcel Dekker, 2000); Trumbull, "The Rise of Consumer Politics: Market Institutions and Product Choice in Postwar France and Germany," Harvard Business School Working Paper Series No. 03-054, 2002.

ownership by American and British investment funds and the alignment of management interests closely with [Large] shareholder value, French companies are largely unconstrained in their response to market signals in the area of finance."[93] At the same time, Alcan's purchase of Pechiney may signal the greater influence of international forces on French managerial control.

Shareholder Protections. As the French system has mutated, some changes in minority shareholder protections have emerged. French listed firms have been rapid adopters of IAS for domestic as well as international reporting: 40 percent of French public firms use IAS, including over one-third of the CAC-40 top firms. Third-party audit is mandatory and widespread, with the Big Four holding the dominant market share, and a reputation for high professional competence. In 1995, accounting standards-setting was moved from the Conseil National de la Comptabilité to the freestanding Comité de la Reglementation Comptable, giving the latter body more independence from the financial authorities.

French listed firms have expanded their use of nonexecutive directors at a rapid pace, from approximately 70 percent in 1989 to 86 percent in 1999. Although these directors are nonemployees, there is some question as to their loyalty to shareholders as opposed to private blockholders, given the high percentage of French firms with a dominant family or entrepreneur owner.

France has, moreover, a set of voting and procedural institutions that hamper minority shareholders in the protection of their rights. These include unequal voting rights for shares (70 percent of firms), voting caps that limit minority voting rights (20 percent of firms), and a variety of procedural roadblocks, including mandatory share-blocking rules during voting. A thicket of antitakeover devices that are widely used mirrors these voting limitations, including poison pills, transfer restrictions, and conditional "golden shares" triggered by changes in control.

Firms controlled by the state as well as those controlled by private blockholders use these barriers. For example, the privatization of France Telecom in 1996 was negotiated with unions by promising to retain them as civil servants (maintaining their status as beneficiaries of preferential civil service pension and retirement benefits), selling 10 percent of the company to employees, applying some proceeds of IPO to the civil service retirement fund, adding employee representation on the board, and retaining state control over the majority of shares, to block any contest for control by foreigners, especially Americans. As of January 2003, there were seven employee representatives on the board, along with 12 civil servants (mostly Ministry of Finance) and one (!) elected by minority shareholders.[94] This makes the odds of a hostile takeover of France Telecom essentially zero.

The employee-managers of privatized SOEs have been pioneers in awarding themselves incentive stock option plans, whereas family-owned firms have been less inclined to incur the dilution costs of such plans. Stock options got a bad name in France from the "l'affaire Jaffré," in which Philippe Jaffré, the head of Elf

---

[93] Goyer 2003a, 8.
[94] http://www.francetelecom.com/en/financials/investors/governance/board.

Acquitaine (an SOE), pocketed $56 million in options when it was acquired by Total Fina (another SOE) in 1999.[95] As noted, the NER bill of 2001 institutionalized some of the shareholder reforms.

The Pension Time Bomb. Pensions and preferences interact in powerful ways: a system heavily dependent on PAYGO will have less interest in corporate governance than one reliant on employee-managed pension funds. France has a complex pension system, with high participation and coverage ratios (80 percent), among the largest in Europe, facing a steep demographic shock. A study performed by the government's Commissariat Générale au Plan in 1986 predicted that between 1990 and 2040, either contribution rates (taxes) must double or benefits must be halved.[96]

Terms are different between private firm employees (68 percent of the labor force), farmers or self-employed (11 percent), and civil servants (21 percent).[97] The two former funds are partially funded; the latter is entirely PAYGO, with more generous benefits than the former. The second-pillar funds are comanaged by labor unions, including the Caisse Nationale d'Assurance Vieillese des Travailleurs Salariés, and the Association pour le Régime de Retraite complémentaire de Salariés.

The pension problem rose in public discourse with the Rocard *livre blanc* of 1991, spelling out the problem and some marginal reform. When Socialist Rocard was replaced by Conservative Balladur as prime minister, more modest change was proposed. In 1995, Juppé proposed equity between civil service and private benefits, but public riots led to abandonment of this line. Thomas then in 1996 proposed expanding funded private firm plans, but this was dropped when the Socialists returned to power in 1997. Another report and another plan, the Charpin Plan, was proposed. In 2000, a social security fund was created to provide partial PAYGO support, and a year later private firm savings plans were adopted. In 2002, the Chirac government proposed another round of reforms, to trim civil servant advantages; these were opposed by unions, who also complained that the Pension Reserve Funds are underfunded.

Because of the lingering problems with the first-pillar scheme, with its IPD of 100 percent of GDP, it is not surprising that pillar 2 and pillar 3 assets amount to between 10 and 20 percent of GDP. As a result, equity holdings by French institutions investors are approximately one-third of those of British investors. French households have hedged the risk of relying on the state retirement system by investing in life insurance policies and private mutual funds.

The growth of private savings has produced some pressures for minority shareholder protection. The firms that manage these mutual fund assets, banded

---

[95] "Cracks in the Wall," *Forbes Global*, May 15, 2000, 102.

[96] The best-case scenario saw rates growing from 18.9 percent to 30.9 percent; and in the worst case, to 41.9 percent.

[97] Didier Blancet and Florence Legros, "France: The Difficult Path to Consensual Reforms," in Feldstein and Siebert 2002.

together under the Association Française de la Gestion Financière (AFG), have pressed the government to reform France's pay-as-you-go pension scheme and to supplement the state system with private pension schemes. AFG issued its own governance code and funded third-party scrutiny of French firms on a collaborative basis through France's two leading third-party fee-based analysis firms, Déminor and Proxinvest.[98]

But France's large institutional investors have been reluctant to criticize managers of the large SOEs or to facilitate hostile takeovers. Here we see the legacy of these large banks and insurance companies serving as the original core of the *noyaux durs*. Although the "hard core" shrank by two-thirds during the 1990s, it remained a potent factor in the control of large firms listed on the Paris Bourse, particularly the former SOEs. As in Japan, many of these financial institutions are guilty of the same governance sins as those they are supposed to monitor and discipline. Their managerial cadres are also homogenous, consisting largely of the same managerial elite from the grande écoles, with prior experience in government ministries before taking the helm of former SOEs. The growth of savings, thus, does not automatically create pressure for monitoring of managers.

Pension reform remains a very high-voltage political issue. In 1995, Juppé provoked the biggest strikes since 1947 by considering pension reform. The right-leaning majority enacted some modest equalization of public-sector rules with private-sector ones, but the topic in France, as in many places, remains politically quite difficult.

Preferences and Political Institutions. What then has caused such substantial change in French practices in corporate governance? The key lies in political shifts. When Mitterrand became the first Socialist president in 1981, he tried to take France in a quite different direction. He and his strong Socialist majority in parliament tried a strategy of activist government and countercyclical policy. Quite soon this proved unworkable: markets reacted quite negatively, and Mitterrand shifted ground. He feared a strong economic backlash that would hurt him politically more than accepting the dictates of the market. Investors have power over the political economy of a market-based democracy, because electorates will punish economic downturn.[99] He started France and the Socialist Party down a policy trajectory to the center-right, which has been a key part of France's policy movement.

Mitterrand lost his Socialist majority and France had cohabitation twice (1986–88 and 93–95) with a prime minister of the center-right and a president on the left. In 1995, the presidency shifted to the right and then for a time the parliament moved left—cohabitation with reversed labels (1997–2002). In 2002, both presidency and parliament moved to the right. The Left's debate

---

[98] "Déminor Rates 300 European Companies Based on Corporate Governance Standards," www.deminor.com.

[99] Among the many explorations of this, Lindblom 1977 remains a classic.

over the role of government has been intense. Reformers wish to "modernize" the economy in new conditions of the European and global competition; the traditional left opposes globalization and any weakening of state aid to the disadvantaged.

A similar debate of great importance is taking place in the right. The French state has been important in France because the owners of property like state activism, and did so long before there was a modern worker left. It has persisted because major forces in the center and right wanted it. French conservatives have also been debating the role of government: many remained attached to a Colbertist role. The move against that model is recent and constantly contested, as the desire for state aid continues. The reasons are familiar and again make France look like the rest of Europe: the opportunities and demands of European integration, adaptation to new economic conditions, the need to cut budget deficits, the desire for higher equity values and flexibility to handle new market conditions and technology.

These political movements confirm the importance of partisan orientation, rather than partisan balance by itself.[100] The left won a lot of elections during this period, but its stance on policy moved toward accommodation of markets; thus key groups shifted preferences. Left-based presidents and parliaments enacted the various laws noted above. At the European level, on the takeover law debate of 2001, French Socialists voted with British Conservatives to support the more market-oriented version.[101] Government policy allowed the evolution of regulation and rules to move away from state control. In the first years of the process, policy did not directly address corporate governance, but it did move the economy toward the market: privatization, looser financial regulation, openness of capital markets, and then, more directly, shareholder protections.

Many observers stress the changing ideas of key civil service elites, who came to believe that France needed liberal economic processes to modernize and be effective.

In this way, they see no direct political debate over corporate governance issues.[102] To them the issues pass under the "radar screen," thus are left to civil service technicians, the classic French mode. That may be quite accurate as a description of the process, but politics plays an important role in allowing it to take place. Letting civil servants write the regulations does not prove groups are not watching them, able to complain if they deviate seriously from what the

---

[100] While his data stresses partisan balance, Roe (2003b) sees this point quite clearly and discusses partisan orientation rather than balance explicitly.

[101] Tiberghien 2002a, chap. 6.

[102] Goyer 2004, 2003a, 2003b; Michel Goyer, "The Transformation of Corporate Governance in France," in *Changing France: Transforming the Democratic Balance among State, Market, and Society*, Peter Hall, Pepper Culpepper, and Bruno Palier, eds. (forthcoming); Culpepper 2004. Tiberghien combines an argument about the importance of politics in the legislative process with a stress on the role of elite civil servants as strategists and leaders at key moments (2002a, chap. 6).

groups want. The analytics of this have been vigorously debated between "delega-tion theorists," who stress the supervisory power of elected officials, including the legislature, and the bureaucratic predominance specialists, who stress autonomy of the bureaucracy. The loci of this debate, not surprisingly, have been Japan and France.[103]

While there may be no open political debate about various details in the devel-opment of MSP and other corporate governance rules, the process takes place in a context that does pass through politics. The decision to privatize, the shift away from big deficits, the rules on labor markets, complying with EU competition rules, ending subsidies for companies—all of this required legislation and thus all moved through the political system overtly. The silence has political founda-tions: the government once had the capacity for intervention and the capacity to use it. The new situation is that it no longer uses this power in the old way—thus a policy change has occurred whether overt or not. While Tiberghien stresses the powers of the bureaucracy, especially the Ministry of Economy and Finance, and the agenda-setting powers of the prime minister and cabinet over the parliamen-tary process, he notes the political context that sets limits: in the NRE bill of 2001, "the ministry (of Finance) had in fact planned to also include drastic reforms of the fiscal treatment of stock options, pension reforms and deeper reforms of the Commercial Code but was forced to back down by the parliamen-tary majority."[104] Overall, the decline of statist ideas on the left and the right seems plausibly to explain the movement of French policy. The change is by no means total: French conservatives have not given up state aid: state power was invoked to prevent the Swiss Novartis from taking over Sanofi/Aventis in phar-maceuticals; and it was used to push the EU to allow France to bail out Alsthom. The Left is divided over the reforms, and Juppé paid the price in fragmented vot-ing during the presidential election of 2002, which pushed him third in the race after Le Pen.

French formal institutions changed little during this period (the term of the president was shortened from seven to five years), so that institutional change by itself cannot account for policy change or behavior toward corporate governance. Institutions may nonetheless influence the process of policy evaluation that does

[103] On Japan, see Chalmers Johnson, *MITI and the Japanese Miracle: The Growth of Industrial Pol-icy, 1925–1975* (Stanford, Calif.: Stanford University Press, 1982); and Mark Ramseyer and Frances Rosenbluth, *Japan's Political Marketplace* (Cambridge: Harvard University Press, 1993); Gary Cox, Frances Rosenbluth, and Michael F. Thies, "Electoral Rules, Career Ambitions, and Party Structure: Conservative Factions in Japan's Upper and Lower Houses," *American Journal of Political Science* 44 (2000): 115–22; Ellis Krauss and Michio Muramatsu, "Bureaucrats and Politicians in Policymaking: The Case of Japan," *American Political Science Review* 78 (1984): 126–46; Ezra Suleiman, *Private Power and Centralization in France: The Notaries and the State* (Princeton: Princeton University Press, 1987); John D. Huber, *Rationalizing Parliament: Legislative Institutions and Party Politics in France* (Cambridge: Cambridge University Press, 1996).

[104] Tiberghien 2002a, 214. See also Yves Tiberghien, "State Mediation of Global Financial Forces: Different Paths of Structural Reforms in Japan and South Korea," *Journal of East Asian Studies* 2 (2002): 103–41.

have an effect, though more indirectly. It may impact pension reform and the development of equity markets.

Presidential power and the single-member district electoral law make France a majoritarian system. When the president and the prime minister are from the same party, the former dominates policy because he dominates the party; when they are split, and cohabitation results, the PM dominates because of his control of the parliamentary majority. But president and PM together have a lot of authority if there is single-party unity. If party balances fragment power, France can acquire some consensual elements, which slow down policy change. French politics also appear quite responsive to protest outside formal political institutions. The public often supports strikes and demonstrations, by farmers, workers, students, and may support them against the conservative government that the public has elected. This may explain the caution in pension system reform.

Societé Bloquée or Transparency Coalition? Not so long ago, France was discussed as a *societé bloquée*, unable to change.[105] This no longer seems an adequate characterization, as much has changed. Politics, markets, and institutions have interacted to produce considerable movement of policy and practice. When market forces showed they disliked Mitterrand's shift to the left, French politicians concluded the public would not like the unemployment that would result if they kept going. Policy shifted, and France began a long process of loosening state control. Each step gradually created a new pattern of interests and of policy preferences. Actors advanced their goals in the marketplace through politics.

A large private sector has emerged, with many of the trappings of the shareholder model: a growing stock market with substantial participation by foreign institutional investors, shareholder relations offices, and other indicators of the diffusion model. Thus it appeared a move to the right pushed France toward the investor pattern, as the class conflict model would predict.

And yet, unlike other investor model countries, the French economy remains strongly connected to using the state as an instrument for action. The French state remains a major consumer of firms' output. One of Alsthom major customers is the SNCF (the public train authority); Dassault's is the French air force; Airbus sells a good share of its planes to Air France; France Telecom does huge business with the state, as does Thomson St Gobain (whose military arm is Thales). The fast trains, telecommunications, and weapons systems are sold to foreign countries as matters of state-to-state negotiation.

Unlike the investor model, managers appear to have substantial autonomy, as the reality of supervision has not caught up with the facts of shareholding. France does not have Germany's system of corporatist interaction by the economic actors, but neither does it have the arm's-length practices of the United

---

[105] Hancké 2002, 333; Ezra Suleiman, *Les resorts cachés de la réussite Française*, trans. Sylvette Gleize (Paris: Seuil, 1995).

States. Shareholder protections do not seem strong. The private savings and pension system has not produced the foundations for a transparency coalition. Without roots in a transparency coalition, or in a vigorous investment one, France maybe headed for the default outcome: managerism. At a minimum it seems in transition: from state leadership to some kind of uncertain and perhaps unstable managerism: one form of monitoring loosened, another not wholly in place.

CONCLUSION

This chapter explores a political cleavage in the politics of corporate governance that has been relatively ignored: labor-related groups joining with external investors to demand stronger MSP.

The transparency coalition is thus grounded in real economic incentives and can coalesce into organized interest group activity and get the attention of politicians. The transparency coalition is a political model that can explain change for greater minority shareholder protections. In this regard it is a complement to the investor model. But the attentive reader may ask whether the transparency coalition is merely the investor model in different clothing. In some ways it is: workers have become more interested in minority shareholder protections for the same reasons the investor model posits: to provide protections to external investors against managerial agency costs. Workers have become investors; therefore they behave like investors.

What are the differences between the transparency coalition and the investor model?

First, the investor model as we derive it from finance theory does not specify the political linkages that go from preferences to politics, from preferences to the specific political activities that bring about a change in regulation. It assumes that preferences more or less automatically turn into policy, in a sort of policymaking "black box." The connection to policy must still be established. To the degree that political bargaining has any effect on shaping this policy, the investor model assumes that rich blockholders can simply "buy" whatever policy they want, with side-payments if necessary—so-called economic pluralism at its purest.

Second, the investor model assumes a unitary view of investors, rather than a fragmented group with diverse interests. Some investors have a substantial interest in blockholding and seek to preserve it, while other investors, external to the firm, seek protections. Some investors are now employees, and as such are now cross-pressured as investors and workers both.

Third, the investor model pays scarce attention to the role of reputational intermediaries and to the governance of pension funds and other institutional investors. The reputational intermediaries and the sometimes mixed motives of money managers matter greatly in connecting worker-voters' interests as investors to policy preferences. In some countries their interests are shut out, fragmented and blocked by the conflicted interests of the fund managers. In this respect, workers as pension beneficiaries face the same collective action problem towards the governance of investment firms that they face as fragmented shareholders in other public firms. In other countries their collective interest has voice: they select fund managers who are responsive to the plan beneficiaries rather than to the managers of firms or the blandishments of reputational intermediaries.

Fourth, the operative time scale is different. It may be that the demographic shifts and battles over IPD take longer than the decade and a half of capital flows associated with the investor model to shift workers' preferences, away from the labor or corporatist compromise model, towards the transparency coalition instead.

The investor model predicts the same outcome as the transparency model, but its political mechanisms for getting there are quite different. It is important with both models to avoid the functionalist fallacy: to assume that an economic interest translates automatically into public policy. If investors want shareholder protections and workers want them via transparency, this still does not explain how these preferences translate into policy outcomes. The transparency model outlines a coalition of actors, in the firm, in the economy, and in politics, who push for this outcome. It calls our attention to the institutional intermediation between asset ownership and the expression of voice; in some structures, worker ownership will have little voice, in other situations, quite a lot. The investor model is generally undeveloped in specifying the political mechanism and the financial institutional structure that link interests to outputs.

Reframing the Actors

Throughout our discussion we have encountered moments where the simplified categories of owners, managers, and workers obscure important distinctions within each group. Treating them as homogeneous, unitary wholes makes it harder to understand coalition formation. Here we offer a brief suggestion as to how researchers might reformulate the categories and explore further the salience of the cleavages within each.

OWNERS: INSIDER/OUTSIDER.

On the side of owners, an important internal division lies between insiders, especially blockholders, and outsiders, especially minority shareholders or those considering whether to purchase a minority stake. Analysis of MSP as the driver of investment strategies focuses on the concerns of the outsiders and assumes the insiders will "accept the bargain." Yet we see considerable resistance from insiders to such deals. Outsiders form the basis of potential bargains with workers to support transparency.

WORKERS: JOBS VERSUS PENSIONS

Employees are split between two identities. On the one hand they seek to preserve their jobs; on the other they seek to protect their pension funds. This may lead to opposing preferences: a concern with job preservation encourages support of blockholding; concern with pensions motivates transparency. In some cases, the job motivation may also push toward transparency: where workers are politically and institutionally able to exercise voice, they may push for transparency, so that workers have a way of evaluating managerial strategies.

MANAGERS: INDIVIDUAL VERSUS THE FIRM

Managers may split along strategies for individual advancement: firm-centered managers may seek to promote preservation of the firm as an entity, and thereby the security of their position in it; individual-centered managers may seek to maximize their financial return by alliance with external investors through maximizing share prices, whatever the risk to the internal coherence of the firm and other stakeholders. The former prefer blockholding, the latter the maximum MSP transparency, including vigorous labor markets.

REPUTATIONAL INTERMEDIARIES

These have not been part of the trinity of players in finance approaches to governance. But it has become clear that they matter vitally in how the system works, especially where investors rely on their monitoring functions in diffusion model systems. We do not know enough about RIs, but one cleavage appears plausible: single-purpose firms versus multifunction firms. All-purpose firms may well have conflicts of interest in their relationship to managers that inhibit vigorous supervision, or at least clarity in the provision of information: their incentives to win contracts from managers for various services reduce the motive to do one service clearly, and may make them allies of managers, not of investors. Conversely, firms built around one function—or around one set of clients—may have stronger motives to play the role that "theory" assigns them. Another important, though overlapping, distinction may have to do with ownership and control in the RIs. Financial institutions controlled by their investors may have incentives with respect to governance different from those controlled by another set of owners seeking to maximize their profits rather than those of their investors.

These subcategories allow us to clarify alliance formation:

Investor and the transparency Coalitions consist of: owners = external; workers = pension funds; managers = financial; RIs = single dimension.

Blockholder/corporatist/labor coalitions consist of: owner = blockholder; worker = employee; managers = firm orientation; RIs = multipurpose.

These are the two big alliance clusters that push for MSP and diffusion outcomes versus blockholder outcomes. The further patterns within these alternatives, of oligarchy or managerism, or corporatism, or labor—turn on the balance of forces among the members of the broader coalitions. The motivations to join in one direction or another will also be influenced by the *degree of coordination* variable we have noted: whether an economy has institutionalized incentives for high coordination of subsystems (the coordinated market economy pattern) or for high flexibility among them (the liberal market economy pattern). The CMEs motivate more interest in blockholding; the LMEs push the same actors the other way.

It will take more research to unravel these distinctions. We risk losing parsimony for accuracy, but the relevance of cleavage within the rough categories compels some moves in that direction.

In sum, as the transparency coalition describes, workers' preferences for corporate governance can become aligned with those of dispersed minority shareholders, for reasons of both job security and pension security. This new coalition of capital and workers can alter corporate governance practices to favor their common interests; they can also fail to do so in the face of managerial entrenchment and self-enrichment, resulting in managerial agency failure.

Which set of actors will triumph? We now have the foundation for contrasting political coalitions across the governance "axis of division" in the political world; political institutions and politicians can aggregate these new preferences into a winning voter coalition.

Pagano and Volpin's formal model predicts this opening as well. They posit a simple "agent" state and a median voting process, under which, say the authors, "we find that the 'vote-weighted equity stake' of society is the key parameter in determining the political outcome. If equity ownership is very diffused among voters, both parties will converge on a platform that favors shareholder rights and grants low employment security."[106]

This chapter described changes in preferences and investigated first-order evidence for lobbying by workers through their institutional investors; it also notes the way institutions aggregate these preferences. But we have not made reference to how those preferences are aggregated by political institutions.

The preceding three chapters have outlined three cleavages (each with a coalitional pair) and six possible outcomes (depending on which side of each pair wins) of corporate governance policy. The chapters focus on the support structures for policy alternatives. That is, they examine the preferences important actors could have for diffusion versus blockholding policy patterns and the coalitions that might form among them. Three models lead to shareholder diffusion: the investor model; the transparency coalition; and managerial agency failure. The other three models sustain blockholding and insider information models, even if there is high-quality law and minority shareholder protections.

We have six possible coalitions. Which prevails in any particular country? The answer is the strongest coalition—but that begs the question of what constitutes strength. This comes from political resources—votes, lobbying ability, direct action such as strikes. Political institutions can play an important role by favoring one coalition over another: thus the fact that consensus institutions favor the corporatist compromise and OMEs while majoritarian ones favor LMEs and either investor or transparency coalitions.

In the next chapter we draw out the implications of what we have observed with the country narratives and the analytic framework.

---

[106] Pagano and Volpin 2001a, 2.

Conclusion: Going Forward

IN THIS CONCLUDING chapter we return to the core questions of this book and sum up the answers we submit, including some brave speculation about the future trajectory of corporate governance. We then frankly acknowledge the manifold shortcomings of our argument and data, in the spirit of humility appropriate to scholars exploring a relatively new area, based on statistics and country cases that are necessarily incomplete. These shortcomings provide guideposts for future research. After declaring these caveats, we close by exploring some of the theoretical and public policy implications of our findings.

QUESTIONS AND ANSWERS: WHAT EXPLAINS VARIANCE?

In this book we have been trying to answer three core questions. What explains variation in corporate governance among countries? What causes these practices to change over time? Are countries converging on a common pattern, or will diversity be sustained?

Question 1: What Explains the Variation in Corporate Governance among Countries?

Recapping the narrative in chapters 1, 3, and 4, we argue that the choice of corporate governance practices in any country expresses the interaction of *economic preferences* and *political institutions*. As the country cases have illustrated, corporate governance arises from incentives created by rules and regulations that emerge from a public policy process, reflecting the power of alternative political coalitions. This has been our mantra throughout this book, that it is the interaction of preferences and institutions that causes policy outcomes, including corporate governance outcomes. This assertion is global; we believe it applies to all the countries in our sample, even in the soft authoritarian and "hard" democracies.

We further argue that corporate governance can be thought of as deriving from two broad packages of rules. First, and most frequently discussed, are *minority shareholder protections*, the range of instruments designed to protect the external investor from appropriation by insiders, be they blockholders, managers, or workers. This is what most academic writers and commentators in the mass media mean when they refer to "corporate governance." High levels of MSP produce high levels of shareholder diffusion.

Second, attracting less attention in the academic literature and even less in the popular media, are the set of rules that we have been calling *degrees of coordination* (product-market competition, price and wage mechanisms, labor relations, and social welfare systems). These also shape the incentives to concentrate shareholding or to sell down to a diffuse shareholding pattern, with highly coordinated markets producing blockholding. Thus ownership patterns—concentration or diffusion—vary across countries in response to the difference in incentives produced by politics. Repeating the mantra: preferences plus institutions equals policy outcomes that shape corporate governance patterns.

At the micro level, the three major actors inside firms with an interest in how the profits of firms are divided—owners, managers, and workers—seek to persuade society at large to provide public policies on corporate governance that favor their interests. Each coalition of players within the firm seeks to mobilize support outside the firm in order to win. It thus tries to build coalitions with other players in its own group, and players in society more broadly, to set the corporate governance packages in its favor.

In moving from the firm to society, these actors can align themselves into different combinations: Owners plus managers versus workers, owners versus managers plus workers, and owners plus workers versus managers. These three different alignments produce a total of six possible outcomes, depending upon which side of the coalitional alignment "wins" by having its corporate governance preferences reflected in rules and regulations. The choice of what sort of shareholder protections to embed in regulations is thus the result of a bargain worked out in society's political system.

In principle, all six coalitional outcomes are possible for a given country at any time. Countries may switch back and forth from one political pattern to the other, reflecting the changing strengths of groups and political institutions. A bit further on we hazard some thoughts on the most common trajectories by which countries move between governance patterns over time.

Question 2: What Causes Corporate Governance Practices to Change?

CHANGES IN A SINGLE COUNTRY

Corporate governance changes occur within any given country when preferences or institutions change. If the policy preferences of one or more of the groups of intrafirm actors—owners, managers or workers—shift enough to upset the ex ante coalition balance, a new alignment ensues. Or political institutions can change, though this is far less common than a change in preferences.

Preferences shift when economic conditions change in big ways—economic competition, the terms of trade, technology, depression, inflation. Institutions change when exogenous forces cause it: revolution, war, or—more peacefully— when policy preferences induce actors to change the political rules so as to alter their output toward their preferences. What new equilibrium results, how quickly this equilibrium changes in response to these shifting preferences, and what sort of negotiations and side-payments are involved in this shift, depends upon domestic political processes in each country.

Changing Preferences: The overall economic situation can change preferences in a variety of ways. To explain the dynamics of change in our period today, we have called special attention to one of these underlying economic situations: pension systems and the onward effects of these systemic choices on the accumulation of pension assets. Pensions and the cross-border mobility of retirement assets through portfolio investment are one of the principal "potentiators" of new equilibrium coalitions. These altered preferences due to pension entitlements are mediated, and sometimes blocked, by the structure of the financial system. There are other factors that can shift preferences that could result in the formation of a transparency coalition, such as rebellion against the cozy ties between chaebol and the authoritarian regime in Korea, or a perception that job security is increasingly tied to shareholder protections in Germany.

As preferences change, each group (and each potential coalition) faces trade-offs in moving from one policy position to another. For example, it is possible that some workers as a group may be better off as part of a corporatist compromise, if the governance practices that result from that alignment include complementary institutions such as joint wage determination, job security, social welfare, or occupational training that may benefit them.

Moreover, the consensual political institutions that are correlated with the corporatist compromise, and which (we argue) are necessary to form and sustain it, do not necessarily produce inferior collective decisions with regard to pensions and pension funding. Indeed, it is striking that two of the countries in Europe that implemented the most thoroughgoing pension reform in the 1990s are also among the most consensual: Netherlands and Sweden. Shifting to "shareholder value" concerns may increase profitability to shareowners, but may lower the average wage to workers.[1]

Conversely the corporatist compromise may have other long-term, dynamic costs that stem from its governance practices in equilibrium. These practices, which favor insiders over outsiders and producers over consumers, run the risk of enhancing the *agency costs of free cash flow*, as well as reducing both factor mobility and price flexibility. This choice tends to stifle job creation and technical innovation, while reducing return on investment. Workers may suffer from fewer jobs, stagnant wages, pressure on social services, and low return on pension funds. As these costs mount, workers may be tempted to defect from the corporatist compromise. The same analysis can be made for other actors in the system. Managers and blockholders have special advantages in the corporatist compromise system, but may also incur long-term losses from economic stagnation and other negative effects of an "insider"-oriented governance system.

Even if these economic pressures develop in ways that alter actors' preferences, they merely make a new coalition possible; they do not make it occur automatically.

---

[1] Anke Hassel and Jürgen Beyer, "The Effects of Convergence: Internationalization and the Changing Distribution of Net Value Added in Large German Firms," Max Planck Institute, Discussions Paper 01/7, November 2001.

What matters most in shaping governance outcomes, preferences or institutions? Based upon this country sample, changes in a country's governance practices are more frequently attributable to shifting preferences than to shifting political institutions. Preferences tend to change faster than institutions, which are sticky over time. In our sample, the altered landscape of corporate governance in only the cases of Chile and South Korea can be traced to overt changes in political institutions. There may well be changes afoot in the political institutions of quasi–authoritarian states such as China, or in "hard" democracies in the sample such as Singapore and Malaysia, but these are hard to measure, and harder still to connect to altered outcomes in corporate governance.

In stable democracies, political institutions change very slowly. There is some feedback effect that "locks in" a constituency for certain governance institutions, but by and large the arrow of causation in our model flows from preferences to political institutions to corporate governance outcomes. We believe that the distributional consequences of different governance outcomes can change preferences over time, but we have not traced thoroughly in any of our country narratives the effects of corporate governance outcomes on political institutions.

CONSENSUS "GLUE" VERSUS MAJORITARIAN "COMPETITION"

In some advanced industrial democracies, a consensual political system tends to keep the parties to the compromise "glued together." It provides the structure to make credible the bargains among the parties, encouraging them to build up interests and ideas that sustain the agreement.

In contrast, a majoritarian system erodes the corporatist bargain because it magnifies small shifts of preference into bigger swings of policy. As a result, a group's investment in a corporatist bargain either does not coalesce in the first place or is undermined, as parties are tempted to defect from their core constituencies (or fear that other parties will defect first) in their pursuit of the loyalties of the median voter. The polarized parties of a majoritarian system compete for a broad coalition of voters, not for specialized interests, thus the outsiders rather than the insiders, the consumers rather than the producers, and—critically—the diffuse mass of minority shareholders rather than the concentrated blockholders.

Thus majoritarian competition tends to move a country's governance system towards enhanced investor protections, which can then take two forms: an investor model, with little involvement of labor, or a transparency coalition, with involvement of labor. If the citizen-voters have a strong stake in good governance by means of funded pension plans, then "lock in" effects can take place to sustain the new equilibrium, as in Chile. If citizen-voters do not have this stake, as in a country heavily weighted towards a pillar 1, unfunded, government-run pension plan, these effects will not lock in.

But the majoritarian path towards pension funding and altered preferences may not be the only road to a transparency coalition. Consensual political systems may also produce a transparency effect in a more indirect way. While these systems sustain many elements of the corporatist compromise, they may also have a higher capacity to carry out pension reform. In a consensual political system, all the major parties have mechanisms for joining in the bargain and risk sharing of reform, the political as well as economic costs. By contrast, in majoritarian systems the "third rail" of social security often hinders political compromise and makes reform a dangerous undertaking for politicians.

Over time, even a consensual political system may generate a constituency concerned with shareholder value and transparency, as appears to be taking place in the Netherlands and Sweden. It remains unclear to us exactly how these political events are sequenced; at least in the Netherlands, the political decisions that created a constituency for enhanced transparency have not had time for that constituency to marshal sufficient political support to offset the bonds of the Poldermodel corporatist compromise that is deeply embedded in domestic political practices.

CHANGES IN MANY COUNTRIES

As we look back over the way that corporate governance has changed in our country sample, and especially in the cases we have examined in the prior three chapters, we observe that change in corporate governance patterns of a country, and in a group of countries, is not an isolated, random process. Corporate governance is just one of many important institutional arrangements hammered out by coalitions in political bargains at the national and, to some degree, regional level (as in the EU). Like other institutional choices, these governance choices are swept along by larger historical currents, and both the underlying preferences and political institutions reflect these broader, deeper currents.

Against this broad sweep of history, from the growth of large limited liability firms in mid–nineteenth century to the present, we detect three broad periods of transformation in corporate governance: 1850–1914, 1914–74, and 1974 to the present. Descriptively we note several important variables that run through these periods: the degree of openness in the world economy, the timing of a nation's entry into the world economy (Gerschenkron's early and late development), the mode of labor incorporation (authoritarian or democratic), and the nature of a country's political institutions.

In these three periods, we can flag several drivers of this process, which shift over time.

PERIOD 1: THE SPREAD OF CORPORATIONS, 1850 TO 1914

The global driver of the first formative period of corporate governance practices was industrialization and capital movement, in western Europe, North America, and Japan. The industrial revolution produced great rewards for investment; these rewards went to those who could accumulate capital and use it wisely and aggressively. They could obtain this capital from their own savings, from groups of people who knew each other, or from the government (through bounties, subsidies, or monopoly rents).

All countries begin with blockholding of owner dominance as founders, with limited roles for managers and workers and the absence of minority shareholders. This fits our knowledge of corporate history across countries. Within a lose framework of rules, "private bonding" mechanisms are essential in accumulating capital to fund the growth of firms. Banks and stock exchanges played this role, as did small personal networks. Banks monitored firms on behalf of their investors. Stock exchanges provided reassurance via listing requirements. Shareholding began, in limited ways through mergers and private arrangements. In response to these incentives, deeper bond and equities markets began to develop.

In this way, all the major industrializing economies of the late nineteenth century fostered corporations with fairly concentrated blockholding governance patterns. Minority investors took risks and bought shares. Equity markets flourished—not only in the United States, but as Rajan and Zingales point out, in Japan and France as well. The rapid growth in the size of firms produced, and demanded, professional managers. In most cases, blockholders monitored these managers directly. Shareholding ran ahead of formal protections.

In this earlier period there were already differences among the countries, which has some bearing on subsequent divergence. Gerschenkron's famous distinction between early and late developers seems applicable here: the United Kingdom as an early developer went down the diffusion path, while Germany, Japan, Russia, the late developers, went down the blockholding path. But by and large in the first period, countries resembled each other more than differed. Political systems were often authoritarian or relatively newly democratic, not well institutionalized, and often heard a narrow range of voices, in response to well-organized elite interest groups.

PERIOD 2: COPING WITH TURMOIL, 1914 TO 1974

The global driver of corporate governance formation in the second period of corporate governance formation (1914–74) was, predominantly, economic and social dislocation. While technology continued to expand the rewards for investment, political forces disrupted markets and trade. War, economic depression, and political dislocation mixed populism with elite reactions against market forces. In most countries, regulation of the economy was the primary response, and this encouraged blockholding, by expanding the powers of government ministries, expanding public ownership, and increasing the role of banks.

In many countries, political change—expanded suffrage, wartime mobilization, and constitutional governments—expanded the voice of a wider range of interests and preferences. In some places this led to democratic collapse and authoritarian regimes; in others countries, it strengthened democratic institutions. Among the major differences across countries is the nature of labor's political "incorporation" in politics: repressed in fascist and communist systems, integrated into Christian and Social Democratic party organizations in "corporatist" democracies, contested in neoliberal countries.

In a few cases like the United States, increased regulation aimed at shareholder protections and diffusion. In continental Europe and Japan, regulation went the other way, as war and economic dislocation produced strong support for government intervention. Banking was reorganized extensively, in some places effectively nationalized even before World War II, in others afterward. Equity markets collapsed. Little was done to develop MSP. Product markets weakened in the face of economic protectionism and extensive restrictions on domestic competition. The welfare state was developed, constructed, extended. Employment protection and social insurance systems grew substantially. In most countries these welfare states relied on pay-as-you-go pension plans, which deferred costs to the future, rather than privately held and fully funded plans (developed late in this period) as in Chile, Malaysia, Singapore, the United Kingdom, the United States, and—recent converts to full welfare funding—the Netherlands and Sweden.

PERIOD 3: GLOBAL CAPITAL FLOWS IN A NEW CONTEXT, 1974 TO THE PRESENT

The third period since the mid-1970s has been marked by a broad liberalization of economic policy and a renewed openness to flows of trade and finance. This period mirrors the openness of the pre–World War I economic system, but with more democratic political systems. A key feature in this third period has been the growth of vast pools of pension assets, as well as private savings generally, moving into global equity markets, thus creating new constituencies—and, we argue, a new and powerful coalition—for the minority shareholder approach to corporate governance across the world.

Trade and domestic patterns of finance changed in important ways that molded corporate governance practices. For example, the United States adopted policies that generated substantial individual and institutional ownership of equities. ERISA steered large pension savings toward stocks—a major transformer of preferences in many countries in our sample. The boundaries that defined financial institutions were loosened, allowing the intermingling of state and national banks, finance and commercial banks, and brokerage houses. Other countries liberalized as well, though not to the same degree. Countries that had nationalized firms now began to privatize extensively.

Liberalized economic relations among countries put competitive pressure on country-level choices of economic institutions. In some countries in Europe and in Japan, the stabilizing features of the corporatist compromise faced competition from producers without restrictions on lowering costs. Firms without pension plans had lower costs. Firms with flexible labor rules could reduce wages. Investors entered national equity markets and demanded attention as minority shareholders. Labor-based organizations with pension fund systems outside the national public retirement structure now entered the game, putting labor's populist voice in the debate.

Are these general global patterns, especially the drivers in the third wave discussed above, inducing conformity of practice in corporate governance—convergence on a single model of "ideal" corporate governance? That leads to our third question.

Question 3: Is the Overall Pattern of Corporate Governance Institutions Becoming Less Varied (Convergence) or More Varied (Divergence)?

Our analytic approach and the evidence from our country sample suggest sustained diversity in corporate governance arrangements, rather than convergence on a single pattern. With preferences of owners, managers, and workers shifting over time, with six different political coalitions to choose from, and a wide variety of political institutions on which they stand, it would be surprising indeed if all countries ended up in the same box.

As we have belabored for the reader, there are three possible alignments, and two possible "winners" in each alignment, thus six possible combinations. Each outcome in corporate governance can have different political foundations. These political alignments can change or oscillate. Many countries at present fall into either the corporatist compromise or transparency coalition buckets (or move between these two conditions), but there is no reason to conclude that countries will all end up in only one of these two end-states. Both the corporatist compromise and the transparency coalition can degrade or break up, reverting to managerism.

Both demographic shifts and capital mobility are likely to continue as exogenous factors altering workers' situations. As worker-citizens acquire assets, they develop preferences for shareholder protections, thus adding pressure to the potential for a transparency coalition.

But the link between worker assets in numerical terms and policy preferences is mediated by institutions, in both finance and in coordinating structures of the economy. Some financial institutions encourage the articulation of a collective voice by pension fund holders (such as a union-controlled pension fund), while other structures may fragment investors' voice, leaving the field to managers and reputational intermediaries to scratch each other's back at the expense of minority shareholders and workers. Some economic structures encourage labor-management cooperation, others encourage friction. And all the preferences will in turn be mediated by the underlying political systems that structure ideas, analysis, interpretation, and coalitional patterns.

Path dependence is at work. Earlier choices shape present ones. We notice two particularly important historical choices. The first, which we have especially stressed here, involves pension plans and funding. The relative weight of the three pension pillars and the subsequent "crowding out" effects of state versus private pensions tends to keep countries moving in one path or another in terms of the coalitional alignments with regard to corporate governance practices. These choices also determine where asset pools are created and, to some degree, where they flow.

In this respect, to understand the future politics of corporate governance debates, we will have to track fights about pension reform. The issue is often presented as a simple question of whether to privatize. This obscures the vital question of how shifting to pillars 2 and 3 would actually occur. Assets in the hands of institutions that are accountable to their owners are likely to pay more attention to governance than are assets in the hands of autonomous managers.

A second historical branch point concerns our degrees of coordination variables, measuring differences among capitalist economies. Countries who constructed highly developed corporatist bargains, supported by CME institutions in consensus political systems are likely to have a different politics for facing global change than are those that have LME structures in majoritarian systems.

The Achilles heel of convergence arguments is the assumption that the selection mechanisms at work in the global economy are so powerful as to erode all the prior existing conditions when the process begins. Glaciers that confront strong mountains are not able to wipe them out. The residue effect is very noticeable. Global economic forces certainly affect the countries we examine, but countries have ways of shaping just how those affects are internalized.

Within the frame shaped by their past, countries engage in political contestation of policies. There is more internal oscillation than strong versions of the "national patterns" approach may imply. The U.S. record on MSP rises and falls as the political balance shifts; Korea shifts course; France strikes out in new directions; the Netherlands in steady fashion changes big pieces of the system. Countries swing back and forth; matching politics to the timing of those swings is another field for research.

SHORTCOMINGS AND GUIDEPOSTS FOR FUTURE RESEARCH

We frankly admit several significant shortcomings to our approach and to our use of evidence in this book. These include the complexity of our causal model and the problems in testability that ensue; data headaches; a couple of simplifying assumptions that we fear will come back to haunt us; the complex, black box of financial and reputational intermediaries; and the plasticity of preferences for corporate governance.

Complexity of the Model

Our definition of corporate governance has been broad, beyond a narrow focus on the mechanics of equity markets, and particularly beyond the mere operation of the board of directors, which has passed for corporate governance in much of the popular business press. Per Claessens, we define corporate governance as the set of obligations and decision-making structures that shape "the complex set of constraints that determine the profits generated by the firm and shape the ex post bargaining over those profits."[2]

Our approach makes politics central to an analysis. In this respect we join Roe, Rajan and Zingales, Pagano and Volpin, Kroszner, and Perotti and von Thadden. They also speak of political parties, interest groups, social classes, and political institutions. We build on their work to develop a typology of groups and preferences that links more directly preferences in the firm to political strategies in the polity.

But this is a complex causal model, as graphically demonstrated by the multiple boxes, lines, and feedback loops in the schema explored in chapter 2. It is

---

[2] Stijn Claessens, "Global Corporate Governance Convergence: The Case of Asia," paper presented to the Global Research Network Meeting, Institute of Corporate Governance of Korea University, Global Corporate Governance Forum of the World Bank, and the International Institute of Corporate Governance, July 2002, Seoul.

famously hard to develop testable, falsifiable propositions in a model that admits of multiple independent variables. Partly as a result of this empirical problem, we have been largely limited to running correlations rather than multiple regressions with controls that can establish less ambiguous arrows of causation.

Data Headaches

There is no canon of what constitutes corporate governance institutions, or—more important—how to measure them objectively. For example, it would be helpful to researchers and practitioners alike to have a generally accepted index of accounting and audit quality for a multicountry sample, perhaps performed under the auspices of the IASB.

This index problem may be solved by the recent emerging market of corporate governance scoring firms. Several firms from the proxy service sector have entered the scoring business, and Standard & Poor's has begun to perform corporate governance evaluations of firms as well. Some firms have been accused of conflicted interests insofar as they also seek revenue from the same business firms they are evaluating. A new firm, Governance Metrics, has entered the fray, while avoiding the problem of conflict by relying on fee revenue from institutional investors, not firm managers.

Our long-run goal is to understand the dynamics of change, how countries evolve from one pattern to another. Much current research is static: it correlates this or that variable with data on concentration. This is valuable, but not enough. We know change has occurred. Rajan and Zingales captured it well with their title, "The Great Reversals." The key next step in the analytic process is to lay out the long-term "longitudinal trajectories" of major country cases, and examine these deep narratives for systematic clues about how countries move between the numerous governance end-states we discuss in this book.

The next step in analyzing trajectories requires laying out in greater detail the patterns of change on both sides of the equation: shifts in ownership patterns and shifts in politics. Here we face a substantial empirical problem: as noted in chapter 3, data on ownership concentration is incomplete and static. It provides at present a snapshot of institutions at a single point. It does not provide points over time. Change has occurred, in some cases quite dramatically in the last few years. For example, a lot of progress has been made in the Asian countries in our sample following the Asian financial crisis of 1997–98, and these changes are not reflected in the accounting quality index that we borrowed from La Porta et al.

The central argument regarding the reaction of blockholders to price incentives proffered by portfolio investors needs to be tested against changes in holdings over time. For this we need at least more recent data sets on ownership concentration. More data within countries over time would help with the small-n problem. The historical reconstruction work being done country by country may contribute substantially to our knowledge in this key area.[3]

---

[3] Morck et al., *The History of Corporate Governance around the World: Family Business Groups to Professional Managers*, forthcoming.

Simplifying Assumptions Haunt Us

In doing so, important elements of political process will become more evident as causes of policy outcomes, factors we and other authors have neglected. Our analysis has stressed preferences and institutions. There is a third piece of the system, what sociologists call "political resource mobilization." Preferences need resources to act through institutions. Workers, owners, and managers need votes, money, organization, ideological articulation, and the capacity to lobby in order to prevail. We look at preferences as they can be inferred from voting and party programs, but we do little with political resources, as they are much harder to measure.

The Black Box of Reputational Intermediaries

Among the most neglected variables in current research on corporate governance is the role of reputational intermediaries and the structure of financial institutions. The reputational intermediaries are clearly quite important players in the system. They are assigned important tasks, especially in the diffusion model, but we lack analysis of the dynamics that cause them to carry these out well or badly.

As the countries of the world deal with their pension crises, the impact of the solutions will turn considerably on the character of the reputational intermediaries. Some structures encourage vigorous monitoring of managerial agency problems and defense of shareholder interests. Others do not. We know too little about this to understand the system well and to understand the policy issues in play.

The Plasticity of Preferences

Closely related is the role of "mediating" structures that link preferences interests and behavior. People's preferences are mediated by the way they understand what is happening. Those understandings are influenced by the mediating financial structures, and by processes that influence ideas: journalists and the economic press; academics and academic writing; political parties and political ideas; think tanks and foundations. All of these generate arguments about good and bad practice concerning regulation, accountability, markets, equality, prices, labor markets, international institutions, and so on. Here collaboration with sociologists would be particularly useful.

Conclusion: Fighting over the Governance Debate

The argument and evidence in this book provide us with ammunition to speculate on, and even forecast, implications of the corporate governance puzzle in several areas of both theoretical and practical interest. These include the idea of a race to the bottom (or race to the top) in terms of corporate governance venues, the validity and tightness of institutional complementarity, the risks and rewards of corporate governance "reform," the shifting role of the state in corporate governance regulation, and the contours of the rhetorical debate over corporate governance.

Race to the Bottom or Race to the Top?

Will the political jostling of shifting coalitions in country markets around the world, against a backdrop of increasing capital and corporate mobility, result in a race to the bottom or a race to the top in terms of shareholder protections?

Our sample countries suggest a race to the top in codes of conduct on behalf of stronger MSPs on a global scale. But actual practice in legislation, rules, enforcement, shareholding patterns, and actual governance practices remains quite varied and unclear. The incentives for enhanced shareholder protections tip countries towards competing for the "stars" of corporate governance rather than attracting a preponderance of "lemons,"[4] and thus to adopt pro-MSP concepts. But other variables enter into play and limit the application of these provisions.

Despite the twin drags of institutional complementarity and institutional inertia, the case of the Netherlands shows how this process of factor mobility can alter outcomes. Both investment capital and firms can migrate across borders if they are not satisfied with the status quo in domestic corporate governance. In the Netherlands, institutional investors such as ABP acquired significant amounts of funds due to the pension fund reforms of the 1980s, but their ability to seek enhanced minority shareholder protections was restricted by the ability of Netherlands managers and workers to foil regulatory changes in that direction—a classic case of resilience of a corporatist compromise equilibrium. In reaction, the investment funds deserted the Amsterdam Bourse en masse and switched their equity portfolios into markets when they got better protections.

Ironically, as domestic investors were fleeing offshore, other European companies were being attracted to Amsterdam listings in order to take advantage of the very same governance rules promoting managerial entrenchment that the investors despised. The most prominent case was Gucci, which switched its base of incorporation from Italy to the Netherlands in order to foil a takeover bid that would have enriched its minority shareholders but which threatened the benefits of control of the existing blockholders.

There are, of course, many more examples of firms migrating away from countries with relatively poor minority protections towards countries with better governance reputations. Many firms from developed markets cross-listed on U.S. or U.K. markets, such as those firms that issued ADRs in New York and London. In parallel, many firms from emerging markets did IPOs on the NASDAQ or cross-listed on the London or Hong Kong exchanges.

Although we noted the relative lack of enthusiasm of many blockholders for cross-listing, there were many examples that made the choice to "defect" from

[4] George Akerlof, "The Market for 'Lemons': Quality Uncertainty in the Market Mechanism," *Quarterly Journal of Economics* 84 (1970): 488–500.

their lower-MSP country to engage in these transactions. The controlling owners or managers of these firms were willing to bind themselves to the stricter governance protections in those listing markets in order to reap the higher price/earnings multiple in the share price that generally resulted; blockholders to make more money, and managers to make more advantageous acquisitions by stock purchases (or avoid being acquired themselves). Indeed, one of the primary motives for Brazil's creation of the Novo Mercado was to keep such "progressive" firms from deserting the São Paulo Exchange completely and listing in New York instead.

In this sense, the reputational intermediaries played a leading role. As investment capital becomes increasingly global and footloose, the stock exchanges in each country stand to gain from attracting the stars and the investment capital that buys into firms with superior corporate governance. Conversely, exchanges in countries whose corporate governance is substandard, such as the Netherlands, stand much to lose from the flight of both capital and listing firms.[5]

As countries with high MSP attract both firms and capital, their exchanges will benefit from the transactions income of higher trading, as well as the long-term benefits of deeper capital markets. Their exchanges will flourish; the immediate gains are concentrated upon the reputational intermediaries, while the long-term gains are widely distributed.

On the other hand, the well-established principle of "lemons" suggests that the costs of attracting mostly lemon firms, while the firms with higher MSP depart, are significant. The short-term losses will fall heavily upon the reputational intermediaries in those countries, whose income will shrivel as their capital markets become thinly traded and shallow; the market discounts assigned to "lemon-rich" markets will fall on all market participants in those countries. Even if the long-term losses are widely distributed, the short-term losses will be concentrated, and it is likely that the gains reaped by lemon firms are unlikely to offset the costs incurred by a shrinking financial sector.

This sequence—the pressure imposed by global funds upon country-level practices—is in essence the investor model. We see the logic of the mechanism, but stress that it is not automatic. Companies may change their practices if they desire. But regulations pass through the political system, and there convergence "up" may encounter resistance. It is likely to be fought by insider blockholders and players in the existing system who fear disruption of their embedded preferences.

Skeptics of our race-to-the-top conclusion may call attention to the United States example concerning competition among governance venues. U.S. firms can incorporate in any state, or shift their "headquarters" from state to state. This mobility may have led to an overall reduction of shareholder protections. *Managers did succeed in getting anti-takeover laws passed in many states, and then migrating their corporate headquarters from investor-friendly Delaware to more friendly venues such as Pennsylvania or Ohio.* State legislators who passed laws diminishing the protections for minority shareholders bore little of the cost from the reduced long-term attractiveness of those firms for investors, because, among other reasons,

[5] Coffee "2002a".

firms headquartered in their location still had the option of listing on U.S. capital markets in New York. The distinction between incorporation and capital markets is important here, as is the notion of concentration of costs and benefits.

State legislators who passed laws diminishing the protections for minority shareholders bore little compensating costs from the reduced long-term attractiveness of those firms for investors, among other reasons because firms headquartered in their location still had the option of listing on U.S. capital markets in New York.

Institutional Complementarity and "Reform"

Governance systems are embedded in a framework of related policies and practices. As many varieties-of-capitalism authors note, patterns of governance interact with practices in worker training, wage determination and price flexibility, employment protections, product-market competition, and exposure to trade. It may be hard to borrow pieces from one model and combine them in another.

How tight is the institutional complementarity that binds corporate governance choices to related institutional choices? Our country cases suggest that institutional complementarity can be quite strong in keeping various coalitional models in their ex ante equilibrium, even in the face of strong pressures that otherwise shift actors' preferences. Our country sample also suggests there may be more flexibility in corporate governance choices than the varieties-of-capitalism notion of strict institutional complementarity allows.

But there is a cautionary note for corporate governance "reformers." Several of our country cases suggest that reforms to corporate governance institutions, particularly in emerging markets, must be careful to deal with both agency and expropriation costs in balance. Governance institutions in complimentary "bundles" appear to interact with each other to mitigate, if not eliminate, both expropriation and agency costs.[6] Changing just one institution at a time, without examining the question of policy complementarity, may have undesirable effects.[7]

For example, efforts to reduce expropriation costs by improvements in NED oversight, in effect levying a heavy "tax on entrepreneurs," may blunt the ability of private blockholders to discipline managers.[8] The unintended consequences of these reforms can be soaring agency costs—with entrenched employee-managers now free to manage badly. Indeed, in the debate over corporate governance in some countries, calls to "professionalize" managers are often a code phrase for "reduce the influence of blockholders." Conversely, efforts to reduce agency costs—changes that open the door to free-for-all takeover contests—may result in high expropriation costs, as blockholders emerge to discipline (or expropriate)

---

[6] Ralph Heinrich, "Complementarities in Corporate Governance: A Survey of the Literature with Special Emphasis on Japan," Kiel Institute of World Economics Working Paper No. 947, 1999.

[7] Katharina Pistor, Martin Raiser, and Stanislaw Gelfer, "Legal Evolution and the Trans: Lessons from Corporate Law Development in Six Countries," unpublished paper, Berkowitz, Pistor, and Richard, 2003.

[8] Boards of directors, even NEDs, are vulnerable to capture by employee-managers.

employee-managers and, in the process, compensate themselves for these efforts at the expense of minority shareholders.[9]

Indeed, blockholding may have many merits, including effective control of managerial agency costs. Yet the investor model implies that blockholding will ultimately be replaced by more "efficient" systems of minority shareholder protections and low concentration.

We are less certain of this. In countries with weak regulation and capacity to enforce, blockholding can provide mechanisms for monitoring. It is difficult and time-consuming to build the ecology of complex laws and practices that are the scaffold of the transparency coalition of the Anglo-American model.

Operational efficiency and shareholding concentration are not necessarily linked. Blockholding firms may perform better at some aspects of a production system than others. Indeed, almost all startups, including the vaunted American high-tech giants such as Microsoft, Oracle, and Google, begin as blockheld firms.

Bringing the State Back In, Again

Our country cases debunk the notion that corporate governance reform is tantamount to deregulation. The role of the state does not necessarily shrink if countries move toward higher MSPs and greater diffusion. Instead it goes in different directions, including its corporate governance regulatory function, the governance choices made in privatizing SOEs, and—above all—the host of policy choices in pension plan structure and funding.

We have discussed at length the critical importance of reputational intermediaries in transmitting (or blocking) pressures for enhanced minority shareholder protections, and the difficulties inherent in effectively regulating these intermediaries. Regulatory capture is always a risk.

The state also plays a key role in governance through the privatization of state enterprises. The managers of privatized or corporatized state-owned firms (SOEs) tend to be more entrenched than managers in firms subject to contests for control. Residual state ownership, "golden shares," and other veto rights effectively insulate these firms from hostile (or even friendly) takeovers in most cases.

Moreover, SOE managers are often skilled at strengthening their "stakeholder" common cause with the SOE workforce, especially if that workforce is unionized and politically mobilized. Many of these firms occupy a commanding position in utilities or transportation, and they also exercise considerable leverage in the financial services sector because they constitute such a large percentage of the equity market cap, once their shares have been floated. Having blunted the forces of financial discipline by neutralizing the risk of contests for control, these employee-managers are likely to work even harder to blunt the forces of product-market

---

[9] Blockholders can expropriate employees by breaking implicit contracts on the sharing of the firm's "quasi rents," or simply by looting their pension funds (as in the Robert Maxwell scandal). See Margaret M. Blair, *Ownership and Control: Rethinking Corporate Governance for the Twenty-first Century* (Washington, D.C.: Brookings Institute Press, 1995).

competition, by resisting continued deregulation or vigorous competition policy that may reduce the rents collected by these SOEs.[10] Thus countries with substantial SOEs remain more likely to continue in the corporatist compromise box of our coalition categories.

As we have said repeatedly in this book, regulations regarding the structure and function of pension plans and mutual funds are a central issue of public policy, with enormous long-term consequences for equity markets generally and for corporate governance specifically. Pension plan regulations may turn out to be the tail that wags the corporate governance dog.

As households and firms assert more control over their pension assets, they will place even more pressure on pension fund managers to seek higher returns domestically and abroad. These changes in pension plans will mobilize a huge amount of previously passive savings into active equity investment, especially in Japan and the EU. Active equity investment leads to a more systematic use of the governance discount (or premium). This could lead to more active monitoring of managers. Or it could go the other way if the firms with the funds have an interest in colluding with managers, or if shareholding is concentrated among few people.

As these funds grow in importance, so will the arguments over how they should exercise their financial (and political) influence: to what end and within what regulatory parameters. For example, CalPERS is a hero institution to many shareholder activists for its leadership in demanding corporate governance transparency. Yet CalPERS is often criticized on Wall Street for using its power for political ends (such as helping unions or Democrat Party politicians) and for sacrificing beneficiaries' economic interest in favor of noneconomic "social ends" of interest to politicians (job bailouts, community development). Indeed, some left activists want pension funds to be used for social ends, such as "sustainable growth," and link shareholder power to that end. Other activists restrict their target to the better performance objective. Managers find it useful to undermine institutions like CalPERS that challenge their autonomy. Many hands will try to push and pull the pendulum of fund regulation in different directions.

Sharing the Gains from Globalization

There are very big stakes in the outcome of this push and pull, against the backdrop of huge sums of investment capital flowing from the developed to the developing world. Over the long run, economic globalization is an engine of vast wealth creation. As we have discussed several places in this book, there are clear winners in the flow of capital and goods across borders—owners of capital in developed countries earn higher returns, workers in developing countries earn higher wages—as

[10] The "grabbing hand" model developed by Shleifer and Vishny suggests that in many cases, politicians can extract as many private benefits from SOEs that are partially or even fully privatized as long as they can retain control over the profits of the firm through discretionary regulations. Depending on the degree to which corruption is tolerated, they will take these private benefits in cash or in terms of excess employment for favored unions or regions. Shleifer and Vishny 1999, 176–78.

well as losers, and the gains should, on average, exceed the loses by a considerable margin, or else globalization would grind to a halt. It shows no signs of doing so.

The wealth created by this more efficient combination of otherwise plentiful resources flows through business firms operating across and within national borders. Owners of capital in the developed world (including pensioners, households, and institutional investors) search for investment opportunities in the developing world, principally equities, preferably in liquid, traded firms, and one of the principal risks they face is the corporate governance of these firms. The magnitude of this MSP risk, how corporate governance changes over time, and how these choices are embedded in domestic political compromises—stable or fragile compromises—will dramatically affect the scale and the locus of globalization's creation of wealth and how it is shared by owners of capital and suppliers of labor.

As a result, the domestic political debate over governance rules in, say, Malaysia or Turkey does matter to the portfolio managers in Tokyo, London, or New York, although the speed of change in those rules in developing world capitals is far slower than the flickering urgency of trading room screens. We wish to underscore the fact that these global investors' partners in that potential gain are not the "crony capitalists" of the developing world, who will see a long-term reduction in their returns as financial globalization continues (as forecast by Stolper-Samuelson), but rather the entrepreneurs, managers, and workers of the developing world. This is the new political context of what we referred to earlier as the third phase (from 1975 until now) in our tripartite periodization of the history of corporate governance.

Rhetoric and the Corporate Governance "High Ground"

Our country cases suggest that it is the victorious political coalition that sets the terms of debate for corporate governance in each country. In corporate governance choices, as in other political contests, there is a drawn-out battle to control the terms of discourse as well as to control the policymaking machinery.

It is no small irony that in a book so focused on economic incentives, rational decision making, and an almost belligerent adherence to the methods of "positive policy economy," we end our story with a discussion of rhetoric and legitimacy. Discourse has an effect, so it becomes an object of contestation, a point made by economic sociologists.[11]

In the course of our research, we sifted through thousands of pages of argumentation over corporate governance choices in dozens of countries (and several languages). We were struck by the stubborn contention over terms. What does *corporate governance* really mean? Many gallons of ink were spilled over this definitional debate. In country after country, and seminar after seminar, we observed a great deal of elaborate rhetoric justifying current coalitional alignments, with

---

[11] See the discussion in chapter 4; Nicolas Véron, Matthieu Autret, and Alfred Galichon, *L'information financière en crise—Comptabilité et capitalisme* (Paris: Odile Jacob, 2004); and Schmidt 2002 on discourses.

the "winners" castigating the "losers," and the losers returning similar rhetorical salvos. Although we performed no systematic content analysis of these debates, we did observe several patterns.

For example, in countries where the political battle lines were drawn at the capital versus labor divide, the investor coalition defined corporate governance in terms of "meeting the challenge of financial globalization," adherence to the OECD *Principles*, fulfilling "international standards of governance in the global competition for capital." Conversely, from the labor power side, blockholders and foreign portfolio investors were castigated as selfish oligarchs in league with the heartless IMF and the faceless gnomes of Zurich.[12] In the corporatist compromise, managers and workers made much of their being in the "same boat" together, of corporate governance choices that ensured that firms "served the nation" in a "stable" economy—with owners dismissed as oligarchs or "speculators." Germany, the Netherlands, Sweden, and especially Japan witnessed much use of this rhetoric. In these countries, the notion of stakeholder (as opposed to shareholder) protections remains quite powerful in public discourse.

Strikingly, the oligarchs (if anyone would care to identify themselves as such) were relatively mute in the struggle to set the terms of discourse. Perhaps this is because oligarchical coalitions tend to set governance choices in authoritarian or early democracies, where the terms of debate don't matter so much. When oligarchs do condescend to issue political justifications for their governance preferences, they tend to borrow the rhetoric of the investor model. For example, Mikhail Khordokovsky frequently invoked the language of shareholder value and good corporate governance, drawing explicit analogies between the accountability of managers to shareholders and the accountability of heads of state to voters—at least until he was tossed into jail by an unamused Vladimir Putin.

Political debate in countries shifting between the transparency coalition and managerism alignment witnessed predictable invocations of corporate governance that protected "the little guy," the "individual investor," the "widow and orphans." Almost every governance speech by SEC commissioners in the United States invokes this mantra. Governance writers from Berle and Means to Monks and Minow have warned darkly of the dangers of managerial entrenchment and managerial enrichment. Journalists delight in combining this rhetoric with splashy images of managerial excess and duplicity.

Meanwhile, across the alignment divide, managers compete to hijack the notion of corporate governance for their own purposes. Few quarterly earnings announcements or analysts' teleconferences in Wall Street, London, or other financial capitals fail to invoke the mantra of "building shareholder value"—even in Japan. Professional managers from countries as diverse as France and South Korea rapidly adopted the notion of shareholder value as the justification for professional autonomy from the meddling of blockholders and workers alike—particularly managers of quasi-privatized SOEs. "Building shareholder value" was among Jean-Paul

---

[12] There was particularly colorful use of this sort of rhetoric in Brazil's presidential election in November 2002, in which populist Luiz Inacio (Lula) da Silva was the victor.

Messier's favorite terms, even as he ran Vivendi into the ground. Many speak of an "investor class" as if this were a unified whole, rather than a fragmented group with quite heterogeneous, often conflicting goals. Shareholder value is partly about efficiency. But there are serious issues of distribution at stake—job security, income inequality, social welfare. There may be many ways to organize an efficient firm.

Market Efficiency and Political Rhetoric

We do not take sides in these rhetorical debates, but we do note a troubling inconsistency in the to-and-fro pattern, a certain reluctance to face the political facts of corporate governance arrangements, by all three actors in our model—owners, managers, and workers.

For example, when managers fail to perform and make money for the shareholders, these managers often embrace broader rhetorical notions of accountability, ranging from employment stability to "sustainable" management, to "serving our stakeholders" rather than mere investors. But when presented with efforts to change the rules of corporate governance to make them more accountable to strictly profit-making definitions of responsibility to the shareholders, these same managers go the other way, embracing narrow rhetorical notions of corporate governance as a strictly economic function—suggesting that governance reforms risk "politicizing" the way firms are run, and thereby open the door to rent-seeking lawyers, bureaucratic meddling, and "populist" forces interested in social agendas, not profit. Blockholders, shareholder groups, and workers and their unions are not above a certain sleight-of-hand in distinguishing between market efficiency and political processes, selecting the ground of the debate over corporate governance with more expediency than consistency.

Settling which forms of corporate governance function most efficiently in economic terms, and with what social effects and political externalities, is beyond the scope of this book, however important that assessment is. But in this book we would like to underline the point that the terms of corporate governance decisions are an explicit political outcome, albeit with important efficiency and other market effects. Corporate governance rules have distributional effects in addition to efficiency ones. Both those who support and those who oppose corporate governance reforms—and those who merely wish to make money along the way—should be, we think, intently aware of the political machinery by which institutional choices are debated and set.

Data Appendix

THIS APPENDIX PROVIDES background support for the data we have used in the book. We plan as well to post the data on a website that can be accessed by other authors.

Like all the researchers in this field, we face substantial challenges in gathering reliable data for all our questions. Again like all the researchers, we rely heavily on the work of others to construct indicators for pivotal measurements such as the MSP index in chapter 3 and the institutional indicator in chapter 4.

We combine data series from several different areas.

- Microeconomic, firm-level data, such as blockholding/diffusion and minority shareholder protections, aggregated to a country level.
- Macroeconomic country variables such as GDP per capita and implicit pension debt, and with
- Country-level political science variables such as indices of political cohesion or left-right alignment.

We have limited our data analysis to straightforward tests such as measurements of dispersion, correlation, and a small number of linear bivariate regressions. Our goal was to perform first-order tests of our hypotheses for the limited sample of countries for which the data was available; we look to future researchers to refine these tests, add new data sources to both the country-specific and cross-country samples, and generally poke holes in our arguments.

We did not insert controls or run additional tests for problems such as collinearity. We are modest in the strength of our assertions of statistical causality between any two sets of data; many of these relationships are endogenous, likely via multiple paths.

Gathering the data sets in a common format for our country sample was remarkably time-consuming, and drew on a wide variety of primary sources, as shown in appendix table 1.

The maximum sample size for our tests was 39 countries; though clearly a subset of all possible countries, these 39 countries cumulatively accounted for 99.5 percent of the global stock market capitalization, measured according to MSCI weights. In other words, we had data on virtually all of the global stock market, across a broad range of income levels, from every continent except Antarctica.

In table 2.1, as noted in the text, we used a variety of studies to compile an index of blockholding for the whole sample. The two right-hand columns in appendix table 2 note the value and source used for our ownership concentration data set; the logic behind these choices is discussed in chapter 2.

Table A.1
Observations and Dispersion

Variable	Observations	Mean	SD	Min	Max
Blockholding	39	46.9	19.4	4.1	90
Minority shareholder protections	39	45.6	19.6	11	97
GDP per capita	39	16681	12085	480	42320
Market capitalization to GDP (%)	39	96.4	80.7	6.7	377
Index of political cohesion	38	0.77	0.58	0	2
Duration of political system	38	33.3	21	4.4	57
Cusack left-right placement (60–96)	16	3.2	0.6	2.2	4
Job security	16	10	5.6	1	21
Implicit pension debt (% GDP)	26	–115.9	75.2	–330	6
Retirement assets to GDP	37	38.5	39	0	127
Pension assets in domestic equities	38	8.4	13.2	0	56.1
Foreign portfolio investors penetration	34	23.3	17.5	3	69.6
Nonexecutive directors	39	19.3	18.3	0	70
Information	39	60.7	16.6	25	89
Oversight	39	27.6	26.2	0	100
Control (La Porta et al.)	39	60.5	28.1	0	100
Incentive	39	33.4	31.6	0	100

In table 3.1, the MSP indices and data on both blockholding and market capitalization covered the full 39-country sample. We discuss the multiple sources of potential estimation error and subjectivity of some of these indices in chapter 2. Our index of MSP draws heavily on work done by the La Porta et al. consortium; though we factor in additional measurements of board independence and executive compensation, the two MSP indices have a correlation of .89.

We were able to obtain data on pension assets on 37 countries, estimates of foreign investor penetration for 34 countries, and estimates of IPD to GDP for 26 countries (shown as tables 7.2, 5.1, and 7.1 in the text). IPD is based on fairly complex calculations performed under the auspices of the OECD, the World Bank, and independent scholars; some of these IPD estimates used different assumptions such as asset rates of return and so they are not strictly comparable.

The data sets of political cohesion and political system duration we obtained for 38 of the countries (Tables 4.2 and A.8). Estimates of left-right placement and job security (tables 5.4 and A.14 by the OECD) were available for only 16 countries.

Table A.2
Data on Ownership Concentration

	World Bank Block holding	La Porta et al. Large	La Porta et al. Medium	Barca and Becht Block holding	Faccio and Lang Block holding	Our Index[a]	Source
Argentina		65	80			72.5	La Porta et al. 1999
Australia		5	50	26		27.5	La Porta et al. 1999
Austria		15	17		52.8	52.8	Faccio and Lang 2002
Belgium		50	40	15	51.5	51.5	Faccio and Lang 2002
Brazil		63				63	La Porta et al. 1999
Canada		25	30			27.5	La Porta et al. 1999
Chile		38				90	Lafort and Walker 1999
China						5	Lin 2000
Denmark		35	40			37.5	La Porta et al. 1999
Finland		10	20		48.8	48.8	Faccio and Lang 2002
France		20	50	30	64.8	64.8	Faccio and Lang 2002
Germany		10	40	26.9	64.6	64.6	Faccio and Lang 2002
Greece		50	100			75	La Porta et al. 1999
Hong Kong	71.5	70	90			71.5	World Bank
India		43				43	La Porta et al. 1999
Indonesia	67.3	62				67.3	World Bank
Ireland		10	13		24.6	24.6	Faccio and Lang 2002
Israel		50	60			55	La Porta et al. 1999
Italy		15	60	20	59.6	59.6	Faccio and Lang 2002
Japan	4.1	5	10			4.1	World Bank
Malaysia	42.6	52				42.6	World Bank
Mexico		67				66	La Porta et al. 1999
Netherlands		20	20	9		20	La Porta et al. 1999

TABLE A.2 (continued)

	World Bank Block holding	La Porta et al. Large	La Porta et al. Medium	Barca and Becht Block holding	Faccio and Lang Block holding	Our Index[a]	Source
New Zealand		25	29			27	La Porta et al. 1999
Norway		25	40		38.55	38.6	Faccio and Lang 2002
Philippines	46.4	51				46.4	World Bank
Portugal		45	50		60.3	60.3	Faccio and Lang 2002
Singapore	44.8	30	40			44.8	World Bank
South Africa		52				52	La Porta et al. 1999
South Korea	24.6	20	50			31.8	Jang 2002, table 10
Spain		15	30	16	55.8	55.8	Faccio and Lang 2002
Sweden		45	60	62	46.9	46.9	Faccio and Lang 2002
Switzerland		30	50		48.1	48.1	Faccio and Lang 2002
Taiwan	45.5	14				45.5	World Bank
Thailand	51.9	48				51.9	World Bank
Turkey		58				58	La Porta et al. 1999
United Kingdom		0	40	5.2	23.6	23.6	Faccio and Lang 2002
United States		20	10			15	La Porta et al. 1999
Venezuela		49				49	La Porta et al. 1999

Source: World Bank; La Porta et al. 1999; Claessens et al. for World Bank, 2,980 public corporations in 9 countries; Barca and Becht 2001; Faccio and Lang 2002, 5,232 listed firms; La Porta et al. 1999, 20 largest firms for "large," 10 largest "small" firms for large.

[a] Table 2.1 presents this index in order of concentration.

TABLE A.3
Table 2.2 Country Variation

	1913	1929	1938	1950	1960	1970	1980	1990	1999
Argentina	0.17				0.05	0.03	0.11		0.15
Australia	0.39	0.50	0.91	0.75	0.94	0.76	0.38	0.37	1.13
Austria	0.76					0.09	0.03	0.17	0.17
Belgium	0.99	1.31			0.32	0.23	0.09	0.31	0.82
Brazil	0.25						0.05	0.08	0.45
Canada	0.74		1.00	0.57	1.59	1.75	0.46	1.22	1.22
Chile	0.17				0.12	0.00	0.34	0.50	1.05
Cuba	2.19								
Denmark	0.36	0.17	0.25	0.10	0.14	0.17	0.09	0.67	0.67
Egypt	1.09				0.16		0.01	0.06	0.29
France	0.78		0.19	0.08	0.28	0.16	0.09	0.24	1.17
Germany	0.44	0.35	0.18	0.15	0.35	0.16	0.09	0.20	0.67
India	0.02	0.07	0.07	0.07	0.07	0.06	0.05	0.16	0.46
Italy	0.17	0.23	0.26	0.07	0.42	0.14	0.07	0.13	0.68
Japan	0.49	1.20	1.81	0.05	0.36	0.23	0.33	1.64	0.95
Netherlands	0.56		0.74	0.25	0.67	0.42	0.19	0.50	2.03
Norway	0.16	0.22	0.18	0.21	0.26	0.23	0.54	0.23	0.70
Russia	0.18								0.11
South Africa				0.68	0.91	1.97	1.23	1.33	1.20
Spain							0.17	0.41	0.69
Sweden	0.47	0.41	0.30	0.18	0.24	0.14	0.11	0.39	1.77
Switzerland	0.58					0.50	0.44	1.93	3.23
United Kingdom	1.09	1.03	1.92	0.86	1.15	1.99	0.38	0.81	2.25
United States	0.39	0.75	0.56	0.33	0.61	0.66	0.46	0.54	1.52

Source: Rajan and Zingales 2003, table 3.
Note: Table 2.2 contains a summary of several country findings; this is the complete table.

TABLE A.4
Figure 3.3 Correlation between Blockholding and Shareholder Protections

	Minority Shareholder Protection		
	Whole Sample	Developed Countries	Developing Countries
Blockholding	−.2467	−.4283**	.3042
Significance ($p > t$)	(0.13)	(0.03)	(0.29)
Number of observations	39	25	14

The table shows that although the sample as a whole shows a negative correlation between block-holding and MSP, the relation is actually reversed depending upon the income level of the country. The key observation is the one in the middle, showing a −.42 correlation between MSP and block-holding for the developed countries, which account for most of the value of the global stock markets.
**$p < .05$.

TABLE A.4A
Descriptive Statistics for Developed Countries (GDP per capita
>$10,000)

Obs	Mean	SD	Min	Max
25	43.62	18.52	4.1	75
25	49.76	20.42	24	97

TABLE A.4B
Descriptive Statistics for Developing Countries (GDP per capita
≤ $10,000)

Observations	Mean	SD	Min	Max
14	52.75	20.13	5	90
14	38.07	16.14	11	67

TABLE A.5
Figure 3.3 Correlation between Blockholding and Shareholder
Protections (20 countries)

	Minority Shareholder Protection
Blockholding	−0.5551**
Significance ($p>t$)	(0.01)
Number of observations	20

$**p<.05.$

TABLE A.6
Figure 3.3: Linear Regression: Shareholder Protections
on Blockholding

Dependent Variable	Minority Shareholder Protection
Blockholding	−0.25
	(016)
Constant	57.28***
	(8.17)
Number of observations	39
$F(1, 37)$	2.4
$Prob>F$	0.13
R^2	0.0609
Adj. R^2	0.0355
Root MSE	19.262

$***p<.01.$

TABLE A.7

Table 4.5 Correlation of Political Cohesion with Blockholding and Minority
Shareholder Protections

| | Modified Index of Political Cohesion | | |
	All	Developed Countries	Developing Countries
Blockholding	0.2043	0.3437	0.2618
Significance	(0.22)	(0.10)	(0.37)
MSP	−0.1654	−0.4617**	0.3317
Significance	(0.32)	(0.02)	(0.25)
Observations	38[a]	24	14

[a] No data for Hong Kong.
**$p < .05$.

TABLE A.8

Table 4.6 Linear Regression: Blockholding and MSP on Political Cohesion

Dependent Variable	MSP	Blockholding
Modified Index of Political Cohesion	−11.3**	12.12**
	(5.04)	(5.02)
Duration of Political System	0.5***	−0.47***
	(0.14)	(0.14)
Constant	36.9***	52.57***
	(5.72)	(5.69)
Number of observations	38[a]	38[a]
$F(2, 35)$	7.25	6.82
Prob > F	0.0023	0.0032
R^2	0.293	0.2804
Adj. R^2	0.2526	0.2393
Root MSE	16.82	16.74

[a] No data for Hong Kong.
**$p > .05$.   ***$p < .01$.

TABLE A.9

Table 4.7: Correlation of Political Cohesion and Private Pension Assets

	Private Pension Assets (% GDP)
Modified index of political cohesion	0.08
Significance	(0.65)
Number of observations	36

Note: The index of political cohesion used here is a recoding of the Beck et al. 2001 material, done to measure our definition of veto players. We recoded the instances of minority parliamentary government from 3 to 1, i.e., from the highest score on the list, to the same score as two-party parliamentary government) The justification for this is that though minority governments are forced to find support from other parties in order to get legislation passed, they have the ability to shop around for that support, and usually only need one other party to get things through. Thus, they are coded by us as equivalent to two party government (IPCOH = 1), rather than multiparty (IPCOH = 2), or even higher as they had initially been (IPCOH = 3).There are several other potential variables from the Beck DPI database that we probed for use as a measure of consensus or majoritarian institutions, including type of election, political fractionalization, and so forth. We believe that the measure of veto players captured by our index is the most effective measure.

TABLE A.10

Figure 5.1 Correlation between Minority Shareholder Protections with Market Capitalization, Foreign Portfolio Investors (FPI) Penetration, Retirement Assets to GDP

	Market Capitalization	FPI Penetration	Retirement Assets
MSP	0.45***	−0.08	0.57***
Significance ($p > t$)	(0.00)	(0.64)	(0.00)
Observations	39	34[a]	37[b]

Note: The table explains the data analysis of correlation coefficient.
[a] No data available for Indonesia, Ireland, Malaysia, Mexico, and the Philippines.
[b] No data available for Turkey and Venezuela.
***$p < .01$.

TABLE A.11

Table 5.6 Linear Regression: Minority Shareholder Protections on Market Capitalization/GDP (%)

Dependent Variable	MSP
Market Capitalization	0.11***
	(0.04)
Constant	35.04***
	(4.47)
Number of observations	39
$F(1, 37)$	9.35
Prob. > F	0.0041
R^2	0.2017
Adj. R^2	0.1801
Root MSE	17.759

***$p < .01$.

TABLE A.12

Table 5.7 Linear Regression Minority Shareholder
Protections on Retirement Assets/GDP (%)

Dependent Variable	MSP
Retirement assets	0.29***
	(0.07)
Constant	35.27***
	(3.85)
Number of observations	37[a]
$F(1, 37)$	16.41
Prob. > F	0.0003
R^2	0.3192
Adj. R^2	0.2997
Root MSE	16.542

[a] No data available for Turkey and Venezuela.
***$p < .01$.

TABLE A.13

Table 5.8 Correlation between Blockholding and Minority
Shareholder Protections with Employment Security Rules

	Blockholding	MSP
Job security	0.73***	−0.73***
Significance ($p > t$)	(0.00)	(0.00)
Number of observations	16	16

***$p < .01$.

TABLE A.14

Table 5.9 Linear Regression Coefficients

Dependent Variable	Blockholding	MSP
Job security	2.35***	−2.73***
	(0.59)	(0.69)
Constant	15.94**	76.13***
	(6.75)	(7.81)
Number of observations	16	16
$F(1, 14)$	15.71	15.83
Prob. > F	0.0014	0.0014
R^2	0.5288	0.5306
Adj. R^2	0.4951	0.4971
Root MSE	12.959	14.981

**$p < .05$ ***$p < .01$.

Table 5.10 Correlation between Blockholding and Shareholder Protections with Income Inequality (GINI)

	MSP	Blockholding
GINI coefficient	0.61**	−0.46*
Significance (p>t)	(0.01)	(0.07)
Number of observations	16	16

*p<.10   **p<.05.

TABLE A.16

Country Descriptive Statistics for Chapter 6

	Blockholding	MSP	IPD (% GDP)	Retirement Assets (% GDP)	Foreign Investors Penetration
China	5.0	11.0		0.0	4.0
Germany	64.6	33.0	−138.0	16.0	23.6
Japan	4.1	37.0	−70.0	41.0	17.4
Malaysia	42.6	67.0		54.0	
Netherlands	20.0	36.0	−54.0	113.0	54.7
Singapore	44.8	84.0		61.0	10.0
South Korea	31.8	37.0	−33.0	13.0	21.1
Sweden	46.9	46.0	−132.0	41.0	32.5
Whole Sample					
Mean	46.9	45.6	−115.9	38.5	23.3
SD	19.4	19.6	75.2	39.0	17.5
Min	4.1	11.0	−330.0	0.0	3.0
Max	90.0	97.0	6.0	127.0	69.6

TABLE A.17

Table 6.2 Corporate Governance and Corporatism: Correlation
Coefficients

	Minority Shareholder Protection (MSP)	Ownership Concentration
H-K corporatism score	−0.7662***	0.4408*
Employer centralization	−0.6187***	0.4735**
Employer coordination	−0.6241***	0.4854**
Enterprise cooperation	−0.7529***	0.4530*
Union density/centralization	−0.3914	0.2552
Bargaining	−0.4675*	0.2962

Note: n = 18 (n = 20 for Coordination).
*p<.10   **p<.05   ***p<.01

Table A.18
Table 6.3 Corporatism: Correlation Coefficients

	H-K Corporatism Score	Centralization of Collective Bargaining	Employer Centralization	Employer Coordination	Enterprise Cooperation
Centralization of collective bargaining	0.6027***				
Employer centralization	0.7465***	0.5765**			
Employer coordination	0.9021***	0.4611*	0.6801***		
Enterprise cooperation	0.7987***	0.4326*	0.5674**	0.6618**	
Union density centralization	0.6504***	0.6294**	0.4959**	0.5290**	0.3073

Note: n = 18.
*p < .10   **p < .05   ***p < .01.

Table A.19
Table 6.4: Bivariate Regression Results (OLS)

	Shareholder Protection	Blockholding
Hicks-Kenworthy corporatism score	−44.89***	22.33*
	(9.41)	(11.37)
Constant	73.27***	26.45***
	(5.79)	(7.00)
$F(1, 16)$	22.74	3.86
Prob. > F	0.0002	0.0671
R^2	0.587	0.1943
Adj. R^2	0.5612	0.144
Root MSE	13.553	16.371

Note: n = 18; Portugal and Spain are missing.
*p < .10   ***p < .01.

Table A.20
Table 6.5: Multivariate Regression Results (OLS)

	Shareholder Protection	Blockholding
Employer centralization	−2.80	7.23
	(6.39)	(7.71)
Union density/centralization	4.67	−1.31
	(5.47)	(6.61)
Hicks-Kenworthy corporatism score	−47.22**	11.94
	(16.76)	(20.24)
Constant	74.35***	31.97***
	(9.28)	(11.21)
$F(1, 16)$	7.37	1.5
Prob. $> F$	0.0034	0.2572
R^2	0.6122	0.2435
Adj. R^2	0.5291	0.0814
Root MSE	14.041	16.959

Note: $n = 18$.
**$p < .05$ ***$p < .01$.

Table A.21
Table 6.6 Bivariate Regression Results (OLS)

	Shareholder Protection	Blockholding
Employer centralization	−15.79***	10.45**
	(5.01)	(4.86)
Constant	49.84***	38.17***
	(3.91)	(3.79)
$F(1, 16)$	9.92	4.62
Prob. $> F$	0.0062	0.0472
R^2	0.3828	0.2242
Adj. R^2	0.3442	0.1757
Root MSE	16.57	16.065

Note: $n = 18$.
**$p < .05$ ***$p < .01$.

TABLE A.22
Table 6.7 Bivariate Regression Results (OLS)

	Shareholder Protection	Blockholding
Employer coordination	−12.45***	8.38**
	(3.90)	(3.77)
Constant	50.22***	37.92***
	(3.88)	(3.76)
Number of obs	18	18
$F(1, 16)$	10.21	4.93
Prob. > F	0.0056	0.0412
R^2	0.3895	0.2356
Adj. R^2	0.3513	0.1878
Root MSE	16.479	15.946

Note: $n = 18$.
**$p < .05$ ***$p < .01$.

TABLE A.23
Table 6.8 Bivariate Regression Results (OLS)

	Shareholder Protection	Blockholding
Enterprise cooperation	−17.85***	9.29**
	(3.90)	(4.57)
Constant	50.21***	37.92***
	(3.27)	(3.83)
$F(1, 16)$	20.94	4.13
Prob. > F	0.0003	0.0591
R^2	0.5669	0.2052
Adj. R^2	0.5398	0.1555
Root MSE	13.881	16.261

Note: $n = 18$.
*$p < .10$ ***$p < .01$.

TABLE A.24
Table 6.9 Bivariate Regression Results (OLS)

	Shareholder Protection	Blockholding
Centralization of Collective Bargaining	−10.77**	5.90
	(5.09)	(4.76)
Constant	51.22***	37.37***
	(4.42)	(4.13)
$F(1, 16)$	4.47	1.54
Prob. > F	0.0504	0.2327
R^2	0.2185	0.0877
Adj. R^2	0.1697	0.0307
Root MSE	18.644	17.421

Note: $n = 18$.
**$p < .05$ ***$p < .01$.

TABLE A.25
Table 6.10 Bivariate Regression Results (OLS)

	Shareholder Protection	Blockholding
Union density/centralization	−9.77	5.51
	(5.74)	(5.22)
Constant	50.32***	37.86***
	(4.57)	(4.16)
$F(1, 16)$	2.89	1.11
Prob. > F	0.1082	0.3068
R^2	0.1532	0.0651
Adj. R^2	0.1003	0.0067
Root MSE	19.408	17.635

Note: $n = 18$.
***$p < .01$.

TABLE A.26
Country Descriptive Statistics for Chapter 7

	Blockholding	MSP	IPD (% GDP)	Retirement Assets (% GDP)	Foreign Investors Penetration
Chile	90.0	54.0		57.0	7.8
France	64.8	52.0	−102.0	16.0	36.1
United Kingdom	23.6	74.0	−24.0	102.0	35.0
United States	15.0	97.0	−23.0	103.0	10.8
Whole Sample					
Mean	46.9	45.6	−115.9	38.5	23.3
SD	19.4	19.6	75.2	39.0	17.5
Min	4.1	11.0	−330.0	0.0	3.0
Max	90.0	97.0	6.0	127.0	69.6

TABLE A.27
IPD Distribution

	n	Mean	SD	Min	Max
Developed	20	119	67	245	6
Emerging	6	134	102	330	37
Total	26	115	75	330	6

Note: See also table 7.1.

TABLE A.28
Distribution of Pillar 2 and 3 Assets

	n	Mean	SD	Min	Max
Developed	25	47	42	1	127
Emerging	12	20	26	0	76
Total	37	38	38	0	127

Note: See also table 7.2.

TABLE A.29
Figure 7.1 Correlation between Blockholding and Minority
Shareholder Protections with Implicit Pension Fund
Deficit (IPD)

	Blockholding	MSP
IPD (% GDP)	0.43**	−0.39**
Significance ($p > t$)	(0.03)	(0.05)
Observations	26	26

TABLE A.30
Figure 7.1 Linear Regression Coefficients

Dependent Variable	Blockholding	MSP
IPD (% GDP)	0.11***	−0.10**
	(0.05)	(0.05)
Constant	32.22***	56.49***
	(6.48)	(6.69)
$F(1, 14)$	5.56	4.37
Prob. > F	0.0269	0.0473
R^2	0.188	0.1541
Adj. R^2	0.1542	0.1188
Root MSE	17.74	18.308

Note: $n = 26$.
**$p < .05$ ***$p < .01$.

TABLE A.31
Figure 7.2 Correlation between Shareholder Protection
and Private Pension Assets (% GDP)

	MSP
Private Pension Assets (% GDP)	0.56***
Significance ($p>t$)	(0.00)
Number of observations	37

***$p<.01$.

TABLE A.32
Figure 7.2 Linear Regression Coefficients

Dependent Variable	MSP	
Private pension assets (% GDP)	0.29***	
	(0.07)	
Pension assets in domestic equities (% GDP)		0.92***
		(0.20)
Constant	35.27***	37.93***
	(3.85)	(3.08)
Number of observations	37[a]	38[b]
$F(1, 35)$	16.41	21.58
Prob.$>F$	0.0003	0
R^2	0.3192	0.3747
Adj. R^2	0.2997	0.3574
Root MSE	16.542	15.922

[a] No data for Turkey and Venezuela.
[b] No data for Venezuela.
***$p<.01$.

BIBLIOGRAPHY

"Accounting Standards to Be Set by Private Institution." 2000. *Nihon Keizai Shimbun*, April 3.

Acemoglu, Daron, Simon Johnson, and James Robinson. 2004. "Institutions as the Fundamental Cause of Long-Run Growth." NBER Working Paper No. 10481.

Adler, Emanuel, and Peter Haas. 1992. "Conclusion: Epistemic Communities, World Order, and the Creation of a Reflective Research Program." *International Organization* 46:367–90.

Adolfsson, Petra, Urban Ask, Ulrika Holmberg, and Sten Jönsson. 1999. "Corporate Governance in Sweden: A Literature Review." Report submitted to the European Commission.

Agnblad, Jonas, Erik Berglöf, Peter Högfeldt, and Helena Svancar. 2001. "Ownership and Control in Sweden: Strong Owners, Weak Minorities, and Social Control." In *The Control of Corporate Europe*. Fabrizio Barca and Marco Brecht, eds. New York: Oxford University Press.

Agosin, Manuel, and Ernesto Pastén. 1999. "Corporate Governance in Chile." Paper for the OECD Development Center, April.

———. 2003. "Corporate Governance in Chile." Central Bank of Chile Working Paper No. 209.

Aguilera, Ruth, and Michal Federowicz. 2003. *Corporate Governance in a Changing Economic and Political Environment: Trajectories of Institutional Change on the European Continent*. London: Palgrave Macmillan.

Aguilera, Ruth, and Gregory Jackson. 2002. "Institutional Changes in European Corporate Governance." *Economic Sociology* 3:17–26.

———. 2003. "The Cross-National Diversity of Corporate Governance: Dimensions and Determinants." *Academy of Management Review* 28:447–65.

Akerlof, George. 1970. "The Market for 'Lemons': Quality Uncertainty in the Market Mechanism." *Quarterly Journal of Economics* 84:488–500.

Albert, Michel. 1993. *Capitalism vs. Capitalism: How America's Obsession with Individual Achievement and Short-Term Profit Has Led It to the Brink of Collapse*. Paul Haviland, trans. New York: Four Walls Eight Windows.

Alchian, Armen A., and Harold Demsetz. 1972. "Production, Information Costs, and Economic Organization." *American Economic Review* 62:777–95.

Amable, Bruno. 2000. "Institutional Complementarity and Diversity of Social Systems of Innovation and Production." *Review of International Political Economy* 7:645–87.

Amable, Bruno, Ekkehard Ernst, and Stefano Palombarini. 2001. "How Do Financial Markets Affect Industrial Relations: An Institutional Complementarity Approach." Unpublished manuscript.

Aoki, Masahiko. 1990. "Toward an Economic Model of the Japanese Firm." *Journal of Economic Literature* 28:1–27.

———. 1994. "The Japanese Firm as a System of Attributes: A Survey and Research Agenda." In *The Japanese Firm: Sources of Competitive Strength*. Masahiko Aoki and Ronald Dore, eds. Oxford: Clarendon Press.

———. 2001. *Information, Corporate Governance, and Institutional Diversity: Competitiveness in Japan, the USA, and the Transitional Economies*. Stacey Jehlik, trans. New York: Oxford University Press.

Aoki, Masahiko, and Hugh Patrick. 1995. *The Japanese Main Bank System: Its Relevance for Developing and Transforming Economies*. New York: Oxford University Press.

Armour, John, Brian Cheffins, and David A. Skeel Jr. 2002. "Corporate Ownership Structure and the Evolution of Bankruptcy Law: Lessons from the UK." *Vanderbilt Law Review* 55:1699–1785.

Barca, Fabrizio, and Marco Becht, eds. 2001. *The Control of Corporate Europe*. New York: Oxford University Press.

Bebchuk, Lucian Arye, Jesse M. Fried, and David I. Walker. 2002. "Managerial Power and Rent Extraction in the Design of Executive Compensation." NBER Working Paper No. 9068.

Bébéar, Claude, and Philippe Manière. 2003. *Ils vont tuer le capitalisme*. Paris: Plon.

Becht, Marco, Patrick Bolton, and Ailsa A. Roell. 2002. "Corporate Governance and Control." European Corporate Governance Institute Finance Working Paper No. 02/2002.

Becht, Marco, and J. Bradford DeLong. Forthcoming. "Why Has There Been So Little Blockholding in America?" In *The History of Corporate Governance around the World: Family Business Groups to Professional Managers*. Randall Morck, ed. Chicago: University of Chicago Press.

Beck, Thorsten, George Clarke, Alberto Groff, Philip Keefer, and Patrick Walsh. 2001. "New Tools in Comparative Political Economy: The Database of Political Institutions." *World Bank Economic Review* 15:165–76.

Becker, Gary. 1968. "Crime and Punishment: An Economic Approach." *Journal of Political Economy* 76:169–217.

Beer, Samuel H. 1965. *British Politics in the Collectivist Age*. New York: Knopf.

Berle, Adolf A., and Gardiner C. Means. 1932. *The Modern Corporation and Private Property*. New York: Commerce Clearing House.

Berger, Suzanne. 2003. *The First Globalization: Lessons from the French*. Paris: Seuil.

Berger, Suzanne, Michael Dertouzos, Richard Lester, and Robert Solow. 1989. "Toward a New Industrial America." *Scientific American* 260:39–47.

Berglöf, Erik, and Ernst-Ludwig von Thadden. 1999. "The Changing Corporate Governance Paradigm: Implications for Transition and Developing Countries." William Davidson Institute Working Paper No. 263.

Berkowitz, Daniel, Katharina Pistor, and Jean-Francois Richard. 2003. "Economic Development, Legality, and the Transplant Effect." *European Economic Review* 47:165–95.

Berle, Adolf A., and Gardiner C. Means. 1932. *The Modern Corporation and Private Property*. New York: Commerce Clearing House.

Besanger, Serge, Nicolas Mottis, and Jean-Pierre Ponsard. 2001. "Value Based Management and the Corporate Profit Centre." *European Business Forum* 8:41–47.

Black, Bernard. 1999. "Creating Strong Stock Markets by Protecting Outside Shareholders." Paper prepared for the OECD Conference on Corporate Governance in Asia: A Comparative Perspective, March 3–5, Seoul.

———. 2001a. "Does Corporate Governance Matter? A Crude Test Using Russian Data." *University of Pennsylvania Law Review* 149:2131–50.

———. 2001b. "The Corporate Governance Behavior and Market Value of Russian Firms." *Emerging Markets Review* 2:89–108.

———. 2001c. "The Legal and Institutional Preconditions for Strong Securities Markets." *UCLA Law Review* 48:781–855.

Black, Bernard, and John C. Coffee. 1994. "Hail Britannia? Institutional Investor Behavior under Limited Regulation. *Michigan Law Review* 92:1997–2087.

Black, Bernard, Hasung Jang, and Woochan Kim. 2003. "Does Corporate Governance Affect Firms' Market Value? Evidence from Korea." Stanford Law and Economics Olin Working Paper No. 237.

Black, Bernard, Reinier Kraakmann, and Anna Tarassova. 2000. "Russian Privatization and Corporate Governance: What Went Wrong?" *Stanford Law Review* 52:1731–1808.

Black, Bernard, and Anna Tarassova. Forthcoming. "Beyond Privatization: Institutional Reform in Transition: A Case Study of Russia." In *The Ecology of Corporate Governance: The East Asian Experience*. Thomas Heller and Lawrence Liu, eds.

Blair, Margaret M. 1995. *Ownership and Control: Rethinking Corporate Governance for the Twenty-first Century*. Washington, D.C.: Brookings Institute Press.

———. 2003. "Post-Enron Reflections on Comparative Corporate Governance." *Journal of Interdisciplinary Economics* 14:113–24.

Blair, Margaret M., and Mark J. Roe, eds. 1999. *Employees and Corporate Governance*. Washington, D.C.: Brookings Institution Press.

Blancet, Didier, and Florence Legros. 2002. "France: The Difficult Path to Consensual Reforms." In *Social Security Reform in Europe*. Martin Feldstein and Horst Siebert, eds. Chicago: University of Chicago Press.

Blasi, Joseph, Maya Kroumova, and Douglas Kruse. 1997. *Kremlin Capitalism: The Privatization of the Russian Economy*. Ithaca, N.Y.: ILR Press/Cornell University Press.

Blasi, Joseph, Douglas Kruse, and Aaron Bernstein, eds. 2003. *In the Company of Owners: The Truth about Stock Options (and Why Every Employee Should Have Them)*. New York: Basic Books.

Bonoli, Guiliano. 2000. *The Politics of Pension Reform: Institutions and Policy Change in Western Europe*. New York: Cambridge University Press.

Botero, Juan C., Simeon Djankov, Rafael La Porta, Florencio López-de-Silanes, and Andrei Shleifer. Forthcoming. "The Regulation of Labor." *Quarterly Journal of Economics* 119:1339–82.

Boutillier, Michel, and Patrice Geoffron. 2001. Vers une convergence des systèmes de gouvernement d'entreprises en Europe? Final Report, Commissariat Général du Plan. December.

Boycko, Maxim, Andrei Shleifer, and Robert Vishny. 1995. *Privatizing Russia*. Cambridge: MIT Press.

Boyer, Robert. 1989. *The Regulation School: A Critical Introduction*. New York: Columbia University Press.

———. 2001. "The Diversity and Future of Capitalisms: A *Régulationnist* Analysis." In *Capitalism in Evolution: Global Contentions—East and West*. Geoffrey M. Hodgson, Makato Itoh, and Nobuharu Yokokawa, eds. Cheltenham, U.K.: Edward Elgar.

Boyer, Robert, and J. P. Durand. 1997. *L'Après-fordisme*. Paris: Syros.

Brancato, Carolyn. 2000. "International Patterns of Institutional Investment." Conference Board Institutional Investment Report, April.

Brewer, John. 1989. *The Sinews of Power: War, Money, and the English State, 1688–783*. New York: Knopf.

Brooks, Sarah, and Estelle James. 2001. "The Political Economy of Structural Pension Reform." In *New Ideas About Old Age Security: Toward Sustainable Pension Systems in the 21st Century*. Robert Holzmann and Joseph Stiglitz, eds. Washington, D.C.: World Bank.

Celina, Karin Knorr, and Alex Poole, eds. 2004. *The Sociology of Financial Markets.* Oxford: Oxford University Press.

Chandler, Alfred D. 1990. *Strategy and Structure: Chapters in the History of the Industrial Enterprise.* Cambridge: MIT Press.

Chang, Sea-Jin, and Jung-Ho Kim. 2000. "The Chaebol Reforms." Paper presented at the Joint International Conference of the Weatherhead Center for International Affairs and Korea University, Cambridge, Mass., March.

Chappel, Randy, and Donald J. Roberts. 1993. "CalPERS and Institutional Shareholder Activism." Stanford Graduate School of Business Case S-BE-12.

Charreaux, Gerard. 2002. "Au-delà de l'approche juridico-financière: Le rôle cognitive des actionnaires et ses consequences sur l'analyse de la structure de proprieté et de la gouvernance." Université de Bourgogne Research Center in Finance, Organizational Architecture, and Governance Working Paper No. 020701.

Cheffins, Brian. 2001. "Does Law Matter? The Separation of Ownership and Control in the United Kingdom." *Journal of Legal Studies* 30:459–84.

———. 2002a. "Corporate Law and Ownership Structure: A Darwinian Link?" *University of New South Wales Law Journal* 25:346–78.

———. 2002b. "Putting Britain on the Roe Map: The Emergence of the Berle-Means Corporation in the United Kingdom." In *Corporate Governance Regimes: Convergence and Diversity.* Joseph A. McCahery, Piet Moerland, Theo Raaijmakers, and Luc Renneboog, eds. Oxford: Oxford University Press.

Chen, Kevin, Zihong Chen, and John Wei. 2003. "Disclosure, Corporate Governance, and the Cost of Equity Capital: Evidence from Asia's Emerging Markets." Paper presented to the Global Research Network Meeting, Institute of Corporate Governance of Korea University, Global Corporate Governance Forum of the World Bank, and the International Institute of Corporate Governance, July, Seoul.

China Securities and Regulatory Commission. 2000. "Information Disclosure and Corporate Governance in China." Paper prepared for the Second OECD/World Bank Asian Corporate Governance Roundtable, May 31–June 2, Hong Kong.

Cho, Lee-Jay, and Yoon-Hyung Kim, eds. 1998. *Korea's Choices in Emerging Global Competition and Cooperation.* Seoul: Korea Development Institute.

Cho, Myeong-Hyeon. 2000. "Corporate Governance in Korea." Paper presented to the Conference on Corporate Restructuring in Korea, University of California, San Diego, October.

Cho, Yoon-Je, and Joon-Kyung Kim. 1997. *Credit Policies and the Industrialization of Korea.* Seoul: Korea Development Institute.

Choy, Jon. 2000. "Tokyo Hesitates on Pension Reform. *Japan Economic Institute Report,* January 28.

Cioffi, John W., and Martin Höpner. "The Political Paradox of Corporate Governance Reform: Why the Center-Left Is the Driving Force behind the Rise of Financial Capitalism." Paper presented to the 2004 Annual Meetings of the American Political Science Association, September 2–5, Chicago.

Claessens, Stijn. 2002. "Global Corporate Governance: The Case of Asia." Paper presented to the Global Research Network Meeting, Institute of Corporate Governance of Korea University, Global Corporate Governance Forum of the World Bank, and the International Institute of Corporate Governance, July, Seoul.

Claessens, Stijn, Simeon Djankov, Joseph P. H. Fan, and Larry H. P. Lang. 1998a. "Diversification and Efficiency of Investment by East Asian Corporations." World Bank Working Paper.

———. 1998b. "Expropriation of Minority Shareholders: Evidence from East Asian Corporations." World Bank Working Paper.

———. 2002. "Disentangling the Incentive and Entrenchment Effects of Large Shareholdings." *Journal of Finance* 57:2741–71.

Claessens, Stijn, Simeon Djankov, and Larry H. P. Lang. 2002. "The Separation of Ownership and Control in East Asian Corporations." *Journal of Financial Economics* 58:81–112.

Clarke, P. F. 1971. *Lancashire and the New Liberalism.* Cambridge: Cambridge University Press.

Clowes, Michael J. 2000. *The Money Flood: How Pension Funds Revolutionized Investing.* New York: Wiley.

Coase, Ronald H. 1937. "The Nature of the Firm." *Economica* 4:386–405.

Coffee, John. 1981. " 'No Soul to Damn: No Body to Kick': An Unscandalized Inquiry into the Problems of Corporate Punishment." *Michigan Law Review* 79:386–459.

———. 1999. "Privatization and Corporate Governance: The Lessons from Securities Market Failures." *Journal of Corporation Law* 25:1–39.

———. 2001. "The Rise of Dispersed Ownership: The Roles of Law and the State in the Separation of Ownership and Control." *Yale Law Journal* 111:1–81.

———. 2002a. "Competition among Securities Markets: A Path Dependent Perspective." Columbia Law and Economics Working Paper No. 192.

———. 2002b. "Understanding Enron: It's about the Gatekeepers, Stupid." Columbia Law and Economics Working Paper No. 207.

———. 2003. "What Caused Enron? A Capsule Social and Economic History of the 1990's." Columbia Law and Economics Working Paper No. 214.

Coutinho, Luciano, and Flavio Rabelo. 2003. "Brazil: Keeping It in the Family." In *Corporate Governance in Development: The Experience of Brazil, Chile, India, and South Africa.* Charles P. Oman, ed. Washington, D.C.: OECD Development Center.

Cox, Gary. 1997. *Making Votes Count: Strategic Coordination in the World's Electoral Systems.* New York: Cambridge University Press.

Cox, Gary, Frances Rosenbluth, and Michael F. Thies. 2000. "Electoral Rules, Career Ambitions, and Party Structure: Conservative Factions in Japan's Upper and Lower Houses." *American Journal of Political Science* 44:115–22.

Crabtree, Susan. 2002. "Hastert Shoots Down GOP Attempt to Block Sarbanes Bill." *Congressional Roll Call,* July 18.

"Cracks in the Wall." 2000. *Forbes Global,* May 15.

"Crusade for Better Governance." 1999. *New Straits Times,* May 4.

Cuervo-Cazurra, Alvaro, and Ruth Aguilera. 2004. "The Worldwide Diffusion of Codes of Good Governance." In *Corporate Governance and Firm Organization.* Anna Grandori, ed. Oxford: Oxford University Press.

Culpepper, Pepper. 2003. *Creating Cooperation: How States Develop Human Capital in Europe.* Ithaca, N.Y.: Cornell University Press.

———. 2004. "Institutional Change in Contemporary Capitalism: Coordination and Change in Finance during the 1990s." Paper presented to the 14th International Conference of Europeanists, Chicago, March 11–13.

Culpepper, Pepper, Peter A. Hall, and Bruno Palier, eds. Forthcoming. *The Politics That Markets Make: Economic and Social Change in France.* London: Palgrave Macmillan.

Curtis, Gerald. 1999. *The Logic of Japanese Politics: Leaders, Institutions, and the Limits of Change.* New York: Columbia University Press.

Cusack, Thomas R. 1997. "Partisan Politics and Public Spending: Changes in Public Spending in the Industrialized Democracies, 1955–1989." *Public Choice* 91:375–95.

———. 1999. "Partisan Politics and Fiscal Policy." *Comparative Political Studies* 32:464–86.

Davis, E. Philip, and Benn Steil. 2001. *Institutional Investors*. Cambridge: MIT Press.

Davis, Gerald F. 1991a. "Agents without Principles? The Spread of the Poison Pill through the Intercorporate Network." *Administrative Science Quarterly* 36:583–613.

———. 1991b. "Networks and Corporate Control: Comparing Agency Theory and Interorganizational Explanations for the Diffusion of the Poison Pill." *Academy of Management Best Papers Proceedings* 1991:173–77.

———. 1996. "The Significance of Board Interlocks for Corporate Governance." *Corporate Governance* 4:154–59.

Davis, Gerald F., Kristina A. Diekmann, and Catherine H. Tinsley. 1994. "The Decline and Fall of the Conglomerate Firm in the 1980s: The De-institutionalization of an Organizational Form." *American Sociological Review* 59:547–70.

Davis, Gerald F., and Christopher Marquis. 2005. "The Globalization of Stock Markets and Convergence in Corporate Governance." In *The Economic Sociology of Capitalism*. Richard Swedberg and Victor Nee, eds. Princeton: Princeton University Press.

Davis, Gerald F., and Douglas McAdam. 2000. "Corporations, Classes, and Social Movements." In *Research in Organizational Behavior 22*. Barry Straw and Robert I. Sutton, eds. Oxford: Elsevier Science.

Davis, Gerald F., and Gregory E. Robbins. Forthcoming. "The Fate of the Conglomerate Firm in the United States." In *How Institutions Change*. Walter W. Powell and Daniel L. Jones, eds. Chicago: University of Chicago Press.

Davis, Gerald F., and Michael Useem. 2002. "Top Management, Company Directors, and Corporate Control." In *Handbook of Strategy and Management*. Andrew Pettigrew, Howard Thomas, and Richard Whittington, eds. London: Sage.

Davis Global Advisors. 2000. *Leading Corporate Governance Indicators, 2000*. December.

———. 2002. *Leading Corporate Governance Indicators, 2002*. November.

———. 2003. "Conflict Patrol." *Global Proxy Watch*, September 5.

de Jong, Abe, and Ailsa Roell. Forthcoming. "Financing and Control in the Netherlands: A Historical Perspective." In *The History of Corporate Governance around the World: Family Business Groups to Professional Managers*. Randall Morck, ed. Chicago: University of Chicago Press.

de Jong, Abe, Rezaul Kabir, Teye Marra, and Ailsa Roell. 2001. "Ownership and Control in the Netherlands." In *The Control of Corporate Europe*. Fabrizio Barca and Marco Becht, eds. New York: Oxford University Press.

de Winter, Jaap. 2004. *FEM Business*, September 13.

Dertouzos, Michael L., Richard K. Lester, and Robert M. Solow. 1989. *Made in America: Regaining the Productive Edge*. Cambridge: MIT Press.

Deutsche für Finanzanalyse und Asset Management. 2000. "Scorecard for German Corporate Governance." July. www.dvfa.de.

Dhanabalan, S. 2002. Speech to Asian Business Dialogue on Corporate Governance. Singapore, October.

Dietl, Helmut. 1998. *Capital Markets and Corporate Governance in Japan, Germany and the United States: Organizational Response to Market Inefficiencies*. New York: Routledge.

Dixit, Avinash K. 2004. *Lawlessness and Economics: Alternative Modes of Governance*. Princeton: Princeton University Press.

Djankov, Simeon, Rafael La Porta, Florencio López-de-Silanes, and Andrei Shleifer. 2002. "The Regulation of Entry." *Quarterly Journal of Economics* 117:1–37.

Djelic, Marie-Laure. 2001. *Exporting the American Model: The Postwar Transformation of European Business*. Oxford: Oxford University Press.

Djelic, Marie-Laure, and Sigrid Quack, eds. 2003. *Globalization and Institutions: Redefining the Rules of the Economic Game*. Cheltenham, U.K.: Edward Elgar.

Dobbin, Frank, ed. 2004. *The New Economic Sociology: A Reader*. Princeton: Princeton University Press.

Dore, Ronald P. 2000. *Stock Market Capitalism, Welfare Capitalism: Japan and Germany versus the Anglo-Saxons*. New York: Oxford University Press.

——. 2002. "Pensioners to the Casino." In *Markets and Authorities: Global Finance and Human Choice*. Marcello de Cecco and Jochen Lorentzen, eds. Cheltenham, U.K.: Edward Elgar.

——. 2004. "Pros and Cons of Insider Governance." REITI Working Paper.

Drucker, Peter. 1976. *The Unseen Revolution: How Pension Fund Socialism Came to America*. New York: Harper and Row.

Dyck, Alexander. 2003. "The Hermitage Fund: Media and Corporate Governance in Russia." Harvard Business School Case 703-010.

Economist Intelligence Unit. 2003. Russia Country Report.

Ellickson, Robert C. 1991. *Order without Law: How Neighbors Settle Disputes*. Cambridge: Harvard University Press.

Ensminger, Jan. 1992. *Making a Market: The Institutional Transformation of an African Society*. New York: Cambridge University Press.

Ernst, Ekkehard C. 2002. "Financial Systems, Industrial Relations, and Industry Specialization: An Econometric Analysis of Institutional Complementarities." OECD, February.

Esping-Anderson, Gøsta. 1989. "The Three Political Economies of the Welfare State." *Canadian Review of Sociology and Anthropology* 26:10–36.

——. 1990. *The Three Worlds of Welfare Capitalism*. Cambridge: Polity Press.

Esteves-Abe, Margarita, Torben Iversen, and David Soskice. 2001. "Social Protection and the Formation of Skills: A Reinterpretation of the Welfare State." In *Varieties of Capitalism: The Challenges Facing Contemporary Political Economies*. Peter Hall and David Soskice, eds. New York: Oxford University Press.

Estienne, Jean-François, and Kiyoshi Murakami. 2000. "The Japanese Experience of Review and Reform of Public Pension Schemes." In *Social Dialogue and Pension Reform: United Kingdom, United States, Germany, Japan, Sweden, Italy, Spain*. Emmanuel Raynaud, ed. Geneva: International Labor Organization.

Faccio, Mara, and Larry H. P. Lang. 2002. "The Ultimate Ownership of Western European Corporations." *Journal of Financial Economics* 65:365–95.

Fama, Eugene, and Michael Jensen. 1983. "Separation of Ownership and Control." *Journal of Law and Economics* 26:301–25.

Fan, Joseph, and T. Wong. 2001. "Corporate Ownership Structure and the Informativeness of Accounting Earnings in East Asia." Center for Economic Institutions Working Paper No. 2001-21.

Federation of European Stock Exchanges. 2002. *Share Ownership Structure in Europe*. http://www.fese.org/statistics/share_ownership/share_ownership.pdf.

Feldstein, Martin. 1996. "Social Security and Saving: New Time Series Evidence." *National Tax Journal* 49:151–64.

Feldstein, Martin, and Horst Siebert, eds. 2002. *Social Security Pension Reform in Europe*. Chicago: University of Chicago Press.

Felton, Robert, Alec Hudnut, and Jennifer van Heeckeren. 1996. "Putting a Value on Board Governance." *McKinsey Quarterly* 4:170–75.

"A Firm's Home May Not Be Sweet for Shareholders." 1999. *International Herald Tribune*, June 12.

Fisher, Lawrence, and James H. Lorie. 1968. "Rates of Return on Investment in Common Stocks: The Year-by-Year Record, 1926–65." *Journal of Business* 41:291–316.

Fiss, Peer, and Edward Zajac. Forthcoming. "Corporate Governance and Contested Terrain: The Rise of Shareholder Value Orientation in Germany." *Administrative Science Quarterly.*

Fligstein, Neil. 2001. *The Architecture of Markets: An Economic Sociology of Twenty-first Century Capitalist Societies.* Princeton: Princeton University Press.

Fligstein, Neil, and Linda Markowitz. 1993. "Financial Reorganization of American Corporations in the 1980s." In *Sociology and the Public Agenda.* William J. Wilson, ed. Newbury Park, Calif.: Sage.

Fohlin, Caroline. Forthcoming. "The History of Corporate Ownership and Control in Germany." In *The History of Corporate Governance around the World: Family Business Groups to Professional Managers.* Randall Morck, ed. Chicago: University of Chicago Press.

Foley, Martin. 1998. "Accounting Adjustments." *China Business Review* 25:22–24.

Franks, Julian R., and Colin Mayer. 1990. "Capital Markets and Corporate Control: A Study of France, Germany, and the UK." *Economic Policy* 5:191–231.

———. 1996. "Hostile Takeovers and the Correction of Managerial Failure." *Journal of Financial Economics.* 40:163–81.

———. 1997. "Corporate Ownership and Control in the UK, Germany, and France." *Bank of America Journal of Applied Corporate Finance.* 9:30–45.

Franks, Julian R., Colin Mayer, and Stefano Rossi. Forthcoming. "Spending Less Time with the Family: The Decline of Family Ownership in the UK." In *The History of Corporate Governance around the World: Family Business Groups to Professional Managers.* Randall Morck, ed. Chicago: University of Chicago Press.

Fredrickson, George M. 1971. *The Black Image in the White Mind: The Debate on Afro-American Character and Destiny, 1817–1914.* Scranton, Pa.: Harper and Row.

Frentrop, Paul. 2003. *A History of Corporate Governance, 1602–2000.* Amsterdam: Deminor.

Frieden, Jeffrey. 1988. "Sectoral Conflict and U.S. Foreign Economic Policy, 1914–1940." *International Organization* 42:59–90.

———. 1999. "Actors and Preferences in International Relations." In *Strategic Choice and International Relations.* David Lake and Robert Powell, eds. Princeton: Princeton University Press.

Gao, Bi. 1997. *Economic Ideology and Japanese Industrial Policy: Developmentalism from 1931 to 1965.* Cambridge: Cambridge University Press.

Garrett, Geoffrey. 1998. *Partisan Politics in the Global Economy.* Cambridge: Cambridge University Press.

Garrett, Geoffrey, and Peter Lange. 1996. "Internationalization, Institutions, and Political Change." In *Internationalization and Domestic Politics.* Robert Keohane and Helen Milner, eds. New York: Cambridge University Press.

Gerschenkron, Alexander. 1962. *Economic Backwardness in Historical Perspective: A Book of Essays.* Cambridge: Harvard University Press.

Gingerich, Daniel W., and Peter A. Hall. 2002. "Varieties of Capitalism and Institutional Complementarities in the Political Economy: An Empirical Analysis." Paper presented to Workshop on Comparative Political Economy, October, Cornell University.

Glaeser, Edward, Simon Johnson, and Andrei Shleifer. 2001. "Coase vs. the Coasians." *Quarterly Journal of Economics* 3:853–99.

Global Corporate Governance Forum. 2002. "Mission Statement and Charter." http://www.gcgf.org/about.htm.

Godeau, Lucie. 2003. "Foreign Investors Shun Russia Despite Growth, BP Deal." *Baltic Times*, February 27.

Goetzmann, William, and Elisabeth Koll. Forthcoming. "The History of Corporate Ownership in China." In *The History of Corporate Governance around the World: Family Business Groups to Professional Managers*. Randall Morck, ed. Chicago: University of Chicago Press.

Go-Feij, Denise. 1999. "Corporate Governance and Technical Innovation in the Netherlands." Report to the European Commission. May.

Goldthorpe, John H. ed. 1984. *Order and Conflict in Contemporary Capitalism*. New York: Oxford University Press.

Gompers, Paul, Joy Ishii, and Andrew Merrick. 2001. "Corporate Governance and Equity Prices." NBER Working Paper No. 8849.

Gordon, Andrew. 1985. *The Evolution of Labor Relations in Japan: Heavy Industry*. Cambridge: Harvard University Press.

———. 1991. *Labor and Imperial Democracy in Prewar Japan*. Berkeley and Los Angeles: University of California Press.

Gourevitch, Peter A. 1977. "International Trade, Domestic Coalitions, and Liberty: Comparative Responses to the Crisis of 1873–1896." *Journal of Interdisciplinary History* 8:281–313.

———. 1986. *Politics in Hard Times: Comparative Responses to International Economic Crises*. Ithaca, N.Y.: Cornell University Press.

———. 1999. "The Governance Problem in International Relations." In *Strategic Choice and International Relations*. David Lake and Robert Powell, eds. Princeton: Princeton University Press.

Gourevitch, Peter A., and Michael B. Hawes. 2002. "The Politics of Choice among National Production Systems." In *l'année de la régulation*, No. 6. Robert Boyer, ed. Paris: Presses des Sciences Po.

Gourevitch, Peter A., and James Shinn. 2001. *Corporate Governance for Beginners*. London: Oxford University Press.

———. 2002. *How Shareholder Reforms Can Pay Foreign Policy Dividends*. New York: Council on Foreign Relations.

Goyer, Michel. 2003a. "Corporate Governance under Stress: An Institutional Perspective on the Transformation of Corporate Governance in France and Germany." Ph.D. dissertation, Department of Political Science, MIT.

———. 2003b. "Core Competencies and Labor: An Institutionalist Perspective on Corporate Governance in France and Germany." In *Global Markets, Domestic Institutions: Corporate Law and Governance in a New Era of Cross-Border Deals*. Curtis Milhaupt, ed. New York: Columbia University Press.

———. 2004. "The Growth of Stock Markets in France and Germany, 1995–2002: The Importance of Work Organization Institutions." Paper presented to the Annual Meetings of American Political Science Association, Chicago, September 2–5.

———. Forthcoming. "The Transformation of Corporate Governance in France." In *Changing France: Transforming the Democratic Balance among State, Market, and Society*. Pepper Culpepper Peter Hall, and Bruno Palier, eds. London: Macmillan Palgrave.

Grandolini, Gloria, and Luis Cerda. 1998. "The 1997 Pension Reform in Mexico." World Bank Policy Research Working Paper No. 1933, Washington, D.C.: World Bank.

Grossman, Sanford J., and Oliver D. Hart. 1980. "Disclosure Laws and Takeover Bids." *Journal of Finance* 35:323–34.

————. 1981. "Implicit Contracts, Moral Hazard, and Unemployment." *American Economic Review* 71:301–7.

————. 1986. "The Costs and Benefits of Ownership: A Theory of Vertical and Lateral Integration." *Journal of Political Economy* 94:691–719.

Groves, Theodore, Yongmiao Hong, John McMillan, and Barry Naughton. 1994. "Autonomy and Incentives in Chinese State Enterprises." *Quarterly Journal of Economics* 109:183–209.

Guillén, Mauro. 2000. "Corporate Governance and Globalization: Is There a Convergence across Countries?" *Advances in International Comparative Management* 13:175–204.

Haas, Peter. 1992. "Introduction: Epistemic Communities and International Policy Coordination." *International Organization* 46:367–90.

Haggard, Stephan. 2000. *The Political Economy of the Asian Financial Crisis*. Washington, D.C.: Institute for International Economics.

Haggard, Stephan, Wonhyuk Lim, and Euysung Kim, eds. 2003. *Economic Crisis and Corporate Restructuring in Korea: Reforming the Chaebol*. Cambridge: Cambridge University Press.

Hall, Peter A., ed. 1989. *The Political Power of Economic Ideas: Keynesianism across Nations*. Princeton: Princeton University Press.

Hall, Peter A., and Robert J. Franzese. 1998. "Mixed Signals: Central Bank Independence, Coordinated Wage Bargaining, and European Monetary Union." *International Organization* 52:505–35.

Hall, Peter A., and Daniel W. Gingerich. 2001. "Varieties of Capitalism and Institutional Complementarities in the Macroeconomy: An Empirical Analysis." Paper presented to the Annual Meetings of the American Political Science Association, August, San Francisco.

Hall, Peter A., and David Soskice, eds. 2001. *Varieties of Capitalism: The Institutional Foundations of Comparative Advantage*. New York: Oxford University Press.

Hancké, Bob. 2001. "Restructuring in French Industry." In *Varieties of Capitalism: The Institutional Foundations of Comparative Advantage*. Peter Hall and David Soskice, eds. New York: Oxford University Press.

————. 2002. *Large Firms and Institutional Change: Industrial Renewal and Economic Restructuring in France*. Oxford: Oxford University Press.

Hansmann, Henry, and Reinier Kraakman. 2000a. "The End of History for Corporate Law." *Georgetown Law Journal* 89:439–67.

————. 2000b. "The Essential Role of Organizational Law." *Yale Law Journal* 110:387–440.

Hart, Oliver H. 1989. "An Economist's Perspective on the Theory of the Firm." *Columbia Law Review* 89:1757–74.

————. 1995. *Firms, Contracts, and Financial Structure*. Oxford: Oxford University Press.

Hartz, Louis. 1955. *The Liberal Tradition in America: An Interpretation of American Political Thought since the Revolution*. New York: Harcourt, Brace.

Hassel, Anke, and Jürgen Beyer. 2001. "The Effects of Convergence: Internationalization and the Changing Distribution of Net Value Added in Large German Firms." Max-Planck-Institute Discussion Paper 01/7, November.

Hawley, James P., and Andrew T. Williams. 2000. *The Rise of Fiduciary Capitalism: How Institutional Investors Can Make Corporate America More Democratic*. Philadelphia: University of Pennsylvania Press.

Heinrich, Ralph. 1999. "Complementarities in Corporate Governance: A Survey of the Literature with Special Emphasis on Japan." Kiel Institute of World Economics Working Paper No. 947.

Herrigel, Gary. 1996. *Industrial Constructions: The Sources of German Industrial Power.* Cambridge: Cambridge University Press.

Hertzfeld, Jeffrey M. 1999. "Russian Corporate Governance: The Foreign Direct Investor's Perspective." Paper presented to the OECD Conference on Corporate Governance in Russia, May 31–June 2, Moscow. http://www.oecd.org/dataoecd/55/47/1921803.pdf.

Hibbs, Douglas A., Jr. 1976. "Industrial Conflict in Advanced Industrial Societies." *American Political Science Review* 70:1033–58.

———. 1977. "Political Parties and Macroeconomic Policy." *American Political Science Review* 71:1467–87.

Hilzenrath, David. 2002. "How Congress Rode a 'Storm' to Corporate Reform." *Washington Post,* July 28.

Hiscox, Michael J. 2001. "Class versus Industry Cleavages: Inter-industry Factor Mobility and the Politics of Trade." *International Organization* 55:1–46.

———. 2002. *International Trade and Political Conflict: Commerce, Coalitions, and Mobility.* Princeton: Princeton University Press.

Hobsbawm, Eric J. 1968. *Industry and Empire: An Economic History of Britain since 1750.* London: Weidenfeld and Nicolson.

Hogfeldt, Peter. Forthcoming. "The History and Politics of Corporate Ownership in Sweden." In *The History of Corporate Governance Around the World: Family Business Groups to Professional Managers.* Randall Morck, ed. Chicago: University of Chicago Press.

Holmstrom, Bengt, and Paul Milgrom. 1994. "The Firm as an Incentive System." *American Economic Review* 84:972–91.

Holzmann, Robert, Robert Palacios, and Asta Zviniene. 2002. *Reporting the Implicit Pension Debt in Low and Middle Income Countries.* Washington, D.C.: World Bank.

Höpner, Martin. 2003a. "European Corporate Governance Reform and the German Party Paradox." Max-Planck-Institute for the Study of Societies Program for the Study of Germany and Europe Working Paper No. 03.1.

———. 2003b. "What Connects Industrial Relations and Corporate Governance? Explaining Institutional Complementarity." Max-Planck-Institute for the Study of Societies Working Paper.

Höpner, Martin, and Gregory Jackson. 2001. "An Emerging Market for Corporate Control? The Mannesmann Takeover and German Corporate Governance." Max-Planck-Institute for the Study of Societies Discussion Paper No. 01/04.

"House GOP Opposition to Senate's Accounting Bill Vanishes." 2002. *National Journal's Congressional Daily,* July 18.

Huang, Yasheng, Kirsten J. O'Neal-Massaro, and Anatoli Miliukov. 2002. "Unified Energy System of Russia." Harvard Business School Case 702-068.

Huber, John D. 1996. *Rationalizing Parliament: Legislative Institutions and Party Politics in France.* Cambridge: Cambridge University Press.

Ibbotson, Roger, and Rex Sinquefield. 1976. "Stocks, Bonds, Bills, and Inflation: Year by Year Historical Returns (1926–1974)." *Journal of Business* 49:11–47.

Iglesias, Augusto, and Robert J. Palacios. 2000. "Managing Public Pension Reserves Part I: Evidence from the International Experience." World Bank Social Protection Discussion Paper No. 0003.

Iversen, Torben. 1998. "Wage Bargaining, Central Bank Independence and the Real Effects of Money." *International Organization* 52:469–504.

Iversen, Torben, and Thomas R. Cusack. 2000. "The Causes of Welfare State Expansion: Deindustrialization or Globalization?" *World Politics* 52:313–49.

Iversen, Torben, and David Soskice. 2001. "An Asset Theory of Social Policy Preferences." *American Political Science Review* 95:875–93.

Iversen, Torben, and Anne Wren. 1998. "Equality, Employment, and Budgetary Restraint: The Trilemma of the Service Economy." *World Politics* 50:507–46.

Jaikumar, Ramchandran. 1986. "Postindustrial Manufacturing." *Harvard Business Review* 64:69–76.

Jang, Hasung. 2003. "Corporate Restructuring in Korea after the Economic Crisis." *Joint U.S.-Korea Academic Studies* 147–84.

Jensen, Michael C. 1986. "The Agency Costs of Free Cash Flow: Corporate Finance and Takeovers." *American Economic Review* 76:323–29.

Jensen, Michael C., and William H. Meckling. 1976. "Theory of the Firm: Managerial Behavior, Agency Costs, and Ownership Structure." *Journal of Financial Economics* 3:305–60.

Johnson, Chalmers A. 1982. *MITI and the Japanese Miracle: The Growth of Industrial Policy, 1925–1975.* Stanford: Stanford University Press.

Johnson, Simon, Rafael La Porta, Florencio López-de-Silanes, and Andrei Shleifer. 2000. "Tunneling." Papers and Proceedings of the One Hundred Twelfth Annual Meeting of the American Economic Association, *American Economic Review* 90:22–27.

Johnson, Simon, John McMillan, and Christopher Woodruff. 2000. "Entrepreneurs and the Ordering of Institutional Reform: Poland, Slovakia, Romania, Russia, and Ukraine Compared." *Economics of Transition* 8:1–36.

Kahler, Miles, and David Lake, eds. 2003. *Governance in a Global Economy: Political Authority in Transition.* Princeton: Princeton University Press.

Kaplan, Steven. 1997. "Corporate Governance and Corporate Performance: A Comparison of Germany, Japan, and the U.S." *Journal of Applied Corporate Finance* 9:86–93.

Katzenstein, Peter, and Takashi Shiraishi, eds. Forthcoming. *Beyond Japan: East Asian Regionalism.* Ithaca, N.Y.: Cornell University Press.

Keefer, Philip. 2005. "Political Credibility, Citizen Information, and Financial Sector Development." Paper presented at the conference Economics, Political Institutions, and Financial Markets, Stanford University.

Keefer, Philip, and David Stasavage. 2003. "The Limits of Delegation: Veto Players, Central Bank Independence, and the Credibility of Monetary Policy." *American Political Science Review* 97 (3):407–23.

Kenworthy, Lane, and Alexander Hicks. 1998. "Cooperation and Political Economic Performance in Affluent Democratic Capitalism." *American Journal of Sociology* 103:631–72.

Kester, W. Carl. 1991. *Japanese Takeovers: The Global Contest for Corporate Control.* Boston: Harvard Business School Press.

———. 1996. "American and Japanese Corporate Governance: Converging to Best Practice?" In *National Diversity and Global Capitalism.* Suzanne Berger and Ronald Dore, eds. Ithaca, N.Y.: Cornell University Press.

Kim, Il-Sup. 2000. "Financial Crisis and Its Impact on the Accounting System in Korea." Korea Accounting Standards Board Manuscript.

Krauss, Ellis, and Michio Muramatsu. 1984. "Bureaucrats and Politicians in Policymaking: The Case of Japan." *American Political Science Review* 78:126–46.

Kremers, Jeroen. 2002. "Pension Reform: Issues in the Netherlands." In *Social Security Pension Reform in Europe.* Martin Feldstein and Horst Siebert, eds. Chicago: University of Chicago Press.

Krozsner, Randall S. 2000. "The Economics and Politics of Financial Modernization." *Economic Policy Review of the Federal Reserve Bank of New York*, October.

Laeven, Luc. 2001. "Insider Lending and Bank Ownership: The Case of Russia." *Journal of Comparative Economics* 29:207–29.

Lamoreaux, Naomi R., and Jean-Laurent Rosenthal. Forthcoming. "Legal Regime and Business's Organizational Choice: A Comparison of France and the United States during the Mid-nineteenth Century." *American Law and Economic Review*.

La Porta, Rafael, Florencio López-de-Silanes, and Andrei Shleifer. 1999. "Corporate Ownership around the World." *Journal of Finance* 54:471–517.

———. 2005. "What Works in Securities Law?" *Journal of Finance*, forthcoming.

La Porta, Rafael, Florencio López-de-Silanes, Andrei Shleifer, and Robert W. Vishny. 1997. "Legal Determinants of External Finance." *Journal of Finance* 52:1131–50.

———. 1998. "Law and Finance." *Journal of Political Economy* 106:1113–55.

———. 2000. "Investor Protection and Corporate Governance." *Journal of Financial Economics* 58:3–27.

———. 2002. "Investor Protection and Corporate Valuation." *Journal of Finance* 57:1147–70.

Lardy, Nicholas. 2002. *Integrating China into the Global Economy*. Washington, D.C.: Brookings Institution Press.

Lefort, Fernando, and Eduardo Walker. 1999. "Ownership and Capital Structure of Chilean Conglomerates: Facts and Hypotheses for Governance." *Revista ABANTE* 3:3–27.

Levy, Jonah. 1999. *Tocqueville's Revenge: State, Society, and Economy in Contemporary France*. Cambridge: Harvard University Press.

Levitt, Arthur, and Paula Dwyer. 2002. *Take on the Street: What Wall Street and Corporate America Don't Want You to Know: What You Can Do to Fight Back*. New York: Pantheon.

Li, David. 2000. "Insider Control, Corporate Governance, and the Soft Budget Constraint: Theory, Evidence, and Policy Implications." In *Financial Market Reform in China: Progress, Problems, and Prospects*. Baizhu Chen, J. Kimball Dietrich, and Yi Fang, eds. Boulder, Colo.: Westview Press.

Lijphart, Arend. 1999. *Patterns of Democracy: Government Forms and Performance in Thirty-six Countries*. New Haven: Yale University Press.

Lin, Cyril. Forthcoming. "Public Vices in Public Places: Challenges in Corporate Governance Development in China." In *The History of Corporate Governance around the World: Family Business Groups to Professional Managers*. Randall Morck, ed. Chicago: University of Chicago Press.

Lindblom, Charles E. 1977. *Politics and Markets: The World's Political Economic Systems*. New York: Basic Books.

Lins, Karl, Deon Strickland, and Marc Zenner. 2000. "Do Non-U.S. Firms Issue Equity on U.S. Stock Exchanges to Relax Capital Constraints?" Research monograph. http://www.cob.ohio-state.edu/fin/dice/papers/2000-5.pdf.

Lipset, Seymour Martin, and Stein Rokkan, eds. 1967. *Party Systems and Voter Alignments: Cross-National Perspectives*. New York: Free Press.

Locke, Richard. 1995. *Remaking the Italian Economy*. Ithaca, N.Y.: Cornell University Press.

Lordon, Frédéric. 2000. *Fonds de pension, pièges à cons ? Mirage de la démocratie actionnariale*. Paris: Raisons d'agir.

———. 2002. *La politique du capital*. Paris: Odile Jacob.

Malkiel, Burton G. 1996. *A Random Walk Down Wall Street: The Time-Tested Strategy for Successful Investing*. 6th ed. New York: Norton.

Magee, Stephen P., William A. Brock, and Leslie Young. 1989. *Black Hole Tariffs and Endogenous Policy Theory in General Equilibrium.* Cambridge: Cambridge University Press.

Maher, Maria, and Thomas Andersson. 2002. "Corporate Governance: Effects on Firm Performance and Economic Growth." *Corporate Governance Regimes: Convergence and Diversity.* Joseph A. McCahery, Piet Moerland, Theo Raaijmakers, and Luc Renneboog, eds. Oxford: Oxford University Press.

Manow, Philip. 2001a. "Business Coordination, Collective Dares, Bargaining, and the Welfare State: Germany and Japan in Historical Comparative Perspective." In *Comparing Welfare Capitalism: Social Policy and Political Economy in Europe, Japan, and the USA.* Bernhard Ebbinghaus and Philip Manow, eds. London: Routledge.

———. 2001b. "Welfare State Building and Coordinated Capitalism in Japan and Germany." In *The Origins of Nonliberal Capitalism: Germany and Japan in Comparison.* Wolfgang Streeck and Kozo Yamamura, eds. Ithaca, N.Y.: Cornell University Press.

———. Forthcoming. *Social Protection, Capitalist Production: The Bismarckian Welfare State and the German Political Economy from the 1880s to the 1990s.*

Manow, Philip, and Bernhard Ebbinghaus. 2001. "Introduction: Studying Varieties of Welfare Capitalism." In *Comparing Welfare Capitalism: Social Policy and Political Economy in Europe, Japan, and the USA.* Bernhard Ebbinghaus and Philip Manow, eds. London: Routledge.

March, James G., and Johan P. Olsen. 1998. "The Institutional Dynamics of International Political Orders." *International Organization* 52:943–69.

Mares, Isabela. 2003. *The Politics of Social Risk: Business and Welfare State Development.* Cambridge: Cambridge University Press.

Martinez, Gebe, and Keith Perine. 2002. "Corporate America Faces Shift in Legislative Landscape." *Congressional Quarterly Weekly,* July 5.

Mayer, Colin. 1996. "Corporate Governance, Competition, and Performance." OECD Working Paper No. 164.

Maurice, Marc, François Sellier, and Jean-Jacques Silvestre. 1986. *The Social Foundations of Industrial Power: A Comparison of France and Germany.* Arthur Goldhammer, trans. Cambridge: MIT Press.

McCall, H. Carl. 2002. Testimony before the Committee on Financial Services. U.S. House of Representatives. March 20.

McCubbins, Mathew D., and Thomas Schwartz. 1984. "Congressional Oversight Overlooked: Police Patrols versus Fire Alarms." *American Journal of Political Science* 28:165–79.

McIntyre, Andrew. 2001. "Institutions and Investors: The Politics of the Financial Crisis in Southeast Asia." *International Organization* 55:81–122.

McKinnell, Henry. 2003. Letter to the Securities and Exchange Commission. October 1.

McKinsey Investor Opinion Survey. 2000. June. www.gcgf.org.

McPherson, James. 1988. *Battle Cry of Freedom: The Civil War Era.* New York: Oxford University Press.

Megginson, William L. "Appendix Detailing Share Issue Privatization Offerings, 1961–2000." http://faculty-staff.ou.edu/M/William.L.Megginson-1/.

Mercer Human Resources Consulting. 2002. Total Remuneration Survey, 2000.

Meyer, John W., and Brian Rowan. 1977. "Institutionalized Organizations: Formal Structure as Myth and Ceremony." *American Journal of Sociology* 83:340–63.

Milgrom, Paul, and John Roberts. 1990. "The Economics of Modern Manufacturing: Technology, Strategy, and Organization." *American Economic Review* 80:511–28.

———. 1992. *Economics, Organization, and Management*. Englewood Cliffs, N.J.: Prentice Hall.

———. 1995. "Complementarities, Industrial Strategy, Structure, and Change in Manufacturing." *Journal of Accounting and Economics* 19:179–208.

Ministry of Welfare. Pension Fund Management Bureau. 2001. "Regarding Basic Asset Management Policy for National Pension and Retirement Savings Accounts." Paper presented to the International Corporate Governance Forum, July, Tokyo.

"Minority Shareholders Watchdog Group looking for a Suitable Model." 1999. Bernama News Agency, August 16.

Minow, Nell. 2003. "When Does a Pay Package Become Too Outrageous?" *Chicago Tribune*, September 14.

Miyajima, Hideyaki. 1998. "The Impact of Deregulation on Corporate Governance and Finance." In *Is Japan Really Changing Its Ways? Regulatory Reform and the Japanese Economy*. Lonny E. Carlile and Mark C. Tilton, eds. Washington, D.C.: Brookings Institution Press.

Moerland, Pieter. 1999. "Corporate Supervision in the Netherlands." Paper presented to the Conference on Convergence and Diversity in Corporate Governance Regimes and Capital Markets, University of Tilburg, November, Tilburg, Netherlands.

Monks, Robert A. G. 1998. *The Emperor's Nightingale: Restoring the Integrity of the Corporation in the Age of Shareholder Activism*. Reading, Mass.: Addison-Wesley.

———. 2001. *The New Global Investors: How Shareholders Can Unlock Sustainable Prosperity Worldwide*. Oxford: Capstone.

Monks, Robert A. G., and Nell Minow. 1991. *Power and Accountability: Restoring the Balance of Power between Corporations, Owners, and Society*. New York: Harper Business.

———. 2001. *Corporate Governance*. 2nd ed. Oxford: Blackwell.

Moore, Barrington, Jr. 1966. *Social Origins of Dictatorship and Democracy: Lord and Peasant in the Making of the Modern World*. Boston: Beacon Press.

Moran, Michael. 2002. "Pension Accounting and Funding: A Roadmap for Analysts and Investors." Goldman Sachs Global Strategy Research. December.

Morck, Randall, Michael Percy, Gloria Tian, and Bernard Yeung. Forthcoming. "The Rise and Fall of the Widely Held Firm: A History of Corporate Ownership in Canada." In *The History of Corporate Governance around the World: Family Business Groups to Professional Managers*. Randall Morck, ed. Chicago: University of Chicago Press.

Morin, Francois. "A Transformation in the French Model of Shareholding and Management." *Economy and Society* 29:36–53.

Mottis, Nicolas, and Jean-Pierre Ponssard. 2002. "L'influence des investisseurs institutionnels sur le pilotage des enterprises." Ecole Polytechnique Laboratoire d'Econometrie Working Paper No. 2002-020, May.

"Move to Improve Corporate Governance." 1999. *Business Times Singapore*, December.

Murphy, Antoine E. Forthcoming. "Corporate Ownership in France: The Importance of History." In *The History of Corporate Governance around the World: Family Business Groups to Professional Managers*. Randall Morck, ed. Chicago: University of Chicago Press.

Naughton, Barry. 2000. "Financial Development and Macroeconomic Stability in China." In *Financial Market Reform in China: Progress, Problems, and Prospects*. Baizhu Chen, J. Kimball Dietrich, and Yi Fang, eds. Boulder, Colo.: Westview Press.

Nesbitt, Steven L. 1994. "Long-Term Rewards from Shareholder activism: A Study of the 'CalPERS' Effect.'" *Journal of Applied Corporate Finance* 6:x–xx.

——. 1995. "The 'CalPERS Effect': A Corporate Governance Update." Wilshire and Associates. July 19.

Nihon Corporate Governance Forum. 1998. "Coporato Gabanansu gensoku: Atarashii nihongata kigyō tōchi o kangaeru." *Coporaato Gabanansu Gensoku Sakutei Iinkai*, May 26.

Nijhuis, Jos, and Jaap van Manen. 2002. "Competing for Capital: Analysts' Perceptions of the Competitive Position of Dutch Companies." PricewaterhouseCoopers Netherlands.

Nishi, Norio. 1998. "The Transformation of the Japanese Pension Market." *National Bureau of Asian Research Publications: Executive Insight*, No. 14.

North, Douglass C., and Barry R. Weingast. 1989. "Constitutions and Commitment: The Evolution of Institutions Governing Public Choice in Seventeenth-Century England." *Journal of Economic History* 69:803–32.

Nye, Joseph S. 2004. *Soft Power: The Means to Success in World Politics*. New York: Public Affairs Press.

OECD Principles of Corporate Governance. 1999. Washington, D.C.: Organization for Economic Cooperation and Development Publications.

OECD Principles of Corporate Governance. 2004. Washington, D.C.: Organization for Economic Cooperation and Development Publications. http://www.oecd.org/dataoecd/32/18/31557724.pdf.

Oi, Jean C., and Andrew G. Walder, eds. 1999. *Property Rights and Economic Reform in China*. Stanford, Calif.: Stanford University Press.

Pagano, Marco, and Paolo Volpin. 2001a. "The Political Economy of Corporate Governance." Centre for Economic Policy Research Discussion Paper No. 2682.

——. 2001b. "The Political Economy of Finance." *Oxford Review of Economic Policy* 17:502–19.

Palmer, Edward. 2002. "Swedish Pension Reform: How Did It Evolve, and What Does It Mean for the Future?" In *Social Security Pension Reform in Europe*. Martin Feldstein and Horst Siebert, eds. Chicago: University of Chicago Press.

Patton, Donald, and Martin Kenney. 2003. "Innovation and Social Capital in Silicon Valley." BRIE Working Paper No. 155.

Perine, Keith. 2002a. "Senate Accounting Industry Regulation Could Get New Legs after Recess." *Congressional Quarterly Weekly*, May 24.

——. 2002b. "Senate Panel Approves Tighter Rules for Accounting Industry." *Congressional Quarterly Weekly*, June 21.

Perotti, Enrico, and Ernst-Ludwig von Thadden. 2003. "The Political Economy of Bank and Market Dominance." European Corporate Governance Institute Finance Working Paper No. 21/2003.

Piñera, José. 1996. "Empowering Workers: The Privatization of Social Security in Chile." *Cato Letter*, No. 10.

Piore, Michael, and Charles Sable. 1984. *The Second Industrial Divide: Possibilities for Prosperity*. New York: Basic Books.

Pistor, Katharina, Yoram Keinan, Jan Kleinheisterkamp, and Mark West. 2002. "The Evolution of Corporate Law: A Cross-Country Comparison." *University of Pennsylvania Journal of International Economic Law* 23:791–871.

Pistor, Katharina, Martin Raiser, and Stanislaw Gelfer. 2000. "Legal Evolution and the Transplant Effect: Lessons from Corporate Law Development in Six Countries." Unpublished paper.

Plihon, Dominique, Jean-Pierre Ponssard, and Philippe Zarlowski. 2001. "Quel scenario pour le gouvernement d'enterprise? Une hypothèse de double convergence." Ecole Polytechnique Laboratoire d'Econometrie Working Paper 2001-008, August.

Porter, Michael. 1990. *The Competitive Advantage of Nations*. New York: Free Press.

———. 1992. "Capital Disadvantage: America's Failing Capital Investment System." *Harvard Business Review* 72:65–83.

Posner, Richard A. 1972. *Economic Analysis of Law*. Boston: Little, Brown.

Rajan, Raghuram, and Luigi Zingales. 2003. "The Great Reversals: The Politics of Financial Development in the 20th Century." *Journal of Financial Economics* 69:5–50.

Ramseyer, Mark, and Frances Rosenbluth. 1993. *Japan's Political Marketplace*. Cambridge: Cambridge University Press.

Rodrik, Dani. 1997. *Has Globalization Gone Too Far?* Washington, D.C.: Institute of International Economics.

Roe, Mark. 1994. *Strong Managers, Weak Owners: The Political Roots of American Corporate Finance*. Princeton: Princeton University Press.

———. 2003a. "Delaware's Competition." *Harvard Law Review* 117:588–646.

———. 2003b. *Political Determinants of Corporate Governance: Political Context, Corporate Impact*. New York: Oxford University Press.

Roeder, Philip G. 1993. *Red Sunset: The Failure of Soviet Politics*. Princeton: Princeton University Press.

Rogowski, Ronald. 1989. *Commerce and Coalitions: How Trade Affects Domestic Political Alignments*. Princeton: Princeton University Press.

———. 1999. "Institutions as Constraints on Strategic Choice." In *Strategic Choice and International Relations*. David Lake and Robert Powell, eds. Princeton: Princeton University Press.

Rogowski, Ronald, and Mark A. Kayser. 2002. "Majoritarian Electoral Systems and Consumer Power: Price-Level Evidence from OECD Countries." *American Journal of Political Science* 46:526–39.

Romano, Roberta. 1990. "The State Competition Debate in Corporate Law." In *Corporate Law and Economic Analysis*. Lucien Bebchuk, ed. Cambridge: Cambridge University Press.

"Russia Launches Corporate Governance Reform." 2000. United Press International, September 7.

"Russia's Lousy Corporate Governance." 1999. *Economist* (U.S.), July 24.

Sakakibara, Eisuke. 1990. *Shihon shugi o koeta Nihon: Nihon-gata shijō keizai taisei no seiritsu to tenkai*. Tokyo: Toyo Keizai.

Salter, Malcolm S., and Joshua N. Rosenbaum. 2002. "OAO Yukos Oil Company." Harvard Business School Case 902-021.

Schieber, Sylvester. 1999. "The Employees Retirement Income Security Act: Motivations, Provisions, and Implications for Retirement Security." Paper presented to the Conference on ERISA after 25 Years: A Framework for Evaluating Pension Reform, September 17, Washington, D.C.

Schmidt, Vivien A. 2001. "The Politics of Adjustment in France and Britain: When Does Discourse Matter?" *Journal of European Public Policy* 8:247–64.

———. 2002. "Does Discourse Matter in the Politics of Welfare State Adjustment?" *Comparative Political Studies* 35:168–93.

Schonfeld, Andrew. 1965. *Modern Capitalism: The Changing Balance of Public and Private Power*. New York: Oxford University Press.

Shinn, James. 2000. "Globalization, Corporate Governance, and the State." Ph.D. diss., Princeton University.

Shiozaki, Yasuhisa. 2003. "Corporate Governance Standards and Capital Markets." Speech presented to the Symposium on Building the Financial System of the 21st Century. October 4, Tokyo.

Shirk, Susan. 1993. *The Political Logic of Economic Reform in China.* Berkeley and Los Angeles: University of California Press.

Shleifer, Andrei, and Daniel Treisman. 2004. "A Normal Country." *Foreign Affairs* 3:20–38.

Shleifer, Andrei, and Robert W. Vishny. 1997. "A Survey of Corporate Governance." *Journal of Finance* 52:737–83.

———. 1999. *The Grabbing Hand: Government Pathologies and Their Cures.* Cambridge: Harvard University Press.

Shugart, Matthew S., and John M. Carey. 1992. *Presidents and Assemblies: Constitutional Design and Electoral Dynamics.* New York: Cambridge University Press.

Sinclair, Timothy J. 2003. "Global Monitor: Bond Rating Agencies." *New Political Economy* 8:147–61.

———. 2004. *The New Masters of Capital: American Bond Rating Agencies and the Politics of Creditworthiness.* Ithaca, N.Y.: Cornell University Press.

Sinn, Hans-Werner. 1999. "The Crisis of Germany's Pension Insurance System and How It Can Be Resolved." NBER Working Paper No. 7304.

Smith, Paul. 1967. *Disraelian Conservatism and Social Reform.* London: Routledge and Kegan Paul.

Smith v. Van Gorkom, 488 A.2d 858 (Delaware 1985).

Söderström, Hans, Erik Berglöf, Bengt Holmström, Peter Högfeldt, and Eva Milgrom. 2003. "Corporate Governance and Structural Change: European Challenges." Studieförbundet Näringsliv och Samhälle Economic Policy Group Report.

Soskice, David, and Torben Iversen. 1998. "Multiple Wage-Bargaining Systems in the Single European Currency Area." *Oxford Review of Economic Policy* 14:110–24.

———. 2000. "The Nonneutrality of Monetary Policy with Large Price or Wage Setters." *Quarterly Journal of Economics* 115:265–84.

Sprenger, Carsten. 2002. "Ownership and Corporate Governance in Russian Industry: A Survey." European Bank for Reconstruction and Development Working Paper No. 70.

Stasavage, David. 2002. "Credible Commitment in Early Modern Europe: North and Weingast Revisited." *Journal of Law, Economics, and Organization* 18:155–86.

Stern, Marc A. 2001. "Pension Reform and Global Equity Markets." Birinyi Associates Inc. Topical Study No. 17, Westport, Conn.

Stiglitz, Joseph E., and Karla Hoff. 2003. "The Transition Process in Post-Communist Societies: Towards a Political Economy of Property Rights." Paper presented to the Annual Meetings of the American Political Science Association, August 30, Philadelphia.

Streeck, Wolfgang. 1984. *Industrial Relations in West Germany: A Case Study of the Car Industry.* London: Heinemann.

Strouse, Jean. 1999. *Morgan: American Financier.* New York: Random House.

Suchman, Mark C. 1994. "On Advice of Counsel: Law Firms and Venture Capital Funds as Information Intermediaries in the Structuration of Silicon Valley." Ph.D. diss., Department of Sociology, Stanford University.

Suchman, Mark C., and Mia L. Cahill. 1996. "The Hired Gun as Facilitator: Lawyers and the Suppression of Business Disputes in Silicon Valley." *Law and Society Inquiry* 21:679–712.

Suleiman, Ezra. 1987. *Private Power and Centralization in France: The Notaries and the State.* Princeton: Princeton University Press.

———. 1995. *Les resorts cachés de la réussite française.* Trans. Sylvette Gleize. Paris: Seuil.

Sundin, Anneli, and Sven-Ivan Sundqvist. 1998. *Owners and Power in Sweden's Listed Companies, 1997.* Stockholm: SIS Agarservice AB.

Suto, Megumi. 1999. "New Developments in the Japanese Corporate Governance in the 1990s: The Role of Pension Funds." *Hamburgische Welt-Wirtschafts-Archiv*, July.

Swank, Duane, and Cathie Jo Martin. 2001. "Employers and the Welfare State: The Political Economic Organization of Firms and Social Policy in Contemporary Capitalist Democracies." *Comparative Political Studies* 34:889–923.

Swenson, Peter A. 1989. *Fair Shares: Unions, Pay, and Politics in Sweden and West Germany*. Ithaca, N.Y.: Cornell University Press.

———. 2002. *Capitalists and Markets: The Making of Labor Markets and Welfare States in the United States and Sweden*. New York: Oxford University Press.

Sykes, Allen. 2000. *Capitalism for Tomorrow: Reuniting Ownership and Control*. Oxford: Capstone.

Thelen, Kathleen. 2004. *How Institutions Evolve: The Political Economy of Skills in Comparative-Historical Perspective*. New York: Cambridge University Press.

Thompson, F.M.L. 1963. *English Landed Society in the Nineteenth Century*. London: Routledge and Kegan Paul.

Thomson, Tracy A., and Gerald F. Davis. 1997. "The Politics of Corporate Control and the Future of Shareholder Activism in the United States." *Corporate Governance* 5:152–59.

Tiberghein, Yves. 2002a. "Political Mediation of Global Economic Forces: The Politics of Corporate Restructuring in Japan, France, and South Korea." Ph.D. diss., Stanford University.

———. 2002b. "State Mediation of Global Financial Forces: Different Paths of Structural Reforms in Japan and South Korea." *Journal of East Asian Studies* 2:103–41.

———. 2003. "Veto Players, Financial Globalization, and Policy Making: A Political Analysis of the Pathway of Structural Reforms in Japan, 1993–2002." Paper presented to the Annual Meetings of the American Political Science Association, August 28–31, Philadelphia.

Towers Perrin. 1999. Worldwide Total Remuneration Report. April.

Trumbull, Gunnar. 2000. "Divergent Paths of Product Market Regulation in France and Germany, 1970–1990." In *Handbook of Global Economic Policy*. Stuart S. Nagel, ed. New York: Marcel Dekker.

———. 2002. "The Rise of Consumer Politics: Market Institutions and Product Choice in Postwar France and Germany." Harvard Business School Working Paper No. 03-054.

Trumka, Richard L. 2002. "Comments on the SEC's Proposal S7-36-02 to Require Mutual Funds to Disclose Their Proxy Voting Policies." Letter to the Securities and Exchange Commission, December 6.

United States Congress. House of Representatives. 2002. *Sarbanes-Oxley Act of 2002*. 107th Congress. H.R. Report No. 107-610 (2002).

United States Securities and Exchange Commission. 2002. *Disclosure of Proxy Voting Policies and Proxy Voting Records by Registered Management Investment Companies*. September 20.

Useem, Michael. 1993. *Executive Defense: Shareholder Power and Corporate Reorganization*. Cambridge: Harvard University Press.

———. 1996. *Investor Capitalism: How Money Managers Are Changing the Face of America*. New York: HarperCollins.

van het Kaar, Robbert. 1998. "Pensions and Pension Funds Become Major Issue in Dutch Industrial Relations." *European Industrial Relations Observatory Online*. August. www.eiro.eurofond.ie.

van Lent, Laurence. 1995. "Pressure and Politics in Financial Accounting Regulations." University of Tilburg, January.

Véron, Nicolas, Matthieu Autret, and Alfred Galichon. 2004. *L'information financière en crise—comptabilité et capitalisme.* Paris: Odile Jacob.

Walter, Carl, and Fraser J. Howie. 2001. *To Get Rich Is Glorious! China's Stock Markets in the '80's and '90's.* New York: Palgrave Macmillan.

West, Mark. 1994. "The Pricing of Shareholder Derivative Actions in Japan and the United States." *Northwestern University Law Review* 88:1436–1507.

Westphal, James D., and Edward J. Zajac. 1998. "Symbolic Management of Stockholders: Corporate Governance Reforms and Shareholder Reactions." *Administrative Science Quarterly* 43:127–53.

Willer, Dirk. 1997. "Corporate Governance and Shareholder Rights in Russia." Centre for Economic Policy Research Discussion Paper No. 343.

Williamson, Oliver E. 1975. *Markets and Hierarchies: Analysis and Antitrust Implications.* New York: Oxford University Press.

———. 1995. *Organization Theory: From Chester Barnard to the Present and Beyond.* New York: Oxford University Press.

Womack, James P., Daniel T. Jones, and Daniel Roos. 1991. *The Machine That Changed the World: The Story of Lean Production.* New York: Harper Perennial.

World Bank. 1993. *The East Asian Miracle: Economic Growth and Public Policy.* New York: Oxford University Press.

Xu, Xiaonian, and Yan Wang. 1997. "Ownership Structure, Corporate Governance, and Firms' Performance: The Case of Chinese Stock Companies." World Bank Working Paper. http://www.worldbank.org/html/dec/Publications/Workpapers/WPS1700series/wps1794/wps1794.pdf.

Yano, Tomomi. 2001. "Nenkinshikin unyô kara mita corporate governance." Paper prepared for the International Corporate Governance Forum, July, Tokyo.

Yoo, Seong-Min. 1997. "Evolution of Government-Business Interface in Korea: Progress to Date and Reform Agenda Ahead." Korea Development Institute Working Paper No. 9711.

———. 1999. "Corporate Restructuring in Korea: Policy Issues before and during the Crisis." Korea Development Institute Working Paper No. 9903.

Yoo, Seong-Min, and Young-Jae Lin. 1999. "Big Business in Korea: New Learning and Policy Issues." Korea Development Institute Working Paper No. 9901.

Yoon, Youngmo. "Chaebol Reform: The Missing Agenda in 'Corporate Governance.'" Paper presented to the Conference on Corporate Governance in Asia: A Comparative Perspective, March 3–5, Seoul.

Zajac, Edward J., and James D. Westphal. 1994. "The Costs and Benefits of Managerial Incentives and Monitoring in Large U.S. Corporations: When Is More Not Better?" *Strategic Management Journal* 15:121–42.

———. 2004. "The Social Construction of Market Value: Institutionalization and Learning Perspectives on Stock Market Reactions." *American Sociological Review* 69:433–57.

Zeigler, Nick. 1997. *Governing Ideas: Strategies for Innovation in France and Germany.* Ithaca, N.Y.: Cornell University Press.

Zingales, Luigi. 2000. "In Search of New Foundations." *Journal of Finance* 55:1623–53.

Zorn, Dirk, Frank Dobbin, Julian Dierkes, and Man-shan Kwok. Forthcoming. "Managing Investors: How Financial Markets Reshaped the American Firm." In *The Sociology of Financial Markets.* Karin Knorr Cetina and Alexandru Preda, eds. Oxford: Oxford University Press.

INDEX

A&P, 251

ABP, 184–85, 185n97, 186, 240, 288

accountant's letter, 36n

accounting and auditing standards, 118n, 171, 200, 221–22, 235

accounting firms, 33, 35, 99, 116

Accounting Society of China (ASC), 195

acquisitions, 39, 113, 129–30, 166, 174

Adelphia, 1

Adenauer, Conrad, 161

Administradora de Fondos de Pensiones (AFP), 230, 230n27

agency costs, 28, 28n4, 32, 209

AGF-Paribas, 265

Ahold, 1, 3, 185n94, 219

Airbus, 272

Air France, 272

AKZO Nobel, 181

Alcan, 267

Alcatel, 212, 212n5

Algemene Bank Nederland (ABN), 185n97

Algemene Oudermans Wet (AGM), 184

Allende, Salvador, 228

Allmänna Tilläggspension (ATP), 145

allocative efficiency, 90

Alsthom, 271, 272

American Airlines, 251

American depository receipts (ADRs), 44n44, 103, 114–15, 288

American Federation of Labor (AFL), 246

American Federation of Labor–Congress of Industrial Organizations (AFL-CIO), 251–52

American model, 5–6, 29, 122

Amsterdam Bourse, 178, 181

Amsterdam Stock Exchange, 182

analytic narratives, 95

Anheuser-Busch, 251

antidirector rights, 46

antitakover devices, 39, 87, 129–30, 267

antitrust rules, 7, 89

Argentina, 18, 110, 111, 114, 188

Armstrong Commission, 2

Arthur Andersen, 117n37, 239

Asian financial crisis of 1997–98, 3, 82, 100, 119, 126, 131, 233, 234–35, 236, 286

asset-stripping, 222

Associação Brasileira das Companhias Abertas (ABRASCA), 108, 108n

Association Française de la Gestion Financière (AFG), 269

Association of Southeast Asian Nations (ASEAN), 232

Association pour le Régime de Retraite complémentaire de Salariés (ARRCO), 268

Assurances Générales de France and PARIBAS (AGF-Paribas), 265

audit practices, 44

Aufsichsrat, 45, 162n25, 163

Australia, 17, 18, 21, 75

Austria, 18, 25, 54

authoritarian systems, 79–83, 187–203

Avon Letter, 251n55

Aznar, José María, 135

Balladur, Edouard, 268

Bank for International Settlements (BIS), 100

Bank of England, 260

Bank of France, 263, 264

Banking Act, 264

Barisan Nasional, 233, 234

Bass brothers, 240

Belgium, 18

Berle-Means separation, 5–6, 245, 246

Berlusconi, Silvio, 135, 199

Big Five accounting firms, 117, 117n37, 118n38, 181, 200, 255, 267

Big Five Chilean families, 229

Big Four, 117, 194n109, 255

Biggs, John, 258

Big Six, 117, 255

binding appointments, 183, 183n86

Blair, Tony, 135, 262

blockholder model, 4–5, 15, 52, 137, 153

blockholding: class cleavage and, 96; in collective action problem, 38; to contain agency costs, 28n4; described, 16; in good governance deal, 99; MSPs and, 162, 301, 302, 303, 308–10; percentage of, 19; political cohesion and, 73, 74–75

BMW, 242

board independence, 45

boards of directors, 45, 115n, 222

Boehner, John A., 255n

Bolsa de Madrid, 110

bond-rating agencies, 35, 99, 116

Borsa Italiana, 110

Brazil, 18, 108, 108n, 110, 111, 188, 289

British Telecom, 240, 262
brokerage firms, 35
Bubble Period of 1985–89, 172
bumiputra, 236
Bundesverband der Deutscher Industrie
    (BDI), 108
Bush, George H. W., 135
Bush, George W., 135, 256–57
Business Accounting Discussion Council
    (BADC), 171n47
business judgment rule, 112
Business Roundtable, 252–53, 255

Caisse Nationale d'Assurance Vieillesse des
    Travailleurs Salariés (CNAVTS), 268
California Public Employees' Retirement
    System (CalPERS), 146, 174n53, 184, 185,
    197n117, 231, 240, 249, 251, 262, 292
Canada, 17, 18, 19, 21, 25, 75
capital, 140
capitalist economics policies (CEPs), 15, 27,
    58–59
Carnegie, Andrew, 242, 243, 250
Carter, Jimmy, 255
carve outs, 115
causal model, 57–59
Center-Right Liberal Democratic Party (LDP),
    168, 175
centralization, 156–57
Central Provident Fund (CPF), 199, 201, 202,
    203, 240
chaebol, 109, 110, 114, 119, 124–31, 188, 189
Chandler, Alfred P., 28, 126, 244
Chandler variables, 125
Charpin Plan, 268
"Chicago school" economy, 228, 229, 230
chief executive officer (CEO), 45, 251,
    253–54, 266
Chile: AFPs options in, 229–30; blockholdings
    in, 110; conglomerates in, 229; corporate
    ownership in, 17, 21; cross-listing in, 114;
    cross-shareholding in, 4; MSPs in, 50, 51,
    112, 229–30; oligarchy in, 188; pension
    reform in, 228–29, 230; Pinochet period in,
    205, 228; privatization in, 228; transparency
    in, 209, 228–32
China: Communist Party in, 193, 194;
    economic systems in, 193–94; MSPs in, 50,
    51; ownership concentration in, 18–19, 21,
    115; pension liabilities in, 198; political
    system in, 80; politics in, 198–99; reputa-
    tional intermediaries in, 197–98;
    selectorate–electorate coalition in, 192–99;
    stock exchanges in, 194n107, 196

China Institute of Certified Public Accountants
    (CICPA), 194, 195
China Securities Regulatory Commission
    (CSRC), 194, 195, 196
Chinese accounting standards (CAS), 194
Chinese Communist Party (CCP), 203
Chirac, Jacques, 264, 265, 268
Christian democratic model, 78n36, 159,
    169n20, 282
Christian Democratic Party (CDU), 3, 161,
    163, 263
Christian Democratic Union, 160
Chung Ju Yung, 124, 129n51, 189, 199
Circulo de Empresarios, 108
Citicorp/Travelers, 239
civil law countries, 83–87
civil servant systems, 215–16
class cleavages, 95–148
class conflict, 11
class conflict models, 23–24, 60–61, 62–64, 95
cleavages, 95–148, 149–204, 205–73
Clinton, Bill, 135
coalitions, 22, 23, 59–67
Code of Takeovers and Mergers, 235
codes of conduct, 288
codetermination, 157–58, 160, 163
Colbertism, 262
Colgate Palmolive, 251
collective bargaining, 157–59, 247, 310
Comité de la Reglementation Comptable
    (CRC), 267
Committee on Company Legislation, 202
Committee on Corporate Governance, 202
Committee on Disclosure and Accounting
    Standards, 202
common law countries, 83–87
Communism, 160, 161
Communist Party, 193
Compagnie des Agents de Change (CAC-40),
    266, 267
Companies Act, 235
companyism, 149n
Compaq, 117
compromesso historico, 159n19
Conable, Barber, 248
Conference Board, 250, 257
conglomerates, 87, 89, 179n72
Congress of Industrial Organizations
    (CIO), 246
Conseil National de la Comptabilité (CNC), 267
consensus systems, 10, 25–26, 71, 72–73,
    76–77, 82
conservative investors, 63
consumers, 77–78

contracterian theory, 37, 38–39, 112
control, 16–20, 43, 46–47
Coordinated Market Economies (CME), 6, 11, 22, 52, 79, 158, 161, 264, 284, 282
coordination index (CI), 53–55
corporate governance: authority in, 30; benefits of, 57; change in, 281–83; convergence versus diversity in, 283–85; corporatism and, 306; country- or firm-level premium in, 102–3; debate over, 3–4, 293; degrees of coordination in, 11, 20, 21–22; described, 3, 285; "legal family" school and, 83–85; measures of, 286; MSPs in, 16, 20–22; patterns of, 15–26; pension plans and, 218–20; policy consequences of, 12–13; political explanation for, 10–12; power and responsibility in, 1–2; rhetoric and legitimacy in, 293; variance in, 4–10, 36–37, 63n10, 277–78
corporate governance law, 4
corporate governance systems, 2–3, 4, 12–13, 16, 20–22
corporate ownership, 16–20
corporate scandals: accountability and, 1, 2; 401(k) effect and, 219–20, 220n18; global, 1, 6; regulation and 35–36n25; reputational intermediary role in, 116, 240
Corporate Sector Transparency and Publicity Act (TransPuG), 162, 163
corporations, 91, 281–82
corporatism, 149, 150, 159–60, 306, 307
corporatist compromise, 207–8, 279, 284
corporatist model, 150–59; authoritarian, 187–203; described, 23, 25, 64–65, 77; measurement in, 25; predictions and testing in, 153–60, 167; preference cleavage in, 150–51; theories of, 151–52
Council of Institutional Investors (CII), 240, 251
Council on Annual Reporting, 182n80
Council on Foreign Relations, 1n2
credible commitment, 76–77
Cromme Commission, 162
crony capitalism, 150
cross-class coalition, 24, 149–87, 246
cross-class coalition model, 206–7
cross-listing of shares, 44n44, 103, 114–15, 288–89
cross-shareholding, 4, 5n7, 13, 18
crowding-out effect, 218
Czech Republic, 86

Daewoo, 124, 127, 129, 129n51, 131
Daimler-Chrysler, 164

Dassault, 272
Database of Political Indicators (DPI), 72, 74
Davis Global Advisors, 162n25
dead hand provisions, 45
defined benefit, 247
defined benefit pension, 215n11
defined contribution pension, 215n11
degrees of coordination (DoC), 11; as CEP component, 15, 27, 58–59; described, 277–78; economic policies and, 20, 21–22; index of, 20, 21–22; MSPs and, 54; variables in, 284
Deloitte Touche Tohmatsu, 117n37
Déminor, 269
democracies, 73–76, 81
Democratic Party, 243, 256
Deng Xiaoping, 193, 292
Denmark, 18, 54, 152
dependent variable, 15, 16–20
depository receipts, 44n44, 103, 114–15, 288
deregulation, 255
Deutsche Asset Management, 117, 163, 163n29, 165
Deutsche Bank, 117, 165, 239
Deutscher Rechnungslegungs Standards Committee (DRSC), 163
diffusion, 4–5, 15, 51–54, 75
disclosure, 211
Disclosure and Accounting Standards Committee (DASC), 200
dislocation, 282–83
Donaldson, Paul, 258
Drexel Burnham Lambert, 250
Drucker, Peter, 248, 249, 259
DSC, 212n5
DSM, 185n94, 181
Dutch East India Company (VOC), 177, 177n67
Dutch financial institution (AEGON Nederland), 185n97

East Asian Tigers, 29, 125
economic sociology, 57, 83, 87–93
economic value added (EVA), 201
efficiency, 57
electoral law systems, 69–71, 75–76
Elf Acquitaine, 267–68
Ellison, Lawrence, 242
embedded economies, 88, 89
Employee Retirement Income Security Act (ERISA), 247, 249, 283
Employees Provident Fund (EPF), 201, 233, 234, 239

Employee Stock Option Plans (ESOPs),
    172–73, 211–12, 212n5, 235, 248
Employee Welfare Pension Insurance
    Scheme, 219
employment insurance, 152
employment security, 136, 305
Enron scandal, 1, 6, 117n37, 219, 220, 256
Enterprise Chamber of the Amsterdam
    Court of Justice, 185
Enzi, Michael, 257
equity index funds, 250
equity markets, 245, 282
equity portfolio managers, 178
Ernst & Young, 117n37
ethnic network, 5
European Community, 3, 166
European Corporate Governance Network, 17
European Monetary Union, 184
European Parliament, 166
European Union (EU), 165, 180, 271, 292
Exxon, 244

Falun Gong, 193
family-held ownership, 17, 109–10
family network, 5
Federal Employees Retirement fund, 219
Federal Ministry of Economics and Research,
    165n33
Federal Reserve, 244, 257
Federation Internationale des Bourses de
    Valeurs (FIBV), 104
Federation of European Stock Exchanges
    (FESE), 109–10
Federation of Korean Industry (FKI), 108, 125
feedback effect, 58
feedback loop, 79
Fidelity Mutual Fund, 249, 252
filibuster rules, 68
Financial Accounting Standards Board (FASB),
    44, 254, 255
financial disclosure, 43
financial forecasting, 91
financial intermediaries, 164–66, 212
Financial Services Act, 260
Financial Services Agency (FSA), 130,
    171n47, 176
Financial Services and Markets Act, 260
Financial Services Authority (FSA), 260
Financial Supervisory Commission (FSC), 129
Finland, 18, 25
first pillar pension plans, 213–15
Fisk, Jim, 245
Ford Motor, 242
foreign direct investment (FDI), 97, 174n55

foreign portfolio investment (FPI), 98, 103–6,
    120, 141, 178, 197, 228, 304
founder-entrepreneurs, 242
401(k) effect, 219–20, 248–49
401(k) plans, 175–76, 216, 225, 225n22, 239
Four Tigers, 233
framing structures, 27–56
France: civil law in, 84, 86; corporate scandal
    in, 3; cross-listing in, 114; economic reversals
    in, 7, 20; future in, 272–73; Matignon
    Accords in, 142; MSPs in, 50, 51, 50, 51;
    overview of, 262–63; ownership concentra-
    tion in, 18, 19, 21, 266; political system in,
    71, 72, 75, 269–72; politics in, 135;
    preferences in, 269–72; privatization in,
    264, 265; reforms in, 152, 268–69;
    shareholder protections in, 267–68; state
    leadership in, 263–67
France Telecom, 267, 272
Free Democratic Party (FDP), 160, 162, 166
Furukawa, 169

game theory, 33
Gates, William, 242
generally accepted accounting principles
    (GAAP), 44, 254
General Motors, 30
General Telephone and Electronics
    (GTE), 251
German model, 161, 165
German Social Democratic Party (SDP), 3,
    160, 161–62, 163, 166
Germany: board membership in, 45; civil law
    in, 84; corporatism in, 25, 157–58, 159,
    160–67; cross-shareholding in, 4; economic
    variance in, 6, 12, 20; financial intermedi-
    aries in, 164–66; ownership concentration in,
    17, 18, 110, 127; pension funds in, 164–65;
    political system in, 71; politics in, 3, 169,
    161–62; postwar occupation of, 163n30, 161;
    reforms in, 152; revival in, 29; training
    system in, 78n35; transparency in, 211;
    unions in, 211; works councils in, 207
Gerschenkron, Alexander, 12, 161, 261
Gerstner, Louis, 257
Gesetz zur Kontrolle und Transparenz im
    Unternehmensbereich (KonTraG),
    162, 163
Glass-Steagall Act, 2, 245
Global Corporate Governance Forum (GCGF),
    119, 119n42
golden shares, 45, 267, 291
good governance deal, 96, 97–99, 101–3,
    110–12, 141, 266

Google, 242, 291
Gould, Jay, 245
governance. *See* corporate governance; corporate governance systems
governance games, 33–34, 37
Governance Metrics, 286
governance patterns, 15–26
government held ownership, 17
"grabbing hand" mode, 292n
Gramm, Phil, 257
Gramm-Leach-Bliley Act, 255
Grasso, Richard, 220
Great Depression, 142, 245
great reversals, 7, 19, 20
Greece, 18
greenmail payments, 240, 251
gross domestic product (GDP), 37, 120, 126, 130, 232, 268, 302
Grove, Andrew, 257
Grumman, 251
Gucci, 288

Handelsgesetzbuch (HGB), 162
Harper & Rowe, 251
Hasan, Bob, 188
Hermes, 262
Hewlett-Packard, 117
Hicks-Kenworthy measure, 25, 153, 154–55, 154n, 308
High Level Finance Committee on Corporate Governance, 234, 235
high-tech entrepreneurs, 116, 254, 291
Historical Compromise, 149
Ho Ching, 201
Hoffa, James, 247
Holland, 180, 279
Hollinger, 1
Hong Kong, 18, 21, 39, 50, 51, 103, 197n116
Hong Kong Bank, 239
Hoogovens, 185n94
hostile takeovers: attempts at, 174n55, 288; banks and, 164; as managerism challenge, 250–54, 269; collective action problem and, 38, 39; protections against, 39, 87, 129–30, 166, 174, 183, 201; worker preferences on, 222–23
hua qiao, 200, 232, 234
Hu Jintao, 193
Hyundai, 124, 127, 129, 129n51, 189

Ibrahim, Anwar, 236
Icahn, Carl, 250
implicit pension debt (IPD), 25, 164, 198, 213–15, 213n9, 218, 226, 268, 274, 311

impression management, 91, 91n69
incentives, 46–47, 89, 195, 223
income inequality, 138, 306
incomplete contracts, 30–32, 35, 36, 38n26
index of political cohesion (IPCOH), 73, 74, 75, 304
India, 18
individually held ownership, 17
Indonesia, 3, 18, 21, 82, 188, 202
information practices, 43–44
initial public offering (IPO), 231, 266, 288
insider kleptocracy, 192
insider knowledge, 111
insiders, 5, 179
Institute of CPAs of Singapore (ICPAS), 200
institutional complementarity, 51–53, 51n, 290–91
institutional investment, 24
institutions, 67–93; consensus, 69–78; interest groups and, 2, 69n22; majoritarian, 69–78; parchment, 68n19; preferences and, 22–26, 57–83, 69n22, 277; role of in corporate governance, 8; types of, 10, 67–83
interest aggregations, 69–71
interest groups, 2, 11, 15
intermediate variables, 15
Internal Revenue Code, 246
Internal Revenue Service (IRS), 246
International Accounting Standard (IAS), 118n, 163, 267
International Accounting Standards Board (IASB), 43, 44, 118n, 182
International Accounting Standards Committee (IASC), 118n
international bond markets, 122
International Data Corporation (IDC), 174n55
Internationale Nederlanden Group (ING), 185, 185n92
International Federation of Accountants (IFAC), 118n
International Federation of Stock Values (FIBV),
international financial organization (IFO), 99–100, 118–19
International Financial Reporting Standards (IFRS), 43–44, 182
International Monetary Fund (IMF), 100, 104, 119, 294
International Organization of Securities Commissions, 118n
International Paper, 251
intervening variables, 15
investment models, 23

investor model: class cleavage in, 96–131;
    conservative support of, 63; contrasted with
    other models, 273–74, 280; described, 61,
    62–63, 206, 289; good governance deal of,
    96–99; labor in, 96–97; pension funds in,
    121; variance in, 100–101
Ireland, 18, 21, 25
Israel, 18, 115
Italy: coalition government in, 70, 264;
    corporate scandal in, 3; cross-listing in, 114;
    employment security in, 136; ownership
    concentration in, 17, 18, 19, 21, 109–10;
    politics in, 135; shareholder protection in,
    50, 51, 108; tax evasion in, 111
iterative game, 33, 34n26, 37
Ito Hirobumi, 168
Iwasaki Totaro, 168, 188

Jaffré, Philippe, 267–68
Japan: banks in, 29, 176–77; bubble period in,
    172; coalition politics in, 135; company
    unions in, 207; consensus system in, 26, 72,
    167–77; corporatism in, 25, 159–60, 167–77;
    cross-shareholding in, 4, 5n7, 13, 18, 52;
    economic growth in, 29; economic variance
    in, 6, 7, 12, 20; great reversal in, 168–71;
    incomplete contracts in, 31; lobbyists in, 108;
    MSPs in, 50, 51, 171–74; ownership concen-
    tration in, 17, 18–19, 21, 54; pensions in,
    175–76, 292; political institutions in,
    174–75; political system in, 70–71; postwar
    occupation of, 149, 163n30, 167, 169; reputa-
    tional intermediaries in, 176–77, 208; VOC
    trade agreement in, 177, 177n67; welfare
    state in, 152
Japan Corporate Governance Association, 174,
    174n53
Japanese Association of Pension Funds, 168
Japanese Institute of Certified Public Accoun-
    tants (JICPA), 171n47
Jiang Zemin, 193, 197n115
job preservation, 209, 210–11, 249
job security, 24, 127, 136–38, 211
Juppé, Alain, 268, 269, 271
Jurong Shipyard, 200

Kabunushi Ombudsman, 172n49
kaisha-shugi, 149n
kansayaku, 171, 173, 208
Kapitalaufnahmeerleichterungsgesetz
    (KapAEG), 162
Keidanren, 108, 168, 169, 171n47, 173–74,
    173n52
keiretsu system, 18, 125, 170

Keizaidantai-rengokai (Keidanren), 108, 168,
    169, 171n47, 173–74, 173n52
Keizaidoyukai, 173
Keppel, 200
Keynesian economic policy, 142, 143
Khordokovsky, Mikhail, 190, 199, 294
Kigyō Kaikei Shingikai, 171n47
Kim Dae Jung, 114, 119, 123, 127, 128, 131
Kim Woo Choong, 124, 129n51
Kim Young Sam, 123, 127
KLM, 185
KMPG Peat Marwick, 117n37
Kohl, Helmut, 135
Koito Manufacturing, 174n55
Koo In Hwoi, 124, 129n51
Korea: and Asian financial crisis, 3, 100, 131;
    chaebols in, 109, 110, 114, 119, 124–31, 188,
    189; class cleavage in, 130; cross-listings in,
    115; democratization in: 2–3, 125, 127, 128;
    foreign investment in, 104; labor unions in,
    127–31; oligarchy in, 124, 125; ownership
    concentration in, 18; reforms in, 107, 119,
    128, 131; shareholder protection in, 99,
    123–24, 123n, 130; shifting preferences in,
    123–31 tax evasion in, 111
Korea Association of Securities Dealers Auto-
    mated Quotation (KOSDAQ), 114, 115
Korea Electric Power (KEPCO), 128
Korean Accounting Standards Board
    (KASB), 129
Korean Financial Accounting Standards
    (KFAS), 129
Korean Stock Exchange (KSE), 104, 114, 126,
    128, 130
Korea Telecom, 128
Korea Tobacco, 128
KPN, 185
Kuala Lumpur Stock Exchange (KLSE), 234,
    235, 236
Kumpulan Wang Simpanan Pekerja, 233
Kwok family, 232
kyōtō keizai, 159n19

Labor, U.S. Department of, 251n55
labor contract, 8
labor markets, 78n36
labor power model, 23, 24, 62, 64, 132–46, 206
labor unions: collective bargaining of, 157–59,
    247; private-sector, 173; reform and, 146;
    retirement benefits and, 216n13; in social
    pacts, 142; strikes by, 127, 169; takeovers
    and, 251
Landis, Judge, 241, 255
Latin America, 70, 188

law-and-economics tradition, 27
Law on Control and Transparency of
    Corporations, 162
Law on Facilitating Raising Capital, 162
Leading Corporate Governance Indicators, 182
Leavitt, Arthur, 254
Lee Byung Chul, 124, 129n51
Lee Hsien Loong, 199, 201
Lee Kuan Yew, 199
left political parties, 132–33
left-right cleavage, 134–36, 137
"legal family" school, 7, 8, 57, 83–87
Legends Program, 118
legislation: antitakeover, 39, 87; job security,
    24; MSP, 39–51; scandal-influenced, 7
Le Pen, Jean-Marie, 271
Liberal Democrats, 135
liberal market economy (LME), 263: centraliza-
    tion in, 158; coordination in, 11, 22, 52, 284;
    diffusion in, 96; education and training in,
    78n36; influence of, 153; politics in, 166
Lieberman, Joseph, 255
limited liability company, 1
Lim Soeliang, 188
Lippo Group, 188
liquidation, 109–10
listing requirements, 34, 99
lobbying, 66, 98, 255, 255n
London Stock Exchange (LSE), 114–15,
    259, 260
Lucky-Goldstar (LG), 124, 129, 129n51

Major, John, 135
majoritarian systems, 10, 25, 69–78; competi-
    tion in, 280–81; credibility in, 76–77; effect
    predictions in, 72–73; measurements of, 72;
    political cohesion in, 82
Malaysia: and Asian financial crisis, 3, 233,
    234–35, 236; diffusion in, 51; ethnicity in,
    232; hostile takeovers in, 39; ownership con-
    centration in, 18, 110; permissive protections
    in, 236–37; political system in, 82, 232,
    233–34; preferences in, 233; privatization in,
    235–36
Malaysian Accounting Standards Board
    (MASB), 235
Malaysian Association of CPAs, 235
Malaysian Chinese Association (MCA),
    234, 236
Malaysian Corporate Governance Code,
    234, 235
Malaysian Institute of Accountants, 235
Malaysian Institute of Corporate
    Governance, 234

Malaysia's generally accepted accounting princi-
    ples (MGAAP), 235
managerial agency costs, 28, 32, 209
managerial agency failure, 66
managerial incentives, 46–47
managerism, 149n, 192, 205, 237–41
managerism model, 23, 25, 62, 66–67, 273–74
managers: as a category, 275; coalition align-
    ments of, 8–9, 23; compensation for, 43,
    195, 201, 223, 237; described, 59, 278;
    discipline of, 112–13; in keiretsu system,
    170, 170n45, 172, 173; monitoring of,
    213–18; public accountability of, 112,
    221–22; preferences of, 59–67
M&A Consulting, 174n55
Mannesmann, 164, 164n31, 165, 165n36
Mao Tse-tung, 193
Marcos, Ferdinand, 188, 202
market capitalization, 103, 104, 304
market control bias, 49n53
market economies, 11
market for control, 38
market power, 132
Matignon Accords, 142
Matsushita, 170
Maxwell, Robert, 291n
McCall, H. Carl, 220, 220n18
McCaw, Craig, 250
media, 1n1
mergers and acquisitions (M&A), 39, 113,
    129–30, 166, 179n72, 243, 259
Messier, Jean-Paul, 294–95
Mexico, 18
microeconomics, 30
Microsoft, 212, 242, 291
Milken, Michael, 250
Millennium Democracy Party, 128
Miller, Zel, 257
Ministry of Economy and Finance, 271
Ministry of Finance (MOF): Chinese, 194, 195,
    195n110, 196; French, 264, 267; Japanese,
    171n47
Ministry of Finance and Economy (MOFE),
    129, 130
Ministry of International Trade and Industry
    (MITI), 140
minority shareholder protection (MSP): block-
    holding and, 301, 302, 303; as CEP propo-
    nent, 15, 27, 54, 58–59; described, 4, 277;
    economic policies and, 16, 20–22; elements
    of, 20–21; employment security rules and,
    305; index of, 48; labor and, 134; in laws and
    regulations, 39–51; market capitalization
    and, 103, 104, 304; ownership concentration

minority (*continued*)
  and, 306; ownership trade-off in, 50; political
  form and, 68; predictions of, 47–51; reform,
  145, 171; resistance to, 108; on retirement
  assets, 305
Minority Shareholder Watchdog Committee,
  234, 235
Mitbestimmung, 45, 163, 167
Mitsubishi, 168, 188
Mitsubishi Bank, 239
Mitterrand, François, 265, 269, 272
Mohammed Mohatir, 233
money managers, 238–41
Monks, Robert, 256n66
Morgan, J. P., 34, 202, 242, 243, 245
Morgan Stanley Capital International
  Index, 49n54
motivation patterns, 90
mutual funds, 224–25, 249, 251–52
Myanmar, 80, 202

National Association of Securities Dealers
  Automated Quotations (NASDAQ),
  103, 113, 115, 288
National Cash Register Corporation
  (NCR), 251
National Front, 233
National Labor Relations Act, 246
National Labor Relations Board
  (NLRB), 247
Naziism, 160, 161
neoliberal models, 63
Neptune Orient, 200
nested authority, 4n3
Netherlands: accounting standards in, 182;
  antitakeover devices in, 182, 183, 185; coalition government in, 70; continuity and consultation in, 184–85; corporate scandal in, 3;
  corporatism in, 160, 177–80; foreign investments in, 178, 179, 181n79; great reversals
  in, 20; industrialization in, 180–81; Japanese
  trade agreement with, 177, 177n67; oversight
  protections in, 182; ownership concentration
  in, 18, 19, 21, 54; pension funds in, 184–86,
  185n97, 240; political system in, 72; sectoral
  conflict in, 177–87; shareholder protections
  in, 21, 50, 51, 178, 279, 288; *structuur-regeling*
  laws in, 181
Netherlands Company Law, 182n82
Neuer Markt, 109, 115, 167
New Deal, 209n
New Economic Regulations, 265
new-money entrepreneurs, 113–14, 115,
  231, 232

New York State Common Retirement Fund
  (NYSCRF), 220
New York Stock Exchange (NYSE), 103, 115,
  117, 117n36, 145
New Zealand, 18, 25
nexus of contracts, 31, 91
Nikkeiren, 168, 169, 173
Nissan, 169
non-bank financial intermediaries
  (NBFI), 126
non-executive director (NED), 45, 100,
  100–101n2, 108, 129, 200, 235, 290
North Korea, 80
Norway, 18, 25, 110
Novartis, 271
Novo Mercado, 115, 289
noyaux durs, 265, 269
NRE bill, 271
Nuovo Mercato, 115

OECD Corporate Governance Principles, 107,
  122, 294
offshore tax shelters, 111
old-money blockholders, 92, 108, 111, 113, 114
oligarchy model, 23, 25, 62, 65, 95, 187–89, 235
O'Neill, Paul, 257
one-off game, 34n20, 37
operating executive system, 172
Oracle, 212, 291
ordinary least squares (OLS), 227, 307–10
organizational capacity, 28
organizational diversity, 13
Organization for Economic Cooperation and
  Development (OECD), 18, 26, 79, 100, 122,
  154, 203
organized market economy (OME), 78n36, 166
outcomes, 12, 16–20, 23, 58
oversight, 43, 45, 182
owners: as a category, 274; coalition alignments
  of, 8–9, 23; described, 59–60, 278; preferences of, 59–67
ownership buckets, 17
ownership concentration, 299–300, 306
Oxley, Michael, 254, 255, 256

Pakistan, 86
Panel on Takeovers and Mergers, 260
parchment institutions, 68n19
Paris Bourse, 265n88, 266
Park Chung Hee, 124, 188, 231
parliamentary system, 70, 71nn27 and 28
Parmalat, 1, 3
party systems, 69–71
path dependence, 29, 284

PAYGO (pay-as-you-go) pension system, 9, 25, 177, 184, 213–15, 268–69
Pechiney, 267
Pension Benefits Guarantee Corporation (PBGC), 247
pension funds: active versus passive, 238, 252; bankrupted, 131; coalitions and, 9; corporatism and, 160, 164–65, 175–76, 177n64 and 65; equity investments of, 66; global, 121; private, 217; raided, 291n; transparency and, 65–66, 145–46
pension plans, 211–13; firm-level, 212, 215–16; individual, 212, 216–18; managerial monitoring and, 213–18; pillars of, 212, 213–16, 311; supplementary, 212, 216; underfunded, 213–15, 247, 268
Pensions Advisory Committee, 175
People's Action Party (PAP), 199, 202, 203
People's Liberation Army, 193
personal retirement account (PRA), 230, 230n27, 231
Peters Commission Corporate Governance Report, 185
Philippines, 18, 82, 188, 202
Philips, 181, 185n91
Pickens, T. Boone, 174n55, 250
Piera, Jose, 230
Pinochet, Augusto, 205, 228
Pitt, Harvey, 255n, 257, 258
Pohang Iron and Steel, 126, 128
poison pills, 5, 45, 87, 89, 267, 292
Poland, 86
Poldermodel, 179
political cohesion index, 73, 74, 75, 304
political economy, 90
political institutions. See institutions
political parties, 75–76
political science, 58, 89
politics: coalitions in, 59–66; elements of, 2, 58; institutions in, 67–83; legal traditions and, 86–87; preferences in, 22–26, 57–67, 69–68; U.S. corporate governance reversals and, 2
populism, 245
portfolio diversification, 106–7
portfolio investors, 98, 102n9
portfolio theory, 32
Port of Singapore Authority (PSA), 200
Portugal, 18, 21, 110, 264
preference: in class cleavage, 95–148; coalitions and, 59–67; corporate governance, 8, 59–68; feedback loop to, 79; institutions and, 67–83, 277; labor, 132–46; political, 16, 22–26; single-country, 278–80; theories of, 60
preferred shares, 183, 183n86

presidential system, 70, 71nn27 and 28
Price Waterhouse Coopers, 117n37
pricing, 91
principal-agent theory, 42, 241
priority shares, 183, 183n86
private bonding, 33–35, 36–37, 261, 281–82
private control bias, 49n53
private equity funds, 110n21
private ordering, 32, 37–38
private ordering guarantee, 97
private ordering model, 97–99
private pensions, 216–18, 226, 312
privatization, 128, 167, 190, 236, 261, 264, 265, 291
privatized pensions, 179, 184
producers, 77–78
profit sharing, 248
property and voice model, 60, 61, 62, 65
proportional representation system, 70n25
Provisional Accounting Regulations for Joint-Stock Limited Enterprises, 194
Proxinvest, 268
Prudent Man Rule, 247
public accountability, 1, 207, 221–22
Public Accounting Oversight Board, 257
public employee pension funds, 215–16, 225, 249, 250
Public Employees Fund, 240
public policy, 2, 8, 16, 20–22
Pure Food and Drug Act, 244
Putin, Vladimir, 190, 294

quality of corporate law (QCL), 24, 39–40, 41n37, 42, 63n10, 134, 139, 166
quasi rents, 209, 291n

rates of return, 249–50
Reagan, Ronald, 89, 135, 248
regulatory market, 6
regulatory policies, 2, 35–36
regulatory reform, 34, 39
religion, 159
Rengō labor federation, 173
replacement effect, 218
Republican Party, 255, 256
reputational intermediaries (RI): ambiguous, 116–18, 287; class cleavage role of, 99–100; conflicted, 38, 239, 239n, 241, 254–56; corporatism and, 176–77; described, 2; in game playing, 34n20; managerial performance and, 5; monitoring role of, 33–35, 241, 254–55, 256; in oligarchic system, 197–98; private bonding and, 34–35; role of, in scandals, 116; single- versus multi-purpose, 275

reputation building, 33–35
residual control, 32–33
residual risk, 32–33
residual state ownership, 291
Rhenish capitalism, 6, 160, 163, 166
Rho Myo Hun, 123
Rho Tae Woo, 125, 188
Ricardo-Viner theory, 151–52, 152n8
Rocard, Michel, 268
Rockefeller, John, 242, 243, 244, 250
Rockwell, 251
Roundtable on Corporate Governance, 1n2
Royal Dutch Airlines (KLM), 185
Royal Dutch Shell, 181
Russia, 150, 189, 190–92, 263

Samsung, 124, 129, 129n51
Sanofi/Aventis, 271
São Paulo Exchange, 289
Sarbanes, Paul, 256
Sarbanes-Oxley Act, 7; debate and lobbying
    over, 220, 243, 251, 256–58; implementation
    of, 118, 254; politics and, 2, 256–58, 256n67
Scandinavian model, 143
Scania, 144
Schröder, Gerhardt, 135
scripts, 92
second pillar assets, 215–16
sectoral cleavage, 11, 149–204
sectoral models, 23, 25, 60, 61, 62, 64–65, 95
Securities and Exchange Act, 2, 243
Securities and Exchange Commission (SEC),
    34, 220, 254; carve out exemptions of, 115;
    lobbying of, 118, 255; on mutual fund proxy
    voting, 251; origins of, 2, 209n, 241, 245;
    prosecution by, 240–41; regulation by, 117,
    255, 258; on shareholder vote, 252
Securities and Investment Board (SIB), 260
Securities Finance Corporation, 173n52
securities firms, 33
securities law, 4
securities lawyers, 35
securities markets, 99
selectorate, 80
self-dealing, 222
self-regulatory organization (SRO), 260
Sembawang, 200
SembCorp, 200
Shanghai Bank, 239
shareholder, 9–10, 67n
shareholder activism, 88, 89, 292
shareholder model, 4–5, 52
shareholder protections, 4, 37, 42–43, 75, 120,
    308–10

shareholder value, 91, 174, 209, 294–95
Shell, 181, 185n91
Sherman Antitrust Act, 2, 7
shikko yakuinei, 172, 244
Shoei, 174n55
Siemens, 164
signaling, 91
Silicon Valley, 88
Singapore: governance approach in, 198;
    hua qiao control in, 200; overview of, 199;
    ownership concentration in, 18, 110;
    pension systems in, 199, 201; politics in,
    202–3; shareholder protections in, 21,
    200–201
Singapore Airlines, 200
Singapore Institute of Directors, 202
Singapore Power, 200
Singapore Stock Exchange (SSE), 200, 201
Singapore Technologies, 200
Singapore Telecom, 200
Single European Act, 264
Snow, John, 257, 258
Sociaal Economische Raad (SER), 185, 186
social democracy, 160, 161–62, 163
social democratic model, 64, 78n36, 132–33,
    133n34, 282
social democratic power, 24
social investing, 249–50
socialism, 269–70
social market, 6
social prestige, 110, 110–11n22
social security, 215, 245
Sōhyō, 173
South Africa, 18, 110
Southeast Asia, 202
South Korea. See Korea
Soziale Marktwirtschaft, 159n19
Spain, 18, 109–10, 111, 135, 264
Spitzer, Elliot, 258
staggered boards, 45
stakeholder, 9–10, 67n
stakeholder capitalism, 6
stakeholder model, 4–5
stakeholder values, 168
Standard & Poor, 286
standard model, 291
Standard Oil Corporation, 244
state-owned enterprise (SOE): ADR use by,
    114; Chinese, 192, 196, 198; French, 265,
    266, 267; governance and, 291–92; liquida-
    tion of control in, 109; in Singapore, 200;
    unions of, 173
state ownership model, 5
State Street Investments, 186

Stichting Corporate Governance Onderzoek voor Pensioenfondsen (SCGOP), 185, 240
Stichting Pensioen Fonds (ABP), 184–85, 185n97, 186, 240, 288
Stichting Pensioenfonds voor de Gezondheid, Geestelijke en Maatschappelijke Belangen (PGGM), 184, 185, 240
stock exchanges, 34, 44, 99–100, 115–16, 117
stock grants, 211–12, 253–54
stock options: employee, 172–73, 211–12, 212n5, 235, 248; executive, 253–54, 266–267; taxation on, 266n92
stock transfer restrictions, 45
Stolper-Samuelson theory, 151–52, 152n8
structural determinism, 30
structuur-regeling laws, 181
Studebaker Corporation, 247
Suharto family, 202
SunKyong (SK), 129
Superintendencia de Seguros y Valores (SVS), 229
supplementary pension plans, 212, 216
sustainable growth, 292
Svenska Arbetgivarforening (SAF), 146
Sweden: coalitions in, 70, 133–34, 152; corporatism in, 25; diffusion in, 51; great reversals in, 20; labor movement in, 140; ownership concentration in, 17, 18, 110, 144; reforms in, 145–46; shareholder protection in, 99, 108, 112, 279; welfare state in, 71n29, 140, 145
Swedish National Pension Insurance Funds, 144
Switzerland, 18, 71n29, 103
Syndicat National des chemins de fers (SNCF), 272

Taft-Hartley funds, 215, 249
Taiwan, 18, 108, 110, 111
takeovers, 39, 113. *See also* hostile takeovers
Tax Equity and Fiscal Responsibility Act (TEFRA), 248
tax evasion, 111
Tax Reduction Act of 2000, 162
Teachers Insurance and Annuity Association–College Retirement Equities Fund. *See* TIAA-CREF
Teamsters Union Central States Pension Fund, 247
Temasek, 199, 201, 202, 203
Temasek listed companies (TLCs), 201
Tennessee Valley Authority (TVA), 245
termination liability method, 213n9
Texaco, 240

Thailand, 3, 18, 72, 82, 189, 234
Thaksin Shinawatra, 189, 199
Thatcher, Margaret, 70, 135, 261, 262
third pillar pension, 216–18
Thomson St Gobain, 272
TIAA-CREF, 230, 240, 249, 258
Tokyo Stock Exchange, 18, 171, 174, 178
tort law, 39, 40–43
torts model, 85
Total Fina, 268
total stock market capitalization measure, 20n
Toyota, 30, 44n45, 170, 291
trade disputes, 13
trade unions, 132
transfer restrictions, 267
transitional systems, 79–83
transparency: in authoritarian systems, 80; class conflict versus, 206–7; in corporatist model, 65, 160; crowding-out effect in, 218; described, 208–10; job security through, 211; managerism and, 237–41; pension patterns and, 213–20; political and economic, 13; prediction and evidence of, 223–28; replacement effect in, 218; shareholding patterns and, 211–213; social pressures and, 80; workers and, 210–11, 220–23
transparency coalition model: changes in, 284; contrasted with other models, 273–74, 280; described, 65–66, 208–10; measures of, 25; preference cleavage in 205–73; reforms in, 145, 142
Treasury, U.S. Department of, 257
trust offices, 183
Turkey, 18, 21
Turner, Ted, 250
two-party system, 70, 70n25
Tyco International, 1, 252, 256

UAP-BNP, 265
unfunded pension plans, 213–15
Unilever, 181, 185n91
Unions des Assurances de Paris and Banque National de Paris. *See* UAP-BNP
United Kingdom (U.K.): common law in, 84–85, 85n44; corporatism in, 25; descriptive statistics for, 310; equity ownership in, 224; great reversals in, 20; hostile takeovers in, 39; institutional investor assets in, 106; majoritarian system in, 69, 70, 75, 259–62; ownership concentration in, 17, 18, 19; pension investments in, 224–25, 240, 262; preferences in, 68n18; shareholder protections in, 21, 50, 51, 262; unions in, 4

United Malays National Organization
    (UMNO), 233, 234, 236
United States (U.S.): blockholding in, 242–46;
    consensus system in, 26, 71n29; corporatism
    in, 25; economic model variance in, 6, 12,
    20; employment Protection in, 136;
    descriptive statistics for, 310; 401(k)
    plans in, 243, 247–48; governance overview
    of, 241–43, 258–59; historical patterns in,
    143–46; hostile takeovers in, 39; incomplete
    contracts in, 31; institutional investor assets
    in, 106; managerial accountability in, 112;
    managerism in, 250–54; oligarchs in, 243,
    244; ownership concentration in, 17, 18, 19,
    54; pensions in, 224–25, 243, 246–47; politi-
    cal system in, 70; reforms in, 356–58; rhetori-
    cal notions in, 295; robber baron period in,
    150; shareholder protections in, 21, 50, 51;
    social investing in, 249–50; stock option issue
    in, 254; unions in, 4; Wall Street, 254–56
Unruh, Jesse, 240

variance, 277–78
varieties of capitalism (VoC), 51–54, 77, 79,
    113n31, 153, 166, 205n, 208, 290
Venezuela, 18
vertical pyramid control, 4
veto gates, 71, 71n27 and 28, 81
veto players, 69, 71, 71n28, 72n30, 175
veto points, 71, 71n28, 234
Vietnam, 202

Vivendi, 1, 3, 219
Vodafone, 164, 164n31, 165, 165n36
voice model, 60, 61, 62, 65, 95
"voice or exit," 187
Volcker, Paul, 255n
Voluntary Code on Takeovers, 201
Volvo, 144
Vorstand, 163
voting caps, 45, 183, 183n86
voting restrictions, 45
voting rights, 45

Wallenbergs, 110, 141
Wall Street, 254–56
Webster, Judge, 258
Weimer Republic, 161
Westminster system, 10, 70n25
Winter, Jaap, 186
Workers: as a category, 274–75; coalition align-
    ments of, 8–9, 23, 25; described, 59, 278; in
    labor power model, 132–46; political influ-
    ence of, 132–34; preferences of, 59–67,
    132–34, 220–21
World Bank, 72, 74, 100, 119, 213n9
WorldCom, 1, 219, 256, 257, 257n69

Xylan, 212n5

Yamagata Arimoto, 168

zaibatsu system, 125, 167, 168, 169, 188